CITIES OF DIFFERENCE

D1315862

Cities of Difference

Edited by

RUTH FINCHER
JANE M. JACOBS

THE GUILFORD PRESS
New York   London

© 1998 The Guilford Press
A Division of Guilford Publications, Inc.
72 Spring Street, New York, NY 10012
http://www.guilford.com

Printed in the United States of America

This book is printed on acid-free paper.

Last digit is print number: 9 8 7 6 5 4 3 2 1

Library of Congress cataloging-in-publication data
is available from the Publisher.

ISBN 1-57230-311-5 (hardcover)
ISBN 1-57230-310-7 (paperback)

Contributors

Kay Anderson, PhD, School of Geography and Oceanography, University College, University of New South Wales, Canberra, Australia

Liz Bondi, PhD, Department of Geography, University of Edinburgh, Edinburgh, Scotland, United Kingdom

Robyn Dowling, PhD, School of Earth Sciences, Macquarie University, Sydney, Australia

Ruth Fincher, PhD, Faculty of Architecture, Building, and Planning, The University of Melbourne, Parkville, Victoria, Australia

Katherine Gibson, PhD, Department of Geography and Environmental Science, Monash University, Clayton, Victoria, Australia

Brendan Gleeson, PhD, Urban Research Program, Research School of Social Sciences, The Australian National University, Canberra, Australia

Jane M. Jacobs, PhD, Department of Geography and Environmental Studies, The University of Melbourne, Parkville, Victoria, Australia

Lawrence Knopp, PhD, Department of Geography, University of Minnesota, Duluth, Minnesota, United States

Eleonore Kofman, PhD, Department of International Studies, The Nottingham Trent University, Nottingham, United Kingdom

Helga Leitner, PhD, Department of Geography, University of Minnesota, Minneapolis, Minnesota, United States

Richa Nagar, PhD, Department of Women's Studies, University of Minnesota, Minneapolis, Minnesota, United States

Geraldine Pratt, PhD, Department of Geography, University of British Columbia, Vancouver, British Columbia, Canada

Lois M. Takahashi, PhD, Department of Urban and Regional Planning, School of Social Ecology, University of California - Irvine, Irvine, California, United States

Preface

In the early 1990s we found ourselves teaching in the same academic place—the Department of Geography at the University of Melbourne. This was—is—a relief, a great support, and a delight. The idea of this volume emerged from our proximity, when it became clear that we could draw on our different international experiences (Jane's in the United Kingdom and Ruth's in North America) and our different perspectives on cities and urban processes to compile a collection that spanned many of the preoccupations of contemporary English-speaking and urban-focused geographies of difference. This book showcases a range of intellectual styles from across the countries and places of English-speaking geography, even as it documents the common project of marking, critically, contemporary encounters between cities and expressions of identity.

We have enjoyed working with the contributors to the book, and thank them most warmly for their interest in the project and for the wonderful chapters they have made available for it. Many kilometers of communication through international cyberspace have been logged up in the organization of this collection, and we have appreciated very much those who deemed it significant even though it was sourced in Australia! Peter Wissoker, our editor at The Guilford Press, has been a model of appropriate support, intervening at precisely the right times and never at the wrong times! We thank him for his continued encouragement. We would also like to thank Jeannie Tang for her careful editorial work. We are grateful for the community of critical geographers—staff and students—in our department at the University of Melbourne, for providing an environment in which this project was feasible. And we have greatly appreciated the presence in Melbourne of a sizable group of feminist geographers, scattered around various institutions and places but meeting regularly.

RUTH FINCHER
JANE M. JACOBS

Contents

CHAPTER 1

Introduction

Jane M. Jacobs
Ruth Fincher

In describing contemporary cities there are many realities and many daily lives to be accounted for. We inhabit different cities even from those inhabited by our most immediate neighbors. Commentators have long recognized the variety of experiences and processes that come to constitute urban life. Social differences are gathered together in cities at unique scales and levels of intensity. Roland Barthes (1981, p. 96), for example, described cities as the "place of our meeting with the other." In a similar vein, Richard Sennett (1990, p. 123) suggests that urban dwellers are always "people in the presence of otherness." From the beginnings of the modern industrialized city, commentators have been enthralled by this diversity: some rejoicing at the energy it injected into everyday life in cities; others blaming it for a loss of community—what they saw to be the modern condition of alienation. Similarly, city governance has vacillated between celebrating and enhancing such diversity, on the one hand, and regulating and repressing it, on the other. Whatever the response, difference is undoubtedly a sustained feature of urban spaces.

Recent developments in contemporary social theory have intensified interest in issues of identity and difference. This sensitivity responds, in part, to the convincing insights of those "others" who have known well the structuring of difference and the importance of identity politics.[1] These voices have challenged singular positions of authority and helped to open out a space in which difference might be theorized in new ways. Along with this enlivened attention to difference has come a new sensitivity to the processes by which identities are constituted and negotiated. These revisions have placed into question the frameworks by which we come to understand urban life and urban processes. "The city" as an object of analysis has been irredeemably unsettled, and many of the more resilient ways urban processes are understood have been rendered problematic. What happens, for example, to the quest for a broadly applicable "theory of urbanization" when we are confronted with the postmodern critique of metanarratives? What happens to our capacity to produce normative models of cities in this context of a new sensitivity to the politics of difference? What happens to studies of housing, suburbia, the inner city, ghettos, gentrification, social polarization, and urban social movements when framed not by a theory of "the city" but by theories of difference? This collection of essays shows how this recent attention to difference has productively contributed to the way contemporary geographers depict and analyze city spaces and city lives.

Taking difference seriously does not simply mean joyously indulging in urban diversity. Nor does it automatically cast one into a form of depoliticized relativism. The engagements with difference contained in this volume do not throw skyward notions of power, inequality, or politics. As Massey (1995, p. 283) notes, power relations contribute to the constitution of identities. Empowerment, oppression, and exclusion work through regimes of difference. The chapters to follow provide insights into the complex ways in which struggles over identity, resources, citizenry, and space are framed in and through differences that are variously constituted and contextually determined. Each chapter in its own way shows the complex entanglement between identity, power, and place. We can conceptualize this interlinking of power and identity not simply as *difference* but as a *located politics of difference.*

The complex processes that produce the arrangements of privilege and marginalization so evident in urban spaces come into sharp focus when conceptualized by way of a located politics of difference. Not least, reductive economistic models for explaining the distribution of "haves" and "have nots" are productively complicated. The lens of difference does not ignore the way in which persistent power structures can unevenly shape urban lives. But it does highlight the ways in which such structures are, in turn, shaped by the contingent circumstances of specific people in specific settings. Emphasizing difference then does not simply mean charting new, more nuanced, uneven geographies of the city. It also means attending to the various ways that specificity—both social and spatial—can transform structures of power and privilege; the ways oppressed groups can, through a politics of identity and a politics of place, reclaim rights, resist, and subvert.

Attending to a politics of difference necessarily collapses the traditional divide between views of city life from cultural and political economy perspectives. This is not simply to say that the lens of difference draws into focus what might once have been thought of as "culturally" defined urban groups such as ethnic or racial minorities. It is, rather, to acknowledge that processes of representation, signification, and performativity are fundamental components of the way identities are constituted and articulated. These processes of defining difference are in a mutually constitutive relationship with the uneven material conditions of everyday life. As Nancy Fraser (1995, p. 72) notes, "even the most material economic institutions have a constitutive, irreducible cultural dimension" and at the same time "even the most discursive cultural practices have a constitutive, irreducible political-economic dimension." In this sense this book contributes to recasting the culture–economy dichotomy into a far more powerful cultural political economy of urban identities and places. For example, in many of the chapters to follow the representation of groups and urban places in public discourses are shown to be complexly entwined with the production and reproduction of the material imperatives of city lives—through urban labor markets and the restructuring of entitlements through the state. Similarly, many of the chapters deal with the way in which contemporary political struggles around rights and entitlements are often as not struggles that cohere around a politics of identity constituted through processes as much cultural as economic.

Many threads link contemporary urban geographies sensitive to difference with the varied urban geographies we have constructed in the past. Geography has a long tradition of attending to how certain social groups come to experience the city in ways different to others. Such concerns are contained within the varied urban geographies of "race," class, gender, and, more recently, disability and sexuality. It is not our task in this introduction to trace the specific lineages of each of these areas of research. Where appropriate, the chapters that follow provide such accounts. But we can note that in recent years these more traditional geographies of social categories have undergone significant transformation. At the very least, the range of identified "groups" whose urban circumstances might be examined and theorized, and whose particular and diverse forms of marginalization or advancement might be publicized, has been extended. In this volume, for example, there is a consideration of life stages, physical disabilities, and religious convictions, as well as analyses of more familiar axes of difference such as gender, class, and race. It will also be clear from the chapters to follow that there is no predetermined or prescribed approach for contemporary urban geographies of difference. The papers in this collection, for example, draw upon varied

paradigms and methodologies. Some have a historical materialist starting point and emphasize how differently identified and resourced
groups are incorporated within the structured material options of urban
living. Others draw more clearly on a cultural perspective that reveals
the moral and ideological frameworks underpinning the constitution of
difference in urban spaces. All demonstrate clearly that geographies of a
located politics of difference compel these once "incompatible" perspectives to come together in productive associations.

It is difficult to trace in any ordered way the trajectories of contemporary thought which have meant that difference is a central (and
yet productively decentering) component of the ways society—including urban society—is now understood. We could point to post-
structuralism, to feminism, to postcolonial criticism, to psychoanalytic theory, to queer theory, each of which has contributed in its own
way to the opening up of the subject of difference. There is much
cross-fertilization between these not-so-distinct bodies of thought that
would further complicate any attempt to pin down origins. This introduction does not attempt to definitively trace the intellectual lineages of a located politics of difference. Others, like Ed Soja (1996),
have already provided such road maps. Rather, we use this introduc-
tory chapter to sketch certain themes that are especially relevant to
how a politics of difference restructures the way cities and urban processes are thought about. They are, of course, also themes taken up
in far greater detail by the various authors who have contributed to
this volume. We begin, below, in the section entitled "Identifying Difference," with rehearsing the significant transformation from thinking about identity (and logically difference) as pregiven and fixed to
something that is socially produced and multiply located. This is followed by a section entitled "(Dis)placing Difference," which deals with
the consequences of this way of thinking about identity for some of
the current commentaries on difference in the city. The implications
of a new emphasis on difference for questions of justice is examined
in the section entitled "Just Difference." Particular attention is given
to the issues that arise when universal notions of justice come into
contact with a politics of difference. Our final section, "Re-placing Difference," suggests the necessity and significance of situating theories and narratives of difference in spatialized frameworks.

IDENTIFYING DIFFERENCE

When we talk of difference we are clearly invoking the idea that there
are distinctions between people and groups. These distinctions may

be marked through gender, race, ethnicity, age, life course, sexuality, or any other referent. More likely, difference will be articulated through a combination of such defining characteristics. Urban studies have long noted differences among urban citizenry and the ways in which such distinctions are evident in city spaces. A usefully illustrative example of how difference has long been factored into accounts of the city is provided by the work of E. W. Burgess and his colleagues in the Chicago School of urban sociology. Of course, Burgess produced the now overexposed concentric zone model of urban growth, a model that was expected to stand as a template for "the city" conceived of as an "organism" with its own internal logic of growth and development. Within the framework of the concentric zone model, Burgess plotted what he saw to be the predictable spatial patterning of ethnic enclaves, racial ghettos, areas of prostitution, and "clean and bright" suburbs. The Chicago School's conceptualization of difference is useful as a point of comparison to demonstrate how ideas of social difference and urban spatiality have recently transformed. This model also helps illustrate the political implication that the identification and charting of difference may have.

In this early and somewhat crude urban model the encounter with "difference"—rudimentary as it is—contains many assumptions and prejudices. A number of these assumptions are quite at odds with the basic premises of contemporary thinking on identity and difference. Most notably, the social distinctions like "race" used in the model were accepted as pregiven and relatively uncomplicated categories that were simply there to be mapped. Others, like monogamous heterosexuality, were so naturalized that they were present only as the invisible norm against which the "deviant" sexuality of prostitution was positioned. Such conceptions of identity are at odds with current views that subjectivity (be it sexualized, gendered, racialized, or whatever) is socially constituted. Subjectivity is constituted by a wide range of discursive practices that label, name, and ascribe. These discourses are part of the means by which subjects come to be known and to know themselves. This is the idea of the interpellated (or "called") subject. From this perspective there is no natural or pregiven subject.

The Burgess model also assumed that in the case of certain groups it was appropriate that they be defined primarily, almost exclusively, by way of one single attribute—be it race, class, sexuality, or criminality. Again, this conceptualization of identity as reducible to one attribute is contrary to our current understanding of identity as multiply and variably positioned; that is, we are racialized, classed, *and* gendered (to select but three possible axes of difference). Furthermore, how these distinct attributes come into play in terms of life chances is by no means given. Current thinking on identity means that describing, or (in the case of the Chicago sociologists) mapping, differences *as if* based around stable and pregiven categories of distinction is problematic. Critical studies of difference must instead chart the varied processes by which difference is constituted. This transformation in perspective is very clearly illustrated in this volume by Lawrence Knopp (Chapter 7), who (revisiting his earlier pathbreaking work on sexuality and cities) explains that geographers have now moved beyond "naive mappings of sexual spaces" (p. 149). In place of such uncritical geographies of (sexual) difference, Knopp proposes geographies of sexuality that attend to the interplay between urban spaces and the complex constitution of sexualized subjectivities.

Another important aspect of current critical perspectives on difference is the assumption that the processes that work to construct gendered, racialized or, say, classed identities are embedded in frameworks of power. Structures of difference are encoded with certain assumptions that variously apportion measures of legitimacy, civility, or authority to the socially constructed subject. Furthermore, through processes of regulation and repetition, these unevenly empowered differences are made to appear natural or, in the words of Judith Butler (1990, p. 33), to have the "appearance of substance." If we rethink the Burgess model of the city in these terms, then what it stands for is radically transformed. In the first place, we can begin to see how it was not an objective description of the city that *indifferently* attended to the social distinctions that occurred there. Rather, this model was one more articulation in the ongoing discursive constitution of those categories of distinction. Furthermore, the Burgess model provides us with an insight into the implications of those differences. This model of the city made specific assumptions about the social categories it mapped. In particular, a number of social groups (such as blacks and prostitutes) were designated as "problematic." The spatial concentration of such groups served as an indicator of the city organism being in a state of malfunction. These concentrations of negatively differentiated groups created what Burgess described as "disturbances" to the urban "metabolism" (Burgess, 1967, p. 52). These "problem" groups deviated from the white, heteronormative ideal embodied in the "clean and bright" outer suburbs. In this sense the Chicago sociologists actually produced an assimilationist model of the city. It was assumed that under the right conditions these "deviant" groups would conform to the characteristics embodied by the suburbs and then the city would become fully healthy. Burgess's map also carried with it the authority of being an academic, social scientific account of urban differences. This contributed to the way in which these constructs of difference and deviancy were legitimized and naturalized. So it is not simply the idea of "the city" that is installed underneath the neat concentric zone of Burgess's model city but also a range of hierarchical structurings of social difference and moral ambitions to assimilate such differences.

It has been a sustained concern of contemporary critical studies of difference to undo the types of fixed categories, moral judgments and assimilationist goals that are so clearly illustrated by Burgess' model of the city. In place of unreflexive descriptions of difference, critical studies of difference concern themselves with the socially constituted subject and the means by which these subjectivities are variously centered and privileged or marginalized and disadvantaged. If one thinks about identity as discursively constituted, then one does away with the notion of a pregiven, essential identity. In its place we must assume that identity comes through the temporary fixing of the array of differences that constitute the embodied person. Judith Butler conceptualizes this process of fixing in terms of "performativity" or "naming as an identity-constituting performance." This is "a specific modality of power" that works through discourse as a means of establishing the parameters of identification by which the subject comes to be known (Butler, 1993, pp. 187–188). An example of this is the way in which, say, the category "woman" comes not from biology but from discursively constituting the sexed body in specific (feminine) ways. Brendan Gleeson, in Chapter 5 on disability, in this book, is particularly illustrative in these terms. Through a historical perspective, he is able to show that disability is something which is "made" from the impaired body under specific historical circumstances. That is, he points to the fact that the relationship between the physically impaired body and the intensely marginalized disabled body is not a necessary or given relationship, but historically contingent.

Gleeson's thinking about impairment and disability demonstrates that to claim that subjectivity is discursively constituted does not mean that it is confined to the sphere of ideas. Discourses are embedded in relational frameworks of power, in institutions, and in structures of governmentality. They have the ability not only to constitute subjectivity but also to demarcate the privileges and rights that embodied subjectivities might enjoy. In this sense, the marking of differences is contingent upon ongoing social processes and is complexly entwined with material conditions (Jones & Moss, 1995, p. 254, after Laclau & Mouffe, 1985). Such an observation is highly relevant to a consideration of cities and difference where the traditions of thinking about difference have often as not centered on issues of rights and access to resources. In the light of nonessentialist conceptions of difference these traditional urban concerns do not disappear but they might need to be thought about and acted upon in new ways.

One of the challenges raised by the idea of the discursively constituted subject is that it suggests identity can be "reduced" to the effects of naming. This is an issue that has been central to recent debates within postcolonial theory, where considerable attention has been given to the ways in which the colonial self was constructed in reference to a colonized (racialized, primitivized, feminized) other. For example, postcolonial theorists might argue that difference in this conceptualization is cast as simply the "subject-effect" of colonial discourses (Williams & Chrisman, 1994, p. 16). But is our acceptance that subjectivity is discursively constituted necessarily limited to "effects"? Is identity so easily stitched into place? Do city dwellers simply succumb to the way society sees them? Kay Anderson, in Chapter 9 of this volume, suggests that urban dwellers are neither fully determined by (say) structures of racialization, class, colonialism, or bureaucracy nor fully outside these processes. They occupy what she calls, taking from Teresa de Lauretis (1987, p. 25), "in-between-spaces" in which it is possible to negotiate the categorizations by which they have come to be known. We might think of this as the open contingency of identity. Yet while is important to admit such complex contingencies, it is also true that many political struggles (and even everyday transactions) are conducted by way of what we would call singularized identity designations—"woman," "race," "ethnicity," and "gayness." That is, there is an urban politics that forms around the very specific identity categories by which subjects have come to be unevenly placed in the sociospatial architecture of the city. Spivak (1990, p. 12) refers to this as a form of "operational" or strategic essentialism in which certain socially ascribed identities become provisional rallying points.

That such singularized political formations occur provisionally and often strategically is significant. The experience of feminism, for example, has shown that alliances that occur around single rallying points like gender have immense strength but also a certain vulnerability. Elspeth Probyn (1990, p. 176) states the problematic in these terms: "in creating our own centres and our own locals, we tend to forget that our centres displace others to the peripheries of our making." Probyn is referring here to the limits of claims for political solidarity around a universalized notion of "woman" and "women's oppression." Such universalist claims set aside alternate vectors of oppression (based on, say, race, class, or sexuality) that mark out one woman's experiences from another. Such singularized rallying points can produce their own exclusions and their own spheres of privilege. An example of this can also be seen when state bureaucracies sensitized to difference become financial supporters of such identity-defined organizations. The "category workers" who are employed as representatives of, say, an ethnic group, disabled people, or women, may find their bureaucratic positioning difficult to reconcile with the diverse requirements of their identified communities (Pettman, 1992, pp. 102–103). So, to conceive of difference as constituted through a more fluid and nonessentialist performativity of identity at once dispenses with some of the more persistent problems associated with "identity politics" *and* poses new problems in terms of the pragmatics of politics and governmentality.

What such political dilemmas point to is the importance of recognizing the sheer multiplicity of differences that may cohere around any one person. Social distinctions are constituted in specific contexts through multiple and interpenetrating axes of difference, what Pringle and Watson (1992, p. 70) usefully refer to as a "chain of differences." At any one time we occupy more than one system of difference (Jones & Moss, 1995, p. 254). And at any one time we may be fixed into or strategically mobilize different aspects of the array of differences through which our embodied selves are known. How we are seen and how we present ourselves to others is, then, always provisional and contextual. As Geraldine Pratt puts it in this volume (Chapter 2), we are often "torn between identifications" and we regularly move "between identifications in different situations and places" (p. 26).

This, then, is a reformulation of identity around not only the notion of interlocking matrices of power relations (Ruddick, 1996, p. 133) but also the provisional and contingent performativity of subjectivity. As productive and necessary as these reformulations are, they do produce certain practical problems for the urban commentator. How does one speak (and write) about such multiply constituted and locationally contingent notions of difference? What are the pertinent dimensions along which different identities are expressed or represented? Should we view people as grouped by class, gender, sexuality, life stage, ethnicity, place, nation, or some combination thereof, and if so which combination and in which contexts? As Bordo (1990, p. 139) asks, "Just how many axes can one include and still preserve analytic focus or argument?" Many of the chapters to follow demonstrate well the intersection of axes of difference, even while they may, for whatever reason, emphasize one axis above others. Often the choice of which identity attribute to be emphasized is determined by the vector of differentiation that most tellingly contributes to that subject's marginalization or empowerment. Other times, the emphasis tends to be prespecified by theoretical questions or intellectual lineages. A number of the contributors to this volume engage in useful reflections on their own efforts to adjust their earlier theoretical convictions in line with new theorizations of difference. For example, Geraldine Pratt (in Chapter 2) recasts her earlier work with Susan Hanson on gender and labor markets and extends these findings through thinking about the multiple differences that constitute located household labor relations. In a similar spirit, Kay Anderson (in Chapter 9) extends her original thinking about the construction of Chinatowns by questioning the reification of race within work influenced by the orientalist tradition and elaborating on the way Chinatowns are also implicated in labor markets where race, gender, and class interconnect. Liz Bondi (in Chapter 8) also revisits her ongoing project of reconfiguring gentrification as something more than a class process. She argues that gendering the gentrification process also necessitates attention to sexuality.

(DIS)PLACING DIFFERENCE

It is easy to critique the now outdated modes of mapping difference that are evident in the Chicago School of urban studies. But in what ways have the current modes of registering difference in contemporary cities incorporated the types of retheorizations we have just outlined? We might begin to answer this question by attending to some of the more dominant (and sometimes related) narratives that attempt, at their boldest, to explain the contemporary city or, more modestly, to simply speak to the specific conditions of contemporary urban life. For while the explanatory capacity of those old models of "the city" might no longer suffice, there is no lack of what might be thought of as blockbuster urban commentaries. For some commentators to speak of the present moment is, necessarily, to begin to speak of cities. The city, at least for some, has come to stand as the paradigmatic site of postmodernity: it is the place where, to paraphrase Ed Soja (1989), "it all comes together."

One feature of contemporary cities that has received considerable attention over the last decade is the phenomenon of social polarization. Social polarization is a term that has come into common currency as a way of explaining the specific social differentiations and inequities apparent in many First World cities. The term is specifically used to describe the trend in which an increasing disparity has been seen to emerge between an expanded and more diversely constituted "underclass" and more affluent groups. It is implied in the term social polarization that the "middle" has dropped away as a significant grouping in the class arrangements of urban societies. As Lash and Urry (1994, p. 160) note: "middle income groups are becoming scarcer as income distribution increasingly assumes a bimodal pattern." Explanations of this heightened differentiation in contemporary urban societies draw primarily on recent economic restructurings—such as the shift from manufacturing to services—which, although globally driven, have distinct local effects. Most notably, social polarization is understood mainly in terms of changes in individual and household capacities, and argues a case for the diminishment or enhancement of these capacities in terms of the character of labor force participation (or, for that matter, nonparticipation). Not surprisingly, then, many of the studies that give empirical flesh to social polarization draw on statistical data sets that illuminate income and labor force participation (for a review and bibliography, see Gibson et al., 1996).

In the case of North American and European cities, these economic (class) disparities are often noted to have specific ethnic, racial, or gender characteristics. Lash and Urry (1994, p. 145), for example, note that "large numbers of immigrants flow" into the new urban underclass (see also Anderson, Chapter 9; Jacobs, Chapter 11; and Kofman, Chapter 12, this volume). Similarly, Saskia Sassen's depiction of the socially polarized "global city" has noted that in the case of New York "the poor are disproportionately black and Hispanic" and large numbers of this racialized poor are also within households headed by a single female parent (Sassen, 1991, p. 264). These accounts of social polarization in contemporary cities do offer a specific register of difference. They demonstrate how, in class terms especially, certain differences are actually being exacerbated in contemporary First World cities. They also indicate how class differences are complexly intertwined with race, ethnicity, and gender. Furthermore, there is considerable local variation in the effecting of global economic change, both in cities that are designated as "global" and in those that are not. As Kofman notes in Chapter 12, these global restructurings incorporate gendered and racialized peoples in different ways.

Complicating the class assumptions of social polarization debates is an important step in chronicling the multiple faces of differentiation within contemporary cities. It is an issue further developed in this volume by Katherine Gibson (Chapter 13), who notes that social polarization arguments approach "difference in a way that sees it as primarily economic . . . , as distinguishing groups that are relatively internally homogeneous and structurally defined by contemporary processes of capital accumulation" (p. 303). Gibson is implying that strict economistic adjudications of difference (even those into which ethnicity or gender might "flow") are inadequate for understanding the complexities of the structuring and negotiation of difference in cities. As Kay Anderson (Chapter 9) suggests, this is as much a methodological as a theoretical issue, arising in part from the dominance of positivist frameworks for detecting difference. Mingione (1993, pp. 325–326) has suggested that social polarization studies may be well served by disconnecting from statistical databases and connecting with alternate methodologies that could better highlight the diverse processes by which difference is constituted.

What are the multiply articulated processes by which disadvantage is made and remade? As Gans (1993, p. 328) argues, it is necessary not only to understand that there is a new urban poor but also to understand how "the poor," in all their internal diversity, are "chosen for victimization, how and by whom." Addressing such questions takes us further than issues of economic advantage or disadvantage. On the one hand, it prompts the posing of optimistic questions about how urban dwellers negotiate their variable positionings in urban society and how they might chart strategic points of political commonality. But, on the other hand, it compels us to consider how disadvantage is made and remade by empowered institutions and the morally laden discursive fields by which specific subjectivities—like "blacks," or "single mothers," or "prostitutes"—come to be known. Several chapters in this volume contribute to the latter project. Fincher (Chapter 3) describes moral narratives that draw on life stage norms to render "youth" (of a particular racialized, gendered, and class-identified variety) in American inner cities a problematic designation, to be contrasted reprovingly with a smugly successful, and adult, suburban norm. Robyn Dowling (Chapter 4) unsettles the contemporary predilection for accounting for diversity among suburbs by way of women's entry into the paid labor force. She argues that suburban lives are negotiated around moral codes of mothering and paid work participation that operate, often in association with diverse religious beliefs and practices, to construct complex between- and within-suburban differences. Lois M. Takahashi (Chapter 6) shows the importance of moral and religious norms in the ways leaders of certain Los Angeles immigrant groups deemed the homeless and those living with AIDS as "inside" or "outside" their communities.

A second and related narrative that circulates in relation to the contemporary city emphasizes the role that consumption now plays in urban transformation. Certainly the commentaries of David Harvey (1989) and Ed Soja (1989) on the conditions of postmodernity give grand testament to this new logic of urban space. The role of consumption is evident in many aspects of the contemporary city: processes of gentrification, the expansion of shopping malls, the new emphasis on image making, and so on. Bondi (Chapter 8), Gibson (Chapter 13), and Jacobs (Chapter 11) each provide explicit critiques of the way difference is depicted in such accounts of the consumption-based (postmodern) city. Within this new cultural logic of urban development, image making and trading in images is paramount. Here difference is registered primarily in terms of how it is appropriated by—and transformed into a commodity within—reoriented processes of capital accumulation. As Gibson puts it, difference becomes something which is "good for business" (p. 309).

As a number of the authors in this volume note, such a scenario is politically debilitating. It assumes that capital has taken over, exhausted, every aspect of city life. Moreover, it is often anticipated that under these new regimes of appropriation political mobilization is thwarted. A politics of difference is transformed into the play of difference. But if a politics of difference were placed into closer contact with these narratives of consumption-led transformation, then it might become evident that the outcomes of these encounters was far from predictable. As Ed Soja's recent book *Thirdspace* (1996) hints, appropriation and political disablement are but two of the modalities that might be assumed. For example, Jacobs (Chapter 11) argues that "playing" with difference does not necessarily compromise urban political mobilizations and can in fact activate a most contested politics precisely around issues of signification and representation. This is a point also emphasized by Knopp in Chapter 7, where he considers the transformation of Gay and Lesbian Mardis Gras from sites of performative resistance to national television events. Such "appropriations" are at the same time amplifications that carry with them gains as well as losses. Indeed, they may even generate a new politics based around what Knopp calls "managing success" (p. 164).

Reexamined through the lens of difference, globalization and social polarization can no longer be simply understood in terms of disembodied and undifferentiated corporate capitalists on some placeless stage, foisting their multinational solutions on powerless local jurisdictions. To challenge this economistic meta-narrative does not, however, do away with issues of economic advantage and disadvantage in the negotiation of a politics of identity and rights. In many of the papers within this volume it is clear that the material resources of groups vis-à-vis others are still a vitally important consideration. This is a theme that resonates with broader debates within feminist and postcolonial writings. For example, Gayatri Spivak (1988) mounts a cogent critique of the desire within poststructuralist theory to incorporate difference by way of the subaltern. She argues that this is an example of the West instrumentally coming into contact with the subaltern in order to better theorize itself, yet notes that these same theorists are unwilling to accept the patently modernist fact that global capitalism has produced most uneven geographies of power and privilege. Indulging in difference is not then an option "enjoyed" in the same way by all (hooks, 1992). For example, Geltmaker (1992) has clearly outlined what we might think of as the uneven enjoyment of difference by way of gay activism for AIDS-related health services. He notes that this is an activism predicated on a class-specific acceptability of being gay that works to ensure that the services secured are primarily directed at those AIDS sufferers within the same economic class. Those with AIDS who are also materially disadvantaged and who might live in less tolerant communities that do not recognize their deservingness of support would never dare to so identify. Our point is to stress that registering difference has uneven outcomes: for some it marks a joyous inclusiveness; for some, a destabilizing contact with otherness; for some, a reminder of the unavoidable materiality of their marginalization.

The influence of material limits and opportunities on the success with which the interests of particular identity groups are acted out on the urban stage is clearly evident in many of the chapters that follow. For example, claims in relation to urban space that are structured around a specific identity politics (such as race, gender, sexuality, or class) are variously restrained or activated, depending on the material resources available. It is clear that economic advantage can assist in guaranteeing particular outcomes or successes for specifically identified groups (see, e.g., Knopp, Chapter 7, and Fincher, Chapter 3). But the relationship between identity-based claims and economic advantage is not always so neatly aligned. A number of contributors to this volume note the importance of "struggle" in the structuring of urban politics and the transformation of urban spaces into more homely places by under-resourced groups (see, e.g., Anderson, Chapter 9, and Nagar & Leitner, Chapter 10).

JUST DIFFERENCE

The reformulations of difference outlined above pose a specific challenge in terms of some of the more enduring political concerns of urban reformists. At stake here is where issues of equity might stand once cities are reconceptualized through the framework of radical difference. Can the political objective of equity be reconciled with the notion of cities of difference? Does producing equity require that difference be obliterated in the name of justice? How can the just city coexist with cities of difference? We can once again turn to feminist theory as a guide here, for it has been within feminism that there has been explicit debate about equality and difference. Joan Scott (1990), for example, has argued against framing equity and difference as irreconcilable on the grounds that this binary is itself disabling in terms of feminist political objectives. She sees equality and difference as interdependent but not exclusive terms. As she so succinctly expresses it, "equality is not the elimination of difference, and difference does not preclude equality" (Scott, 1990, p. 136). Anne Phillips (1992, p. 25) further elaborates by considering the issues which arise from replacing the universal citizen as the subject of justice with differentiated persons and groups. For her the issue is "how far one would want to go; and in this case what balance one might hope to achieve between the ideals of the universal citizen and the reality of group differentiation."

Significant in this debate has been the work of Iris Marion Young, who has provided a more complex conceptualization of oppression. Her notion of the variable vectors of power and the oppressions they produce is explained in terms of "five faces of oppression" (Young, 1990, p. 39). Young's "plural explication of the concept of oppression" incorporates such explicit axes of oppression as racism, sexism, ageism, and homophobia but reformulates them into broader modalities of power, which she labels as exploitation, marginalization, powerlessness, cultural imperialism, and violence (1990, p. 42). In reconceptualizing oppression in this way Young is attempting to dismantle neat alignments between singularly identified oppressed groups and tyrannically cast oppressors (e.g., black/white; women/men; homosexuality/heteronormativity). Drawing on Foucauldian ideas of power, she argues that oppression is the consequence of complexly structured regimes of difference that are "systematically reproduced in major economic, political and cultural institutions" (Young, 1990, p. 41). This may even include the oppressive consequences of well-meaning practices like education, bureaucratic administration, medicine, and even some of the more inclusionary forms of governmentality. Young's project is explicitly directed at attempting to adjust older notions of justice based around equity for a universal citizen so they are more responsive to difference. Like Joan Scott, she mounts a sustained challenge to an "ideal of justice" that presumes the necessity of the "transcendence of group difference" (Young, 1990, p. 157; see also Fraser, 1995). This older, Enlightenment framework of justice is, she poses, assimilationist. In its place she proposes "an

egalitarian politics of difference" that attends to difference not by
way of essentialist conceptions of those group distinctions but by way
of difference defined "more fluidly and relationally" (Young, 1990, p.
157).

In reconceptualizing the relationship between justice and the politics of difference Young draws specifically on city life and on a well-
established tradition of viewing public spaces in cities as potentially
democratic (Ruddick, 1996, p. 134). For Young, cities are sites defined by "the being together of strangers," a concept that raises specific issues in terms of justice and difference (Young, 1990, p. 237;
Gibson, Chapter 13, this volume). As Young (1990, p. 163) sees it,
urbanization actually amplifies "particularistic affiliations" and reinforces "group solidarity and differentiation." In short, the city challenges the Rousseauist ideal of community, built as it is around the
notion of copresent subjects that are "transparent" to each other and,
because of this, enjoy certain levels of mutual understanding and sympathy. Young describes this idea of community as a dream that presumes a number of basic forms of social relations, such as face-to-face
contact, which have long been absent from urban life. For Young, city
life is not structured around known-ness and transparency but around
social relations between "both seen and unseen strangers" (1990, p.
237), around casual encounters and the brushing together of opaque
groups and individuals. It is within this social context that the uneven
distributions of advantage and disadvantage, privilege and
marginalization, are embedded.

The dilemma of seeing city life in this way, of course, is that it
begs the question of how, in the jumble of identity politics that exists
in city spaces, power between strategically identifying groups actually
will be exercised. As Phillips (1992, p. 25) says, unless we interpret
politics as an activity in which we act "outside of ourselves," consciously
beyond our own positions, then there will be a "battle between vested
interests which the larger groups will inevitably win." What must be
avoided, as Neil Smith cogently argues, is an assumption of the "auto-
matic equivalence of different oppressions," or a ranking of oppressions by appeal to histories of relative suffering (Smith, 1994). A close
examination of "real cities," Pratt and Hanson (1994, p. 7) shows us,
makes it very clear that

> different groups and inequalities are structured relationally; a
> celebration of alterity (especially one premised on the denial
> that different groups can or even should understand each other)
> would seem to draw attention away from the relations of power

and domination that structure difference and the very real *connections* that exist between groups. (emphasis in original)

If city life is understood not as a community, but as a site structured around the actual, not imagined, "being together of strangers" joined through uneven power relations, then this has direct implications for the ways justice might be instituted in urban space. In particular it compels us to rethink a pragmatics of justice built around redistributive interventions aimed at delivering equity. It may well be that Henri Lefebvre's concept of the right to the city, as outlined by Eleanore Kofman (Chapter 12, this volume) can provide a guide to a reconfiguring of justice in cities of difference. She argues that new formulations of social citizenship should enshrine, as a right, respect for diversity and difference, for it is such an integral aspect of urban life, the use of city space, and the decisions that are made about that space.

Nancy Fraser (1995, p. 69) suggests that justice now needs to be built around both redistribution and recognition (of difference). She proposes an alternate framework for urban "remedies" that is structured around "affirmation" and "transformation." Affirmative remedies effect equity without doing away with the fundamental structures of difference around which inequity may have been built. This might include, say, multiculturalism or a gay rights politics that revalues and gives new legitimacy to previously marginalized groups. It is easy to see how in the contemporary polity of cities such redistributive strategies can cojoin with a politics of affirmation. Indeed, in those cities that retain some semblance of welfare governmentality, this is precisely the way in which justice is being restructured. But Fraser warns against some of the perverse and unseen outcomes of such recognitions of difference. These redistributive programs can create what she calls "stigmatized classes of vulnerable people" who are then resentfully perceived as being the beneficiaries of special compensatory measures.

There is presently plenty of evidence of resentment, expressed in complex ways and with diverse justifications, among distinct sectors of urban society. The problems posed for redistributive reforms in such urban contexts is specifically addressed in this volume in Chapter 5 by Gleeson and Chapter 6 by Takahashi. Lois M. Takahashi deals with local responses to the placement of service delivery points for AIDS sufferers and the homeless. Her paper reveals the deep antipathy that urban residents can express when human service provisions for "undesirable" groups move into in their neighborhood. Her chapter demonstrates clearly that the "trouble" surrounding human services delivery in contemporary cities is not simply a matter of a misrecognition of the diverse axes of oppression that the client group may face. Rather, it is the way in which human services must negotiate an often antipathetic and defensive NIMBY ("not in my backyard") politics. Brendan Gleeson (Chapter 5) also points to the way in which aversions between "strangers" intersects with the processes of deinstitutionalization that have seen facilities for the disabled become the "unwanted neighbors" (p. 99) of normative homeowners. He notes that these localized expressions of antipathy are regularly shored up by centralized policies which assume that facilities for the disabled will impact negatively on property values. This, he argues, points not to cities of difference but to "cities of (in)difference" (p. 100).

It is certainly true that much of the recent restructuring of the welfare state evident in North America, Europe, and other First World regions is based precisely upon this type of misperception and the resentments it seems to generate. Once recognizably marginalized and disadvantaged groups are now seen to have "too much": too many special rights, too much government assistance, and so on. Neil Smith (1994, pp. 3–4), for example, suggests that the U.S. city of the 1990s is "increasingly the revanchist city in which the reassertion of rigid, conservative, legal, cultural and ideological statutes has been startling . . . [resulting] from a series of political and economic back-lashes, backed by state power, against alternative visions and realities of social justice." And Robert Lake (1994, p. 601) has noted the re-duction in size of the contemporary American public sphere and the simultaneous growth of mean-spiritedness, particularly at the local scale at which exclusionary modes of democracy prevail. This is an aspect of the policies toward single mothers in North American cities described by Ruth Fincher in Chapter 3 of this volume.

It is perhaps more necessary than ever before to think about how justice might be reconfigured through the radical transformations that attending to difference brings. Transformative remedies, as Nancy Fraser sees them, depend upon a radical fracturing of the generative frameworks of difference around which inequity has been built. This would entail deconstructing the binary notions of, say, white and black or hetero- and homosexuality. Fraser (1995, p. 83) sees this transfor-mative politics not as a mechanism for dissolving difference entirely but as a way of opening out possibilities for sustaining "multiple, debinarized, fluid, ever-shifting differences." Or does David Harvey's (1996, p. 362) reformulated universality, one which is "construed in dialectical relations with particularity," provide a realistic and realiz-able political option? Harvey suggests that political futures must rec-ognize that "some are more other than others" and that radical politics must work to draw different groups together into strategically formed alliances in order to ensure that justice prevails in relation to those who are so deeply marginalized. But is Harvey's political vision of "synthesis" (1996, p. 431) just as elusive as Fraser's radical fracturing?

The problematic posed by the located accounts of difference charted in the chapters to follow is that even as we may theorize such political possibilities, there are residual, nonprogressive structures of power and difference that are deeply embedded in city spaces and that resist such radical transformations. It is difficult to imagine how one might begin to reconcile a theorization of fractured and positional identities with an urban politics that is so routinely expressed by way of oppositional frameworks. It is difficult to imagine how a revised notion of justice might resurrect itself in contexts where difference plays a key role in the way marginalized or disenfranchised groups compete for the diminished resources of the welfare state. In part this is a task that involves attending to the diverse structures of urban politics, an issue of interest to a number of the contributors to this volume.

RE-PLACING DIFFERENCE

Theories of difference assume that contingency, or context, is significant. In the writings on difference this contingency is often conceptualized with recourse to spatialized metaphors, and particularly the notion first mobilized by Adrienne Rich (1986) as a "politics of location." Rich's term has been widely taken up by geographers concerned with rethinking identity politics and relational differences (see, e.g., Smith & Katz, 1993; Pile & Thrift, 1995; Rose, 1993, 1994). It has provided a way of moving from universalizing spatial visions toward geographies that are open to that which is cast as minor, marginal, or other. Elspeth Probyn (1990, p. 177) has considered the routine way in which this new openness to difference articulates itself as a "cry for the 'local.' " Probyn (1990, p. 186) concludes that it is fundamentally important in the project of a "politics of location" to look at "the construction of locale" and how it is implicated both in the reproduction of social difference and in the way our experiences of specific places are circumscribed by a politics of location. Many geographers have been engaged in just such a project for many years. They have been able to demonstrate that place and space are far more than "neutral backdrops or uncomplicated stages for people's lives," more than "containers within which social relations develop" (Pratt &

Hanson, 1994, p. 25). Instead, these geographies have shown how place and social processes are complexly intertwined.

One of the clearest statements of the relationship between "placement" in a locale and the construction of social identities and diversity was made by Pratt and Hanson (1994) in the opening article of the feminist geography journal *Gender, Place and Culture*. Based on their important study of women at work in Worcester, Massachusetts, Pratt and Hanson (1994, p. 6) found that contests over identity occurred in and through the spatial relations of places. Their focus on place worked against rigid and static conceptualizations of difference along lines like class, gender, and sexual alliance. In their view the use of geographical metaphors in feminist writing fails to explore fully the ways that complex configurations of identity emerge in place. Using a detailed empirical study of the social relations of workplaces and of the exhibited preferences of employers for certain "types" of worker in their firms, Pratt and Hanson were able to substantiate their point that community and identity are not accounted for solely "in movement, in the ability to disidentify, and dislodge privilege" (Pratt & Hanson, 1994, p. 25). Instead of this more mobile theorization of identity, their work suggests that there is a "stickiness to identity grounded in the fact that many women's lives are lived locally." This point returns us to the tension that exists between the radically fragmented notions of identity (which current theorizations of difference stress) and the less transformative and transforming lived realities. As Pratt and Hanson (1994, p. 25) note:

> Many people simply do not move through the city in the way that [some] feminists suggest, at least not within certain spheres of their lives—especially in relation to labour and housing markets. . . . At the very least, this simple observation suggests that feminist theorists must work with a more complicated set of geographical constructs to conceptualise adequately subjectivity and community.

Many chapters in this book develop the point that people's relationships with places help construct their identities like their relationships within class, gender and ethnic groupings. Nagar and Leitner (Chapter 10) demonstrate that the appropriation of place and the control exercised over urban spaces by powerful groups is an important pivot in struggles that shape identities. Pratt (Chapter 2) continues her project of showing how "urban space orders grids of social difference" (p. 44), using an analysis of the lived realities of multicultural space in Vancouver, British Columbia. She indicates not only the complexity of the relationships between identity and place but also the limits of those arguments that see city space as borderless and zoneless. Anderson (Chapter 9) claims that contests around identity and poverty actively transform urban space into place. Other contributors look at the significance of representations of city spaces, in the constitution of identities in public discourse (see Fincher, Chapter 3, Knopp, Chapter 7, and Bondi, Chapter 8).

Doreen Massey argues that a conceptualization of space through the lens of difference "inherently implies the existence in the lived world of a simultaneous multiplicity of spaces: cross-cutting, intersecting, aligning with one another, or existing in relations of paradox or antagonism" (1994, p. 3). Places are open to the presence of social relations crafted at all spatial scales. In this vein, growing emphasis is being placed on the intersection of differently scaled processes in the construction of identity, with various geographers situating their sustained interest in the local in terms of its full range of broader and narrower spatial contexts. Smith (1993), for example, has noted the particular identities that seem to adhere to social processes at the scales of the body, home, local community, city, region, nation, and globe. Similarly, Ruddick (1996, p. 140) has demonstrated how an apparently "local" urban public square is also at the same time "situated in a liminal space of a global city" and may consequently play a "more pivotal international role in the production and dissemination of social identities [or] mythologies, than entire regions or nations in other parts of the world." These geographers are suggesting that internationally broad social configurations are forged with reference to local places, that local spaces are not limited in their relationships to local identities.

Several chapters in this collection extend this emphasis in the geographical literature on the complexity of spatial scales that flow through "place": the ways in which the local is always also a national or an international space, or the way in which "local" identities are always also constituted through nonlocal processes, or the way in which place-based identities are tied to the micropolitics of the home or the body. Pratt, for example, in Chapter 2 notes the diverse outcomes that arise from the presence of those from beyond Canadian borders in the multicultural spaces near to Vancouver's gentrifying inner-city neighborhoods. Dowling (Chapter 4) registers a different spatial scale at work in the constitution of suburban space. She demonstrates how apparently "minor" codes around modes of mothering can spill out of the confines of the house and constitute the moral geographies of neighborhoods, establishing broader-scaled patterns of inclusion and exclusion. In a related fashion, Bondi (Chapter 8) demonstrates how study of processes of neighborhood gentrification cannot be sealed off from study of the politics of the sexed body.

A number of the chapters extend this theme of the spatial complexity of cities by drawing our attention to the links between urban localities and geopolitical processes such as nation building, colonialism, and postcolonialism. Kofman's account in Chapter 12 of migrant labor in the "global" cities of Europe, for example, shows clearly that city spaces are also transnational spaces and that "urban" rights are complexly entwined with broader, nationally constituted issues of citizenship. In a different vein, Knopp (Chapter 7) traces the unlikely relationship between the articulation of gay identity in and through urban spaces to processes of nation building. Nagar and Leitner (Chapter 10) emphasize the way in which structures of power and difference constituted under colonialism continue to shape the everyday politics of urban space in a supposedly postcolonial city. Jacobs (Chapter 11) extends this intersection of urban space and geopolitics by arguing that many of the features associated with postmodern cities are unavoidably linked to struggles over how (post)colonial nations and their citizenry come to see themselves.

* * *

The essays collected in this book chart varied paths through the differences so apparent in city spaces. Each in their own way shows how a place-related focus on difference can reveal new complexities to be unraveled in matters considered the traditional substance of urban studies. The production and consumption of material life, long a preoccupation of critical urbanists in their work on built environments, labor markets, and capital movements, is unsettled in difference-directed geographies. Such concerns are not done away with, but they are productively complicated. And to these traditional preoccupations are added new urban geographies that not only document previously ignored urban lives but also reveal the complex intertwining of axes of difference. These new urban geographies attend to the variable and contextually constituted formation of difference and to the moral and material infrastructures around which such differences are built. This is a view of urban life that unavoidably fractures the idea of "the city." We invite you to make your own pathways and connections through these cities of difference.

NOTE

1. We draw on such work later in this chapter, as do many of our contributors. We are thinking, as examples, of the general influence of feminist theory as well as the important contribution of subaltern theorists like Gayatri Spivak and Homi Bhabha, the writings of women of color like bell hooks and the border writings of, say, Gloria Anzaldúa. A geographical overview of these and many other such theorists has been provided by Ed Soja in his book *Thirdspace* (1996).

REFERENCES

Barthes, R. (1981). Semiology and the urban. In M. Gottdiener & A. P.

Lagopoulos (Eds.), *The city and the sign: An introduction to urban semiotics* (pp. 87–98). New York: Columbia University Press.

Bordo, S. (1990). Feminism, postmodernism, and gender-scepticism. In L. J. Nicholson (Ed.), *Feminism/postmodernism* (pp. 133–156). London and New York: Routledge.

Burgess, E. W. (1967). The growth of the city: An introduction to a research project. In R. E. Park & E. W. Burgess (Eds.), *The city* (pp. 47–62). Chicago: University of Chicago Press. (Original work published 1925)

Butler, J. (1990). *Gender trouble: Feminism and the subversion of identity.* London and New York: Routledge.

Butler, J. (1993). *Bodies that matter.* London and New York: Routledge.

De Lauretis, T. (1987). *Technologies of gender: Essays, films and fiction.* London: Macmillan.

Fraser, N. (1995). From redistribution to recognition? Dilemmas of justice in a "post-socialist" age. *New Left Review, 212,* 68–93.

Gans, H. (1993). From underclass to undercaste: Some observations about the future of the postindustrial economy and its major victims. *International Journal of Urban and Regional Research, 17*(3), 327–335.

Geltmaker, T. (1992). The queer nation acts up: Health care, politics and sexual diversity in the County of Angels. *Environment and Planning D: Society and Space, 10,* 609–650.

Gibson, K., Huxley, M., Cameron, J., Costello, L., Fincher, R., Jacobs, J., Jamieson, N., Johnson, L., & Pulvirenti, M. (1996). *Restructuring difference: Social polarisation and the city.* Melbourne: Australian Housing and Urban Research Institute, Working Paper 6.

Harvey, D. (1989). *The condition of postmodernity.* Oxford: Blackwell.

Harvey, D. (1996). *Justice, nature and the geography of difference.* Oxford: Blackwell.

hooks, b. (1992). Representing whiteness in the black imagination. In L. Grossberg, C. Nelson, & P. Treichler (Eds.), *Cultural studies* (pp. 338–346). London and New York: Routledge.

Jones, J. P., & Moss, P. (1995). Democracy, identity, space. *Environment and Planning D: Society and Space, 13,* 253–257.

Keith, M., & Pile, S. (1993). Introduction, part 2: The place of politics. In M. Keith & S. Pile (Eds.), *Place and the politics of identity* (pp. 22–40). London and New York: Routledge.

Laclau, E., & Mouffe, C. (1985). *Hegemony and socialist strategy: Towards a radical democratic politics.* London: Verso.

Lake, R. (1994). Democracy and the transformation of the public sphere. *Urban Geography, 15*(7), 601–602.

Lash, S., & Urry, J. (1994). *Economies of signs and space.* London: Sage.

Massey, D. (1994). *Space, place, and gender.* Minneapolis: University of Minnesota Press.

Massey, D. (1995). Thinking radical democracy spatially. *Environment and Planning D: Society and Space, 13,* 283–288.

Mingione, E. (1993). The new urban poverty and the underclass: Introduction. *International Journal of Urban and Regional Research, 17*(3), 324–326.

Pettman, J. (1992). *Living in the margins: Racism, sexism and feminism in Australia.* Sydney: Allen & Unwin.

Phillips, A. (1992). Universal pretensions in political thought. In M. Barrett & A. Phillips (Eds.), *Destabilizing theory: Contemporary feminist debates* (pp. 10–30). London: Polity Press.

Pile, S., & Thrift, N. (Eds.). (1995). *Mapping the subject: Geographies of cultural transformation.* London and New York: Routledge.

Pratt, G., & Hanson, S. (1994). Geography and the construction of difference. *Gender, Place and Culture, 1*(1), 5–29.

Pringle, R., & Watson, S. (1992). "Women's interests" and the post-structuralist state. In M. Barrett & A. Phillips (Eds.), *Destabilizing theory: Contemporary feminist debates* (pp. 53–73). London: Polity Press.

Probyn, E. (1990). Travels in the postmodern: Making sense of the local. In L. J. Nicholson (Ed.), *Feminism/postmodernism* (pp. 176–189). London and New York: Routledge.

Rich, A. (1986). Notes towards a politics of location. *Blood, bread and poetry* (pp. 210–231). New York: Norton.

Rose, G. (1993). *Feminism and geography: The limits of geographical knowledge.* Cambridge, UK: Polity Press.

Rose, G. (1994). The cultural politics of place: Local representation and the oppositional discourse in two films. *Transactions of the Institute of British Geographers, 19*(1), 46–60.

Ruddick, S. (1996). Constructing difference in public spaces: Race, class and gender as interlocking systems. *Urban Geography, 17*(2), 132–151.

Sassen, S. (1991). *The global city: New York, London, Tokyo.* Princeton, NJ: Princeton University Press.

Scott, J. (1990). Deconstructing equality-versus-difference; or the uses of poststructuralist theory for feminism. In M. Hirsch & E. Fox Keller (Eds.), *Conflicts of feminism* (pp. 134–146). New York and London: Routledge.

Sennett, R. (1990). *The conscience of the eye: The design and social life of cities.* New York: Knopf.

Smith, N. (1993). Homeless/global: Scaling places. In J. Bird et al. (Eds.), *Mapping the futures: Local cultures, global change* (pp. 87–119). London and New York: Routledge.

Smith, N. (1994, March). *Social justice, gentrification and the revanchist city.* Paper presented at the Conference on Social Justice and the City, Oxford University, Oxford, UK.

Smith, N., & Katz, C. (1993). Grounding metaphor: Towards a spatialized politics. In M. Keith & S. Pile (Eds.), *Place and the politics of identity* (pp. 67–83). London and New York: Routledge.

Soja, E. W. (1989). *Postmodern geographies: The reassertion of space in social critical theory.* London: Verso.

Soja, E. W. (1996). *Thirdspace: Journeys to Los Angeles and other real-and-imagined places.* Cambridge, MA: Blackwell.

Spivak, G. (1988). Can the subaltern speak? In C. Nelson & L. Grossberg (Eds.), *Marxism and the interpretation of culture* (pp. 271–313). Urbana and Chicago: University of Illinois Press.

Spivak, G. (1990). *The post-colonial critic: Interviews, strategies, dialogues.* London and New York: Routledge.

Williams, P., & Chrisman, L. (Eds.). (1994). *Colonial discourse and postcolonial theory: A reader.* New York: Columbia University Press.

Young, I. M. (1990). *Justice and the politics of difference.* Princeton, NJ: Princeton University Press.

CHAPTER 2

Grids of Difference

PLACE AND IDENTITY FORMATION

Geraldine Pratt

When I was taught urban social geography in the 1970s, I learned about the city as a mosaic of social worlds, an exciting array of enclaves in the inner city (ethnic villages, gay ghettos, artist enclaves, elite neighborhoods) ringed by homogeneous middle-class, family-oriented suburbs. Part of my interest in the subject stemmed from the understanding that different areas of the city sustained radically different ways of life. Worlds apart in social terms, they stand as neighbors in space. I am still fascinated by the geographical premise of Tom Wolfe's novel (1987) about New York City, *The Bonfire of the Vanities*: that the space between two freeway ramps divides the Bronx from Park Avenue, and that by missing one turnoff you can emerge into a social world that operates with different codes, where other sets of identities are performed and where your identity is out of place.

With recent theorizing about identity and place, this view of the city now seems outdated. Rather than thinking about identities as solidified around one or two social traits such as ethnicity, or gender, or stage in the life cycle, or sexuality, identities are conceived as a process, as performed, and as unstable. Current theories call attention to the fact that we have multiple and sometimes contradictory subject positions and are sometimes torn between identifications, often moving between identifications in different situations and places. This notion of subjectivity has been articulated by Kathy Ferguson through the metaphor of mobile subjectivities: "I have chosen the term *mobile* rather than *multiple* to avoid the implication of movement from one to another stable resting place, and instead to problematize the contours of the resting one does" (1993, p. 158). "Class," she notes, "like race, gender, erotic identity, 'etc.,' can be crucial but still temporary and shifting resting places for subjects always in motion and in relation" (p. 177).

So too, it has been argued that it is inappropriate to view places as bounded because any boundaries are permeable, the global flows through the local, and the local is always dynamic (Massey, 1994). Moreover, there is a deep suspicion about mapping cultures onto places, because multiple cultures and identities inevitably inhabit a single place (think of the multiple identities performed under the roof of a family home) and a single cultural identity is often situated in multiple, interconnected spaces. Gupta and Ferguson (1992) argue against assuming the isomorphism of space, place, and culture. They resist the conventional view that cultures are localized and bounded in space and that cultural difference can be represented through a spatial grid of discrete and separate places. They reject, in other words, a vision of the city as a mosaic of spatially discrete and spatially bounded social worlds.

While convinced of the need to rethink the links between place and identity, many theorists are wary of tendencies simply to invert the isomorphism of place and identity, that is, to conceive of mobile identities as *de*-territorialized. Despite her metaphor, Ferguson herself recognizes (1993, p. 162) that subjectivities do get anchored and that understanding this process requires careful attention to the specifics of geography and particular locales. In this, she anticipates Angelika Bammer's criticism of contemporary writing that universalizes displacement, with the effect of "elaborating a new, postmodernistically hip version of the universal subject" (1994, p. xiii; see also Kaplan, 1987; Morris, 1990; Wolff, 1993). Bammer calls for work that puts "the 'place' [and historical specificity] back into 'displacement' " (p. xiv). Gupta and Ferguson (1992) direct attention to processes of re-(as opposed to de-)territorialization.

This chapter is a partial exercise in thinking within this middle ground, by considering the many and different ways that identities are territorialized in contemporary North American cities and the varying scales at which boundaries are produced. The denial of the reality of boundaries would seem to be a luxury affordable only to those not trapped by them. (The same is probably true for the romanticization of them.) My argument is that borders in space and place are tied up with social boundaries (the formation of identity and its complement, the production of difference) but that there are multiple grids of difference and complex and varied links between place and identity formation. It is important to understand these processes of boundary formation in order to create opportunities for imagined and actual alliances across them.

IDENTITIES ARE STILL BOUNDED

Accepting that identities are a process, a "project," and a "performance" is compatible with an understanding that a stable identity is reenacted through daily life. In my recent research and writing with Susan Hanson, we have been interested in how particular places not only enable but exact the performance of particular gender, class, and racial identities. We have argued that employers and employees in Worcester, Massachusetts (Figure 2.1), both intentionally and unintentionally conspire in boundary projects by creating extremely local labor markets within the metropolitan area, which have the effect of enabling and imposing different family and gender relations, as well as class and racial identities, on individuals living in different parts of

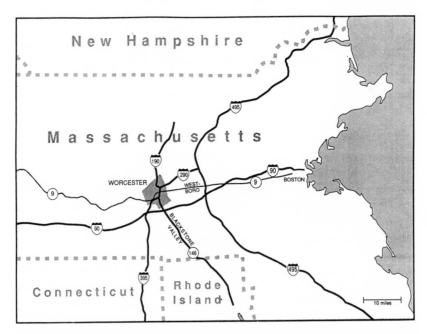

FIGURE 2.1. Worcester in its region. Worcester straddles Route 9, a route dating to colonial times, but is poorly connected to Interstate 90 (the Massachusetts Turnpike), constructed in the 1950s. From Hanson and Pratt (1995). Copyright 1995 by Routledge. Reprinted by permssion.

the city (Hanson & Pratt, 1995). At the extremes of intentionality and containment, employers to the southeast of the city in the Blackstone Valley were rumored to have prevented transportation linkages and improvements in order to maintain control of the local (white, working-class, low-waged) labor supply, while blocking other employers from coming into the region. Less obvious in intent but equal in effect, employers' propensity (in all areas studied) to advertise locally and hire through word of mouth, paired with the local job searches of many employees (especially women and workers in "lower" occupational grades), served to create locally bounded and distinctive labor markets (Figure 2.2). The fact that so many women, in particular, look for jobs close to home is not a matter of unmediated choice. Women with the heaviest domestic workloads were the most likely to find work close to home; power relations in the home thus played an important role in producing bounded labor markets.

These bounded labor markets make a difference to the identities enacted by women living in different parts of the city. They provide different resources, in terms of types of jobs available, hours and schedules of work, and wages paid for comparable work. Two individual case histories make this point. First, the place-bound restrictions on occupational class identity are illustrated by the case of one woman with whom we spoke in the Blackstone Valley. The Blackstone Valley had few clerical jobs, relative to a middle-class area that we studied. The circumstances of this one woman demonstrate the effects of the limited number of clerical jobs available there. This woman, 50 years old when interviewed in 1989, had migrated to the Blackstone Valley in the late 1960s from England with her husband. She had worked as a clerical worker before migrating and sought this type of work when her husband was laid off in 1970. Given that she had young children and no car, she needed to find work close to home, with "mothers' hours." Like so many women with whom we spoke, she found out about her job through neighborhood contacts—in this case from a woman neighbor who knew of an opening for a clerical job at her own workplace. When computers were brought into her workplace, the woman we interviewed told us that she "couldn't get it" and she was moved into production to work as an assembler. The new job was clearly a demotion, and not only in terms of status: it involved a shift from salary to waged work, and reductions in both pay and benefits. This woman preferred office work and returned, throughout the interview, to her loss of status: "Now I'm on the same level as everyone else at the plant today. I'm just assembly. If a machine is down, I do another [assembly] job." She described her current job as "a bore . . . It's just a paycheck." Of particular interest is this woman's

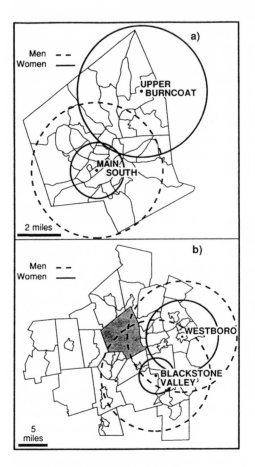

FIGURE 2.2. Locally bounded labor markets are demonstrated by median journey-to-work distances for women and men living in four local areas in Worcester, Massachusetts. (a) City of Worcester; insufficient numbers to show median travel times for men in Upper Burncoat. (b) Worcester MSA (Metropolitan Statistical Area). From personal interviews, Worcester MSA (1987), and Pratt and Hanson (1994). Copyright 1994 by Carfax Publishing Company, P.O. Box 25, Abingdon, Oxfordshire OX14 3UE, United Kingdom. Reprinted by permission.

recognition that her present circumstances were in large part dictated by her residential location. When she got a car, she said that "I looked around a little, but the majority of things that interested me, they were mostly around Worcester." Though these jobs were less than 10 miles away, she judged them to be too far and opted to stay (despite her dissatisfaction) in her job as assembler. The reputation of the Blackstone Valley, as home to poorly paid, well-disciplined factory workers, became a reality for this woman.

One gets the same sense of an identity congealing around an individual, in large part because of residential location in a spatially circumscribed labor market, in the case of a woman who had recently migrated from Puerto Rico and was presently living and working in Main South, an inner-city, low-income area of Worcester, home to large numbers of Latino and Vietnamese households. She lived in an area around Piedmont Street, a notorious and stigmatized street in the eyes of middle-class residents of Worcester, and worked in a nearby industrial laundry with many of her neighbors: "About 12 people who work here live where I live. All my good friends [at the laundry] live near me in the building that I'm talking about. I started working, and then cousins came and friends came, and all started working." She characterized her job as "suitable for dogs": the hours were long (a 10-hour day was not unusual) and wages low (in general, firms in Main South paid the lowest wages for comparable work, relative to firms in three other areas that we studied); and she very much wanted to find another job within the year. It is important, however, to note that the preceding quotes are translations of her words in Spanish. This woman lived and worked almost exclusively with Spanish-speaking Worcesterites and, working long hours, her opportunities to learn English were extremely limited. Her low wages minimized opportunities to move to another part of the city (where rents are higher), and yet a number of employers told us that her address alone would disqualify her from a job in their establishment. Again, the qualities and resources of her neighborhood seem to stabilize a poor Puerto Rican identity from which it seems extremely difficult to move away.

Within feminist and postmodernist writing there has been some resistance to the type of narrative that Susan Hanson and I, and many others, have constructed around stabilized identities and bounded places. We do not, however, see bounded places and spatialized identities as natural and static; our point has been to reveal the processes and power relations that produce bounded areas and the implications of these for those who are contained and enact their identities within them. While this provides the rationale for examining the relation between identities and bounded places, the feminist poststructuralist literature constructively sensitizes one to the inevitable partiality of these narratives, in terms of identities of both places and individuals. There is also a danger of missing the relationship between identities formed in different places. As a way of thinking about relationality and fragmented subjectivities, as well as responding to the empirical reality of international migration, a number of feminists (and others) have been drawn to tell stories about movement and identity formation.

CROSSING BOUNDARIES AND IDENTITY FORMATION

Writing about her experience of migrating from Romania to the United States, Marianne Hirsch (1994, p. 73) describes a fusion of geography and identity shifts associated with adolescent development:

> That is why it is so hard for me to write about the period of transition—my adolescence. My childhood remained in [Romania]. It is in Vienna that I had my first period, my first crush, wear my first stockings, try on lipstick. My first date, my first kiss, my first dances and parties, are all in Providence. That's where I lose my pudginess, grow another two inches (or is it two centimeters?), have my teeth straightened, become a teenager. But which of those changes are due to chronology, which to geography?

In instances where developmental changes are of less obvious significance, the geography of identity shifts is clearer. Feminists writing about 19th-century British travel writers in Africa, for example, have considered how different aspects of identity come to the fore in different contexts (Blunt, 1994; McEwan, 1994; Mills, 1994). Writing about Mary Kingsley, Alison Blunt (1994) describes how she was positioned as a *woman* travel writer in Britain, while her whiteness and class position overran her gender to some extent in West Africa. Ill of health in Britain, Mary Kingsley seemed to abandon these unfortunate trappings of femininity when she resumed her travels: in West Africa (beyond enjoying excellent health!) she moved between masculine and feminine codes of conduct. Other feminists have described how travel has altered their own sense of self, seeing differing aspects of identity and another grid of difference in a new context. Teresa de Lauretis (1988, p. 128) tells of the importance of immigration to the United States for her awareness of ethnic difference: "[My] first (geographical) dis-placement [from Italy to the United States]," she writes, "served as a point of identification for my first experience of cultural difference (difference not as simple distinction, but as hierarchized)." Through traveling to Cuba from the United States, Johnetta Cole (Bateson, 1990, p. 45) describes how she came to understand herself in gendered and not just racialized terms: "There I was," she says, "seeing for the first time the possibility that the race thing was not forever and ever; and then the other ism [sexism] was right up there saying, what about me?"

Along with simply highlighting another grid of difference, travel across boundaries can produce new identities. At an urban scale, bell hooks (1990) has articulated how movement across bounded places can sharpen an oppositional consciousness and in a sense unify an identity politics because societal contradictions and inequities become visible through travel; hooks writes about her experiences growing up in a small Kentucky town, where the railroad tracks divided the residences of African Americans—shacks and unpaved roads—from the town of whites. African Americans would cross those tracks, as service workers, and she argues that it is the recognition of this movement between margin and center—the knowledge and experiences of both separation and connection—that engenders oppositional consciousness (for additional examples from the secondary literature, see Rose, 1993). Moreover, hooks herself envisions a new identity space beyond the old polarities of difference (e.g., black and white) (Soja & Hooper, 1993). In this she resonates with postcolonial theorists such as Bhabha who are searching to articulate "strategies of selfhood—singular or communal—that initiate new signs of identity and innovative sites of collaboration, and contestation" (1994, pp. 1–2). Crossing boundaries figures prominently in his conception of these strategies: "It is in this sense that the boundary becomes the place from which something begins its *presencing*" (Bhabha, 1994, p. 5; emphasis in original).

Bhabha, as do others, historicizes these new subjectivities as a fin de siècle phenomenon and, as a postcolonial theorist, focuses on hybridity beyond grids of racial difference. There is room to explore arguments such as these within other grids of difference and, in a short vignette that follows, I again turn to the work that Susan Hanson and I have done in Worcester, Massachusetts, to experiment with the possibilities of exhausting the polarities of class identities among some groups of women.

In our writing about women's lives in Worcester, Susan Hanson and I have tried to think about how crossing class boundaries might spawn progressive politics among "middle-class" women (Pratt & Hanson, 1988). We start with the observation that there is a spatialization to the fragmentation of many women's identities.[1] The argument builds from the recognition that most women still find work in traditionally female-dominated occupations that tend to have relatively low status, poor benefits, and low remuneration. This means that many women, while living in middle-class households (defined in terms of their partners' jobs[2]) in relatively affluent neighborhoods, work in working-class occupations. As an index of this, using 1980 census data from Worcester and looking only at households in which women and men are employed, in one-quarter of the households in which the male's job is classified as managerial and professional, the woman is employed in a so-called nonskilled white-collar job. This would be a job like telephone operator, cashier, waitress, or retail clerk. One could argue that these women literally move through class locations during the day. At their jobs they are working class, at home they are middle class. For most men in our societies, residential location reinforces work class location; for many women, there is a radical disjuncture between these two class experiences. Of course, the two experiences are nonetheless linked: the working-class status of middle-class wives can be read, in part, as an extension of their subordinated position in the family.

There is something very interesting about the fact that many women live out the fragmentation of this part of their identity both temporally and spatially. The implications of this for exhausting the binary of working- and middle-class identities is intriguing. It may be that contradictions thrown up by multiple-class locations are managed by compartmentalizing different parts of one's life and identity, and that the spatial separation of home and workplace encourages this. Rosemary Pringle (1988), for example, notes that the relations of home and work are lived differently for "middle-class" (to some extent in terms of their own jobs and through their husbands' class standings as managers) and "working-class" Australian secretaries (who tended to be employed in "lower secretarial" jobs and to be married to men in the trades). The former tended to compartmentalize the two parts of their lives more completely: "As far as they were concerned, their home life was not relevant to what they did at work: they assumed a separation" (p. 227). Pringle observed that middle-class women were reluctant to bring their private lives to work—"their 'middle-classness' required that they be able to resist intrusions on their 'private' lives" (p. 226)—while working-class secretaries spoke openly and predominantly about their families and social activities. This difference may be tied to attempts on the part of middle-class secretaries to manage their experiences of class disjuncture.

Alternatively, different class locations may disrupt each other, and the fact that many women experience different class locations may have transformative effects.[3] Working women may bring back to their middle-class residential communities a knowledge of a greater range of experiences and needs. This may partially explain the gender gap in electoral politics and women's greater support for social services, which have been noticed in the United States at least since 1980 (Klein, 1984). We get clues of how these gender differences might translate into the transformation of urban places from a large survey conducted in the Greater Vancouver region in 1990 (Hardwick, Torchinsky, & Fallick, 1991). Women were much more likely than were men to support statements such as "Housing developments should contain a variety of income groups"; "The single family house is not essential for a 'true' family life"; or "I like the variety and stimulation one finds in the city." They were less likely to agree with a statement like "Attempting to mix lifestyles in any one part of the city leads to friction." (Unfortunately, differences among women were not pursued.)

My causal scenario for why many women are seemingly more accepting than are men of cultural and architectural diversity is extremely speculative, but—given the potential significance of these patterns for the places in which we live—they are well worth speculating about. I am tracing an argument about how class-based residential segregation, and the fact that many middle-class women track across different class positions during the course of their days, may transform our cities by encouraging the creation of more diversity in place. Movement across class boundaries may find concrete, material expression in our built environments.

UNSETTLING GENERALIZATIONS

It would be unwise, however, to overgeneralize the identity effects of crossing boundaries and to settle into new assumptions about isomorphisms between identity and place (e.g., crossing boundaries = new in-between identities). Boundary crossings can also disempower, fragment identity, and protect privilege, and bounded communities may have progressive effects.

In thinking about this I put my ongoing research on domestic workers in Vancouver, British Columbia, in tension with Bhabha's claims about the empowerment of Filipino/a migrants: "In their cultural passage as migrant workers . . . they embody the Benjaminian 'present': that moment blasted out of the continuum of history. Such conditions of cultural displacement and social discrimination—where political survivors become the best historical witnesses—are the grounds on which Frantz Fanon . . . locates an agency of empowerment" (Bhabha, 1994, p. 8).

It is important also to remember that these are the grounds of disempowerment. In Canada, large numbers of women come from the Philippines to work as domestic workers for Canadian families (6,400 entered through the Foreign Domestic Movement Program (now the Live-in Caregiver Program) in 1990 alone (60% of all women who came to Canada through this program in 1990 were Filipinas) (WCDWA, 1993; for details see Bakan & Stasiulis, 1995). In my interviews with nanny agents and government officials in the summer of 1994 it was patently clear that these gatekeepers hold no illusions that Canadians will do this work. One government official who administers the Live-in Caregiver Program through a local employment office put it succinctly: "The reason that we have to bring in [nannies] from abroad is that the occupation is so poorly paid that no one wants to do it." It is arguable, however, that Canadians are cleansed of guilt about hiring "Third World" women to do this work under conditions intolerable to Canadians, on the grounds that Filipinas are using the Live-In Caregiver Program as an immigration strategy: "Filipinos have a very different motivation [compared to European nannies]. . . . [T]hey are coming to immigrate to get citizenship, to bring in their families. They will put up with a lot in order to have a clean record, which makes for a whole other set of problems. But it means that they're likely to stay on the job" (nanny agent). A knowledge that the program enables Filipinas to cross international boundaries offers some justification, then, for labor conditions unacceptable to Canadians (see also Arat-Koc, 1990). So too, it is arguable that spatial separation shields Canadians from the day-to-day reality that many Filipinas have left their own children in the Philippines to care for Canadian families; 29% of the 144 domestic workers interviewed in a survey done under the auspices of the West Coast Domestic Workers' Association (WCDWA) in 1992/93 reported having at least one child in the Philippines (Mikita, 1994). A number of employers whom I have interviewed addressed this issue through a First World/Third World frame and, empathetic with Filipinas in these circumstances, find a comfortable space for themselves in the knowledge that these women are enacting their role of "good mother" by making the sacrifice of leaving their children. One woman whom I interviewed chose to sponsor a Filipina with an infant in the Philippines instead of an older, single Filipina, on the grounds that leaving an infant was a sign of deep maternal love and signaled the capacity to love her [the employer's] Canadian children. Thus, while border crossings may raise Filipinas' consciousness, they also effectively shield Canadians from making connections and/or legitimate social and employment relations that might otherwise raise some discomfort.

The ways in which border crossings can maintain old identity classifications and grids of difference, as well as privilege, are also apparent in an interview that I carried out in the summer of 1995 with parents who employ domestic workers. In writing about just one interview, I sketch the outlines of their childcare history and then "let the tape run" at length in order to unravel some of the complexities that emerge in thinking about identities and places.

This couple lives in a gentrifying inner-city neighborhood, adjacent both to Vancouver's "skid row" and "Chinatown," and home to a good number of Chinese and Vietnamese residents. The couple with whom I spoke were white professionals who owned a home in the area. That identities are crafted from fragmented and often contradictory subject positions was evident from the remarks made by the woman (Teresa), who seemed less comfortable living in her multicultural neighborhood when her children's childcare was involved. They had taken their first child to a day-care center outside the neighborhood, close to Teresa's workplace, until he was 18 months old. Because of a bureaucratic mishap, their child lost his day-care space at this age. This is the point at which the real dilemmas of living in a multicultural neighborhood began to be debated in the household. Teresa first looked into a family daycare arrangement in her neighborhood, run by an Italian woman in her home. She tapped into her multicultural networks to check this out: "I have a friend who is Italian so I asked: 'How does this woman check out?,' wanting as much collateral as possible. 'Can I trust this person with my child?'" The woman was recommended highly, which meant that Teresa "just felt worse after being there": "I went to visit on a very bright sunny snowy morning. The TV was on. The curtains were drawn. There were about six kids all sort of bouncing off each other, in a very bold way." She rejected the day-care arrangement because "the sort of sensory deprivation put me off." She felt that she had exhausted her networks and "advertising was the very last thing that we wanted to do," so her husband (Tom) started to inquire through his networks. Eventually, a friend knew of a "fellow" worker who might want the job: "That's how we met up with the other woman. . . . She brought her own [8-month-old] child to be here. And that situation lasted for about a year and a half [until their next child was born]. And it was a very very good situation."

TERESA: It was great. She came over the first time and she was younger than I had imagined this person should be. But she was mature. Early twenties. Really confident. And energetic and had lots of experience.

TOM: And she and [her daughter] had lovely manners.

TERESA: Both really gentle.

TOM: With her own child and with [their son].

As the discussion about this caregiver progressed, it became clear to me that a norm of similarity was very important to Teresa.

TERESA: We had sort of agreed at the beginning about discipline, and sort of philosophy.

G.P.: How did you agree?

TERESA: I had taken the Parent Effectiveness Training course. I'll show
    you the book later. But it's very clear about giving kids choices.
    And preserving self esteem. Let them experience competencies.
    So I sort of talked to her about the highlights that were impor-
    tant to me in this book. And our philosophy was in common.
    Just sort of . . . I don't know . . . comfortable with each other. And
    her spirituality was similar. And all that stuff. And she was pretty
    well vegetarian. I'm not vegetarian. That's not really important
    to me. But she had good food choices. She wasn't going to fill
    the kids up with candy, and chips and pop and stuff, which I
    could see happening with other baby-sitters. And so that part
    was important to me as well.

When their second child was born, they had to rearrange childcare.

TERESA: One option that keeps coming up from living in this area,
    which has a lot of Chinese and Vietnamese people, was that many
    people have the old Chinese grandmother looking after their
    kids. The woman across the park who is Caucasian and both her
    kids have had this older Chinese lady looking after them. . . . But
    I felt really like I didn't want to do that because I didn't want to
    have anyone here who I couldn't communicate with.

TOM: I did want it. But we didn't agree.

G.P.: Because you weren't worried so much about . . . ?

TOM: No, I felt it would have been a great situation. But it wouldn't
    have been a great situation if Teresa was worried. So I couldn't
    pursue it. But I thought that would be great.

G.P.: Because of the language?

TOM: Yes. And being able to stay in the home. And there is a network
    in the park of grandmothers and kids.

TERESA: The downside is that, while learning Cantonese would be great
    and learning about another culture, but what I also observe is
    that the old ladies don't have a lot of energy for stimulating the
    kids. So on rainy days they are all kind of in front of the televi-

sion, and behavior is dealt with by either yelling or bribing with
candies. So it didn't meet my kind of standards.

G.P.: [Directed toward Tom] So you kind of liked the connectedness of the neighborhood?

Tom: That's one of the reasons why we live here. The neighborhood has a great sense of community. That for me would have just been another way of living that way. But if Teresa wasn't going to be comfortable with it, it wouldn't have worked.

G.P. And there is a different balance [between you]. Because they are different priorities.

Teresa: Yes.

Tom: Mmmm.

So it becomes evident, in listening to Teresa speak, that although she feels comfortable living in the neighborhood herself, she is less comfortable with cultural difference when it affects her children's care. Eventually, after hiring a Filipina nanny to care for their children in their home, two spaces became available at their son's original day-care center. They accepted those spots, even though this arrangement cost roughly $300 more a month and required car transport. (Tom in particular expressed a commitment to a carless lifestyle and mentioned the sacrifices in this regard that went along with their childcare choice.) It is also interesting to note that a number of middle-class parents in the area transport their children out of the neighborhood for childcare. Teresa estimated that eight children within a two block radius of their home go to their sons' day-care center, a migration precipitated by their enthusiasm for it (As Tom put it, "I think it's just a question of, a sort of snowballing thing"). There is a day-care center in the neighborhood, but it is on Hastings Street (skid row) "and no one wants to use it because it is part of the Hastings traffic" (Teresa). The Hastings Street day-care center undoubtedly is used by some parents in the area (or it would be closed) but seemingly not by middle-class parents in their neighborhood.

There are several aspects of this interview that point to the complexities of theorizing the links between identity formation and place. First, Teresa appears to be divided in relation to her neighborhood—we see the fragmentation of identity in play—and, second, the multicultural neighborhood eventually works for her (and evidently a good number of other white middle-class families) because she is able to cross outside of it in one part of her life (her role as a mother). Her privilege allows her to do this, and being able to do so allows her to enact middle-class child-rearing standards. Further, by taking their children out of the neighborhood, these families possibly reproduce a new generation of social and cultural boundaries among children in the neighborhood. But, third, this interview demonstrates how a geographical boundary can sustain an openness to cultural difference. Tom's acceptance of cultural difference is very much tied to a sense of neighborhood. He embraces the Chinese grandmother option because it is a way of living as part of the community. Further, he was exploring an exchange with a Mandarin-speaking neighbor, offering English instruction in exchange for Mandarin instruction for his children. Tom was much less receptive to the idea of hiring a Filipina caregiver, not because of her cultural identity, but because she was coming from outside their local networks: "I felt less um . . . When we hired [the Filipina caregiver] the whole process of deciding whether to have someone to come in somehow wasn't comfortable. I felt. . . . It's complicated. I felt like we would be passing over our children to some other person who we had no idea about at all. Even with the references, there was part of me saying it didn't feel quite right. . . . I wasn't going to block it, but when the decision was made to put them in [day care], I felt much better."

This makes the simple but critical point that boundaries and a commitment to the local are not necessarily politically regressive. In this instance, they nurtured a willingness to cross boundaries of identity and culture. The boundedness of the local opens possibilities to create relationships across differences. The complexities of place and identities are such that it seems unwise to expect a necessary or uncomplicated relationship between identities and places. It is possible to imagine ideals of community that envelope difference and bounded spaces that foster multicultural ideals. Madan Sarup (1994, p. 103) asks, "At present the norm stresses similarity, but what would happen if the norm changed and if the norm stressed difference? What would happen if there was a recognition of the diversity of subjective positions and cultural identities?" And can we ask, in what spaces might this norm of diversity be practiced?

MULTICULTURAL SPACES

Implicit in at least some writing about "decentered," "in-between," "hybridized" identities, and a multiculturalism that exists through a norm of difference is the sense that this identity may find expression within globalized, multicultural cities. So, as an example of "a broad-minded acceptance of cosmopolitanism," Gupta and Ferguson quote a "young white reggae fan in the ethnically chaotic neighborhood of

Balsall Heath in Birmingham" (1992, p. 10). The geographical iden-
tifier is worth noting. As a way of articulating the norm of difference,
Iris M. Young imagines the ideal of the nonoppressive city, in which
individuals from different social groups enjoy experiencing each others' cultures without the pretense or presumption of belonging to or
fully understanding those other cultures: "We witness one another's
cultures and functions in such public interaction, without adopting
them as our own. The appreciation of ethnic foods or professional
musicians, for example, consists in the recognition that these tran-
scend the familiar everyday of my life" (1990, p. 319). Iain Chambers
(1994a, 1994b) speculates that the globalization of contemporary cities serves to destabilize the centrality of a single identity:

> The idea of cultural complexity, most sharply on display in the
> arabesque patterns of the modern metropolis—and that includes
> Lagos as well as London, Beijing and Buenos Aires—weakens
> earlier schemata and paradigms, destabilises and decentres pre-
> vious theories and sociologies. Here the narrow arrow of pro-
> gressive time is displaced by the open spiral of heterogeneous
> collaborations and contaminations, and what Edward Said has
> recently referred to as "atonal ensembles." (1994a, p. 93)

> This encourages me to contemplate living with the responsibil-
> ity for the always provisional nature of fabricated habitats that
> are never realized but are always in the process of becoming. In
> this I begin to learn the art of losing myself (as opposed to merely
> getting lost) and thereby gain the opportunity of falling through
> the gap in my consciousness, rationalism and inherited verdicts,
> to begin learning the languages of silence and a capacity for
> listening. (1994b, p. 249)

As compelling as this urban imaginary may be, I think that we
should be cautious about the freedoms and diversity of actual cities,
based on an awareness that boundaries are drawn and redrawn at
very fine spatial scales. I rely on a final empirical vignette, from
Williams's (1988) ethnography of one block in a racially integrated,
rapidly gentrifying inner-city neighborhood in Washington, DC, to
make this point. Most of the whites living on the block studied by
Williams were relatively recent arrivals. In occupational terms, they
are classified as political activist lawyers, environmental activists, university professors, or newspaper reporters. These people bought into
the area, in part, because they were attracted by its varied racial composition and an ideal of multiculturalism. Despite the attractions of

racial heterogeneity, the realities of labor market segmentation were translated starkly into the housing market and strict racial segregation persisted: all of the white households owned row houses on the one side of the street, while long-term African American residents lived in rental apartments facing them. Members of neither group had entered the homes of the other.

Williams's analysis of the television-viewing habits of these residents is particularly interesting to me because it demonstrates the process of boundary formation in a multicultural space, and the interplay between material and cultural boundaries. While mass television could be taken as an index of the nationalization and indeed globalization of culture and as a vehicle for crossing boundaries, in fact residents on one side of the street rarely watched the same programs as those on the other. Instead, they watched each other through programs that seriously distorted each other's lives and perpetuated stereotypes of race and urban living. African American women living in the apartments, who did most of the television viewing in their households, watched programs like *Dallas* and *Dynasty,* dramas of wealthy, troubled white families living in large houses. The white homeowners watched what Williams terms gentrified television, programs like *Hill Street Blues* and *St. Elsewhere.* Although these latter programs have been represented as self-conscious attempts to undermine racial and gender stereotypes and to portray urban life in realistic ways, Williams argues that they simply reproduce these stereotypes and a vision of city life as chaotic, violent, and unpredictable, in which liberal, well-intentioned people are vulnerable to attacks from gangs and drug addicts, and where lower-income people live uniformly sordid and violent lives. She sees these programs as "extraordinary urban vehicles for cross-class communication" that "guide assumptions" that the white homeowners make about everyday life. These programs "lead [the homeowners] to interpret and frame ambiguous scenes with more unease, fear, and distrust [than they might otherwise]. These programs thus speak powerfully to the uncertainties of [the] new owners, although a direct connection between watching them and growing more hostile [to their neighbors across the street] might be difficult to prove" (1988, p. 112). Liberal whites are attempting to live in a multicultural place, but the cultural representations that they watch on television portray a dichotomous cultural urban space that then partially structures, through fear and hostility, their relations in their neighborhood, reproducing dichotomized urban places.

The television preferences of the African Americans can be interpreted as a sign of their contradictory status, drawn to the ethics of home ownership but unable to gain entrance to these property relations. Their in-between and contradictory status is apparent in their relations with Latino families within their building. In recent years about a half dozen extended Latino families, refugees from El Salvador, had moved into the apartment building inhabited by African Americans. There was a fair amount of conflict between African American and Latino residents, articulated through their different ideas of how the building should be used. The categories of race and difference were signified and worked through the material use of the building. Many African Americans attributed declining conditions within the building to the presence of Latino families. They were critical of what they perceived to be overcrowding on the part of Latinos, as well as the tendency of Latinos to domesticate semipublic spaces, such as the laundry and halls. As one African American woman put it, "Spanish people use the hall like a porch." In appealing to the management company, African American residents distinguished themselves from Latino families and employed the rhetoric of home ownership, citing their personal morality, concern about the building, and residential stability. Williams writes that "black women tenants argue that by settling in and taking an active moral interest in a building you can act like a homeowner. This ethos then frames the rhetoric through which they demand particular privileges and services" (1988, p. 68). By tying African Americans so closely to the ideals of home ownership, Williams positions them within the same ideological space as the homeowners across the street.

The boundaries on this one street are multiple and drawn in different places in different ideological spaces. Material boundaries (homeowner/renter; different traditions of drawing lines between public and private spaces) underline racial categories. Cultural representations of race reproduce material divisions. I am struck not only by the multitude of boundaries but by the loss of political agency that flows from them. As the deterioration of living conditions, possibly due to disinvestment on the part of the landlord, is interpreted as the consequence of racial difference among tenants, the potential for effective tenant organizing is undermined. As the white residents, whose gentrifying impulse is prompted by the ideals of a type of multiculturalism (bracketing the material consequences of this impulse for their neighbors across the street and the responsibility that they may bear for any disinvestment on the part of the landlord), burrow into the security of their private homes, a vision of urban living that seeks out difference is lost. Sorting through the boundaries and overlapping ideological spaces—seeing the boundaries and points of intersection—is a very preliminary step toward building alliances that might work against the homogenizing forces of gentrification.

One of the points of interest of this case is that, if the residents have any hope of retaining the social and economic diversity of their neighborhood, they will likely have to move beyond "enjoying" difference to actually engaging with it by pursuing a common political project located in space. In this instance, a multicultural space localizes the political project, but it certainly does not ensure a multicultural space of identity formation or political practice.

CONCLUSIONS

The last vignettes raise the issues of what we mean by multiculturalism and how ideals of multiculturalism relate to urban space. Shohat and Stam (1994, p. 47) argue that multiculturalism "has become an empty signifier [on to] which diverse groups project their hopes and fears. . . . For us, the word 'multiculturalism' has no essence; it points to a debate." They hope to prod the debate towards a radical critique of power relations, to a multiculturalism that makes connections and decolonizes through reordering and equalizing power relations between communities.

With our long history of studying the ways in which urban space orders grids of social difference, social geographers have much to contribute to this debate, at the very least by continuing to detail the material and cultural boundaries that permeate the city. As Shohat and Stam (1994, p. 358) put it, multiculturalism is not simply "nice": "like a suburban barbecue to which a few token people of color are invited"; it involves seeing and taking responsibility for histories of social and economic inequalities. It seems to me that efforts toward this kind of multicultural "space" are not advanced by representations that conceive of cities as blurred, chaotic, borderless places; these representations of urban space potentially screen hierarchized grids of difference. One must understand the multiple processes of boundary construction in order to disrupt them, in order to build toward multicultural spaces of radical openness and radical politics, what Shohat and Stam (1994, p. 359) term "mutual and reciprocal relativization."

At the same time, processes of border construction and the "reterritorialization" of identity are clearly complex, far more complex than the metaphor of "a mosaic of social worlds" suggests. Through various empirical vignettes I have tried to show how bounded places can stabilize identities or, alternatively, open up the potential for cross-cultural communication. Some individuals are contained by places; others move across boundaries and enact different aspects of their identity in different places. Crossing boundaries can have transformative effects or protect the status quo. The most consistent message of this chapter is that the relations between place and identity are complex and variable. There is therefore a persistent need to examine the specificity of these processes, in time and place, and to resist overgeneralizing one set of relations or effects. There is a need to take seriously the historical geography of identity formation.

ACKNOWLEDGMENTS

I thank Jennifer Hyndman for her very helpful comments on a draft of this chapter and Ruth Fincher and Jane Jacobs for their invitation to contribute to this volume and their careful editing. The two vignettes from Worcester owe much, of course, to a long and productive association with Susan Hanson. The empirical material for the crossing boundaries and multicultural spaces sections of this chapter were first written for a paper ("Travelling Theory and Spatial Metaphors") presented at the Making Worlds: Metaphor and Materiality in the Production of Feminist Texts Conference, sponsored by Southwest Institute for Research on Women (SIROW), at the University of Arizona, Tucson, October 1993. A reworked version of the conference paper appears as "Geographic Metaphors in Feminist Theory" in S. Aiken, A. Brigham, S. Marston, and P. Waterstone (Eds.), *Making Worlds: Metaphor and Materiality in the Production of Feminist Texts*. Tucson: University of Arizona Press, 1997. The research on domestic work has received generous support from the Social Sciences Humanities Research Council (SSHRC Grant No. 5-57335). I thank Trina Bester for her careful transciption of the parent interview.

NOTES

1. I do not want to overgeneralize my claims about gender. I, for example, do not experience the class rupture that I describe here.

2. I recognize the difficulties associated with this class positioning (Pratt & Hanson, 1991). I am drawing attention to the fact that many working-class women live in higher-income residential areas because of their husbands' class standing.

3. On the other hand, the politics that result from this disruption may be less "progressive." The multiplicity of class locations inhabited by women in the same occupations may, for example, impede workplace organization. This is precisely what Cho (1985) concludes from her participant observation study of women working at Microtek, Inc., in Silicon Valley. Most of the unskilled assembly jobs at Microtek were filled by women, but—if one takes into consideration the rest of their lives and identities—these women were situated in diverse class circumstances: "One Korean woman worker's husband was a medical doctor, while one American woman's boyfriend was a

fabrication operator at a firm in Silicon Valley. . . . In general, a significant number of the married women's husbands had high-income jobs, such as chemical engineering. There were also quite a few single women who had two jobs to meet their living expenses" (pp. 200–201). Cho argues that the diverse cultural and class backgrounds discouraged women from discovering and pursuing their common interests as assembly workers. She reports that many of the married women "never read [their paychecks] with care" (p. 201) and it was therefore not surprising that it was a single mother who discovered that the company was violating its own regulations by failing to pay overtime.

REFERENCES

Arat-Koc, S. (1990). Importing housewives: Non-citizen domestic workers and the crisis of the domestic sphere in Canada. In S. Arat-Koc, M. Luxton, & H. Rosenberg (Eds.), *Through the kitchen window: The politics of home and family* (pp. 81–103). Toronto: Garamond.

Bakan, A., & Stasiulis, D. (1995). Making the match: Domestic placement agencies and the racialization of women's household work. *Signs: Journal of Women in Culture and Society, 20,* 303–335.

Bammer, A. (Ed.). (1994). *Displacements: Cultural identities in question.* Bloomington and Indianapolis: Indiana University Press.

Bateson, M. C.(1990). *Composing a life.* New York: Plume.

Bhabha, H. (1994). *The location of culture.* London and New York: Routledge.

Blunt, A. (1994). *Travel, gender, and imperialism: Mary Kingsley and West Africa.* New York: Guilford Press.

Chambers, I. (1994a). *Migrancy culture identity.* London and New York: Routledge.

Chambers, I. (1994b). Leaky habitats and broken grammar. In G. Robertson, M. Mash, L. Tickner, J. Bird, B. Curtis, & T. Putnam (Eds.), *Travellers' tales* (pp. 245–249). London and New York: Routledge.

Cho, S. K. (1985). The labor process and capital mobility: The limits of the new international division of labor. *Politics and Society, 14,* 185–22.

de Lauretis, T. (1988). Displacing hegemonic discourses: Reflections on feminist theory in the 1980s. *Inscriptions, 3/4,* 127–144.

Ferguson, K. (1993). *The man question: Visions of subjectivity in feminist theory.* Berkeley: University of California Press.

Gupta, A., & Ferguson, J. (1992). Beyond "Culture": Space, identity, and politics of difference. *Cultural Anthropology, 7,* 6–23.

Hanson, S., & Pratt, G. (1995). *Gender, work, and space.* London and New York: Routledge.

Hardwick, W., Torchinsky, R., & Fallick, A. (1991). *Shaping a livable Vancouver region: Public opinion surveys* (B.C. Geographical Series, No. 48). Vancouver, British Columbia, Canada.

Hirsch, M. (1994). Pictures of a displaced girlhood. In A. Bammer (Ed.),

Displacements: Cultural identities in question (pp. 71–89). Bloomington and Indianapolis: Indiana University Press.

hooks, b. (1990). *Yearning: Race, gender, and cultural politics.* Toronto: Between the Lines.

Kaplan, C. (1987). Deterritorializations: The rewriting of home and exile in Western feminist discourse. *Cultural Critique, 6,* 187–198.

Klein, E. (1984). *Gender politics: From consciousness to mass politics.* Cambridge, MA: Harvard University Press.

Massey, D. (1994). *Space, place and gender.* Cambridge and Oxford, UK: Polity Press.

McEwan, C. (1994). Encounters with West African women: Textual representations of difference by white women abroad. In A. Blunt & G. Rose (Eds.), *Writing women and space* (pp. 73–100). New York: Guilford Press.

Mikita, J. (1994). *The influence of the Canadian state on the migration of foreign domestic workers to Canada: A case study of the migration of Filipina nannies to Vancouver, British Columbia.* Unpublished M.A. thesis, Department of Geography, Simon Fraser University, Burnaby, British Columbia, Canada.

Mills, S. (1994). Knowledge, gender, and empire. In A. Blunt & G. Rose (Eds.), *Writing women and space* (pp. 29–50). New York: Guilford Press.

Morris, M. (1990). Banality in cultural studies. In P. Mellencamp (Ed.), *Logics of television: Essays in cultural criticism* (pp. 14–43). Bloomington: Indiana University Press.

Pratt, G., & Hanson, S. (1988). Gender, class and space. *Environment and Planning D: Society and Space, 6,* 15–35.

Pratt, G., & Hanson, S. (1994). Geography and the construction of difference. *Gender, Place and Culture, 1,* 5–29.

Pringle, R. (1988). *Secretaries talk.* London and New York: Verso.

Rose, G. (1993). *Feminism and geography: Disciplinary discourse and difference.* Cambridge, UK: Polity Press.

Sarup, M. (1994). Home and identity. In G. Robertson, M. Mash, L. Tickner, J. Bird, B. Curtis, & T. Putnam (Eds.), *Travellers' tales* (pp. 93–104). London and New York: Routledge.

Shohat, E., & Stam, R. (1994). *Unthinking Eurocentricism.* London and New York: Routledge.

Soja, E., & Hooper, B. (1993). The spaces that difference makes: Some notes on the geographical margins of the new cultural politics. In M. Keith & S. Pile (Eds.), *Place and the politics of identity* (pp. 183–205). London and New York: Routledge.

WCDWA (West Coast Domestic Workers' Association) (March, 1993). Supporting documentation for WCDWA brief to Employment Standards Act Review Committee. #302, 119 West Pender St., Vancouver, British Columbia, Canada.

Williams, B. (1988). *Upscaling downtown.* Ithaca, NY: Cornell University Press.

Wolfe, T. (1987). *The bonfire of the vanities.* New York: Bantam.

Wolff, J. (1993). On the road again: Metaphors of travel in cultural criticism. *Cultural Studies, 7,* 224–239.

Young, I. M. (1990). The ideal of community and the politics of difference. In L. Nicholson (Ed.), *Feminism/postmodernism* (pp. 300–323). New York: Routledge.

CHAPTER 3

In the Right Place at the Right Time?

LIFE STAGES AND URBAN SPACES

Ruth Fincher

> [T]he public ideal of leisured and paced
> mainstream middle-class childhood, adolescence,
> young adulthood and adulthood, often portrayed
> in the media, lies outside the realm of possibility
> for those who grew up in inner cities anywhere in
> the world at the end of the twentieth century.
> —MCLAUGHLIN AND HEATH (1993, p. 215)

Life stages, the times of our lives with which certain statuses, behaviors, activities, or achievements are associated, are socially constructed, as are notions of gender, ethnicity, race, and place. We expect things of ourselves and of others at named times in our lives. Societal institutions—schools, bureaucracies, media, workplaces—predict certain characteristics of people at different life stages as well, usually generalizing to us all from the "middle-class mainstream" alleged above. Within these general expectations, people carve out their individual life courses idiosyncratically (see Katz & Monk, 1993).

Geographical studies now accept people's shifting and multiple identities, and refer more routinely to the ways interactions between people's ethnicity, gender, or class frame their experiences across the meaningful places of their lives. In this chapter I suggest some ways in which urban spaces are associated with, and interpreted by, constructions of people's life stages as well as by other aspects of their identities and difference.

Of course urban geographies of different age groups have long been made. They have focused on the perceptions or activities of a range of age groups in varying urban circumstances and the reasons that these take the form they do. Such work has occurred across the shifts in fashionable paradigms within urban studies. Decades ago in research on children, for example, perceptions of urban spaces were shown to vary with the age and cultures of the users of those urban spaces (Lynch, 1970; Downs & Stea, 1973) and the spaces used by elderly urban residents were contrasted with the spaces of their imaginations and memories (Rowles, 1980). In the behavioral studies of the 1970s, people's residential choices were modeled and contrasted on the basis of the different life stages at which they occurred—with or without children (Preston & Taylor, 1981). A good deal of the study of gentrification has focused on the lifestyles and demographic characteristics of those choosing residence in restructured inner-city environments (Smith & Williams, 1986), with recent work finding that those lifestyles and stages are not so easy to generalize in the 1980s and 1990s as perhaps they were previously (Ley, 1992). In frameworks focusing on the constraints posed by urban built environments on the choices of residents of cities, the difficulties faced by women accompanying small children around cities have been noted (Tivers, 1988). Furthermore, it is not just the actions and perceptions of individual consumers or residents that have been viewed in terms of life stages. For example, Laws (1993) described the promotion by developers of residential landscapes in the United States that are exclusively for elderly residents who can afford to buy into them. Mullins and Rosentraub (1992) show the efforts of local jurisdictions in that country to "capture" wealthy elderly taxpayers, despite the fact that the wealthy elderly are not always the fiscal bargain they may seem, requiring more services than local governments may have anticipated!

In this chapter, I focus on ways that life stage assumptions are present in the interpretations or understandings of urban spaces made by policymakers and urban analysts. Normative views about what should go on at certain stages of people's lives and the places in which these life stages should be lived often guide policies and public statements about cities.

I take two spatial fixtures of American urban analysis and interpretation—the inner city and the suburb—and show some of the ways that academic and public discussion of them presently depicts the gendered and racialized *life stages* of their residents, rather than just the gendered and racialized *characteristics* of their residents. The first two sections of the chapter will make this point. They show in particular how teenage African American men and women have been rendered in analysis the "problem" inhabitants of inner cities, from a focus in the young women's case on out-of-wedlock births and in the young men's case on their involvement in violent and criminal behavior. In contrast, the American suburb is depicted as the site of heterosexual adulthood where grownups live in owned, single-family housing, in a place and mature life stage to which all in the youthful phase (and in the inner city) should aspire.

In a third section I take a different slant on the question of life stages in urban space, considering and querying the way life stage norms are adopted by Australian women of different age groups, as evidenced in their use of urban services and the activism they engage in to produce or extend those services. This material highlights the ways that analysts' ("outsiders'") notions of the performance of life stages can be like or unlike the lived realities of those life stages for the individuals and groups living them.

Anticipating the discussion to follow, it will be apparent that space is associated with life stages in a number of ways in this chapter. One approach is in much of the literature cited on inner cities, where those inner cities are conceived (often implicitly) as bounded areas containing, concentrating, and therefore helping to constitute the activities of residents in certain "immature" life stages. A second association between urban space and life stages sets the built landscapes of suburban housing and their housing tenure characteristics as a frame through which an adult life stage identity is established in suburbs. In a third way of linking people and urban locations, the imagined spaces of activity of older women are contrasted to those of younger women, in the Australian material of the chapter's final section.

YOUTH IN THE AMERICAN INNER CITY

Segregation, separation, zoning, the spatial severing of certain people from certain places, increasing differentiation between forms of labor market participation and social resources among groups that are divided spatially—these are the messages of contemporary American urban geographies of inequality. Economic processes have captured those people living in inner-city areas who previously worked in nearby manufacturing plants, grouping them together in places inaccessible by public transport to new sites of suburban jobs (Kasarda, 1990, pp. 237–239). Most affected by the loss of jobs in these altering inner-city labor markets have been African American men, whose "joblessness" relative to other gendered and racialized groups is, in many accounts, associated with inner-city and community dysfunction. It is certainly the case that American inner cities are now home to greater concentrations of people who are severely disadvantaged than in the past.

These economic and spatial differences are overwhelmingly racialized in the posing of the situation in academic and public policy writing, and no doubt in the lived realities of it. The "race issue" is, however, generally perceived to be the divide between white and black, European American and African American (Galster & Hill, 1992, p. 1), despite the presence of a range of other ethnic groups that are variably resourced and spatially integrated in American metropolises. Racialized differences often frame discussions of the formation of an American "underclass" and the reasons and responsibilities for this (see Ricketts, 1992). Some analysts, however, place greater stress on the motivations and behaviors of those in poverty, reinvoking notions of a "culture of poverty" more common to academic and policy discussions in the 1960s (see Zinn, 1989; Ricketts, 1992). In the work of William Julius Wilson (1987) these two understandings of concentrated disadvantage seem fused. Wilson's definition of the underclass is still regularly quoted:

> [It is] that heterogeneous grouping of families and individuals who are outside the mainstream of the American occupational system. Included in this group are individuals who lack training and skills and either experience long-term unemployment or are not members of the labor force, individuals who are engaged in street crime and other forms of aberrant behavior, and families that experience long-term spells of poverty and/or welfare dependence. (1987, p. 8)

The legislative and constitutional capacity of local authorities within American cities to restrict access to "unlike" families or households sustains the differences between residents of suburban and inner-city jurisdictions. Galster (1992) cites the U.S. President's Commission for a National Agenda for the Eighties to show that the divisions and their implications are understood by people and their governments but that little has changed in order to remove them: "Middle-class whites—and middle-class blacks—guard their social and physical separation from the urban underclass. An array of political forces (zoning regulations, building codes) supports an approach that keeps the poor where they are" (p. 197).

Households experiencing greatest poverty are those headed by female single parents, while those reaping greatest economic rewards more typically contain two adult wage earners. Goldsmith and Blakely (1992, p. 38) conclude that "the burden of poverty falls disproportionately on women with children, especially on African American women with children." African Americans make up almost half the poor in central cities. Having two parents in a family is not necessarily a guarantee of higher income for people in racial minority groups, however. Research shows that much poverty in single-parent African American households follows the split up of two-parent households that were just as poor (Zinn, 1989, p. 862).

Understandings of the inner-city spaces of American metropolises, then, often identify residents racially, and by income and employment status. Inner-city peoples are, even if implicitly, presented as the bearers of certain collective attributes and behaviors. Gendered life stages are profoundly significant in this, as are racialized expectations of what these gendered life stage progressions will be. The emphasis in many accounts describing the populations of inner cities, for example, is on households headed by young women and on their childbearing practices in particular. The youthful demography of inner cities is portrayed as a "problem," something which reduces the likelihood that these neighborhoods and their residents will redeem themselves in some more "adult" future. There is also frequent association of the young African American male with American inner cities, most often as a dangerous person for whom an appropriate "adult" future is unlikely.

How, then, is youth present in the usual descriptions of the poor residents of American inner cities, and is this mention of age and life stage judgmental, anticipating behaviors and reduced capacities that should not be assumed on the basis of age? Are there present in these descriptions judgments of inner-city residents' lifepaths that are too inflexible, stereotypically racialized or sexualized? I argue that particular gendered constructions of youth are embedded in the racialized inner cities of much academic and public writing. Young men and young women have certain "problems" in this view. Further, their problematic status is seen as the greater because of their perceived lack of capacity to proceed from this "youthful" stage (where irresponsibility, however defined, is to be expected) to the next life stage, that of "adulthood."

The following list quotes one author—Krumholtz (1992, p. 36)—to demonstrate the manner in which sets of numerical indicators about inner-city neighborhoods are typically used to show the "problems" of a place. The inner-city place being described in this list is in Cleveland. Note how many of the indicators refer to the youth of the neighborhood's inhabitants, with age, childbearing, and lack of homeownership singled out. Says Krumholtz (1992, p. 36) of this Cleveland neighborhood:

It is . . . the city's most troubled residential neighborhood by
nearly every measure of deterioration, poverty, unemployment,
crime, and social dislocation. . . . Central is also the most isolated neighborhood in Cleveland, a factor that reduces the ability of its residents to overcome their poverty and distress. . . .
Central's 1980 statistics outline the extent of the problem.

- Median family income was $4,280.
- Unemployment rates were by far the highest in the city.
- Seventy percent of households were one-parent, female-headed
  households, as opposed to a 29 percent city-wide rate.
- Birth rate was the highest in the city.
- Sixty-two percent of adults, 25 years of age or older, had not
  finished high school.
- Median age was 24.6 years, 31 percent of the population was
  14 years of age or younger, making Central the "youngest"
  city neighborhood.
- Between 1960 and 1970, 49 percent of the population left
  Central, the highest rate of loss in the city and more than
  three times the city-wide loss of 14 percent. Between 1960 and
  1980, nearly 30,000 residents left this area of less than one
  mile in radius. Most out-migrants moved to better black neighborhoods like Hough and Glenville.
- Median sales price of homes during 1980–1983 was about
  $4,000.
- Violent crime, as measured by rate per thousand of homicide,
  rape, and assault, was the highest in the city and was typically
  three to four times higher than the city-wide rate. Homicide
  was the leading cause of death among black young men aged
  25–35.
- Only 4.3 percent of housing units were owner-occupied, compared with 44 percent city-wide.
- Because of high crime rates, poor maintenance, and widespread vandalization of property, over 20 percent of CMHA
  [Cleveland's Cuyahoga Metropolitan Housing Authority]'s
  apartments were vacant.

In the measures shown in the list above, the picture presented of
women is of unemployed, young, single heads of household, living in
rented housing and giving birth to many children. For males, similarly unemployed and not homeowners, the suggestion of the statistics shown is that they are young and involved in violent crime, principally among themselves. We have young people here in disproportionate numbers, characterized by undesirable behaviors. These
statistics are certainly "valid," but nevertheless are selected, not inno-
cently, for presentation to describe the area's "problems." The asso-

ciation of young people with crime (males) and with female-headed households and births outside marriage (females) means, in one account, that "much of what has gone awry in the inner city is due in part to the sheer increase in the number of young people, especially young minorities" (Wilson, 1987, p. 37), and "the importance of this jump in the number of young minorities in the ghetto, many of them lacking one or more parents, cannot be overemphasized" (Wilson, 1987, p. 142).

With regard to African American young women, discussions of the "problems" of inner cities frequently invoke their fertility and their decisions to breed young and, particularly, without a permanent male mate. Wilson (1987, p. 20) compiles a list of the symptoms of inner-city troubles in which the characteristics of households he associates with women's reproductive activity are frequently lumped together with practices one would think of as much more threatening: one example is his comment that "the rates of crime, drug addiction, out-of-wedlock births, female-headed families and welfare dependency have risen dramatically in the last several years." At worst this is criminalizing out-of-wedlock births; at best, rendering them dysfunctional. The geographer Holloway (1990) goes right along with this problematizing of young women having children outside marriage, setting out to "explicitly examine two of the social dislocations that are typically associated with the underclass—adolescent unwed childbearing and single-parent families." Even when his own statistical analysis fails to confirm that "female-headed households should be more prevalent in metropolitan areas with lower status and greater economic deprivation" (1990, p. 338), Holloway seems unable to expose the ideological nature of linking high rates of teenage pregnancy and household formation solely to dysfunctionalized, inner-city "underclasses."

Much more sensitive and accurate are Rose and Deskins (1991), also embarking on a statistical trek to test the relationship between teenage pregnancy and economic restructuring, here in a neighborhood-level analysis of Detroit. Pointing out how the term "underclass" is ideologically loaded, and also that teenage pregnancy is not confined to African American youth, they are able to conclude that the extent to which teenage pregnancy should be seen as a long-term problem depends on the resources of those having the children. Thus, they are keen to separate the moral or ethical judgments often made about young women's childbearing from the actual long-term consequences of this. This is a view recently supported by Kristin Luker (1996). Young women with fewer resources are more likely to bear children while in their teens, she says, and their poverty means that they are more likely to have difficulties in their lives subsequently. Luker (1996, p. 85) points out as well some facts that are often left out in discussions linking African American young women with high rates of teenage pregnancy: there is a large and growing proportion of unmarried mothers in the United States who are not teenagers; illegitimacy rates among black American women are stable or falling, whereas those among white American women are increasing; and most teenagers giving birth are aged 18 or 19 years, rather than being the very young teenagers of popular myth.

In their positioning of young African American women, then, some studies imply that inner-city poverty can be explained with reference to the absence of certain "proper" family-forming behaviors. Feminist authors, however, have exposed the gendered assumptions underpinning criticisms of women's behavior at particular life stages (as well as women's behavior in general) (Zinn, 1989; Collins, 1989).

In both those "culture of poverty" explanations of inner-city poverty that see the poor as having family values inconsistent with achievement and those "structural and economic" explanations that locate the marginality of inner-city populations with shifting labor market opportunities, links are made between the (typical) underemployment of inner-city African American men with the head-of-household status of African American women (even if the women are also underemployed) (Zinn, 1989). In both these explanations, the strategy for rectifying the poverty of American inner-city residents revolves around making *men* breadwinners again, having them live with the mothers of their children, and having those children in two-parent, traditionally gendered families. There is little suggestion associated with either explanation of where employment for inner-city males is likely to be found, and no mention of employment options for inner-city women. So the burden of ameliorating poverty in these accounts rests, though more implicitly in the structural accounts than in the culture of poverty accounts, with the reassertion of male power within heterosexual-couple households, and with women taking a backseat and relinquishing their head-of-household status.

How then is this masculinized and heterosexist view of the prospects for poverty reduction also one which rests on particular norms about life stages, about what women should be doing in their youth when presently many young women are giving birth to children outside stable relationships with men? It rests in interesting and conflicting ways on gendered life path assumptions, what it is deemed appropriate and ethical to do when one is a teenaged woman.

First, women *are* seen as family formers in this view, as producers of children for male breadwinners. It is just that this is not seen as a role for female *teenagers,* who are envisaged still as children in transition to adulthood, going through a well-paced set of life stages. When the discussion of single-parent families refers to older female heads of household, the assumption is that it would be better if the households took on a male breadwinner head; where the discussion refers to teenage mothers, the intention is that this parenting should cease. As Wilson (1987, p. 3) notes approvingly of the earlier 20th century, single-parent African American families were fewer and were headed "not by unwed teenagers and young adult women but by middle-aged women who usually were widowed, separated, or divorced."

Secondly, there is no recognition that the youth of a middle-class childhood might have eluded these teenage mothers. Motherhood-in-childhood, this "problem" or oxymoron, may not be how these young women interpret their own situations. As McLaughlin and Heath (1993, p. 216) indicate, "adult responsibilities and realities push themselves on youngsters early in inner cities," and "young people often have to develop their own metaphors and rules for how sex relates to 'manhood' and 'womanhood' " (p. 26).

Precisely how teenage pregnancy and childbirth come to seem rational in some places and for some people has been a subject of considerable study (e.g., by Jacobs, 1994; Kelly, 1994; Luker, 1996, chap. 6; see also Rose & Deskins, 1991). Such teenage pregnancy does make many lives in poverty harder than they otherwise might have been. My point is, however, that a life stage assumption may be criticized if it holds, on the basis of a moral or normative judgment that adolescence and parenting are in all circumstances better experienced separately. "Youth" is not itself problematic because of this frequent linking. As Ruddick (1992, p. 3) says, "adolescents are generally considered too young to be reasoned actors in the sense that one might consider adults. When it comes to any form of sustained and serious agency, adolescents are depicted as awkward, simple minded—'stupid and contagious.' They live in a state where agency is continually denied them."

For inner-city men, the suggestion of Krumholtz's (1992) statistics about inner Cleveland, quoted earlier, is of disproportionate involvement in violent and criminal activity. There is reinforcement in the American mass media almost every day of the association between violent and criminal activity, young African American men, and inner cities. Newspaper reports of the Million Man March held in Washington, DC, in late October 1995, in which hundreds of thousands of African American men marched against the feared image of themselves in the American public mind and heard speeches exhorting them to change their own masculine lives, presented these links more thoughtfully than is often the case (e.g., see *Los Angeles Times,* October 17, 1995, pp. A1, A10; *Watts Star Review,* September 28, 1995, pp. A-1, A-7). Alongside constant public discussion of how to make young people less susceptible to gang recruiters, there is a also a literature explaining the reasons why young, unemployed men would find the strict codes of conduct and "family" ties of a gang appealing and what social policies could possibly build on these ties (Vigil, 1993).

So where, then, in the public discussion of African American men, are questionable associations between youthfulness and dangerous activity in inner cities to be found? There is clear evidence that inner-city populations, especially minority groups within them, are young compared to populations of other areas. The gangs they form, which receive so much publicity for their aberrant acts, are made up of young people—people are not generally gang members when they are well into adulthood. It is also evident that young people, among whom minorities are disproportionately represented, contribute greatly to urban crime; as Wilson (1987, p. 37) describes, "66 per cent of all those arrested for violent and property crimes in American cities in 1980 were under twenty-five years of age."

The point is not to dispute that youthfulness is a demographic constant in this situation, but rather to expose the particular interpretation of what youthfulness *should* be that is being used in accounts interpreting the problematic nature of young men's behavior and its causes. If young people in inner cities are behaving in their teenage years in ways deemed unacceptable to others (for very good reason when violent and abusive behaviors are involved), then is this attributable primarily to youth, to teenagerhood, and is this juvenile behavior being tolerated less than at other times, in other places, and among other class and racial groups? Ruddick (1992, p. 96) claims that "in spite of the rising publicity on youth violence, violent crimes among youth, both nationally and in the state of California, have been decreasing." She also notes that "while lower class behaviors of youth were simply tolerated in premodern times, and in the modern era were presumed to lead to delinquency, they are increasingly treated as evidence of potential criminality" (p. 85). "Images of youth as the 'dangerous classes' are becoming fixed," she says (p. 271). There is reason, then, to situate the public and analytical associations between male youth and dangerous behavior in inner cities in their precise political and historical context.

ADULTHOOD AND HAPPY FAMILIES
IN THE AMERICAN SUBURBS

A different set of gendered and racialized life stages is present in academic and legislated understandings of American suburbs. Zoning and building codes (and property values) set aside many suburbs for those "unlike" the residents of the inner cities.

Despite increasing suburban diversity from the 1970s, certain American suburban values are argued to have been sustained by a "dominant ethos"—in Ashton's (1978) terms—about suburbs, a belief that in the autonomous suburbs residents will be able to seek out and maintain certain consumption and reproduction practices. Walker (1981, p. 392) names the characteristics of contemporary suburban life as the "so-called nuclear family, the single-family home, homeownership, the neighborhood school, and a certain limited type of 'community,' conjoined with a localized political jurisdiction." Here, dominant values and practices emphasize families in which adults are the actors and youth is associated with lack of agency. Such notions are enshrined in family-oriented zoning ordinances.

Zoning in American suburbs specifies land uses for designated areas, in what is interpreted to be the local interest. These are accompanied by subdivision regulations (about provision of infrastructural services to land, siting of houses on parcels of land, landscaping, etc.) and building codes that regulate construction (Danielson, 1976, p. 50). Very common are severe restrictions on the number and type of apartments, large lot specifications for single-family housing and minimum-size rules for buildings, and the prohibition of prefabricated and mobile housing. No growth policies are also popular among conservationists, opponents of high local taxes, and those interested in excluding lower-income or particular racial groups from the suburb (Danielson, 1976, p. 64; Pincetl, 1992).

Ritzdorf (1985, p. 15) makes an important point about research on exclusionary zoning:

> Research into the exclusionary uses of municipal zoning ordinances has focused on the exclusion of minority and low-and moderate-income residents from American communities by limitations upon or exclusion of alternatives to large lot single-family housing, yet the family definitions affect an even wider variety of people.

She describes the struggles of state courts to designate an appropriate definition of "family," and the entry of the U.S. Supreme Court into the zoning debate (Ritzdorf, 1985, p. 16). One landmark case before the Supreme Court in 1974 concerned the zoning restrictions of Belle Terre, a village on Long Island, New York. Its local government wished to use zoning regulations to prevent the rental of a house to six students attending a nearby college. Unfortunately, the Supreme Court decided not to use the case to examine the use of local zoning for exclusionary purposes; rather it upheld the local rule as a legitimate exercise of local police power. So, restrictive definitions of family persist—and may vary from treating single households as "families" to the requirement that individuals sharing a house be legally related by blood, marriage, or adoption. Choices of living arrangement that might be at variance with local zoning might include those of elderly people to live collectively or those of single-parent families to share accommodation and therefore ease the burdens of the double day. Single-parent households would not be excluded, but their choice to share living arrangements with others might be.

The urban anthropologist Constance Perin (1977, 1988) has argued with great skill and clarity that norms about life stages and progress through the "ladder of life" are basic to the understandings of the American suburb held by professionals designing and selling suburban housing and land as well as those who live in the resulting suburbs. "These 'habits of thought' [as she calls them] do not, of course, explain social or economic systems . . . [but they show] assumptions we all share as social scientists, consumers, policy-makers—as Americans" (Perin, 1977, p. xiii). They shed light on the (middle-class) logic that links the social characteristics of people with particular types of housing tenure and that sees their spatial separation by land-use regulation as desirable. In her 1977 study, Perin spoke at length to people regulating the local development process in Houston and Philadelphia: professionals and executives in private sector firms involved with land and housing development, municipal officials and public figures. Her own words (1977, p. 32) best summarize the ways life stage norms were embedded in their thinking about suburbs and the ways they designed suburban life in consequence:

> The people I talked to make the proposition that the life cycle is composed of a sequence of events to be lived out in a correct order, each stage matched by appropriate marital status, amount of income, ages of children, school years completed, leisure tastes, tenure form, and housing type. In distinguishing between the characteristics of renters and of owners, they see the correct sequence of the life cycle as being an intrinsic feature of these differences—first a renter, then an owner.

A "ladder of life" is climbed as one moves through the different housing tenures and types, and through the parts of the city they occupy. "In taking the ladder rung by rung, the movement is altogether upward, an evolutionary progress as well, toward salvation from 'lower forms' to a 'final, divinely ordained form' " (Perin, 1977, p. 47).

In this normative narrative of life stages, youth is associated with renting, not necessarily in suburban locations. But it is assumed that the housing tenure type and nonsuburban location of youth is a transient stage in a trajectory that ultimately ends in the suburbs. Heterosexual adulthood is associated with owning a detached house in a suburb, having "arrived" at adulthood and its most appropriate spatial expression. Perin detected the strongly held view among her interviewees that in this context "the market" of people buying homes "[doesn't] want the houses mixed up with the apartments" (1977, 51).

Such views are bolstered by a family ideal that distributes certain gender roles within the perfect suburb—the life stages envisaged are gendered (adult) ones. The ideal depends on the presence of husbands and fathers for legitimacy for its realization; widows, divorcees, and never married women often experience stigma and hostility because they are aberrations, imperfect people in this suburban setting (Perin, 1988, p. 40). The gender roles of the nuclear family, where woman is wife and preferably concentrating on domestic duties in the home, are important as a norm here (if less a reality in these times of middle-class households having two adult incomes). Urban/suburban stereotyping applies to men, as well: "there is only one complete unblushing male in America: a young, married, white, urban, northern, heterosexual, Protestant father of college education, fully employed, of good complexion, weight and height and a recent record in sports" (Perin, 1988, p. 145). Note that men have the privilege to be judged largely with reference to their roles outside the home and a wide range of their identity attributes, rather than primarily with respect to their relationships with women.

I am aware that the tendency of some feminist social science to polarize concepts and realities into opposites has been rejected as a classificatory and explanatory strategy. Certainly the formation and use of any set of opposites risks masking the many ways such regularities are disrupted in lived realities. Nevertheless, such sway do the terms "inner city" and "suburb" hold in American discussion of metropolitan areas and their characteristics and "problems" that a comparison of the way those two spatial terms are threaded with normative assumptions about the social characteristics of their residents seems justified, in making an argument that the problematizing of life stages in the understanding of metropolitan circumstances should be revealed. People may negotiate individual life courses, but these stereotypes nevertheless inhabit and structure processes of production and regulation of urban places. So, it is important to compare the satisfied adulthood of suburban life, as it exists in public, legislated, and academic assumptions, with the concern felt about inner-city transience, *which does not seem likely to "grow up"* into that appropriate suburban adulthood.

ADOPTING LIFE STAGE NORMS: ACTIVISM ABOUT URBAN SERVICES IN AUSTRALIA

It is one thing to allege, as do the previous sections, that assumptions about life stages suffuse many public accounts of urban characteristics and problems, and are embedded in the ways other identity categories are invoked. But it is always a valid criticism that the generality of such allegations parallels the generality of the claims being criticized! There is also the point that an outsider's generalization about life stage norms in certain public statements does not comprehend the way that those living out the lives represented actually understand their own identified life paths or negotiate ascribed positionings. Whether or not the public stereotyping of people's lives in the places they live actually matters to those people's well-being, and how they may contest these generalizations or appropriate them, is a matter for continued empirical investigation.

In my own Australian research in outer Melbourne on the provision of services for the dependents of employed women, it is clear that women do negotiate the life stage assumptions made about them in public policy. Decades of women's activism in Australia have had an impact upon the ways women are positioned publicly. On the other hand, some life stage groups of women have engaged more than others in activist debate with governments, shaping public policy about themselves more effectively than have those groups of women who have not become so involved. The contrasting nature of women's activism over services to help them care for dependents who are frail and aged, as opposed to women's activism for government support in caring for able-bodied, pre-school-age dependents, is very clear. In consequence, the provision of regulated childcare services has increased markedly over the last two decades, supporting employed women with children in particular (see Fincher, 1993). The provision of services to assist those caring for older dependents has increased far less.

In my own statements on this subject, I have argued a social policy inequity in this—that women caring for dependents, no matter what their life stage, deserve the same opportunities for government support. This has sometimes been met with the response, especially from older women, that "you don't understand: we want to care for our older kin." It is an interesting question whether those who have taken on and reshaped the state to a lesser degree, that is, women who are caring for the frail aged, have in fact agreed with the views of themselves held by government and as certain cultural mores—that they *should* be at home caring for their kin independently, rather than expecting major government support in this activity. What does seem to be the case is that the spatial imaginaries of women involved or uninvolved in activism toward local governments diverge. That is, the self-positioning of older groups of women caring for their kin puts them in a less trusting relationship than does the self-positioning of younger caregiving women with those institutions of local government supposedly representing their interests most closely in the neighborhood places they inhabit. Local space, as a regulated place, is less empowering for the older group than for the younger.

In this section I will briefly describe the apparent adoption of life stage norms by Australian women of different ages, and the varied interpretation of caregiving associated with these norms that is expressed in their activism about urban services provision. I do this keeping in mind that, first, all women who are caring for kin do not have the same view of themselves in that role. Second, even if there are characteristic views of women's responsibilities within different life stage groups, there will nevertheless be women within those groups who feel uncomfortable with that positioning.

State-directed activism is certainly one way that younger women have negotiated a new life stage identity for themselves. Their efforts to extend state provisions for childcare have differed in form and extent, however, from activism relating to care for aged dependents. No doubt this is causally linked to the varied "official" views in Australia of caring for kin at different life stages. As Franzway, Court, and Connell (1989) have it, caring as mothering has been cast into the sphere of public dependency. Caring for the frail aged is consigned largely to family members, to the sphere of private dependency, and the actual work involved in this caring has been rendered invisible.

Central to Australian battles to entrench childcare in government policy have been participants in the women's movement from the 1970s, often young-adult Anglo women entering the paid workforce and demanding support for themselves in the care of their young children. Femocrats (feminist bureaucrats) in government, charged with representing women's interests and often representatives themselves of the young-adult life stage group of full-time female labor force entrants, championed this cause along with matters like equal employment opportunity (see Franzway et al., 1989). Yeatman (1990) has detailed the particular women's interests represented by femocrats and the consequent clashes between them and members of the women's movement seeing themselves as differently positioned. Day-care centers have served in greatest numbers parents of the urban Anglo middle class.

Activism for the establishment and expansion of services to support women with aged dependents, to allow women who are primary caregivers for such dependents more lifestyle options, including that of regular paid work, has been far less prevalent. Older women, with different caregiving responsibilities and employment characteristics, have not negotiated an identity for themselves to challenge government views of their proper roles. They seem in this to have accepted the norm so prevalent in social policy that women should be caregivers in private households, taking care of their kin relatively unaided. Very recent actions by community organizations, however, have helped give voice to women, especially those women caring for dependents with Alzheimer's disease. The comments of staff of these organizations show that many older women accept their caring obligations, but also that some disagree with this positioning. Some women are willing to use expanded government services (if these were provided) so as to reduce their own caregiving commitments, but are fearful that other government benefits they receive might be withdrawn if they "rock the boat" by participating in activism toward this end.

From their experience working with women caring for their aged kin, the directors of two Melbourne organizations stated when interviewed (in 1993), for example, that most people want to care for their relatives for as long as possible. But many of these caregivers are reluctant to admit that they cannot cope with an aged dependent and need help caring for him or her. Community organization coordinators represented their members as thinking it much more acceptable to place children in childcare than to admit that one's elderly parents are unmanageable at home: "They see it as a failure, especially women. They see it as being defeated." The community organization staff felt that caregivers' own unwavering sense of responsibility for the care of their dependents has had an enormous impact on the relative lack of organized lobbying from the local, grassroots level, an influence compounded by many caregivers' ignorance of available services.

In part because use of caring assistance for aging family members is a far less "public" issue for many than use of assistance for childcare, those caring for elderly dependents are a more fragmented, isolated, and very private group of people. Those in outer urban locations of middle-income, low-density living can find their spatial location contributing to this: active use of local social services is less visible here than in inner areas of mixed-income households. Their own nervousness about the consequences of seeking better services contributes too: one community services manager in an outer Melbourne municipality described those caring for aged kin as disempowered:

> They're fearful about the consequences of complaining and I think that they have very traditional ideas about where a service is at. . . . [For example,] people think like this. If I complain about the home care worker, maybe I won't be able to access that service again and that means I'll have to come down once a week and clean Mum's bathroom . . . but I can't because I've got three kids, a job and other commitments on top so I won't complain . . . [so] better this than nothing.

And this comment came from a community services worker at another Melbourne outer urban location: "aged services lobby is State-based. . . . [Local] people don't lobby actively. We don't hear from many local groups." The local scale of aged services provision, then, is disempowering for isolated, potentially activist caregivers. Unsure if their receipt of local services would be threatened if they complained about them locally, they rely on State-wide organizations to present these arguments outside the local government context.

At this later life stage, one could hypothesize, many caregivers in the 1990s attribute meaning to caring for kin themselves that differs from the meaning of caring attributed by younger adults to their tasks of looking after their children. Of course this is a generalization: young adults of some backgrounds, in households where women are not expected to participate in paid employment if it can be avoided financially, will often wish to care for their own children without government assistance. And it may well be the case that in the future, when the current users of childcare services reach the age at which they must decide upon the care of their own aged dependents, many will decide to reject the decision to undertake the care themselves that has been a familiar "choice" of their mothers.

The brief evidence presented here about how and why older women caring for their kin act as they do, however, belies the interpretation that their manner of caring is a clear lifestyle "choice." Some older women have adopted norms that it is a private responsibility to care for their dependents; others are less comfortable with this. Similarly, with younger women caring for dependents, many have adopted the norms of the femocrats responsible for the design of Australian childcare policy. But many have not done so and continue to press for recognition of the value of caring for children in the private home. So women's understanding of their own experiences and responsibilities do vary across and within life stage groups (and across groups of other identity categories, of course). No official or outsiders' view can ignore this in designing the delivery of services so that broad options are open to people within and across different age groups.

CONCLUSION

Judgments about the behaviors and characteristics of people at different stages of their lives are present, but unremarked, in much public discussion of contemporary urban issues. This chapter has indicated the presence of these judgments in analyses of American inner cities and suburbs. I have also suggested that the meanings for people of their life stages are important for urban researchers to discover analytically and to use in reflection upon the adequacy of public stereotypes and the policy thinking associated with them. Examples of the provisions of the Australian state for women with dependents suggest that women of different life stages may frequently view the task of caring for dependents in different ways, contributing to their presence in or absence from political activism on this issue and to their view of their locality as a regulated place that they might influence (or not).

Of course the focus of this chapter on representations and understandings of the life course should not be taken to suggest that other aspects of identity and difference are less important. Any one aspect of identity and difference is expressed and understood through others—gender being mediated by class and ethnicity, racializing being carried out in varied ways according to class and gender and place, and so on. My claim in this chapter has been that assumptions and norms about life stages are often silently influential in policy and public discussions that treat racial and gender issues more explicitly, as well as in the way people understand their own activities, and that this should not go unnoticed.

ACKNOWLEDGMENTS

The financial support of the Australian Research Council is gratefully acknowledged. Jane Jacobs, Natalie Jamieson, Janice Monk, and Valerie Preston have made helpful suggestions, for which I am also very grateful.

REFERENCES

Ashton, P. J. (1978). The political economy of suburban development. In W. K. Tabb & L. Sawers (Eds.), *Marxism and the metropolis* (pp. 64–89). New York: Oxford University Press.

Collins, P. H. (1989). A comparison of two works on black family life. *Signs, 14*(4), 875–884.

Danielson, M. N. (1976). *The politics of exclusion.* New York: Columbia University Press.

Downs, R., & Stea, D. (Eds.). (1973). *Image and environment: Cognitive mapping and spatial behavior.* Chicago: Aldine.

Fincher, R. (1993). Women, the state and the life course in urban Australia. In C. Katz & J. Monk (Eds.), *Full circles: Geographies of women over the life course* (pp. 243–263). London: Routledge.

Franzway, S., Court, D., & Connell, R. (1989). *Staking a claim: Feminism, bureaucracy and the state.* Sydney: Allen & Unwin.

Galster, G. C. (1992). A cumulative causation model of the underclass: Implications for urban economic development policy. In G. C. Galster & E. W. Hill (Eds.), *The metropolis in black and white* (pp. 190–215). New Brunswick, NJ: Rutgers University Center for Urban Policy Research.

Galster, G., & Hill, E. W. (1992). Place, power and polarization: Introduction. In G. C. Galster & E. W. Hill (Eds.), *The metropolis in black and white* (pp. 1–18). New Brunswick, NJ: Rutgers University Center for Urban Policy Research.

Goldsmith, W. W., & Blakely, E. J. (1992). *Separate societies: Poverty and inequality in U.S. cities.* Philadelphia: Temple University Press.

Holloway, S. R. (1990). Urban economic structure and the urban underclass: An examination of two problematic social phenomena. *Urban Geography, 11*(4), 319–346.

Jacobs, J. L. (1994). Gender, race, class, and the trend toward early motherhood. *Journal of Contemporary Ethnography, 22*(4), 442–462.

Kasarda, J. D. (1990). Structural factors affecting the location and timing of underclass growth. *Urban Geography, 11*(3), 234–264.

Katz, C., & Monk, J. (Eds.). (1993). *Full circles: Geographies of women over the life course.* London: Routledge.

Kelly, M. P. F. (1994). Towanda's triumph: Social and cultural capital in the transition to adulthood in the urban ghetto. *International Journal of Urban and Regional Research, 18*(1), 88–111.

Krumholtz, N. (1992). The Kerner Commission twenty years later. In G. C. Galster & E. W. Hill (Eds.), *The metropolis in black and white* (pp. 19–38). New Brunswick, NJ: Rutgers University Center for Urban Policy Research.

Laws, G. (1993). "The land of old age": Society's changing attitudes toward urban built environments for elderly people. *Annals of the Association of American Geographers, 83*(4), 672–693.

Ley, D. (1992). Gentrification in recession: Social change in six Canadian cities 1981–1986. *Urban Geography, 13*(3), 230–256.

Luker, K. (1996) *Dubious conceptions: The politics of teenage pregnancy.* Cambridge, MA: Harvard University Press.

Lynch, K. (1970). *The image of the city.* Cambridge, MA: MIT Press.

McLaughlin, M. W., & Heath, S. B. (1993). Casting the self: Frames for identity and dilemmas for policy. In S. B. Heath & M. W. McLaughlin (Eds.), *Identity and inner city youth: Beyond ethnicity and gender* (pp. 210–239). New York: Teachers College Press, Columbia University.

Mullins, D. R., & Rosentraub, M. S. (1992). Fiscal pressure: The impact of elder recruitment on local expenditure. *Urban Affairs Quarterly, 28*(2), 337–354.

Perin, C. (1977). *Everything in its place: Social order and land use in America.* Princeton, NJ: Princeton University Press.

Perin, C. (1988). *Belonging in America.* Madison: University of Wisconsin Press.

Pincetl, S. (1992). The politics of growth control: Struggles in Pasadena, California. *Urban Geography, 13*(5) 450–467.

Preston, V., & Taylor, S. M. (1981). Personal construct theory and residential choice. *Annals of the Association of American Geographers, 71*(3), 437–451.

Ricketts, E. (1992). The nature and dimensions of the underclass. In G. C. Galster & E. W. Hill (Eds.), *The metropolis in black and white* (pp. 39–55). New Brunswick, NJ: Rutgers University Center for Urban Policy Research.

Ritzdorf, M. (1985). Challenging the exclusionary impact of family definitions in American municipal zoning ordinances. *Journal of Urban Affairs, 7*(1), 15–25.

Rose, H. M., & Deskins, D. R., Jr. (1991). The link between black teenage pregnancy and economic restructuring in Detroit. *Urban Geography, 12*(6), 508–525.

Rowles, G. (1980). Toward a geography of growing old. In A. Buttimer & D. Seamon (Eds.), *The human experience of space and place* (pp. 60–75). London: Croom Helm.

Ruddick, S. M. (1992). *Redrawing the maps of meaning: The social construction of homeless youth in Hollywood.* Unpublished Ph.D. dissertation, Graduate School of Architecture and Urban Planning, University of California, Los Angeles.

Smith, N., & Williams, P. (Eds.). (1986). *Gentrification of the city.* Boston: Allen & Unwin.

Tivers, J. (1988). *Women attached: The daily lives of women with young children.* London: Croom Helm.

Vigil, J. D. (1993). Gangs, social control, and ethnicity: Ways to redirect. In S. B. Heath & M. W. Milbrey (Eds.), *Identity and inner-city youth: Beyond ethnicity and gender* (pp. 94–119). New York: Teachers College Press, Columbia University.

Walker, R. A (1981). A theory of suburbanization: Capitalism and the construction of urban space in the United States. In M. Dear & A. J. Scott (Eds.), *Urbanization and urban planning in capitalist society.* London: Methuen.

Wilson, W. J. (1987). *The truly disadvantaged: The inner city, the underclass, and public policy.* Chicago: University of Chicago Press.

Yeatman, A. (1990). *Bureaucrats, femocrats, technocrats.* Boston: Allen & Unwin.

Zinn, M. B. (1989). Family, race and poverty in the eighties. *Signs, 14*(4), 856–874.

CHAPTER 4

Suburban Stories, Gendered Lives

THINKING THROUGH DIFFERENCE

Robyn Dowling

For some, the presence of a chapter on suburbs in a volume about difference is incongruous to say the least. Suburbs are more often thought about and described in terms of homogeneity, not difference and heterogeneity (Gold & Gold, 1989). This is especially the case with respect to gender. It is commonly argued that the physical form and dominant cultural meanings of suburbs are only supportive of gender relations associated with the traditional nuclear family (e.g., England, 1991). Alternative constructions of masculinity, femininity, and sexuality, such as gay and lesbian families (Valentine, 1993), single parenthood (Wekerle, 1984), or maternal employment (England, 1991) are, so the story goes, neither apparent nor supported in suburban environments.

Such accounts of uniform suburban gender relations are no longer valid, and my first aim in this chapter is to document the diversity of genders, and specifically femininities, lived in suburbs. Using feminist critiques of essentialism as an organizing framework, I will relate the rich stories of multiple forms of suburban gender relations currently being told. Elements of homogeneity nevertheless remain in these accounts, for some axes of difference are allowed while others are suppressed. Only transparent, across-category differences are elaborated, and significant heterogeneities within suburbs, classes, and genders are masked. Specifically, middle-class femininity is assumed to be unitary and geographically invariant, while the differences within practices of motherhood beyond participation in paid employment are overlooked. These criticisms guide the second aim of the chapter, which is to produce a more multitextured story of suburban gender relations. Research in Canada, in Vancouver, British Columbia, underpins an exploration of two other axes of difference—motherhood and within-place diversity—in the lives of women in two suburban neighborhoods. Women's participation in paid employment is not the only factor differentiating their suburban femininity, for it is overlain and mediated by cultural constructions of motherhood. Also important are the substantial differences *within* these suburban places that relate to religious practices. These multiple and often subtle axes of difference, therefore, can produce a more heterogeneous suburban tale.

DIFFERENCE, SUBURBS, AND GENDER

Although theories of difference have not been explicitly used to produce more heterogeneous stories of gender and suburbs they can be insightfully used to read recent suburban scholarship. Theories of difference have underlain the recent concern with identity, culture, and power in feminist geography (Rose, 1993). They have many strands and many conceptual sources (Barrett, 1987; Scott, 1990), but one strand is especially relevant to suburban stories. Critiques of essentialism are shared among theories of difference and provide a useful window onto them. Since, as Grosz (1990) outlines, essentialism has at least three meanings, theories of difference enunciate three critiques. First is the invalidity of biological essentialism, or the view that gender—masculinity or femininity—is prescribed by nature. Gender is neither pregiven nor transparent, but culturally and socially constituted. As a result, a sole focus on the activities of men and women, or on demographic statistics, is clearly inadequate. Instead, attention is more productively placed on the social construction of gender, the production and maintenance of socially prescribed definitions of what it is to be male (masculinity) and female (femininity) (McDowell, 1991). Second is the critique of universalism, which is the position that categories like woman and femininity are invariable across time, space, and social location. Femininity varies by, for example, class and race (Collins, 1994), and what it means to be a woman is historically and geographically contingent. Finally, there is the critique of an essentialist "subject" or identity. An individual's identity is neither whole nor unitary, but fragmented and unstable (Smith, 1989). One woman's femininity, for instance, has a number of sometimes contradictory components.

The first critique of essentialism is clearly identifiable in suburban scholarship. Feminist scholars have been carefully highlighting the cultural constitution and negotiation of gendered identities in suburbs. Suburbs are not naturally places for the nuclear family, and women do not automatically re-create mothering femininities. Marsh (1990) shows the role of an ideology of separate spheres in informing the creation of late-19th- and early-20th-century suburbs in the United States. Women's identities as mothers and wives, she argues, were not natural but were constituted by them, their husbands, the state, and the land development industry. Johnson (1993) locates the persistence of separate spheres in 1990s Australia through the continued privileging of the nuclear family in house designs. England (1993) points out the active participation of women in constructing suburban gender identities, and Dyck (1990) documents the negotiation of mothering identities and practices in and through suburban locales. These works have provided important counterpoints to the essentialist notion that suburbs are naturally associated with nuclear-family gender relations. Instead, the associations are socially constructed and negotiated.

The universalizing tendencies of understandings of suburban femininity have also been scrutinized, akin to the second critique of essentialism. Representing all suburbs as middle class and constituted only by a nuclear-family model of gender is acknowledged to be empirically untenable. It is widely accepted that suburbs do not now, and maybe never did, closely resemble their portrayal as homogeneous, middle-class, and nuclear-family-focused environments (Saegert, 1980). In the American case, O'Connor (1985) and Marsh (1990) have shown that there have always been many different types of suburbs, especially in terms of class and ethnic composition. Strong-Boag (1991) paints a similar portrait for suburban Canada in the 1950s. Immigrants to Canada and working-class families were often suburban settlers, she argues, and suburban lives varied significantly across Canada. Morton's (1994) analysis of a working-class suburb in Halifax, Nova Scotia, further refutes the middle-class basis of suburban life. Ideals of family, respectability, and homeownership, often identified as middle class, were clearly evident in the Halifax suburb of Richmond, despite the persistent poverty of residents. Morton's findings are echoed in Australia through Peel's (1995) analysis of 20th-century public housing on Adelaide's suburban fringe. Similarly, the contemporary Canadian suburb, according to Evenden and Walker (1993), is characterized by a complex social geography of class, race, and gender, a mosaic that is still overlain by regional differences. Suburban life and suburban places are not the same in every place and time, and not always and everywhere white and middle class.

The homogeneity implicit in the category *suburban woman* has been similarly disaggregated. Not all suburban women are the same, nor do they share some essential attribute (Grosz, 1990; McDowell, 1991). There is no such thing as the "suburban woman," the story goes, because many different types of women, living in many different family arrangements, populate and create suburban landscapes. Law and Wolch (1993) show, for instance, that many different household and family forms occupy suburban space, evincing different forms of gender relations. The practice and construction of gender in a single-parent household or in a household consisting solely of couples without children is necessarily different than in a nuclear family consisting of a heterosexual couple and their children. Suburban femininity is therefore multiple rather than singular. The life cycle is also important, with gender relations and identities varying with the age of both parents and children (Pratt & Hanson, 1993; Richards, 1990). It may be the case, for instance, that a hardening of gender identities and difference occurs while children are young, and a loosening of the rigidities of gender occurs as children get older. Suburban gender relations also vary across class (Rubin, 1994). For example, since working-class women are more likely to participate in the paid labor force than middle-class women, different class-based femininities are constructed. There is thus not one model of familial-related femininity in suburbs but many, dependent upon, among other factors, class, race, and life course.

Despite these contributions, remnants of essentialism remain in relation to the breaking up of the categories *middle-class femininity* and *suburban neighborhood* (or *place*). Difference has been demonstrated *across* rather than *within* categories; the third critique of essentialism is not apparent. We now know, for instance, that suburbs are not only middle class and that family life also varies by class. But we remain largely unaware of fissures within suburban, middle-class, familial experience. What of the differences internal to these categories? Where suburban women's experiences within the middle-class family have been disaggregated, it has been narrowly, according to their paid labor force participation. For example, England (1993) uses the differential labor force participation rates of suburban women and their varied strategies for combining home and work to demonstrate multiple suburban gendered identities. Breaking down suburban femininity in this way, however, remains limiting in a number of important respects.

First, paid work is only one component of suburban femininity. Mothering practices, religious affiliation, family connections, choice of childcare and residential history all differentiate constructions of suburban femininity. More complex suburban geographies therefore need to acknowledge axes of difference in addition to paid work. Second, a focus on paid employment draws attention away from the work women do in suburbs, especially in relation to mothering. Motherhood may be broadly defined as practices of caring for children, practices that are infused with cultural meaning and dominate women's lives in suburban locations. Women's identities as mothers are crucial both in their self-definition (Dyck, 1990) and in social and cultural debates about femininity (Glenn, 1994; Kaplan, 1992). Despite its importance, mothering is ignored in geographical analyses of suburbs and gender, with the exception of Dyck's (1989, 1990) exemplary work. Thus the neglect of mothering practices erases an important component of suburban women's lives and therefore a potential source of difference. Third, a focus on paid work essentializes, or assumes a sameness within, women's experiences of motherhood. Lack of consideration of practices and ideologies of motherhood implies that these do not vary beyond accommodations between home and work. Yet mothering is as diverse as femininity (Glenn, 1994), and its heterogeneity cannot only be traced to different forms of, and relations to, paid employment. Indeed, women's participation in paid work, as well as their interpretations and experiences of it, are partially determined by, and experienced through, cultural constructions of mothering. The decision not to engage in paid work, for instance, is ideologically charged, as is its experience. Fourth, attention to mothering can insightfully open up internal fissures within femininity. Motherhood is a contested concept (Kaplan, 1992), and involvement in it produces tensions and accommodations for many women. A focus on mothering discourses and practices can mitigate some of the essentialism remaining in contemporary suburban scholarship, thereby addressing a neglected issue and helping produce a more complexly textured suburban story.

It is not only femininity whose variations have been inadequately noted in contemporary suburban stories. Remnants of essentialism also remain in approaches to place. Acknowledgment of the social construction of place has been central to critiques of the "naturalness" of suburban gender relations, for the production and reproduction of place is crucial in the constitution and negotiation of femininity (England, 1993). As Hanson, Pratt, Mattingly, and Gilbert (1994, p. 233) note, "the strategies women develop in leading their daily lives, particularly for combining home and paid employment, are embedded in, and actively shape, their local cultural and economic context." In other words, gender is experienced in and through place; place is more than a container for gender difference. Resources available within the immediate environment are drawn upon and recreated in constructing gender identities. Dyck (1989) demonstrates, for instance, how women develop local networks to aid their mothering work, in the process constituting the street as a safe space. Local cultural meanings circulating in and through the neighborhood are also part of women's interpretations of the meanings of motherhood (Dyck, 1990).

Many evocations of the geographical construction of suburban gendered identities are themselves limited, however, for they rely upon an essentialist or unitary conception of place, insofar as they assume that the meanings and social relations circulating within a place like a neighborhood are singular rather than multiple, that all residents share a similar relation to, and sense of, that place. England (1993), for instance, does not disaggregate the locales in her case studies, and Hanson et al. (1994) show difference *across* rather than *within* suburbs. Dyck (1989) acknowledges that her conclusions are based on a case study where values with respect to mothering were homogeneous and shared, but she leaves open the implications of a neighborhood where values were heterogeneous. Yet holding onto a singular and fixed conception of place is no longer tenable, for at least two reasons. First, it is conceptually invalid, a point most clearly articulated by Massey (1994). Massey uses poststructuralist critiques of identity to think about the concept of place differently. Just as identity is multiple, so too is place. She argues (p. 121) that places are open and porous networks of social relations with multiple meanings and interpretations. Massey therefore draws our attention to the varied social networks within a suburban neighborhood and the multiple readings and constructions of its cultural meaning. A second problem is that an essentialist conception of place fetters representations of suburban diversity. If we see suburban neighborhoods as unitary rather than multiple, then it will likely follow that a singular construction of femininity is located there. Conceptualizing place in a nonessentialist way facilitates an awareness of the potential for different gender relations and identities *within* one site and is therefore more likely to produce a heterogeneous suburban story.

Thus, despite recent scholarship on difference in suburban gender relations, the fluidity and heterogeneity within the category *suburban middle-class femininity* remains incompletely elaborated and the diversity of suburban landscapes and identities remains misrepresented. In the rest of this chapter I use the two entry points of mothering and nonessentialist senses of place to produce a more complex and nuanced suburban story. At the center of this story are differences in practices of mothering and interpretations of paid work between and within suburban places.

TABLE 4.1. Social Profiles of Glenwood and Berkshire, British Columbia, 1991

Characteristic		Glenwood		Berkshire	
Total population		1,140		2,810	
Family type (% families)					
Husband–wife without children at home		29		37	
Husband–wife with children at home		60		58	
Lone parent		5		5	
Owned dwellings (%)		95		92	
Percentage of children aged					
0–5 years		30		35	
6–14 years		41		38	
15–17 years		8		7	
18–24 years		15		14	
Over 25 years		6		5	
Labor force participation rate of					
Women with children at home		61		68	
Women with children under 6 years		57		75	
Women with children under and over 6 years		55		67	
Women with children over 6 years		72		68	
Median family income ($)		59,492		51,499	
Percentage of labor force employed in		Women	Men	Women	Men
Managerial, professional	36	32	29	25	
Clerical, administrative		39	9	44	10
Sales, service		20	28	23	21
Manual, construction		0	29	8	39

Note. Data from Statistics Canada (1994). Income is in Canadian dollars.

The story is based on interviews with residents in two "single-family subdivisions" in suburban Vancouver. The two neighborhoods fit a conventional suburban description, each consisting of approximately 100 single-detached houses that were built and marketed for homeowners (generally couples) with children. All houses were constructed at the same time 8 years ago. In terms of social composition the two neighborhoods exhibit similar profiles (see Table 4.1): the nuclear family with two or three children per family is predominant in both places, as is the detached dwelling. Residents of both places can be described as "middle class" (Savage, Barlow, Dickens, & Fielding, 1992) in the sense that both men and women worked in professional, managerial, scientific, or clerical occupations, all were homeowners, all had above-average incomes, and all drew part of their class identity from consumption, especially the home. Moreover, all residents interviewed (30 in each neighborhood) were strongly committed to "traditional" family values and consistently expressed belief in the desirability and benefits of a nuclear family over and above other family forms. Both men and women in the household were interviewed (separately). Interviews lasted from 1 to 3 hours and were transcribed verbatim. The interview material presented here represents the themes of the interviews, distilled from transcripts. Thus all the points I make refer to sentiments shared by at least a majority of residents. However in the analysis a few quotations are presented to exemplify the major points.

CULTURES OF MOTHERING IN SUBURBAN VANCOUVER

The heterogeneity of women's suburban lives in two Vancouver neighborhoods does not solely revolve around differences in their paid labor force participation. Nevertheless, paid work is an important differentiating element. In Glenwood, one of the neighborhoods, two-thirds of the women interviewed were not currently employed in the paid labor force either full- or part-time, nor were they contemplating a return to the labor force. In the other neighborhood, Berkshire, three-quarters of the women worked full or part time. But these discrepancies in no way exhaust women's experiences there. Reasons for, interpretations of and consequences of, paid employment decisions were also not the same in the two neighborhoods.

For the women and men of Glenwood, it was important that motherhood (not fatherhood) not be disrupted by paid employment. Since participation in the labor force was seen to jeopardize the quality and quantity of mothering, it was cast as undesirable. As distilled by one man, "I think bringing up the kids is too bloody important to pass off to day-care centers or baby-sitters." "Being there" for children, quantity as well as quality, was deemed to be most important, evident in Debby's (a pseudonym, as are all names) description of her definition of a "good" mother:

> "A lot of available time for them, doing lots of different things. I just bought my son and I tickets for *Joseph,* spending time camping, spending time going to a play like that."

A certain independence was desired, according to Ruby:

> "Friends would say I could use someone to help me out [with four children under 5 years old] but all I could think of was that this is something I would like to do for myself, they couldn't do what I do, you know they wouldn't take the same interest as me and I wouldn't want anyone in my home anyway."

These models of motherhood are in some ways unremarkable. They are expressions of more pervasive notions of the desirability of a conventional nuclear family (Stacey, 1994), and the women's work they entailed (Milroy & Wismer, 1994) formed the basis of a strong sense of community cohesion. What is notable is the way this mothering work was conceptualized, or the meaning given to and constituting this work. Mothering work was performed and understood in a businesslike or professional manner. Raising children for these Glenwood women was not less caring or emotionally attached than in other places. But these bonds were articulated to me, and understood individually, in terms of work. Phrases, words, and ways of organizing more commonly associated with business and the workplace were used to represent family life.

For women with school-age children, the local elementary school was a focus of activity. Women described and structured their school-based activities in terms of work—committees, meetings, tasks, goals, and projects. This is Kathy's description of a typical day:

> "[O]ften I would walk the kids to school even though I'm only like a minute away; it's sort of a social thing to do to get up in the morning and walk the kids to school. The kids like it, and then you'll see all the other ladies there and stop and have a chitchat and there might be a coffee afterwards. And often those coffee meetings that we had would have a purpose, you know they would be a meeting of a committee, many times in the morning I'd get the kids off to school, quickly come in, clean up the kitchen, then head off to a coffee meeting and that would usually last till 11:30. . . . Sometimes it would go on till 2:30 and so a lot of hours in the day were spent with the other people in the area, on school-related business."

Notice Kathy's use of "committee," "meeting," and "business," terms more usually associated with paid work. Professional motifs were used to describe mothering activities. Another woman actually called her school work a "job," and allocated at least one morning a week to the task.

Worklike attitudes also structured many of the school-related activities these committees organized, such as fund-raising for extra school equipment like computers and playground equipment, garage sales, and neighborhood social gatherings. According to Anne, her neighbors "can definitely get the job done. They can organize, they can plan, they can implement, they get a lot of stuff happening."

She was speaking about finishing work on the local park, where a committee of three women met regularly, delegated tasks, had the materials donated, and arranged for the male residents to erect playground equipment and landscape the park. Mothering in Glenwood was thus constituted and understood as a job. Responsibility for the care of children was seen to be more reliably achieved through formalized, worklike, labor-intensive activities.

Professional motifs also extended to the activities and supervision of children. The spaces and activities of children were tightly controlled, beyond the extent identified by Dyck (1989). Good mothering here meant children's constant involvement in formal extracurricular activities. These activities, it was felt, were essential to give children the "best start in life" and also keep them off the streets and away from problematic influences. Some of these activities were school related, like "Kumon Math." Several children regularly attended this program, marketed on the basis of using Japanese teaching methods to improve a child's mathematical abilities. Children's afternoons commonly consisted of arranged activities like music lessons and sport. Such activities are not uncommon in middle-class families. More noteworthy are the preferences that these activities be run formally and professionally, rather than haphazardly and informally.

Professional motifs were also used by mothers in their governance of children's activities and their use of space. Children's social contacts, even within the neighborhood, were characterized by arranged, formal play. According to Libby:

"I find that if she has to go more than four or five houses either way, it is more an arranged event, as opposed to just popping over. She may go across the street, but not in the same way."

Most but not all mothers would arrange appointments in advance for play for their children, as described and criticized by Jennifer:

"[M]ost kids her age (7) are not even allowed out of their house alone, period. So it's not like they can all play together, you have to make appointments."

Children's use of space and those they came into contact with were thus tightly controlled and organized. Fears for children's safety supply a partial rationale for this practice. As Libby noted, "we do tend to guard our children a bit." What is also notable, however, is the extent of organization, like in a corporation. Children's play was to be supervised, not left to chance.

In sum, participation in the paid labor force only partially encapsulates mothering identities and femininity in Glenwood. At-home mothering was infused with workplace understandings and motifs, and conducted in a businesslike manner. A high level of involvement in children's lives, a structure to their days, and constant exposure to formal influences beyond the neighborhood were seen to constitute good mothering practices. Hence the meanings surrounding paid work and motherhood provide an important window onto suburban women's lives.

Paid labor force participation is also an inadequate axis of difference in Berkshire, another Vancouver neighborhood. Instead of a preponderance of professionally organized activities and lives, a casualness of practices and social relations was more common. Mothering and femininity were defined and practiced in terms of accommodation and fluidity. It was not that women held carefree, irresponsible attitudes toward the care and nurture of children. Like Glenwood mothers, the women of Berkshire were concerned and devoted to the well-being and future of their children. I am, however, pointing out that different strategies and interpretations of this work were employed, strategies that were more laissez-faire than strictly regulated.

Cultural evaluations of paid work and home-based work were characterized by accommodation. Neither paid work nor at-home motherhood were viewed in entirely favorable terms; each had its advantages and disadvantages. These feelings were most clearly articulated by Marie, who works on weekends and occasionally in the evening. With two grandmothers close by, baby-sitting is not a problem; she works these shifts to maximize the amount she earns for the time she works. For her, staying at home is "just as hard as a job," because "it's hard dealing with kids." She continues:

> "[L]ike I have three [children] and sure they fight and they're bored and you have to keep them out of trouble, they fight over what to watch on TV. This one (4-year-old) will watch videos all day, I have to play with her, thank goodness they're in school all day and thank goodness their Dad's home on the weekend to keep them entertained too."

Working full time would be similarly problematic:

"I couldn't work full-time and do all this, I don't think, I don't know what kind of life that would be, if I worked full-time and he [her husband] worked full-time, we'd get up, get the kids to [day care] and come home, make supper and stuff, I don't know, I don't think I could do that."

The experience of Sharon almost exactly mirrors that of Marie. A sales assistant who returned to part-time paid work when her first child was 7 weeks old, she would not work full-time because:

"They're only small once, you only have them little once. I could work full-time but I don't want to do that."

She also didn't want to leave the paid labor force:

"I don't want to quit. I like getting out, but I get bored at home, that's mainly why I went back and I wanted money. For the bills and stuff."

Thus unlike Glenwood it was seen to be both possible and desirable for Berkshire mothers to literally, rather than solely culturally, meld paid work with mothering work.

Such accommodations can also be found in the activities of children. Berkshire children's involvement in after-school activities was minimal compared to children in Glenwood. Music and sports were less important and sometimes not participated in at all. Indeed, some parents, like Ingrid and Henry, felt that too many activities were detrimental rather than beneficial. For their eldest son:

"[H]e's a very competitive child. And for that reason we didn't want him in team sports or a lot of extracurricular things because he's already quite anxious about school so his frustration level is quite high."

Further, since a "temporal treadmill" (Law & Wolch, 1993) was more pervasive in Berkshire, parents often did not have the time to spend their afternoons and evenings driving children around.

This hesitancy toward institutions and formality flowed into women's attitudes toward, and relations with, the local elementary school. For a variety of reasons it was seen to be best that formal education be left to the school, without considerable parental involvement. One woman even went so far as to be critical of the school's expectations of her. As she puts it:

"Parents have enough trouble finding time to help their children with homework, then you get notices about field trips. I don't have time."

According to another woman, volunteer work at the school was a luxury she and others couldn't afford. Instead, she says, "I think you should put all that effort [i.e., school volunteer work] into getting some money." Thus by default the school was not a focus of mothering activity in Berkshire. As a result, formal education was defined as the school's responsibility, with limited volunteer involvement.

A similar fluidity characterized parents' perceptions and children's use of neighborhood space. Within set boundaries beyond the house children were free to roam. This was especially the case with cul-de-sacs, which dominated the built landscape of both Berkshire and Glenwood. As one woman put it, "the cul-de-sac's not the street. Its just another extension of the driveway, its a big driveway." Consequently, according to one of her neighbors,

"Because it is a cul-de-sac they do play on the road a lot, just with other kids and stuff, like our kids they play in the backyard when they're by themselves but with other kids they usually play in the cul-de-sac."

One cul-de-sac was thus occupied by what Mark described as "the pack": "they're like birds, wherever one goes the other one goes." Full of children,

"you'll see every kind of thing that has wheels will be going around the cul-de-sac at varying speeds and varying times, but they're all out there doing it together."

Play with neighbors beyond the cul-de-sac was also less controlled than in Glenwood. Although not free to roam anywhere, children's "safe space" was much larger in Berkshire than the four or five houses it comprised in Glenwood. As long as parents knew where their children were and that they would be supervised there, they were free to go on their own rather than be driven there. Three or four streets were seen to be the limit. One woman was concerned, for instance, that one of her children's friends was moving from one street to four streets away. This would mean that the children would have be driven to each other's house rather than walk on their own.

Two subtly different constructions and practices of mothering are thus evident here. Differences in the paid labor force participation of women were a component of, but do not exhaust, these differences. The symbolic meanings of home and work and everyday practices were equally important. Home and work intermingled in a cultural rather than practical sense for women in Glenwood, with children's activities and play controlled and organized in a professional, businesslike manner. In Berkshire, women's lives consisted of a practically fluid relation between home and work, and a belief that children's lives should be correspondingly fluid. In particular, neighborhood space was less tightly controlled and education was left up to the school system. Thus a focus on mothering practices both complicates understandings of suburban women's relation to paid employment and highlights an important source of difference in suburban lives: constructions of mothering.

RELIGION AND TRADITIONAL FAMILIES IN SUBURBAN VANCOUVER

Although useful in showing the inadequacies of a sole focus on paid work as a source of suburban difference, this chapter so far has also been complicit with another form of essentialism. Like other suburban scholarship, it has shown difference across rather than within places. In this section I use a nonessentialist conception of place to produce a more complex suburban story, drawing out two distinct mothering networks and practices within Glenwood.

Mothering practices in Glenwood differed along religious lines. With few exceptions (e.g., Cooper, 1994), religion is largely invisible in urban and feminist scholarship and "remains peripheral to modern, academic geography" (Park, 1994, p. 1). Feminist suburban scholarship reproduces this situation, for it neither mentions religious affiliation nor acknowledges the possibility of its influence on women's lives. It appears that religion has not been "looked for," not found, and hence assumed to be an unimportant element of identity and difference. This invisibility of religion is increasingly problematic. Religiosity can influence sense of place, social relations, and neighborhood interactions (e.g., Cooper, 1994). It is therefore an element that may be important in suburban lives. Moreover, recent scholarship has highlighted the importance of religion in debates over the family and the constitution of motherhood. Stacey's (1990) analysis of postmodern families in the United States, for instance, identifies evangelical Christianity as an important explanatory element. To understand working-class motherhood and family relations in Silicon Valley, she argues, religious beliefs must be taken into account. In my interviews in Glenwood, religion emerged as an important element differentiating the neighborhood and mothering practices. Thus in this section I focus on attitudes toward and practices of motherhood that are associated with evangelical Christianity, to open up differences within that place and demonstrate the insights offered by a nonessentialist conception of place.

Within the Glenwood subdivision there were not one but two overlapping social networks and mothering practices. The first network was the one described in the previous section, revolving around the professionalization of at-home mothering. The second was focused around a religious school in a nearby neighborhood. Some residents had moved to Glenwood explicitly because of the school, and it was their Christianity and this school that tied them to, and was a source of identification with, the neighborhood. The private school, and the nondenominational church subsequently started there, fostered ties among families with strong religious beliefs. For these women (of which three were interviewed), the private school and church were the focus of their days and their mothering. For instance, Ruby felt isolated and alone in Glenwood until the church began. She states:

> "Since we've found this church that people in the neighborhood are attending, and so I'm finding other couples, like with little kids and having babies, wow, I didn't know these people three years ago and we've all been living here around the same time but none of us knew each other and it's the church that brought us together. . . . Basically I met all these people, we all have the same things in common since we started going to the church and that's what brought us together."

Thus two different social networks existed in the neighborhood, focused around the two schools and religious affiliation. To a large extent the adults and children of the two networks did not mix. As one woman explains:

> "A case in point—one year we were raising money to put up a playground behind the school and we were selling fresh orange juice and I went down to one family that lives at the other end of the road and I know the lady fairly well and she's got a few kids, and I mean who doesn't need fresh juice when they have little kids, but she said no, she wasn't interested in buying any and I said it was for a playground and she said my children won't be going to the public school, they'll be going to the Christian school and I said it's not just for the school, it's the playground,

and you'll be able to make use of it, and she just said no, my
children won't be playing in that area."

The two cultures of mothering coalesced in a number of ways, most
notably around the nonpaid labor force participation of women. It
was widely held by both groups that children were primarily women's
responsibility and that women should remain at home with children.
Differences were also apparent. Women in the religious network came
to decisions about family and motherhood via Christianity rather than
through an extended evaluation of the advantages and disadvantages
offered by differing mothering models. Remaining at home with children was seen to be naturally desirable and the only possible decision. Children's use of space and the extent of outside influences
were similarly more rigidly controlled. Home was clearly demarcated
as a haven from the secular world. One woman, Julie, believed and
policed the notion that home was sacrosanct. All outside influences
were prohibited from the house, including television and videos.

The two networks also entailed different models and practices of
motherhood: a more consumption-oriented, professional model, and
a "back to basics" Christian model practiced by religious families. The
public school network was consumption oriented, with home decora-
tion and material possessions like boats or motor homes and holidays
to Disneyland as high priorities. Opposite values were held by Christian families, and it is here that the role of the two models in materially affecting the construction of gender becomes apparent. Julie's
awareness and criticism of the nonreligious families in Glenwood re-
affirmed her beliefs. When I asked her about her involvement with
her neighbors she replied:

> "No, I don't really have a lot, don't talk to them much, don't
> have much discussion. They're all talking about things that are
> important to them, like what size boats they own, where they
> went on holidays, I don't want to be caught up in that, I don't
> think that's what life is about."

For Julie, her Glenwood neighbors represented all that she disliked
socially and economically. Her Christian-derived social conscience and
antimaterialism led her to distance herself from other mothers in the
neighborhood. She explicitly enrolled her eldest child in the Christian school on the assumption that it would take her child away from
the materialism that was rife throughout Glenwood. In this respect,
Julie was tapping into a well-known division in Glenwood. Moreover,

her identity as mother was partially constructed through her opposition to, or difference from, others in the neighborhood.

Multiple gender identities were thus sustained *within* this suburban site. Two different social and mothering networks were built around the two schools in Glenwood, each consisting of different but overlapping models of femininity. Participation in either of these networks, and their coexistence in one place, supported at-home mothering through reinforcement of shared beliefs in traditional constructions of motherhood. At the same time, within-place diversity materially affected women's mothering-related identities by cementing the subtle distinctions between religious and nonreligious practices.

SUMMARY

Theories of difference provide substantial insights into the variability and construction of gendered identities, especially femininity, in sites that are called suburban. In their wake stories of suburban homogeneity almost disappear and are replaced by accounts of the multiple gender identities constructed in and through suburban environments and the nuances and complexities embedded in the local context. Thinking about gender and suburbs in nonessentialist ways has facilitated an analysis that views neither suburbs nor their associated gender identities as transparent, homogeneous categories. Instead, the diversity, contradictions and dynamics internal to these categories surface. Thus in this chapter I have told multiple stories of the diversity of suburban women's lives: across space and in place, within and across class, including and extending beyond participation in paid employment. The focus on mothering has also opened up, albeit partially, an important facet of suburban women's lives. In particular, I have extended Dyck's (1989, 1990) work, demonstrating that where values with respect to mothering are heterogeneous (the Glenwood case) the local context matters but not in an entirely supportive way. Alternative notions of mothering within the one neighborhood are used oppositionally to reaffirm individual's own values.

The place of mothering in suburban lives and stories has been far from exhausted in this chapter. The third critique of essentialism, namely, the multiple and sometimes contradictory subjectivities within individuals, has only been partially elaborated. I have touched upon multiplicity through a consideration of women's rationales for their participation in paid employment but have not explored them fully.

As a contested and multifaceted ideal and practice, motherhood assumes and produces many tensions for women not addressed here but that could be taken up in a number of ways. For instance, the two case studies, though far from representative, suggest that the ideal of the nuclear family is far from dead. The internal fissures produced through men's and women's attempts to live this ideal in the 1990s need to be examined in more depth. Further critical scrutiny of the practices and ideologies of motherhood is therefore required to ensure the continued production of heterogeneous suburban stories.

ACKNOWLEDGMENT

I am grateful to Ruth Fincher and Jane M. Jacobs for their thoughtful comments on a previous draft.

REFERENCES

Barrett, M. (1987). The concept of difference. *Feminist Review, 26,* 62–75.

Collins, P. H. (1994). Shifting the center: Race, class and feminist theorizing about motherhood. In E. N. Glenn, G. Chang, & L. R. Forcey (Eds.), *Mothering: Ideology, experience, and agency* (pp. 45–60). London and New York: Routledge.

Cooper, A. (1994). Negotiated dilemmas of landscape, place and Christian commitment in a Suffolk parish. *Transactions of the Institute of British Geographers, 19,* 202–12.

Dyck, I. (1989). Integrating home and wage workplace: Women's daily lives in a Canadian suburb. *The Canadian Geographer, 33,* 329–341.

Dyck, I. (1990). Space, time and renegotiating motherhood: An exploration of the domestic workplace. *Environment and Planning D: Society and Space, 8,* 457–483.

England, K. V. L. (1991). Gender relations and the spatial structure of the city. *Geoforum, 22*(2), 135–147.

England, K. V. L. (1993). Changing suburbs, changing women: Geographic perspectives on suburban women and suburbanization. *Frontiers, 14*(1), 24–43.

Evenden, L. J., & Walker, G. E. (1993). The changing geography of the suburbs. In L. Bourne & D. Ley (Eds.), *The changing social geography of Canadian cities* (pp. 234–251). Montreal and Kingston: McGill–Queen's University Press.

Glenn, E. N. (1994). Social constructions of mothering: A thematic overview. In E. N. Glenn, G. Chang, & L. R. Forcey (Eds.), *Mothering: Ideology, experience, and agency* (pp. 1–32). London and New York: Routledge.

Gold, J. R., & Gold, M. M. (1989). Outrage and righteous indignation: Ideology and imagery of suburbia. In F. Boal & D. Livingstone (Eds.), *The behavioural environment: Essays in reflection, application and re-evaluation* (pp. 163–181). London and New York: Routledge.

Grosz, E. (1990). Conclusion: A note on essentialism and difference. In S. Gunew (Ed.), *Feminist knowledge: Critique and construct* (pp. 332–344). London and New York: Routledge.

Hanson, S., Pratt, G., Mattingly, G., & Gilbert, M. (1994). Women, work, and metropolitan environments. In I. Altman & A. Churchman (Eds.), *Women and the environment* (pp. 227–253). New York and London: Plenum Press.

Johnson, L. (1993). Textured brick: Speculations on the cultural production of domestic space. *Australian Geographical Studies, 31*(2), 201–213.

Kaplan, E. A. (1992). *Motherhood and representation: The mother in popular culture and melodrama.* London and New York: Routledge.

Law, R. M., & Wolch, J. R. (1993). Social reproduction in the city: Restructuring in time and space. In P. L. Knox (Ed.), *The restless urban landscape* (pp. 165–206). Englewood Cliffs, NJ: Prentice Hall.

Marsh, M. (1990). *Suburban lives.* New Brunswick, NJ: Rutgers University Press.

Massey, D. (1994). *Space, place and gender.* Cambridge, UK: Polity Press.

McDowell, L. (1991). The baby and the bathwater: Diversity, deconstruction and feminist theory in geography. *Geoforum, 22*(2), 123–133.

Milroy, B. M., & Wismer, S. (1994). Communities, work and public/private sphere models. *Gender, Place and Culture, 1*(1), 71–90.

Morton, S. (1994). *Ideal surroundings: Domestic life in a working-class suburb in the 1920s.* Toronto: University of Toronto Press.

O'Connor, C. (1985). Sorting out the suburbs: Patterns of land use, class and culture. *American Quarterly, 37*(3), 382–394.

Park, C. (1994). *Sacred worlds: An introduction to geography and religion.* London and New York: Routledge.

Peel, M. (1995). *Good times, hard times: The past and the future in Elizabeth.* Melbourne: Melbourne University Press.

Pratt, G., & Hanson, S. (1993). Women and work across the life course: Moving beyond essentialism. In C. Katz & J. Monk (Eds.), *Full circles: Geographies of women over the life course* (pp. 27–54). New York and London: Routledge.

Richards, L. (1990). *Nobody's home: Dreams and realities in a new suburb.* Melbourne: Oxford University Press.

Rose, G. (1993). *Feminism and geography: The limits of geographical knowledge.* Cambridge, UK: Polity Press.

Rubin, L. (1994). *Families on the faultline: America's working class speaks about the family, the economy, race and ethnicity.* New York: HarperCollins.

Saegert, S. (1980). Masculine cities and feminine suburbs: Polarized ideas, contradictory realities. *Signs, 5*(3), 96–111.

Savage, M., Barlow, J., Dickens, P., & Fielding, T. (1992). *Property, bureaucracy and culture: Middle-class formation in contemporary Britain.* London and New York: Routledge.

Scott, J. (1990). Deconstructing equality-versus-difference; or, the uses of poststructuralist theory for feminism. In M. Hirsch & E. F. Keller (Eds.), *Conflicts in feminism* (pp. 134–48). New York and London: Routledge.

Smith, P. (1989). *Discerning the subject.* Minneapolis: University of Minnesota Press.

Stacey, J. (1990). *Brave new families: Stories of domestic upheaval in late twentieth-century America.* New York: Basic Books.

Stacey, J. (1994). Scents, scholars and stigmas: The revisionist campaign for family values. *Social Text, 40,* 51–75.

Statistics Canada. (1994). *Profile of enumeration areas in British Columbia—Part A* (Reference No. A9105). Ottawa: Author.

Strong-Boag, V. (1991). Home dreams: Women and the suburban experiment in Canada, 1945–60. *Canadian Historical Review, 72*(4), 471–504.

Valentine, G. (1993). (Hetero)sexing space: Lesbians and experiences of everyday spaces. *Environment and Planning D: Society and Space, 11,* 395–413.

Wekerle, G. (1984). A woman's place is in the city. *Antipode, 63,* 11–19.

CHAPTER 5

Justice and
the Disabling City

Brendan Gleeson

THE SOCIAL OPPRESSION OF DISABILITY

In her recent critique of universalist ideals of justice, the American philosopher Iris Marion Young (1990) argues that *domination* and *oppression* must replace material distribution as the central politico-theoretical concerns for progressive social movements. For Young, established "welfarist" notions of justice are premised on a misleading social ontology that elides human difference by instating an abstract "citizen subject" as the beneficiary (or otherwise) of material distributions. As Young shows, the political and institutional practice of distributional justice by capitalist welfare states in the postwar era was hardly a universally beneficial project, and in fact enshrined the economic and cultural privilege of dominant identities, notably white, middle-class men. While Young's alternative vision for justice remains inchoate, she certainly provides a powerful theory of *in*justice that condemns welfarism and its institutionalized denial of the domination and oppression that marginalized social groups have suffered and resisted for decades in capitalist societies.

Among the many social groups that the "universalist" project has excluded, Young identifies women, gays, indigenous populations, and disabled people as "marginal identities." Young notes that all marginalized "groups are not oppressed to the same extent or in the same ways" (1990, p. 40). Her fivefold schema of oppression—the "faces," exploitation, marginalization, powerlessness, cultural imperialism and violence—is analyzed as a set of separate delimitations which marginalized social groups experience in distinctive ways. For

89

example, disabled people certainly suffer economic marginalization in the manner described by Young (1990), given the devalorization of their labor power in capitalist production (Gleeson, 1993). However, unlike women or gays, disabled people are probably not subjected to systematic violence in capitalist societies (leaving aside the question of often horrific medical interventions).

The aim of this chapter is to demonstrate the singularity of disability as a form of oppression that occurs in capitalist cities. The evidence here is drawn from North American, British and Australasian urban contexts that, notwithstanding local politico-economic specificities, broadly reflect the challenges of city life confronting disabled people in all capitalist societies. Disabled people have certainly suffered discrimination in other, noncapitalist urban settings (see, e.g., McCagg & Siegelbaum, 1989, on the former Soviet Union). It is argued here, however, that the socially oppressive features of capitalist societies for disabled people—especially those sourced in commodity labor markets—require a specific theoretical and empirical consideration. In short, while disabled people have been oppressed in most recent societies, the diversity of origins and forms for these experiences means that there can be no all-embracing analysis of this oppression.

"Disability" is a term that has many different uses in various places and is therefore impossible to define objectively. Disability may be used to refer a considerable range of human differences—including those defined by age, health, physical and mental abilities, and even income status—that have been associated with some form of social restriction or material deprivation. This chapter will adopt the more focused sense of the term often used in the social sciences: here "disability" refers to the social experiences of people with some form of physical impairment to a limb, organism, or bodily mechanism (Oliver, 1990).

Thus, the sense of disability used here encompasses disabilities that have an organic basis, including those which manifest as physical and intellectual impairments. The chapter will not focus on the question of mental illness, a specific set of health-related conditions and sociospatial experiences that can be distinguished from physical disability. However, in examining the urban geographical dimensions of disability, the chapter will briefly review at various points the considerable geographical work that has been undertaken on mental illness, much of which has relevance to the spatial consideration of physical impairment.

The chapter has three main sections. The first section highlights the contemporary urban context of disablement (the experience of disability). Here three principal aspects of the urban social oppression of disabled people are identified: inaccessibility, poverty, and sociospatial exclusion. These separate but structurally linked dimensions of urban disablement are then considered in theoretical context, through a critical appraisal of the disability analyses produced in the spatial sciences. This theoretical appraisal is undertaken from a historical-geographical perspective (cf. Harvey, 1990, 1996), which locates the origins of disablement in the material organization of capitalist cities. After this, a historical-geographical view of disability is outlined and applied in a brief analysis of the historical genesis of disablement in the capitalist city. The chapter concludes by briefly considering the potential role that geographers might play in the emancipatory struggles of disabled people.

CITIES OF OPPRESSION

From the voluminous policy and theoretical literatures produced by the disability movements of Western countries in recent years, it is clear that disabled people share a common, if not completely homogeneous, experience of social oppression.[1] It is also clear that this oppression takes a distinctive form in cities and that certain general urban characteristics—notably urban design, employment patterns, and the distribution of land uses—entrench social discrimination against disabled people. (It must be admitted that the phenomenon of rural disablement has been little explored in scholarly literature and that frequently the only basis for comparison for urban disability research is analysis undertaken at the national scale.) Disabled people, their advocates, and occasionally governments have identified three main dimensions of what may be termed "urban disablement": physical inaccessibility, poverty, and sociospatial exclusion in institutionalized forms of social care.[2] As will be argued later, these aspects of urban disablement take specific sociospatial forms but nonetheless have a common genesis in the economic and cultural devalorization of disabled people in capitalist societies.

Physical Inaccessibility

A critically disabling feature of capitalist cities is their inaccessible design. This means that the physical layout of cities—including both macro land use patterns and the internal design of buildings—discriminates against disabled people by not accounting for their mobility requirements. Practically speaking, this discrimination takes the following form:

1. Physical barriers to movement for disabled people, including broken surfaces on thoroughfares (streets, guttering, paving) that reduce or annul the effectiveness of mobility aids (e.g., wheelchairs, walking frames).
2. Building architecture that excludes the entry of anyone unable to use stairs and hand-opened doors.
3. Public transport modes which assume that passengers have a common level of ambulance

The above list is not exhaustive but does point to some of the more common discriminatory aspects of the built environments of contemporary Western cities.

Even allowing for the distinctive morphologies, economies, cultures, and planning policies of Western cities, the international breadth of concern raised by disabled people concerning inaccessibility (see Wrightson, 1989) demonstrates that this is a pervasive feature of urban life. As Hahn observes: "In terms of ease or comfort, most cities have been designed not merely for the nondisabled but for a physical ideal that few human beings can ever hope to approximate" (1986, p. 273). For disabled people, these pervasive mobility handicaps are more than simply the quotidian urban frictions (e.g., public transport delays, road blockages, freak weather, periodic crowding) that irritate the lives of nondisabled people. Rather, discriminatory design is a critical manifestation, and cause, of social oppression because it reduces the ability of disabled people to participate fully in urban life. More particularly, mobility constraints in the contemporary capitalist city are serious impediments to one's chances of gaining meaningful employment and are hence linked to heightened poverty risk. In addition, an inaccessible built environment reduces disabled people's capacity both to engage in political activities and to establish and maintain affective ties. It is not surprising therefore that Hahn (1986, p. 274) sees inaccessibility as a threat both to "principles of democratic freedom and equality for citizens with disabilities."

Although most Western countries now have in place some form of building and planning legislation that attempts to counter the problem of inaccessibility, there is accumulating evidence to show that such policies are generally failing to reduce or prevent discriminatory urban design (Bennett, 1990; Imrie, 1996; Vujakovic & Matthews, 1994). Access legislation is often opposed by development capital, and governments tend to be less than rigorous in its enforcement. Recently in the United States, powerful corporate interests have argued before the federal judiciary that the Americans with Disabilities Act, by requiring businesses to provide wheelchair access, is an unnecessary restriction upon private property rights, and therefore an infringement of the Fifth Amendment (Helvarg, 1995).

In Britain, Imrie and Wells (1993a) have shown how the Thatcher government during the 1980s progressively relaxed central controls on accessibility standards and encouraged a mood of regulatory voluntarism among local authorities (which bear the primary responsibility for enforcing access codes). The authors argue that many local authorities subsequently gave little policy priority and few resources to accessibility responsibilities. The national lethargy on access policy was attributed in part to the flourishing climate of local growth politics and the consequent anxiety of individual councils that "superfluous" building regulations would frighten away increasingly mobile development capital (Imrie & Wells, 1993a).

Like Britain, New Zealand has enacted accessibility legislation, in the form of amendments to its Building Act (1991), which aim to make that country's cities more accessible to disabled people. However, in one major New Zealand city, Dunedin, disability advocacy groups have argued that local government has failed to enforce the accessibility standards in the building legislation. Reflecting the British experience portrayed by Imrie and Wells (1993a, 1993b), Dunedin disability activists have recently argued that the city's local government has neglected its accessibility policy responsibilities by underresourcing its building standards inspectorate (*Otago Daily Times,* September 11, 1994, p. 5). In late 1993, after some press exposure of activists' complaints, the city council's building control manager publicly admitted that "resources are being stretched" and attached the familiar bureaucratic codicil for inaction by remarking that "the requirements [of the Building Act] are being enforced as far as is reasonably practicable" (*Dunedin Star Midweek,* November 10, 1993, p. 1). In a further admission this same officer acknowledged that the city council had not required a particular commercial establishment to install a lift during a major refit, although the building legislation may have required this. He then attempted to reassure the city's disability community with the observation that "this place can still be accessed by people with disabilities who are not confined to a wheelchair" (*Dunedin Star Midweek,* November 10, 1993, p. 1), thereby demonstrating a highly arbitrary and selective notion of disability that conflicted with the inclusive aim of the legislation.

Poverty and Unemployment

A further major feature of urban disablement is poverty, due largely to the exclusion of disabled people from mainstream employment markets (Oliver, 1991). Alcock (1993, p. 175), citing Groves (1988), observes that "Poverty is disability's close companion" and, like Liachowitz (1988) and Oliver (1991), traces this relationship back to the growth of urbanization in 19th-century Europe. As I have argued elsewhere (Gleeson, 1993), the motive force for this urbanization was the rise of competitive capitalism, a mode of production that fashioned workplaces, and entire cities, around industrial labor markets that excluded "slow" or "incapable" workers. The economies of contemporary capitalist cities thus reveal a legacy of discriminatory industrial labor markets by continuing to valorize nondisabled labor power over all other forms. Both Liachowitz (1988) and Alcock (1993) argue that contemporary capitalist cities both reflect and entrench disablement through their physical inaccessibility and discriminatory labor markets. Alcock (1993) draws particular attention to the link between inaccessibility and poverty, arguing that there are many "additional costs of coping with a disability in the able-bodied world" (Alcock, 1993, p. 188). Inaccessibility also often means that disabled people are unable to engage in mainstream consumption activities, thereby reducing their capacity to purchase goods and services at optimal prices. These goods and services include major urban consumption items, such as housing, education, transport, and finance (Oliver, 1991).

For many disabled people, employment in mainstream work settings is the key to achieving both personal dignity and social inclusion. A recent New Zealand survey of more than 1000 disabled people revealed that many respondents (49%) regarded "money" as the overriding reason why employment was important to them (Hillary Commission and Workbridge, 1994). Moreover, nearly 20% of respondents mentioned their aspirations for "social contact" and the chance to "play a part in society" through paid work. However, the employment aspirations of most disabled people remain unrealized in Western countries (Alcock, 1993; Lunt & Thornton, 1994). The unsaleability of disabled labor power is stark. British figures show that during the 1980s disabled people were three times more likely to be unemployed than nondisabled people (Barnes, 1992). Figures reported by Oliver (1991) confirm that most disabled people in the United Kingdom are unemployed. This is acknowledged as a significant underestimate, given that labor force participation among disabled people is generally low.

For the relative few that do find employment, exploitation frequently awaits in sheltered workplaces or lowly paid jobs in open employment settings (Alcock, 1993). In Australia, for example, the exploitation of impaired people in sheltered workshops has been documented (e.g., Ronalds, 1990), but this form of oppression continues. In 1990, the National Department of Social Services in that country estimated that 53% of sheltered employees were earning less than $A20 (Australian dollars) per week (Ronalds, 1990). Similarly, in Britain, disabled men in full-time work currently earn almost a quarter less per week than their nondisabled equivalents. Even worse, disabled women workers earned almost a third less per week than did disabled men workers, suggesting—not surprisingly—that gender plays an important role in determining the relative oppressiveness of disablement (Barnes, 1992).

While the vast majority of disabled people are poor, the degree of immiseration tends to be hidden or mediated by state welfare payments and family support. (Alcock, 1993, estimates that 75% of British disabled adults rely on some form of state support.) There is little published research on the economic impacts of disablement for households with a disabled member in certain Western countries. However, some indication of the extent of this "silent poverty" is given by Barnes's estimation (1992) that, in 1985, British families with a disabled (nonpensioner) adult member received on average only 72% of the incomes of families without disabled adults. Oliver's (1991, p. 133) bleak summary assessment of disablement is that it is "a situation of unemployment, underemployment and poverty."

Sociospatial Exclusion

In addition to their exclusion from mainstream employment settings, disabled people also experience barriers to choice in their preferred living environment in the contemporary Western city (Dear, 1992; Steinman, 1987). These two areas of sociospatial injustice present difficult policy challenges, to say the least, for Western governments, most of which have struggled to lessen the constraints experienced by disabled people in obtaining both employment and a valued living setting (Gleeson & Memon, 1994; Glendinning, 1991; Jenkins, 1991; Lunt & Thornton, 1994; Minister for Health, Housing and Community Services [Australia], 1991; Oliver, 1991).

Large institutions have provided both residential "care" and "sheltered" employment for disabled people for much of the 20th century. The oppressive experience of institutionalization by disabled people was frequently characterized by, inter alia, material privation, brutalizing and depersonalized forms of "care," a lack of privacy and individual freedom, and separation from friends and family (Horner, 1994; Shannon & Hovell, 1993). The failure of institutions as socialized forms of care for disabled people exposes, among other things, the inadequacy of the welfarism (cf. Young, 1990), which has broadly framed the urban social policies of Western states since World War II. Institutions may have distributed a very minimal level of material support to disabled people (which admittedly improved in many countries over time), but they also ensured the sociospatial exclusion of disabled people from the mainstreams of social life, thus entrenching the political invisibility and powerlessness of this social group.

In recognition of these inadequacies, Western governments have sought to deinstitutionalize support for disabled people, usually involving the closure of large-scale residential centers and their replacement with small, dispersed community care units. This restructuring of care has been overdetermined by other political dynamics that have little to do with therapeutic ideals and civil rights, including the desire of neoliberal governments from the 1970s to reduce welfare budgets and desocialize care of the dependent (Dear & Wolch, 1987; Eyles, 1988).

The social geographical consequences of deinstitutionalization have been thoroughly documented for North America in a set of landmark studies by Michael Dear and Jennifer Wolch. *Landscapes of Despair* (Dear & Wolch, 1987) traced the construction of new urban "zones of dependence," these being clusters of service-dependent groups and facilities designed to support them, usually located in declining inner-city areas (see also Joseph & Hall's [1985] examination of clustering in Toronto). Both this and a follow-up study, *Malign Neglect* (Wolch & Dear, 1993), emphasized how poor public funding and community opposition had forced many deinstitutionalized people into homelessness and "ghettoization" in the emerging zones of dependence. Milligan's recent (1996) analysis examined the applicability of these North American findings to Scotland. Milligan concluded that while deinstitutionalized people suffer sociospatial exclusion in Scotland, this marginalization is different from that which commonly occurs in North America due to the influence of different legislative mechanisms, policy structures, and service provision forms.

Has the transition to community care (where it has been realized) reduced the social oppression of disabled people by offering them greater freedom in the choice of preferred living environment? As the work cited above suggests, the experience of several Western countries in trying to deinstitutionalize both residential care and employment of the socially dependent suggests that such strategies cannot eliminate the exclusion of disabled people from valued areas of community life—in particular, mainstream workplaces and residential settings. A critical social dynamic has impeded the ability of deinstitutionalization to secure "locational freedom" for disabled people: pervasive opposition to community care facilities, in the form of the NIMBY ("not in my backyard") syndrome (Dear, 1992). Young (1990) identifies localized opposition to community care homes as a source of injustice for disabled people. For her, "zoning regulations that limit . . . location choices" are institutional sources of injustice for disabled people (Young, 1990, p. 255).

Much of the early investigation of NIMBY reactions to care homes was undertaken in North America, where deinstitutionalization has been underway for at least three decades. The pioneering work of Wolpert (e.g., 1976), Dear (e.g., 1977, 1981, 1992) and collaborators (e.g., Dear, Fincher, & Currie, 1977; Dear, Taylor, & Hall, 1980; Dear & Taylor, 1982), and C. J. Smith (e.g., 1977, 1978, 1984, 1989) was important both in charting the course of deinstitutionalization policies and in developing a critical geographical analysis of the NIMBY syndrome as a particular form of urban locational conflict. In recent years both the NIMBY phenomenon and scholarly interest in it have grown within a range of Western countries, including the United Kingdom (e.g., Burnett & Moon, 1983; Locker, Rao, & Weddell, 1979; Moon, 1988), Australia (e.g., Foreman & Andrews, 1988) and New Zealand (Gleeson, Gooder, & Memon, 1995).

Much of this geographical analysis of NIMBY and locational conflict has centered on reactions to facilities for people with mental illnesses. It will be argued later in this chapter that this literature may not fully appreciate the singularity of locational conflict issues that surround disabled people and the support facilities provided for them. While many of the broad findings of these locational conflict studies are relevant to the question of disability, there is a need for further analyses that can identify the distinct patterns of community receptiveness toward physical impairment and mental illness. In most Western countries the distinctiveness of these issues is reflected in separate, if sometimes overlapping, policy regimes for disability support and psychiatric care.

NIMBY sentiments are rooted in the structure of the capitalist land economy and thus represent a strong and enduring potential impediment to the realization of community care for disabled people. As Walker (1981) explains, the commodified nature of residential land in capitalist societies is a powerful influence on homeowners' (and home purchasers') social interests. Locational conflicts are often expressed as defensive reactions by homeowners confronted with land uses that are perceived as threats to residential amenity (the putative "character" or "quality" of a residential environment). In fact, the notion of "residential amenity" is heavily coded with concerns for land as a commodity capable both of storing value and rendering capital gain (profit) (Walker, 1981). Seen from this perspective, homeowners' sensitivity toward amenity, and land uses that may threaten this, is an outward expression of their deeper social interests as commodity purchasers and owners who are concerned to safeguard the exchange value of their principal capital possession, residential land. Hence, "NIMBY sentiments" are often the phenomenal form of deeply embedded class interests, namely, the concern of homeowners to safeguard the exchange value of their principal asset, residential land (Plotkin, 1987; Walker, 1981).

This would suggest that areas with high concentrations of homeowners (as opposed to other land uses and other residential tenure types) would be most likely to resist the "intrusion" of perceived noxious facilities (Dear, 1992; Beamish, 1981). As Taylor (1988, p. 234) found in his Toronto study with Dear, "Greater opposition to facilities was associated with stable neighborhoods with relatively large proportions of families with children and relatively higher socioeconomic status." Such "opposition" will take the form of NIMBY reactions in which homeowners pursue an important common interest—the protection of residential exchange values—through collective actions that curb the entry of unwanted facilities into their neighborhoods (Dear & Taylor, 1982; Beamish, 1981). These collective NIMBY actions are most often pursued through local government development control systems (Gleeson & Memon, 1994).

A recent empirical analysis in New Zealand (Gleeson, 1995c) suggests that the increasing flexibilization of planning regulation, common to a number of Western countries, may well enhance the power of local communities to exclude land uses that they see as undesirable. In the case of New Zealand, a survey of its 20 largest urban district councils found that urban planners often had little knowledge both of deinstitutionalization and the potential of new, flexible planning regulations to restrict the locational range of community care homes (Gleeson, 1995c).

A series of recent court rulings in Western countries has illustrated the enduring political-economic potency of NIMBY sentiments and their capacity to constrain disabled people's choice of living environment. In September 1995, the British High Court ruled that a set of neighbors were entitled to compensation for a fall in property values after a local health authority had established a care home in their immediate vicinity. The broader implications of this ruling were not immediately clear, but health authorities feared that the fiscal impacts of the decision would jeopardize all community care programs in the United Kingdom (*The Times*, September 21, 1995, p. 2).

Also in 1995, the U.S. Supreme Court ruled that cities may not use local zoning ordinances to exclude group homes for disabled people from residential areas. The court ruled that exclusionary zoning violated the rights of persons, including disabled people, protected under the antidiscrimination provisions of the federal housing laws (*AAMR News and Notes*, May/June, 1995, p. 1). However, Zipple and Anzer (1994) had earlier reported how city authorities had anticipated such a ruling by switching to other regulatory modes, notably building codes, in order to achieve exclusionary zoning outcomes. On the basis of the U.S. experience, it seems difficult to conclude that mainstream human rights legislation is sufficient to protect disabled people against NIMBY discrimination.

Clearly, the prospects for successful deinstitutionalization are limited by the twin facts of the capitalist land economy, which encourages among property owners an endemic hostility toward perceived sources of disamenity, and the continuing social devalorization of disabled people. One potential strategy for counteracting NIMBY reactions toward care homes and residents might be public employment policies aimed at revalorizing the labor power, and thus social identities, of disabled people. However, the comments made earlier on the employment difficulties facing disabled people suggest the magnitude of the public policy effort required to realize this strategy. Given the neoliberal character of many contemporary Western governments (Lipietz, 1992), such a spectacular intervention in national labor markets seems highly unlikely in the present conjuncture.

THE URBAN GEOGRAPHY OF DISABLEMENT

Thus far, I have highlighted the main dimensions of disablement in the contemporary capitalist city. In the following discussion, these distinct urban aspects of disablement are considered theoretically, drawing upon the spatial social science literature that has considered the question of disability. The literature review is sourced in historical materialism, a theoretical framework that has given rise to certain social constructionist explanations of disability (Oliver, 1990). In general, the historical-materialist approach opposes those perspectives that see disability as a product purely of ideologies (idealism), the physical environment (crude materialism), or individual physiology (methodological individualism) (Abberley, 1987, 1991a; Gleeson, 1995a; Oliver, 1990). Against these viewpoints, historical materialism posits disability as a product of society, an oppressive experience that emerges from the discriminatory organization of material and cultural life in contemporary capitalist societies. After the critical apprais-

als that now follow, this materialist critique is broadened into a historical-geographical account of urban disablement.

Cities of (In)difference

Anglophonic urban geography has hardly considered the question
of disability (Chouinard, 1994; Golledge, 1993; Hall, 1994), though
considerable attention has been given to closely related issues such as
mental illness (e.g., Dear, 1977, 1981; Dear & Taylor, 1982; C. J. Smith
& Giggs, 1987; Wolpert, 1976) and access to state social services (e.g.,
Pinch, 1985, 1987; Wolch, 1980, 1990). In the past, few geographers
have attempted a systematic consideration of disability in their research endeavors, though Golledge (1990, 1991, 1993) is a notable
exception here. Indeed, one of the most thoughtful geographical
analyses of disability to appear in recent years was authored by a political scientist (Hahn, 1986). Moreover, there have been other, more
recent attempts by nongeographers to consider the environmental
context of disability, focusing upon inherently spatial concerns such
as physical access in cities (e.g., see Wrightson, 1989; and the collection edited by Swain et al., 1993).

There are several recent published analyses of disability within
the sociospatial disciplines—including planning (e.g., Bennett, 1990;
Imrie & Wells, 1993a, 1993b), architecture (e.g., Kridler & Stewart,
1992a, 1992b, 1992c; Lebovich, 1993; Leccese, 1993), and geography
(e.g., Gleeson, 1995a, 1995b; Golledge, 1993). To date, however, these
analyses remain relatively isolated from each other, rather than integrated as a critical discourse, and tend to address debates within the
nonspatial social sciences. Human geographers, in the main, have
overlooked the fact that disability is a profoundly sociospatial issue.
Ignorance of a condition that, at any given time, probably affects 10–
15% of national populations (Golledge, 1993) is a disturbing feature
of a discipline claiming to explain the geographical dimensions of
human affairs (cf. Johnston, Gregory, & Smith, 1994).

Interestingly, there is a considerable, if largely invisible, tradition of postgraduate research on disability that exists as a set of isolated investigations undertaken in many Anglophonic geography and
planning departments (e.g., Cook, 1991; Dodds, 1980; Dorn, 1994;
Gleeson, 1993; Lawrence, 1993; McTavish, 1992).[3] For some reason(s),
these student investigations of disability have never matured as an
explicit academic agenda, perhaps partly because some of these students are disabled themselves and experience barriers to academic
development. One could speculate on other reasons, including, perhaps, a general unwillingness of the discipline to recognize disable-

ment—the experience of disability—as a profoundly geographical experience.

Against this continuing "disciplinary silence," a small but growing community of geographers is arguing that disability must be a critical concern for geography (e.g., Butler, 1994; Chouinard, 1994; Cook, 1991; Gleeson, 1993, 1995a, 1995b; Golledge, 1990, 1991, 1993; Hall, 1994; Imrie & Wells, 1993a, 1993b; Imrie, 1996; Vujakovic & Matthews, 1994). These advocates, however, hold radically different assumptions concerning how disability is to be conceived, socially and spatially, and concerning the potential contribution that geographers can make in transforming the lives of disabled people. For instance there is a fundamental conflict between behavioralist geographies, which locate the cause of disability in the impaired body (e.g., Golledge, 1993), and crude (viz., asocial) materialisms (mostly in other spatial sciences, such as architecture), which see disablement as primarily a problem of reduced physical access in the urban environment (e.g., Kridler & Stewart, 1992a, 1992b, 1992c). In contrast to these spatial understandings of disability, a historical-geographical approach is emerging that locates the origins of disablement in the material organization of capitalist society (e.g., Gleeson, 1995a; Hall, 1994; Imrie, 1996). The following subsections demonstrate both these disciplinary silences and theoretical differences through separate considerations of the three aspects of urban disablement highlighted above. Following these three critical deliberations, an outline is sketched of an alternative historical-geographical account of disability.

Theorizing Access

The spatial sciences have produced several examinations of the inaccessibility problem that confronts disabled people in contemporary cities. Many of these studies have emerged from spatial social sciences outside geography, including planning (e.g., Bennett, 1990; Imrie & Wells, 1993a, 1993b) and architecture (e.g., Kridler & Stewart, 1992a, 1992b, 1992c). These investigations have certainly influenced public urban policies on disability issues in the form of access legislation and inclusive building codes. However, from a historical-materialist perspective, a major criticism of the access literature is its frequent tendency to reduce the social oppression of disablement to a built environment problematic.

Indeed, the general treatment of the spatial question within disability studies has tended to display a crude materialism in which the arrangement of the built environment is seen as the principal source of disablement. In this view space is reduced to an inanimate configuration of material objects, and its sense of sociality—its character as a dimension of dynamic human relations—is lost to analysis. The implied phenomenal form of space, the city, simply becomes a static diorama, freed from the social structures that created it, and the issue of disablement is reduced to a dilemma of access.

The geographers Imrie and Wells (1993a, 1993b), have produced analyses that recognize the importance of political economic factors in preventing the successful implementation of public access policies. However, in one such analysis they suggest, after Hahn (1986), that the capitalist city is "characterised by a thoughtless lack of design and planning in public and private building" (1993a, p. 213). This remark seems to deny the possibility that physical inaccessibility arises from a sociostructural origin. Inaccessibility is reduced here to a sociospatial contingency whose diffuse genesis is merely the inadvertently discriminatory decisions of individual actors (i.e., planners, architects, developers) in the land economy. The discriminatory design of capitalist cities appears then to be an environmental "accident," which the state must correct through accessibility legislation, rather than the phenomenal form of deeper material and ideological structures of oppression.

The recent influential work of Golledge (1990, 1991, 1993, 1996) also critically examines the inaccessibility of the contemporary Western city for disabled people. His approach departs from a historical-geographical perspective in several important ways. Golledge argues that disabled people inhabit "distorted spaces" (e.g., 1993, p. 64): in fact, he envisions a unique "world of disability" (e.g., 1993, p. 65) that corresponds to the constricted time–space prism of the disabled individual. In another recent geography of disability, Vujakovic and Matthews (1994, p. 361) echo this sociospatial ontology with their stress on the "contorted, folded and torn" environmental knowledges of disabled people. This perspective offers the appealing idea that disabled people are actually creators of their own space, in that they are seen to transform actively the general geographical landscape in their everyday lives and reproduce this as their own experiential world. The motive force, however, for this transformation is the disabled, primordially limited body itself, which encounters the urban landscape and magnifies otherwise quotidian physical objects and surfaces to the extent that they become daunting barriers to effective social participation. The result of this encounter is the production of "distorted spaces . . . which these populations *must endure*" (Golledge, 1993, p. 64, emphasis added).

Not all blame is placed on disability as the source of spatial distortion, for Golledge clearly sees disablement as a state of social disadvantage. Therefore, he argues at several points that the physical urban environment is structured in ways that exacerbate the distorting effect of disability, through careless design and signage, for example, which inhibit the access and mobility of disabled people.

Nonetheless, this approach contrasts with the "social constructionist" perspective because these so-called worlds of disability are seen to have a primarily pathological genesis, located in the deficiencies of the disabled body rather than in social phenomena. These deficiencies are exaggerated, but not caused, by the social arrangement of space. Environmental modifications that seek to increase access for disabled people are explained as "efforts to *compensate for* disability" (Golledge, 1993, p. 64, emphasis added). The clear implication is that disability is a set of physiologically given deficiencies, rather than socially created limitations, for which society seeks to compensate the individual through environmental design concessions. The "spatial problem" of disability is seen to reside first with the disabled individual, whose physical deficiencies are primordially assumed. Only then is society problematized, with an assumption that it needs to improve the arrangement of space in order to compensate disabled people for their deficiencies.

The Economic Geography of Disability

The theoretical review for this aspect of urban disablement is necessarily short: geography has simply ignored the issues of poverty and employment among disabled people. One searches without result through the major texts and journals dealing with economic and industrial geography for any mention of disability in the analyses contained therein (see also Hall, 1994). The influential *Dictionary of Human Geography* (Johnston et al., 1994, p. 147) defines the field of economic geography as "A geography of people's struggle to make a living." Is it not then extraordinary that economic geographers have ignored a sizeable social group whose very existence is overshadowed by profound material struggle? This represents a serious elision in the economic geography discourse and demonstrates geography's own complicity in the marginalization of disabled people from the mainstreams of social life, including, in this case, authoritative realms of knowledge.

Feminists in recent years have criticized economic geography for ignoring nonclass cleavages—notably, gender—in the social relations that underpin economic activity in capitalist societies (e.g., Rose, 1993). The same argument can be made for disability, a social identity that, as was shown earlier, is characterized by a specific set of economic realities, including poverty, labor market exclusion, exploitation, welfare dependence, and low pay. Although these economic conditions resonate with those that commonly define the experience of many women in capitalist societies, disability and gender are certainly not identical materialities. Although, for example, biology–physiology can be a source of labor-power devaluation for both women and disabled people, the latter experience labor markets in highly specific ways.[4] One critical distinction in the general economic experiences of women and disabled people is the exclusion of many of the latter in special industrial realms, frequently known as "sheltered workshops" (Alcock, 1993).

The sheltered workshop emerged within Western cities in the early 20th-century as a "humane" solution to the problem posed by the pool of disabled labor power that industry largely refused to absorb (Ronalds, 1991). However, a range of commentators have noted that sheltered workshops are sites both of marginalization and exploitation of workers within the economies of contemporary cities. Both Alcock (1993) in Britain and Ronalds (1991) in Australia have pointed out that sheltered workshops promote the exclusion of disabled people from mainstream employment settings and also frequently subject their workers to low pay and poor labor conditions. However, the problems facing disabled workers in sheltered work settings have been poorly documented (Ronalds, 1991). There is a pressing need for analyses that can assess both the internal labor regimes of sheltered workshops and the more general role of these distinctive sites of production within the broader industrial landscape. In terms of the latter, exogenous consideration, it could be hypothesized that these cellular low-pay regimes might have aggregate or at least sectoral effects on the rate and type of technological change within certain labor-intensive industries (e.g., packaging) (see Oliver, 1991).

In summary, then, economic geography has ignored the issue of disability, thereby limiting its own claim to be a geographical specialism that investigates the human struggle for material existence. However, as part of the foregoing critique, it was suggested that the phenomenon of sheltered workshops is both poorly understood and of wider potential economic significance than social science has hitherto acknowledged. The sociospatial issue of sheltered labor suggests an obvious investigatory starting point for an economic geography of disablement.

Institutional Geographies

There is now a wealth of geographical literature on human service institutions and the restructuring of this mode of social care in Western countries since World War II.[5] This literature, inspired by work in philosophy (notably, Foucault, 1975, 1979) and social history (especially Ignatieff, 1978; Rothman, 1971) has charted historical aspects of institutional care for socially dependent people. These historical geographies (e.g., Dear & Wolch, 1987; Driver, 1993; Philo, 1995, 1996) have illustrated the rise from the 19th century of a "carceral landscape"—made up of hospitals, asylums, and workhouses—to which was exiled a growing estate of socially dependent groups including orphans, the mentally ill, and the elderly.

Geographers have also studied the more recent shift in most Western countries from institutional to community-based modes of social care, a process known as "deinstitutionalization" (e.g., Dear, Wolch, & Wilton, 1994; Dear & Wolch, 1987; Kearns, Smith, & Abbott, 1992; and the collection edited by C. J. Smith & Giggs, 1988). As mentioned earlier, much of the geographical work concerning deinstitutionalization has investigated patterns of local community resistance to the neighborhood-based care facilities that are replacing large asylums and hospitals in most Western countries (e.g., Dear & Taylor, 1982; Gleeson & Memon, 1994; Moon, 1988). In addition, geographers have shown how poorly executed community care programs have meant that many deinstitutionalized people continue to suffer poverty and sociospatial isolation as part of the burgeoning homeless populations of many Western cities (e.g., Dear & Gleeson, 1991; Wolch & Dear, 1993).

One important criticism that can be made of the body of geographical work on institutions and community care is that it has focused upon particular forms of social dependency—notably, homelessness and mental illness—to the exclusion of physical and intellectual disability. Allowing for confusions that arise through international variations in the terminology of social dependency, a distinction must be drawn between mental illness, a disorder of the mind, and physical disablement, which relates to physiological difference. Both the geography of institutions and the broader field of medical-health geography have tended to focus the discipline's attention on issues of mental health, with physical and intellectual abilities receiving scant attention.

Disabled people and mentally ill people have not experienced deinstitutionalization in identical ways, and there is a need for geographical analysis that is sensitive to this difference. As Dear (1992) acknowledges, popular perceptions of service-dependent peoples are highly variegated, and he points to a "pecking order" of community preferences for various socially marginalized groups. At the "highest" end of the pecking order are those social groups that arouse most fear (rational or otherwise) among communities in Western cities, including the mentally ill and people with AIDS. Dear (1992, p. 289) rightly observes thus that "the intensity of NIMBY sentiments vary widely, depending upon the specific service clients." Dear (1992) goes on to note that physically disabled people are probably one of the lowest placed groups on the scale of popular anxiety, but he does not cite examples of geographical analyses of community reactions to physically disabled people. However, such an analysis was conducted in the United Kingdom by Moon (1988), whose study of NIMBY attitudes found that hostels for "physically handicapped" people were seen as less "noxious" by communities than were facilities for a variety of other social groups, including the homeless, drug users, and women seeking refuge from domestic violence. While Moon's study did not measure attitudes to facilities for the mentally ill, he is certain that "findings would have been more negative in the case of mental illness" (1988, p. 213).

In view of the foregoing, it seems important to further sensitize the already considerable and insightful geographical knowledge of the NIMBY syndrome through new studies of community reactions to the establishment of care networks for "less noxious" groups such as disabled people, the elderly, and children. Work has been undertaken on community acceptance of these social groups in other areas of social science (e.g., Balukas & Baken, 1985; Berdiansky & Parker, 1977; Currie, Trute, Tefft, & Segall, 1989), but none of these studies have fully developed the important spatial concepts—such as externality and distance decay[6]—that geographers have used to understand the NIMBY syndrome. Without such analytical discrimination between social groups, there is a danger that geographical knowledge will contribute to public policies that wrongly presume the existence of general community attitudes toward all service-dependent peoples. A practical consequence of this erroneous generalization might be inhibited program planning by agencies that provide residential community care for disabled people.

HISTORICAL-GEOGRAPHICAL MATERIALISM AND DISABILITY

A Social Constructionist Approach

The preceding critiques reflect a historical-geographical understanding of disability that emphasizes the distinctive material and cultural qualities of this form of social oppression. The following elaborates a view of disability and space that is sourced in historical-geographical materialism (cf. Harvey, 1990, 1996). The historical-geographical view of disability can be closely related to certain social constructionist perspectives in the field of disability studies.

Materialist scholars of disability in Britain have argued for a social constructionist definition of disability which emphasizes the sociopolitical and cultural forces that shape the experience of physical impairment (see, e.g., Abberley, 1987, 1991a, 1991b; Finkelstein, 1979; Oliver, 1990). These theorists have insisted upon an important conceptual distinction between *impairment*, which refers to the absence of part of or all of a limb or having a defective limb, organism, or bodily mechanism, and *disability*, which is the socially imposed state of exclusion or constraint that physically impaired individuals may be forced to endure (Oliver, 1990). From this, disability is defined as a social oppression that any society might produce through its sociopolitical and cultural organization of everyday life.

This is not to say that this social constructionist position ignores the real limits that nature, through impairment, places upon individuals. Rather, the perspective separates, both ontologically and politically, the oppressive social experience of disability from the unique functional limitations (and capacities) that impairment can pose for individuals. Impairment is a physiological fact that certainly embodies a given set of limitations and abilities, which then places real and ineluctable conditions on the social capacities of certain individuals. However, the social capacities of impaired people can never be defined as a set of "natural" and historically fixed "functional limitations." The capacities of impaired people are conditioned both culturally and historically and can only be understood through concrete spatiotemporal analyses.

The historical-geographical view recognizes that different societies may produce environments that liberate the capacities of impaired people while not aggravating their limitations. It is certainly possible to point to historical societies where impairment was sociospatially reproduced in far less disabling ways than has been the case in capitalism. The historical analyses of Dorn (1994), Finkelstein

(1979), Morris (1969), Ryan and Thomas (1987), and Topliss (1979) have all opposed the idea that capitalist society is inherently less disabling than previous social forms.

The Sociospatial Production of Disability

The postpositivist position accepted by most contemporary human geographers (Johnston et al., 1993) problematizes an absolute view of space and the belief this encourages of urban geographical change as primarily the rearrangement of objects on a flat, isotropic surface. Historical-geographical theorists (e.g., Harvey, 1990, 1996; N. Smith, 1984; Soja, 1989) and other postpositivist geographers have argued for a view of space as socially produced—a sociospatial dialectic, which sees society and space as mutually constituting material dynamics. In this view, capitalist social space arises from the territorialization of, among other things, deep structural forces such as commodity relations, which in the process of materialization are themselves mediated by existing spatial patterns. Critically, the historical-geographical view locates the origins of disablement in capitalist society at the unseen and dynamic structural level of sociospatial transformation: a dialectic of social and spatial change that has devalued the capacities of impaired people.

One historical example of this dialectic is the growth of commodity relations in late feudal society that slowly eroded the labor power of impaired people. Market relations, and the commodification of labor, introduced a social evaluation of work—the law of value—into peasant households. Heretofore, these households had been relatively autonomous production units, largely clustered in small rural communities (cities and large towns were few in number—most Europeans in the Middle Ages lived in hamlets and villages).

The increasing social authority of the law of value meant the submission of peasant households to an abstract external force (market relations) that appraised the worth of individual labor in terms of average productivity standards. From the first, this competitive, social evaluation of individual labor power meant that "slower," "weaker," or more inflexible workers were devalued in terms of their potential for paid work (see also Mandel, 1968). Impaired workers thus entered the first historical stage of capitalist accumulation handicapped by the devaluing logic of the law of value and competitive commodity relations. Also, under the impress of commodity relations and urbanization, sites of production were themselves evolving (in fact, convulsively by the late 18th century), and were re-creating as urban social spaces that were compelled by the logic of competition to seek the most productive forms of labor power. The "original handicap" that early commodity relations bestowed upon impaired people was crucial in setting a trajectory of change in both the social relations of production and their sociospatial settings (e.g., factories) that progressively devalued their labor power.

The twin processes of labor commodification and urbanization resulted in the production of increasingly disabling environments in Britain and its colonies. As was observed earlier, the emergence of the industrial city in the late 18th century crystallized the sociospatial oppression of disabled people that had been slowly increasing after the appearance of commodity relations in the late feudal era.

One disabling feature of the industrial city was the new separation of home and work, a sociospatial phenomenon that was all but absent in the feudal era. This disjuncture of home and work created a powerfully disabling friction in everyday life for physically impaired people. In addition, industrial workplaces were structured and used in ways that disabled "uncompetitive" workers, including physically impaired people. The rise of mechanized forms of production introduced productivity standards that assumed a "normal" (i.e., usually male and nonimpaired) worker's body and disabled all others.

As Marx (1981) pointed out at the time (the 1870s), one result of these changes was the production of an "incapable" stratum of labor, most of which was eventually incarcerated in a new institutional system of workhouses, hospitals, asylums, and (later) "crippleages." Industrialization and urbanization, he believed, "produced too great a section of the population which is . . . incapable of work, which owing to its situation is dependent on the exploitation of the labor of others or on kinds of work that can only count as such within a miserable mode of production" (p. 366). For impaired people, then, the social history of capitalism appears as a sociospatial dialectic of commodification and spatial change that progressively disabled their labor power. Given this sociospatial genesis of disablement, it is appropriate to question the key assumptions that have underpinned many geographies of disability.

First, the historical-geographical dialectic exposes the inadequacy of relying solely upon environmental modification as a strategy for eradicating the deeply embedded social oppression of disability. Such a strategy, where it can be successfully pursued (see the analyses of Imrie & Wells, 1993a, 1993b, which point to the difficulty of this), may improve the employment chances of some disabled people. On its own, however, environmental modification offers no lasting solution to disablement, as it cannot transform the dynamic and embedded sociospatial dynamics that oppress impaired people. Better building standards and new modes of mobility, for example, will not on their own revalue the labor power of all physically impaired people. Such strategies can reduce the friction of everyday life for disabled people, and must be defended for this, but they will not solve the dynamic sociospatial oppression of disablement. To reduce the struggle against disablement to such "spatial fixes," is to invite a Sisyphean political labor where any environmental improvements will constantly be destroyed or remade in disabling ways by commodity relations that produce space in order to facilitate average productivity standards.

From the historical-geographical view, the built environment thus appears as the phenomenal form of substructural processes that devalue physically impaired people. This is not to reduce the built environment to an inert or passive role in the process of disablement, but to assert that urban environments reinforce, rather than cause, the social marginalization experienced by physically impaired people (Imrie & Wells, 1993a). A great entrapment for policy practice is the tendency to reduce the dynamic sociospatial nature of disablement to a built environment problematic, so that disability merely becomes a problem of physical inaccessibility in a thoughtlessly designed environment. This perspective commonly leads activists to pursue the modification or adaptation of built environments through planning regulations as a means for reducing or even eliminating disablement (see, e.g., Bennett, 1990; Kridler & Stewart, 1992a, 1992b, 1992c). While such strategies have a great value in reducing the mobility friction in everyday life for many physically impaired people, they do not address the deeper sociospatial dynamics, such as the commodity labor market or the land economy, which produce disabling environments. This form of reductionism, or "spatial fetishism," fails to consider the social processes that create built environments and the role of these forces in disabling impaired people.

TOWARD AN ENABLING GEOGRAPHY

Landscapes of Injustice

The capitalist city is certainly a landscape of injustice for most disabled people. Using a materialist interpretation of Young (1990), this injustice can be described as a specific bodily oppression that is chiefly characterized by poverty, powerlessness, and sociospatial marginalization from economic and political life. As Abberley (1991b), Alcock (1993), and Oliver (1991) have shown, the central injustice for disabled people in highly urbanized, capitalist societies is material poverty. To this must be added the failure of welfare capitalism to secure the participation of disabled people in mainstream urban social life, an injustice which the incarceration of mentally and physically impaired people in remote institutional settings exacerbated rather than ameliorated. Thus Young's (1990) inclusive formulation of social justice could be restated in more specific terms for disabled people as (1) an end to material deprivation and (2) the elimination of sociospatial exclusion.

Such conditions for justice may appear quixotic, given the analysis of the earlier section that pointed to the power of commodity relations to produce disabling urban environments. Nonetheless, these conditions certainly reflect the concerns for social emancipation that disabled people in Western countries have demanded through both policy (e.g., Disability Alliance, 1987a, 1987b; Eastern Bay of Plenty People First Committee, 1993; Ronalds, 1991) and academic (e.g., Abberley, 1991a, 1991b; Lonsdale, 1986; Oliver, 1990) forums.

Certainly, the failure of welfare states to eliminate the urban social oppression of physically impaired people (indeed, welfarist public policies frequently entrenched it) lends cogent historical support to the above argument that the injustice of disability cannot be solved merely by (re)distributional means (i.e., through state transfer payments to socially dependent people). Welfarist justice cannot address the causes of oppression for disabled people, and it may actually worsen their position by codifying the relationship between disability and social dependency.

A Geography for Disabled People?

This chapter noted that the question of physical disability has long been ignored by urban social geographers. It was also observed, however, that a growing community of geographers are now taking the issue of disability seriously in their investigations of city life and social difference in capitalist societies. Nonetheless, the discipline cannot deny its enduring complicity with institutional structures that have marginalized disabled people and their concerns from public political and intellectual life. There is much that needs to be done by geographers, both in terms of analysis and political engagement, before the discipline can reasonably claim that it has embraced the pervasive oppression of disabled people as a central concern.

As part of the foregoing discussion, a historical-geographical framework was outlined for the analysis of disablement in capitalist societies. The historical-geographical approach connects the heretofore separate cultural materialist analyses of space and disability in an explanatory framework that sees disability in capitalist societies as a singular social oppression, sourced, inter alia, in the commodification of labor power. The historical-geographical perspective provides a critical theoretical framework for sociospatial investigations of disability in particular urban policy contexts (e.g., employment, institutions, or accessibility). However, a postpositivist perspective warns against any theories that fail to define the terms of political engagement with their subject matter. Theorization cannot, of itself, define how geographers, particularly nondisabled geographers, should politically engage both the phenomenon of disablement and those who endure it. The political articulation of geography and disability presents a challenge that cannot be ignored. Consequently, there is a need within the discipline for a debate on how this engagement could be realized.

Chouinard (1994) has recently argued for a reconstructed and democratized radical geography that embraces the multiple concerns and experiences of socially marginalized groups, including disabled people. For her, this new and expansive radicalism demands that geographers connect practically and politically with the experiences of marginalized social groups:

> This means putting ourselves "on the line" as academics who will not go along with the latest "fashion" simply because it sells, and who take very seriously the notion that "knowledge is power." It means as well personal decisions to put one's abilities at the disposal of groups at the margins of and outside academia. This is not taking the "moral high ground" but simply saying that if you want to help in struggles against oppression you have to "connect" with the trenches. (Chouinard, 1994, p. 5)

This then highlights the practical implications of the foregoing historical-geographical analysis of the urban context of disability: geographers must participate in the political struggle against sociospatial structures and formations that oppress impaired people.

Golledge (1993) calls for geographical research that can enhance the ability of impaired people to cope with the experience of disability. By contrast, the materialist position is that disability must be opposed at a deeper sociopolitical level, namely, at the level of processes that create social space and condition social actors. In particular, structures such as the commodity labor market and the capitalist land economy can be identified as critical realms of emancipatory struggle, given their importance in creating landscapes that marginalize many social groups, including disabled people.

The challenge in short is to pursue a geography with disabled people that seeks an inclusive, but not homogeneous, ideal of social justice. After Young (1990), this ethical ideal must seek both material fairness and sociopolitical inclusion as its central political objectives. However, both objectives cannot be achieved through simply the promulgation of universal moral standards, but must be won through political engagements that presume social difference and seek thereby to articulate and satisfy the variety of human needs that exist in contemporary capitalist societies. This demands that geographers seek a political encounter with disability—a major form of social difference—within the struggles of disabled people themselves. This is a critical point—not about political credibility, but about the validity of social scientific knowledge. When geographers speak on disability, we must not pronounce on or even for disabled people. Rather, we must, as Young (1990) observes, speak with the oppressed "other." It is surely this capacity to share the empowering potential of knowledge with the socially marginal that will define an enabling geography.

NOTES

1. See Oliver (1991) and the collection edited by Swain, Finkelstein, French, and Oliver (1993) for overviews of these literatures.

2. There is a voluminous literature that both supports these assertions and highlights the pervasiveness of these discriminations in Western cities generally. This literature cannot be surveyed in entirety here; however, useful starting sources are Swain et al. (1993) (United Kingdom); Minister for Health, Housing and Community Services (1991) (Australia); and Eastern Bay of Plenty People First Committee (1993) (New Zealand). Lunt and Thornton (1994) also provide an authoritative overview of employment and disability in 15 Western countries.

3. I am indebted to the work of Dorn (1994), which alerted me to the existence of some of this research.

4. It is important to note here how the separate discriminations arising from gender and disability can overlap within individual social identities, causing what some feminists have called a "double handicap" for disabled women (see Lonsdale, 1990).

5. This literature is simply too voluminous now to be cited here exhaustively. Good overviews of the work on institutional care by geographers are to be found in Dear and Wolch (1987), Philo (1996), and the collection edited by C. J. Smith and Giggs (1988).

6. An "externality" is the spillover effect from any land use activity. "Distance decay" refers to the tendency of externalities to decline in intensity with increasing distance from their point of origin.

REFERENCES

Abberley, P. (1987). The concept of oppression and the development of a social theory of disability. *Disability, Handicap and Society, 2*(1), 5–19.

Abberley, P. (1991a). *Disabled people: Three theories of disability* (Occasional Papers in Sociology 10). Bristol, UK: Bristol Polytechnic, Department of Economics and Social Science.

Abberley, P. (1991b). *Handicapped by numbers: A critique of the OPCS disability surveys* (Occasional Papers in Sociology 9). Bristol, UK: Bristol Polytechnic: Department of Economics and Social Science.

Alcock, P. (1993). *Understanding poverty.* London: Macmillan.

Balukas, R., & Baken, J. W. (1985). Community resistance to development of group homes for people with mental retardation. *Rehabilitation Literature, 46*(7–8), 194–197.

Barnes, C. (1992). Disability and employment. *Personnel Review, 21*(6), 55–73.

Beamish, C. (1981). *State, space and crisis: towards a theory of the public city in North America.* Unpublished MA thesis, McMaster University, Hamilton, Ontario, Canada.

Bennett, T. (1990). Planning and people with disabilities. In J. Montgomery & A. Thornley (Eds.), *Radical planning initiatives: New directions for planning in the 1990s* (pp. 259–269). Aldershot: Gower.

Berdiansky, H. A., & Parker, R. (1977). Establishing a group home for the adult mentally retarded in North Carolina. *Mental Retardation, 15,* 8–11.

Burnett, A., & Moon, G. (1983). Community opposition to hostels for single homeless men. *Area, 15,* 161–166.

Butler, R. E. (1994). Geography and vision-impaired populations. *Transactions—Institute of British Geographers, 19*(3), 366–369.

Chouinard, V. (1994). Reinventing radical geography: Is all that's left right? *Environment and Planning D: Society and Space, 12,* 2–6.

Cook, I. (1991). *Drowning in see-world? Critical ethnographies of blindness,* Unpublished Master's Thesis, Department of Geography, University of Kentucky, Lexington.

Currie, R. F., Trute, B., Tefft, B., & Segall, A. (1989). Maybe on my street: the politics of community placement of the mentally disabled. *Urban Affairs Quarterly, 25*(2), 298–321.

Dear, M. (1977). Spatial externalities and locational conflict. In D. B. Massey & P. W. J. Batey (Eds.), *Alternative frameworks for analysis* (London Papers in Regional Science 7). London: Pion.

Dear, M. (1981). Social and spatial reproduction of the mentally ill. In M. Dear & A. J. Scott (Eds.), *Urbanization and urban planning in capitalist societies* (pp. 481–497). New York: Methuen.

Dear, M. (1992). Understanding and overcoming the NIMBY syndrome. *Journal of the American Planning Association, 58*(3), 288–299.

Dear, M., Fincher, R., & Currie, L. (1977). Measuring the external effects of public programs. *Environment and Planning A, 9,* 137–147.

Dear, M., & Gleeson, B. J. (1991). Attitudes towards homelessness: The Los Angeles experience. *Urban Geography, 12*(2), 155–176.

Dear, M., & Taylor, S. M. (1982). *Not on our street: Community attitudes to mental health care.* London: Pion.

Dear, M., Taylor, S. M., & Hall, G. B. (1980). External effects of mental health facilities. *Annals, Association of American Geographers, 70*(3), 342–352.

Dear, M., & Wolch, J. (1987). *Landscapes of despair: From deinstitutionaliztion to homelessness.* Cambridge, UK: Polity Press.

Dear, M., Wolch, J., & Wilton, R. (1994). The human service hub concept in human services planning. *Progress in Planning, 42*(3), 174–271.

Disability Alliance. (1987). *Poverty and disability: Breaking the link.* London: Author.

Dodds, A. G. (1980). *Spatial representation and blindness.* Unpublished PhD thesis, Nottingham: University of Nottingham, Nottinghamshire, UK.

Dorn, M. (1994). *Disability as spatial dissidence: A cultural geography of the stigmatized body.* Unpublished master's thesis, Department of Geography, Pennsylvania State University, University Park.

Driver, F. (1993). *Power and pauperism: The workhouse system, 1834–1884.* Cambridge, UK: Cambridge University Press.

Eastern Bay of Plenty People First Committee. (1993). *People first conference report 1993.* (Available from People First, PO Box 3017, Ohope Eastern Bay of Plenty, New Zealand)

Eyles, J. (1988). Mental health services, the restructuring of care, and the fiscal crisis of the state: The United Kingdom case study. In C. J. Smith & J. A. Giggs (Eds.), *Location and stigma: Contemporary perspectives on mental health and mental health care* (pp. 36–57). Boston: Unwin Hyman.

Finkelstein, V. (1979). *Changing attitudes and disabled people: Issues for discussion.* Unpublished manuscript, Open University, Milton Keynes, UK.

Foreman, P. J., & Andrews, G. (1988). Community reaction to group homes. *Interaction, 2*(5), 15–18.

Foucault, M. (1975). *The birth of the clinic.* New York: Vintage Books.

Foucault, M. (1979). *Discipline and punish: The birth of the prison.* New York: Vintage Books.

Gleeson, B. J. (1993). *Second nature? The socio-spatial production of disability.* Unpublished PhD thesis, Department of Geography, University of Melbourne, Parkville, Victoria, Australia.

Gleeson, B. J. (1995a). Disability—a state of mind? *Journal of Social Issues, 29*(1), 10–23.

Gleeson, B. J. (1995b). A geography for disability? *Transactions—Institute of British Geographers, 21*(2), 387–396.

Gleeson, B. J. (1995c). The commodification of planning consent in New Zealand. *New Zealand Geographer, 51*(1), 42–48.

Gleeson, B. J., Gooder, H. F., & Memon, P. A. (1995). *Community care facilities: A guide for planners and service providers.* Dunedin, New Zealand: University of Otago, Environmental Policy and Management Research Centre.

Gleeson, B. J., & Memon, P. A. (1994). The NIMBY syndrome and community care facilities: A research agenda for planning. *Planning Practice and Research, 9*(2), 105–118.

Glendinning, C. (1991). Losing ground: Social policy and disabled people in Great Britain, 1980–90. *Disability, Handicap and Society, 6*(1), 3–19.

Golledge, R. (1990). Special populations in contemporary urban regions. In J. F. Hart (Ed.), *Our changing cities* (pp. 146–169). Baltimore: Johns Hopkins University Press.

Golledge, R. (1991). Tactual strip maps as navigational aids. *Journal of Visual Impairment and Blindness, 85,* 296–301.

Golledge, R. (1993). Geography and the disabled: a survey with special reference to vision impaired and blind populations. *Transactions—Institute of British Geographers, 18*(1), 63–85.

Golledge, R. (1996). A response to Imrie and Gleeson. *Transactions—Institute of British Geographers, 21*(2), 404–411.

Groves, D. (1988). Poverty, disability, and social services. In S. Becker & S. MacPherson (Eds.), *Public issues and private pain: Poverty, social work and social policy.* London: Insight.

Hahn, H. (1986). Disability and the urban environment: A perspective on Los Angeles. *Environment and Planning D: Society and Space, 4,* 273–288.

Hall, E. C. (1994). *Researching disability in geography.* (Spatial Policy Analysis Working Paper No. 28). Manchester, UK: School of Geography, University of Manchester.

Harvey, D. (1990). Between space and time: Reflections on the geographical imagination. *Annals, American Association of Geographers, 80*(3), 418–434.

Harvey, D. (1996). *Justice, nature and the geography of difference.* Oxford: Blackwell.

Helvarg, D. (1995, January 30). Legal assault on the environment. *The Nation,* pp. 126–127.

(The) Hillary Commission and Workbridge. (1994). *Listening to people with disabilities.* Wellington, New Zealand: The Hillary Commission.

Horner, A. (1994). Leaving the institution. In K. Ballard (Ed.), *Disability, family, whanau and society* (pp. 159–184). Palmerston North, New Zealand: Dunmore Press.

Ignatieff, M. (1978). *A just measure of pain: The penitentiary in the industrial revolution, 1750–1850.* New York: Columbia University Press.

Imrie, R. (1996). *Disability and the city.* London: Chapman.

Imrie, R. F., & Wells, P. E. (1993a). Disablism, planning and the built environment. *Environment and Planning C: Government and Policy, 11*(2), 213–231.

Imrie, R. F., & Wells, P. E. (1993b). Creating barrier-free environments. *Town and Country Planning, 61*(10), 278–281.

Jenkins, R. (1991). Disability and social stratification. *British Journal of Sociology, 42*(4), 557–580.

Johnston, R., Gregory, D., & Smith, D. M. (Eds.). (1994). *The dictionary of human geography.* Oxford: Blackwell.

Joseph, A. E., & Hall, G. B. (1985). The locational concentration of group homes in Toronto. *Professional Geographer, 37*(2), 143–155.

Kearns, R., Smith, C. J., & Abbott, M. (1992). The stress of incipient homelessness. *Housing Studies, 7*(4), 280–298

Kridler, C., & Stewart, R. K. (1992a). Access for the disabled, 1. *Progressive Architecture, 73*(7), 41–42.

Kridler, C., & Stewart, R. K. (1992b). Access for the disabled, 2. *Progressive Architecture, 73*(8), 35–36.

Kridler, C., & Stewart, R. K. (1992c). Access for the disabled, 3. *Progressive Architecture, 73*(9), 45–46.

Lawrence, D. (1993). *Being without seeing.* Unpublished research project, Department of Geography, University of Waikato, Hamilton, New Zealand.

Lebovich, W. L. (1993). *Design for dignity: Studies in accessibility.* New York: Wiley.

Leccese, M. (1993). Is access attainable? *Landscape Architecture, 83*(6), 71–75.

Liachowitz, C. H. (1988). *Disability as social construct: Legislative roots.* Philadelphia: University of Pennsylvania Press.

Lipietz, A. (1992). *Towards a new economic order.* Cambridge, UK: Polity Press.

Locker, D., Rao, B., & Weddell, J. M. (1979). The community reaction to a hostel for the mentally handicapped. *Social Science and Medicine, 13A,* 817–821.

Lonsdale, S. (1986). *Work and inequality.* London: Longman.

Lonsdale, S. (1990). *Women and disability: The experience of physical disability among women.* Macmillan: London.

Lunt, N., & Thornton, P. (1994). Disability and employment: Towards and understanding of discourse and employment. *Disability and Society, 9*(2), 223–238.

Mandel, E. (1968). *Marxist economic theory.* London: Merlin.

Marx, K. (1981). *Capital: A critique of political economy* (Vol. 3). London: Penguin. (Original German edition of Vol. 3 published posthumously 1894, edited by F. Engels; original English edition published 1909)

McCagg, W. O., & Siegelbaum, L. (1989). *The disabled in the Soviet Union: Past and present, theory and practice.* Pittsburgh: University of Pittsburgh Press.

McTavish, F. (1992). *The effectiveness of people with disabilities in the policy process: The total mobility scheme example.* Unpublished master's thesis, Department of Geography, University of Otago, Dunedin, New Zealand.

Milligan, C. (1996). Service Dependent Ghetto formation—a transferable concept? *Health and Place, 2*(4), 199–211.

Minister for Health, Housing and Community Services (Australia). (1991). *Social justice for people with disabilities.* Canberra: Australian Government Publishing Service.

Moon, G. (1988). Is there one around here?—Investigating reaction to small-scale mental health hostel provision in Portsmouth, England. In C. J. Smith & J. A. Giggs (Eds.), *Location and stigma: Contemporary perspectives*

CITIES OF DIFFERENCE

118

on mental health and mental health care (pp. 203–223). Boston: Unwin Hyman.

Morris, P. (1969). *Put away.* London: Routledge & Kegan Paul.
Oliver, M. (1990). *The politics of disablement.* London: Macmillan.
Oliver, M. (1991). Disability and participation in the labor market. In P. Brown & R. Scase (Eds.), *Poor work: Disadvantage and the division of labor* (pp. 132–146). Milton Keynes, UK: Open University Press.
Philo, C. (1995). Journey to asylum: A medical–geographical idea in historical context. *Journal of Historical Geography, 21*(2), 148–168.
Philo, C. (1996). *"Across the water": Reviewing geographical studies of asylums and other mental health facilities.* Manuscript in preparation. (Copy supplied by the author, Department of Geography and Topographic Science, University of Glasgow, Scotland)
Plotkin, S. (1987). *Keep out: The struggle for land use control.* Berkeley: University of California Press.
Ronalds, C. (1990). *National employment initiatives for people with disabilities— A discussion paper.* Canberra: Australian Government Publishing Service.
Ronalds, C. (1991). *Report of the national consultations with people with disabilities.* Canberra: Australian Government Publishing Service.
Rose, G. (1993). *Feminism and geography: The limits to geographical knowledge.* Cambridge, UK: Polity Press.
Rothman, D. J. (1971). *The discovery of the asylum: Social order and disorder in the new republic.* Boston: Little Brown.
Ryan, J., & Thomas, F. (1987). *The politics of mental handicap.* London: Free Association.
Shannon, P. T., & Hovell, K. J. (1993). *Community care facilities: Experience and effects.* Unpublished report, Dunedin City Council and the Otago Area Health Board, Dunedin, New Zealand.
Smith, C. J. (1977). Geography and mental health. *Association of American Geographers Commission on College Geography, Resource Paper No. 76-4.*
Smith, C. J. (1978). Problems and prospects for a geography of mental health. *Antipode, 10*(1), 1–12.
Smith, C. J. (1981). Urban structure and the development of natural support systems for service dependent populations. *The Professional Geographer, 33,* 457–465.
Smith, C. J. (1984). Geographical approaches to mental health. In H. Freeman (Ed.), *Mental health and the environment.* London: Churchill Livingstone.
Smith, C. J. (1989). Privatisation and the delivery of mental health services. *Urban Geography, 6,* 88–99.
Smith, C. J., & Giggs, J. A. (Eds.). (1988). *Location and stigma: Contemporary perspectives on mental health and mental health care.* Boston: Unwin Hyman.
Smith, N. (1984). *Uneven development.* Oxford: Blackwell.
Soja, E. (1989). *Postmodern geographies: The reassertion of space in critical social theory.* London: Verso.
Steinman, L. D. (1987). The effect of land-use restrictions on the establish-

ment of community residences for the disabled: A national study. *The Urban Lawyer, 19*, 2–37.

Swain, J., Finkelstein, V., French, S., & Oliver, M. (Eds.). (1993). *Disabling barriers—enabling environments.* London: Sage.

Taylor, S. M. (1988). Reactions to deinstitutionalization. In C. J. Smith & J. A. Giggs (Eds.), *Location and stigma: Contemporary perspectives on mental health and mental health care* (pp. 224–243). Boston: Unwin Hyman.

Topliss, E. (1979). *Provision for the disabled* (2nd ed.). Oxford: Blackwell.

Vujakovic, P., & Matthews, M. H. (1994). Contorted, folded, torn: Environmental values, cartographic representation and the politics of disability. *Disability and Society, 9*(3), 359–374.

Walker, R. (1981). A theory of suburbanisation: Capitalism and the construction of urban space in the United States. In M. Dear & A. J. Scott (Eds.), *Urbanization and urban planning in capitalist societies* (pp. 383–430). New York: Methuen.

Wolch, J. (1980). The residential location of the service-dependent poor. *Annals of the Association of American Geographers, 70*, 330–341.

Wolch, J. (1990). *The shadow state: Government and voluntary sector in transition.* New York: The Foundation Center.

Wolch, J., & Dear, M. (1993). *Malign neglect: Homelessness in an American city.* San Francisco: Jossey-Bass.

Wolpert, J. (1976). Opening closed spaces. *Annals, Association of American Geographers, 65*, 24–35.

Wrightson, W. (1989). *From barrier free to safe environnments: The New Zealand experience.* New York: World Rehabilitation Fund.

Young, I. M. (1990). *Justice and the politics of difference.* Princeton, NJ: Princeton University Press.

Zipple, A., & Anzer, T. C. (1994). Building code enforcement: New obstacles in siting community residences. *Psychosocial Rehabilitation Journal, 18*(1), 5–13.

CHAPTER 6

Community Responses to Human Service Delivery in U.S. Cities

Lois M. Takahashi

Community opposition toward certain forms of human services provision has been on the rise across cities in the United States. Communities which identify themselves racially or ethnically, in particular, are becoming more involved in locational conflict over human service facility siting. This chapter focuses on the attitudes of such communities toward human services (in particular, those services concerned with homelessness and AIDS), and uses the notion of "difference" to explore perceptions in Orange County, California.

To provide a context for discussing community perceptions of homelessness and AIDS in the United States, the changing character of human service delivery in cities is outlined. A conceptual framework is then provided that explores three aspects of "difference" or "otherness" directly attributed to homelessness and AIDS: perceptions of nonproductivity associated with homelessness and AIDS; beliefs concerning danger and potential threat; and the degree of personal culpability attributable to homeless persons and people living with HIV and AIDS. Interviews with Latino/a and Vietnamese residents in Orange County illustrate these three aspects and suggest that the dynamics underlying attitudes toward homelessness and AIDS are very much influenced by cultural norms, religious institutions, and family and kinship networks.

HUMAN SERVICE PROVISION IN U.S. CITIES

The need for human services has grown dramatically in the United States over the past few decades. Massive demographic change in the United States has resulted in an increasing number of households living at or below the poverty line. The widely acknowledged aging of the population, for example, has played several distinctive roles. The aging of the baby boom generation has meant that more individuals are competing for jobs in an increasingly competitive labor market. This cohort has been subject to an expanding two-tier wage system that developed during the past decade because of the elimination of many middle-level management positions and because of an ongoing decline in the manufacturing sector (Harrison & Bluestone, 1988; Phillips, 1990). In addition, elderly persons now face a rising risk of poverty and homelessness, due to the rapid growth in the size of the elderly population. Approximately 40% of the single-person households in 1990 were over 64 years of age, indicating a significant population of elderly persons who have limited access to social support and kinship networks (Keigher, 1991; Wolch & Dear, 1993). This limited access to support means that these elderly individuals experience an increasing vulnerability to economic, personal, and medical crises.

The broader disintegration of close-knit family and kinship networks can also be traced to wider changes in the structure of the family due to divorce, (im)migration, and domestic violence. The disintegration of kinship obligations has meant that some individuals have fewer resources and options in terms of dealing with housing and resource deprivation (Rowe & Wolch, 1990). Single women and female-headed households have been particularly affected; the feminization of poverty has counted an increasing proportion of single women and female-headed households among the poverty ranks (J. P. Jones & Kodras, 1990; Ringheim, 1990).

The pressures placed on those social networks that remain intact and supportive have been intensified by the outcomes of global economic change. Global economic restructuring over the past few decades has affected growing numbers of labor force participants in varied ways. One primary characteristic of economic restructuring has been the expanding dependence of private firms on flexible work organization to cope with globalized competition. Through strategies promoting flexibility and adaptability, the U.S. labor force has become increasingly part-time and contractual (bolstering the rapidly expanding service sector), the influence of unions has weakened, real wages have declined, and benefits that had been attached to employment (such as health insurance) have been reduced or eliminated (Harrison & Bluestone, 1988). The deindustrialization resulting from economic restructuring, as well as the increasing mobility of firms, has created a varied geography of employment and production at the national, regional, and intraregional levels (Hanson & Pratt, 1995; Massey, 1984). Overall trends emanating from this geography of employment and production point to an increasingly bimodal distribution of income, instability in employment opportunities, and fewer resources emanating from the private sector to support employees and their families (Phillips, 1990). The growing instability in income and employment opportunities has been especially acute for low-income and inner-city urban residents.

The declining economic opportunities for urban residents, particularly those living in inner-city metropolitan areas, have meant that more persons have turned to the public sector for help in coping with economic deprivation. However, human service delivery at the federal, state, and local levels has been fundamentally altered by recent welfare state reorganization. At the federal level, reorganization of the U.S. welfare state has been realized through national strategies of privatization, cutbacks in programs and funding, and changes in eligibility requirements for receiving benefits. The overall result of these strategies has been a transfer of program and funding responsibilities to the state and municipal levels, this generating what have been described by scholars as "new federalism" policies largely associated with the Reagan–Bush administrations (Palmer & Sawhill, 1982).

State and municipal governments have largely been unable, and unwilling, to compensate for federal contraction in the welfare state. Local governments in large cities have often been overwhelmed by the demand for human services, which often becomes intensified in inner-city skid row areas where services already exist. The expanding population of persons in need has frequently been drawn to existing networks of services, which through historical and policy circumstances have tended to be located in skid row areas of large cities (Dear & Wolch, 1987). The uneven distribution of human services, service-dependent persons, and developing fiscal crises at municipal and state levels of government have all acted to fuel intergovernmental conflict.

Beyond the intensifying conflict among varying tiers of government, the transfer of responsibility for human service delivery and efforts at privatization have meant that human services are increasingly provided through a chaotic system of private, nonprofit, and informal sector sources. States have responded to the transfer of responsibility from the federal level by allocating responsibility for indigent persons to municipal governments and by turning to more privatized systems of for-profit and nonprofit service providers. California, for example, in the early 1980s, in its reorganization of the federally funded and state-funded Medi-Cal benefits system, turned to a privatized system of hospital contracts for medical diagnosis and treatment services and shifted responsibility to the county level for medical care for indigent clients (Wolch & Dear, 1993). In turn, municipalities have recently begun to look to managed care[1] to control the spiraling costs associated with a growing number of medical clients without health insurance.

Past institutional shifts have also been instrumental in expanding the numbers of persons needing human services and in creating a system of human services inadequate for their needs. In particular, deinstitutionalization, or the movement initiated during the 1950s and 1960s to transfer mentally disabled individuals out of large-scale institutionalized care to community-based care, has long been criticized for not fulfilling its mission (Dear & Wolch, 1987). A lack of community-based services has been implicated in the growth in the number of mentally disabled persons who have become homeless.[2] To counteract these negative trends, the reinstitutionalization of mentally disabled persons through an expansion of state hospitals has increasingly been touted as a viable solution to the mismatch between client need and available services. In practice, however, reinstitutionalization has more often meant the placement of mentally disabled persons in already overcrowded prison systems than in new forms of institutionalized mental health care (Abrahamson, 1991).

One primary issue associated with the perception that deinstitutionalization has contributed to the expansion of homelessness in the United States during the 1980s and 1990s is the lack of affordable housing for mentally disabled persons and other service-dependent populations. The lack of affordable housing has meant that for many low- and very-low-income urban residents, the contemporary housing market acts as a game of "musical chairs," where particular households will consistently be left out of the housing market because of the very limited number of available units. This undersupply of adequate and affordable housing units has caused many to live in overcrowded conditions to remain housed and forced others onto the streets (Burt, 1992; Myers, Baer, & Choi, 1996). The reasons for the shrinking number and rising cost of housing units include gentrification and urban renewal, demolition of single-room-occupancy hotels, and the conversion of low-rent units into luxury apartments and condominiums (Baer, 1986; Hoch, 1991). Federal housing policy during the 1980s and early 1990s did little to counteract these market trends, instead moving to contract the state's role in the housing market by reducing budget appropriations and federally funded housing construction, as well as to incorporate market mechanisms such as vouchers (Gilderbloom & Applebaum, 1988).[3]

In addition to the limitations created by a lack of affordable housing, the existing system of traditional human services has often been unable to respond in efficient and effective ways to the growing size, dispersion, and diversity of the service-dependent population. Part of its inability to respond relates to the institutional form of the human service delivery system. The shelter and social service system in many cities contains what Wolch and Dear (1993) term gatekeeper services (points of entry into the human service system that usually focus on emergency shelter, food, and income maintenance services), coping services (health care, advocacy, meals, clothing, and other services that facilitate daily survival), and other human services (the remaining social services in any given system). Such services are provided by the public, nonprofit, and private sectors, with the nonprofit sector tending to dominate in terms of service delivery (Burt & Cohen, 1989). Such services often act independently of one another, with the varying sectors overlapping or even in conflict. Although the need is great for housing, health, and other human services among varying service-dependent populations, several studies have indicated that this existing structure of services is underutilized. Beyond the institutional constraints indicated by the lack of coordination of existing services, this underutilization may be due to the types of services offered and the location of facilities and programs.

Location in particular plays a significant role in the degree of access to services. There is an uneven distribution in the number and types of facilities, which often coincides with the spatial boundaries defined by economic class. More affluent communities tend to have facilities with universal access (such as libraries and recreation centers), whereas lower-income neighborhoods tend to contain greater shares of the shelter and service system used by homeless individuals, substance abusers, and people living with HIV and AIDS (Wolch & Dear, 1993). While concentrations of facilities in specific locales may have agglomeration benefits for clients and facility operators, the location and composition of "service-rich" areas may also prevent many service-dependent individuals from obtaining the services they need. That is, even relatively "service-rich" areas often do not contain, or are limited in supplying, all the services needed by individuals, leading either to necessary trips between "service-rich" areas or to attempts to cope without the absent services. The location and composition of services are therefore critical, especially given the limited mobility experienced by much of the service-dependent population (Wolch, Rahimian, & Koegel, 1993).[4]

The spatial distribution of shelter and services has been constrained by federal, state, and local legislation, and has been influenced by community support or rejection of specific facility-siting proposals (Laws, 1992). Municipal governments have long used the land use planning apparatus (through zoning ordinances and restrictive covenants) to exclude facilities or limit their possible locations (Dear & Laws, 1986; Mair, 1986). Recent federal legislation has been used to counteract this exclusionary use of zoning and restrictive covenants. The Fair Housing Amendments Act of 1988 and the Americans with Disabilities Act of 1992 (often referred to as ADA) have made housing and employment discrimination of persons with mental or physical disabilities illegal. This wide-reaching legislation has been interpreted as including persons with mental disabilities, individuals who are physically disabled, and people living with HIV or AIDS. The ADA has been challenged in the courts, with decisions tending to favor the rights of service providers and clients over community and municipal protests in locating facilities and shelter.

Municipalities and residents have engaged in other strategies to reduce the number of local facilities and the size of the service-dependent population. For example, municipal governments have increasingly turned to the criminalization of homeless activities to move homeless persons from their jurisdictions (Fischer, 1988). The City of Santa Ana in Orange County, California, recently passed a local ordinance banning camping by homeless persons. The anticamping ordinance was challenged by legal advocates on behalf of the homeless population and was made void by an Appeals Court decision (DiRado, 1994; Goldberg, 1994). In a later decision, however, the California Supreme Court upheld the city's right to impose such a restriction, and now other cities are following suit to deal with homelessness in their jurisdictions (Dolan, 1995).

Local residents and businesses have also significantly influenced the spatial distribution of facilities and clients. Community opposition, generally known as the NIMBY (or "not in my backyard") syndrome, has been particularly effective in directing facilities away from specific communities (Dear & Gleeson, 1991; Dear, 1992). For affluent communities, such opposition need not be expressed through overt public demonstration. Instead, residents may use existing channels of political influence to block the siting of undesirable facilities (Graham & Logan, 1990).

The NIMBY syndrome has emerged as one of the more vital factors in the changing geography of human service delivery. The importance of the NIMBY syndrome for human service delivery at the local level has led geographers and other urban scholars to search for appropriate methods and conceptual frameworks that explain the processes underlying community opposition toward human services and that point to alternatives to address these escalating tensions. Many of these approaches are formulated using attitude–behavior models. These models have served to identify the potential mechanisms that spark organized community opposition toward human service facilities; they have led to typologies of communities likely to reject such facilities and clients.

UNDERSTANDING COMMUNITY OPPOSITION

Geographers and other urban scholars have often looked to attitude–behavior models to explain opposition to controversial human service and environmental facilities. Attitude–behavior models explaining community opposition focus on perceptions and evaluations of perceived risk and threat, and then predict behavior based on assumptions concerning either the minimizing of this perceived threat or the compensation for exposure to these risks. Using such models, geographers have conceptualized opposition to human service facilities and their clients as the end point in a process beginning with individual characteristics and beliefs and ending with behavioral intentions and behavior.

The foundational work in geography using this framework to explore human service facility siting and community rejection sought the linkages between sociospatial and attitudinal attributes, on the one hand, and rejecting and accepting behavior, on the other (Dear & Taylor, 1982; Smith & Hanham, 1981). Significant findings from this research (which built upon public facility location models and incorporated social-psychological approaches concerning perception and behavior) indicated that specific types of residents (such as suburban residents and homeowners) tended to reject human service facilities and clients, that facility characteristics significantly influenced the perception of risk to the community, and that proximity was a primary determinant of the degree to which residents rejected or accepted facilities (Green, McCormick, & Walkey, 1987; Segal, Baumohl, & Moyles, 1980). These were groundbreaking studies in that they worked to clarify and categorize many of the particularities of resident response. Researchers hypothesized that community opposition reflected the reasoned actions of individuals based on their attitudinal predispositions, rather than attributing community opposition to the selfish, irrational response of residents to controversial facilities.

This work also suggested that perceptions toward varying service-dependent groups changed over time. Researchers focusing on perceptions toward clients and facilities have often expressed the relative changes in acceptance and rejection over time by comparing hierarchies of acceptance, which consist of rankings of client groups or facility types according to their relative acceptability in the neighborhood (Dear, 1992). Although they constitute highly simplified representations of the dynamic underlying shifts in perception concerning clients and facilities, such rankings do provide a relatively quick method of assessing the degree of change in attitudes over time. A 1970 study, for example, suggested that the least acceptable group was composed of "alcoholics," "ex-convicts," and "mentally ill" individuals (Tringo, 1970). People who had physical disabilities or ailments (such as ulcers and asthma) were the most acceptable. A later study in 1980 indicated that elderly persons and the physically disabled were much more acceptable than "mentally ill" persons, "alcoholics," and "drug addicts" (Solomon, 1983). The variation in sampling and survey methods preclude detailed comparisons, but what is clear is that these hierarchies tend to remain defined over time by the perception of difference from socially established norms. Those persons considered to be the most different from "normal" are consistently located at the bottom of the hierarchy. There is also evidence of change over time in researchers' definitions of controversial client groups. The inclusion of "drug addicts" in the 1980 study and their absence from the 1970 study indicate the shifting nature of human service client groups over time. In the 1980 study, "drug addicts" established a new benchmark by which the rest of the client groups could be evaluated.

Recent national survey data in the United States on perceptions of human service facilities, collected in late 1989, indicate that newer facility types had differential effects on the perception of more established and familiar facility types and that specific facility types remained highly rejected (Takahashi, 1997a; Takahashi & Dear, 1997). The relatively new facility types in this 1989 national survey included homeless shelters and group homes for persons with AIDS, neither of which were included in the 1970 and 1980 studies. These recent survey data indicate that the most acceptable facility types included schools, daycare centers, nursing homes for elderly persons, medical clinics treating eyes or allergies, and hospitals. Less accepted by the national sample were group homes for mentally retarded persons, alcohol rehabilitation facilities, homeless shelters, and drug treatment centers. The least accepted human service facilities in this survey largely focused on mental disability and AIDS. Group homes for persons with AIDS were the least-accepted facility type in this survey. These results indicated that although AIDS, substance abuse, and homelessness have all become increasingly important over the past two decades, the facilities addressing these populations were perceived very differently by the respondents. Facilities for persons with AIDS were much less acceptable than facilities providing substance abuse or homeless services.

These national survey data also suggest that a large proportion of the respondents had not participated in community opposition or support of facilities in their neighborhoods. Less than 10% of the respondents reported participating in either supportive or oppositional activities concerning a proposed facility. This result tends to support earlier studies which suggest that community opposition is composed of relatively small, often well-organized groups. Thus, rather than reflecting the widespread rejection of facilities and clients across a neighborhood, researchers have argued that community opposition represents their rejection by a highly vocal minority (Dear & Taylor, 1982).

These attitude–behavior studies have proved very useful for policymakers and service providers in trying to predict what types of communities might be more likely to respond with opposition, and to what types of facilities. Survey data have been particularly useful in tracking changes in the dynamics of perception concerning human services and their clients. When such methods are employed, however, the analysis of such changes tends to remain somewhat descriptive. Survey data may indicate that changes have occurred and that variation across space does exist, but they are less successful at untangling the reasons for these changes. The reasons for the limitations of survey data, which include but are not limited to surveyor and respondent bias, have been widely discussed and comprise substantial sections in survey methods texts (Alreck & Settle, 1985).

There are also substantive reasons to look more broadly than is possible with attitude–behavior models at the issue of community opposition toward human service facilities. With the increasing size and variation in the service-dependent population and the growth in local activism concerning many issues, these categorizations may be less useful. Varying types of communities are becoming enmeshed in local opposition (other than the stereotypical suburban, homeowning

population). In addition, the size, dispersion, and diversity of the service-dependent population may make the use in surveys of highly
charged labels such as "mentally ill" inadequate indicators of the wider
population's potential response to human services. The issue of labeling and broader issues of representation and identity have proved
increasingly salient with ongoing debates in social theory concerning
"difference." With these conceptual discussions, there are now new
avenues with which to discuss and analyze not only the outcomes of
the process of community opposition but also the socially constructed
reasons for differentiated rejection and acceptance. The variation and
changes in the social construction of homelessness and AIDS over
time and space lead to a dynamic of distinction, where "difference"
and "abnormal" are defined in radically different ways across communities. This dynamic of distinction is reflected in varied types of
communities opposing facilities, and different types of service-dependent individuals being rejected. It has led to our understanding of
community opposition as a complex process reflecting a varied geography of community opposition, locational politics, and urban life.

Of particular importance in this dynamic is the growing participation of groups that self-identify racially or ethnically in the politics
of controversial facility siting and land use. A growing and thoughtful
literature continues to explore the nuances of community mobilization in such communities over the inequitable distribution of environmental hazards (Bullard, 1994; Pulido, 1996). There has been
much less work, however, in relation to the response by communities
identifying themselves racially/ethnically to human service delivery
in U.S. cities. Survey data have provided one method of analyzing the
distinctions in response among groups which self-identify themselves
racially. The 1989 national survey of attitudes for example suggested
that, after controlling for sociodemographic and locational variations,
there were specific differences in attitudes among "black," "Hispanic,"
and "white" respondents (Takahashi, 1997b).[5] However, as scholarly
and policy debates concerning identity politics and "race" have indicated, such categorizations of respondents by racial grouping are
highly problematic and, moreover, may serve to cloud the dynamics
of distinction that influence community response rather than illumi-
nating them.

The exploration of the complexity underlying the dynamics that
drive community opposition in such communities and broader human service delivery can be daunting. One obvious issue is that of
defining what is a just policy concerning the distribution of human
services across space. Communities that identify themselves racially
or ethnically, many of which have historically been marginalized across

multiple dimensions (political, economic, and social), are increasingly organizing to oppose facilities for service-dependent individuals and families who have been subject to often similar (and sometimes different) processes of marginalization. This example indicates that a description of variation in perception by "race" is just the first step in understanding community response. A substantive investigation of community response demands that we search deeper into the dynamics underlying difference than the attitude–behavior models might allow.

EXPLORING DIFFERENCE AND COMMUNITY RESPONSE TO HUMAN SERVICES

The intensification in community rejection of facilities that provide human services may be due in large part to the representation in the popular media and within the wider populace of service-dependent populations and how that representation influences public consciousness. Although there have been ongoing efforts by researchers, advocates, and the media to portray service-dependent populations in all their diversity in the popular media, in lectures and public testimony, and in published research, there remains in public discourse a highly stigmatized understanding of such groups. For example, even with efforts to change the widespread understanding of homelessness, the term "homeless person" continues to be associated with laziness, alcoholism, drug abuse, mental disability, criminalism, and even perversion (Gallagher, 1994). The tenacious linkage of labels describing service-dependent populations to negative images and attributes reflects a deeply embedded social phenomenon of stigmatization and marginalization. Community opposition to human service facilities should not then be judged as being merely selfish and exclusionary responses by residents but should also be understood as the product of structural processes that serve to stigmatize and marginalize specific groups.[6]

Social theory debates concerning the notion of "difference" provide one way to untangle the complexity of responses by communities self-identifying racially/ethnically to human services and their clients. Here I pay particular attention to human services related to homelessness and AIDS; both have garnered national attention over the past few decades and have been especially significant for groups identifying themselves racially/ethnically. Exploring the understanding within self-identifying racial/ethnic communities of persons who are homeless or living with AIDS may provide vital clues for explaining the varied community response to homeless and AIDS facilities (Blasi, 1994; MacKinnon, 1992). The three interrelated aspects characterize contemporary understanding of homelessness and AIDS: the perceived lack of productivity of homeless persons and people who are HIV positive or living with AIDS; perceptions of the danger posed by these individuals and groups to the wider community; and the assessment of personal culpability attached to becoming homeless, HIV positive, or contracting AIDS.

The marginalization of those deemed nonproductive emanates to a large degree from the broader structure of social relations. Within capitalist societies, productive individuals are those participating in the labor force and production processes; they are accorded privileged status in comparison with seemingly nonproductive persons such as homeless individuals or persons with AIDS. Nonproductive individuals do not participate significantly in the labor force or production processes. Their (perceived) lack of productivity means they fail to contribute to maintaining privileged social relations and, indeed, may even threaten their continuing reproduction. This leads to the devaluation of nonproductive persons (in this case, homeless persons or people living with HIV or AIDS) by wider society and their consequent characterization as threats to collective consumption and communal life (Cox, 1989). Minimal participation by these individuals in the important social relations of capitalist production both reinforces and is reinforced by this perception of threat, creating an understanding of homeless persons and persons with AIDS as lacking value for their own sakes or for their potential contributions to a community. Thus, they become marginalized because of their perceived lack of productivity and contribution to society.

Persons with AIDS are often viewed as nonproductive because of the common image in the popular media of persons living with AIDS as hospitalized, ill, and on the verge of death. Illness and death have become primary points of characterization of people who have AIDS by many members of the wider society and even many persons living with HIV/AIDS (Pomerance & Shields, 1989; King, 1993). The person living with HIV or AIDS is viewed as an extension of the condition itself, embodying the essence of disease and death (Gilman, 1988; Herek & Glunt, 1988; MacKinnon, 1992). Thus, once a person is diagnosed as being HIV positive or having AIDS, not only is his/her own self-image profoundly altered but also to the wider society he/ she often changes from being a particular individual to being a "person with AIDS." Since persons with AIDS are largely viewed as being bearers of disease and on the verge of death, such individuals are deemed nonproductive. Similar characterizations concerning nonproductivity serve to define homeless persons. A recent national Gallup Poll conducted on behalf of the Los Angeles Mission indicated, for example, that approximately 78% of respondents believed that most or all homeless persons were unemployed and 67% believed that the loss of employment was a primary cause of homelessness (Gallup Organization, 1995).

The public's understanding of homelessness and AIDS as nonproductive is related to the second aspect of "difference" framing community response—that homeless individuals and persons living with HIV or AIDS present a danger to community members' quality of life and property. When groups are perceived as threats to collective consumption and communal life, there is a process of stigmatization where residents rationalize this perceived danger. Through stigmatization, service-dependent groups become defined as essentially different from the rest of the population. This definition as essentially different is socially constructed and becomes a widely shared negative evaluation (Ainlay & Crosby, 1986), such that homeless persons and people living with HIV/AIDS become viewed as undesirable, uncontrollable, and dangerous to residents and businesses (Hopper & Baumohl, 1994).

Perceptions of danger are particularly important in the stigmatization of persons living with HIV and AIDS. The perception of the degree of danger posed by persons living with HIV or AIDS to others can be understood using the metaphor of invasion concerning the transmission of AIDS. Major sources of anxiety spring from the perception that AIDS threatens to cross the border between that which is imagined to be polluted to that which is presumed to be pure. Residents who do not perceive themselves as being part of a high-risk group (socially, economically, or spatially) tend also to perceive themselves as being part of a community uncontaminated by the threat of AIDS. A penetration of this border constitutes an invasion of the condition from "polluted" sources. Suburban communities, for example, tend to see themselves as safe from the threats and dangers faced in large metropolitan inner-city environments. Therefore, suburban communities might perceive persons with AIDS as representing an invasion from polluted, dangerous places. As well, from a geopolitical point of view, AIDS has often been viewed as an invasion from outside national borders, resulting in calls for limits on immigration from specific countries and for AIDS testing of immigrants (MacKinnon, 1992). At the community level, AIDS has been seen as an invasion of the well by the sick, as a pollution of the heterosexual by the homosexual, and an invasion of the general population by the deviant (Sontag, 1988).

Scholars may have inadvertently reinforced or even created images of service-dependent populations as "different." Past research on homelessness may have contributed to this process of distinguishing homeless persons by characterizing homelessness as distinct from poverty, emphasizing the presence of substance addiction and mental disability within the homeless population, and promoting the notion that being "homed" has more positive normative value than being "homeless" (Veness, 1993; Blasi, 1994). More broadly, the negative societal evaluation of homeless persons as dangerous may be a combination of the negative perceptions associated with mentally disabled persons, substance abusers, and other populations deemed to comprise substantial proportions of the homeless population (see, e.g., Smith & Giggs, 1988; Fink & Tasman, 1992). The "difference" of homeless persons consequently prevents their acceptance by the public and leads to the added negative characterization of their being, or potentially being, highly dangerous.

The stigma of danger is linked to additional traits, such as high visibility, incurability, disruptiveness, unpleasant aesthetics, and personal culpability (Goffman, 1963; E. E. Jones et al., 1984). How much individuals can be blamed for their circumstances very much influences the acceptability of service-dependent individuals. In particular, the degree of personal culpability for becoming homeless has remained a vital element in our understanding of the causes and possible solutions for homelessness (Baumohl, 1989; Dear & Gleeson, 1991). When the definition of homelessness is primarily confined to "individual deficiency," the public is much more likely to blame homeless individuals for their problems. Conversely, if homelessness is understood as emanating from other than individual sources, the public might be less likely to blame individuals for their homelessness. While recent attitudinal studies in the United States have indicated that there is a wider acknowledgment among the populace that homelessness derives in large part from structural and institutional changes that homeless individuals cannot control (Lee, Lewis, & Jones, 1992; Toro & McDonell, 1992), there remains the perception that many homeless persons are to some degree personally responsible for their becoming homeless or, more importantly, for their remaining homeless. The greater the perception that individuals are personally culpable for becoming or remaining homeless, the less acceptable they tend to be to community residents.[7]

Views about personal culpability also influence people's evaluations of the acceptability of persons living with HIV and AIDS. Public perceptions concerning HIV and AIDS are still largely influenced by the metaphor of deviance, implying willful behavior on the part of the person who has AIDS. Persons living with HIV or AIDS are often viewed as being personally responsible for acquiring the condition (Blendon & Donelan, 1989). The more responsible individuals are perceived to be for acquiring HIV and AIDS, the less acceptable those individuals tend to be to the wider public.

Several elements in the deviance metaphor identify subgroups perceived to be likely to acquire AIDS: homosexuality, promiscuity, and substance abuse. There is still the widespread belief, for example, that AIDS is confined solely to the homosexual community (Rogers, Singer, & Imperio, 1993). Recent studies have indicated that in the United States and elsewhere, the stigma associated with homosexuality is still a vital factor in negative public responses toward persons living with HIV and AIDS (McDevitt, Sheehan, Lennon, & Ambrosio, 1990; Kunkel & Temple, 1992). The association of promiscuity and substance abuse with AIDS has also contributed to the social construction of the definition of "groups at risk of contracting AIDS," which is becoming the language used by service providers to describe subgroups likely to contract HIV. While such identification seems necessary for developing education and prevention strategies appropriate for "at risk" groups, the labeling of such groups presents a potential boundary delineating "difference" (those more at risk of contracting HIV and AIDS) from the wider population (those less at risk).

These three aspects form cognitive spaces of stigma, where the degree of nonproductivity, danger, and personal culpability attributed to those homeless and living with HIV/AIDS lead to degrees of rejection. The least-stigmatized cognitive spaces (and therefore the most acceptable) contain productive, nondangerous, and blameless persons. Individuals who can be characterized in this space of stigma are perceived as contributing to the local community and to society at large. They are the productive members of society, working for wages, paying their taxes, volunteering for neighborhood activities and other social causes, and not exhibiting significant and visible evidence of deviance from social norms. Homeless persons and people living with HIV or AIDS are defined by the most extreme expression of spaces of stigma.

These cognitive spaces of stigma often become translated onto landscapes of stigma, where particular communities and locales are viewed as threatening by the wider population because they represent or house these service-dependent groups (e.g., skid rows, gay/lesbian enclaves, low-income neighborhoods). In communities that are not defined as landscapes of stigma, the encroachment of a human service facility brings the threat associated with service-dependent individuals and families into their midst. Thus, the facility becomes a condensate of the negative images of service-dependent individuals and becomes the flashpoint for community mobilization in defense of amenities, turf, and local quality of life.

ATTITUDES TOWARD HOMELESSNESS AND AIDS AMONG COMMUNITIES IN ORANGE COUNTY, CALIFORNIA

One means of accessing the ways in which cognitive spaces of stigma are defined is to explore people's attitudes toward homelessness and AIDS. There has been limited research on perceptions toward homelessness and AIDS of individuals who self-identify racially or ethnically, but there has been even less work on how such individuals define landscapes of stigma. That is, scholars know little about how communities who self-identify racially or ethnically define and view locales that are threatening. To explore these issues, this section presents excerpts from semistructured interviews I conducted with Latino/a and Vietnamese residents living in Orange County, California, during the fall of 1994. These residents were selected, with the help of researchers and human service providers, because of their informal influence among the wider Latino/a and Vietnamese communities. Thus, rather than representing formal political institutions, these individuals, many of whom were highly respected religious or civic leaders, were chosen as representatives of prevailing attitudes within these two communities which identify themselves by race.[8]

The three aspects of "difference" described in the previous section are used here to explore the understanding of homelessness and AIDS in these two communities. Understandings of nonproductivity, danger, and personal culpability affect perceptions of service-dependent populations in distinct ways. While these varied understandings often contribute to the marginalization and exclusion of homeless persons and people living with HIV/AIDS, they also provide opportunities for sympathy, caring, and inclusion.

In expressing views on people living with HIV or AIDS, in particular, the fact that their lack of productivity is brought about primarily through illness is often used as a rationale for overlooking the "deviance" associated with contracting the condition. While religion and traditional norms clearly dictate that specific behaviors are unacceptable (although these are less related to productivity and more related to danger), religious groups and cultural family support networks also promote sympathy and caring for the sick. There is a complex interaction between this religious-based caring and sympathy, on the one hand, and the exclusion of behavior defined as unacceptable by traditional norms, on the other. In specific situations, the caring facet of cultural norms and religious doctrine overrides the exclusionary dictates with respect to persons living with HIV or AIDS. Some religious leaders, for example, spoke about AIDS as if it were equivalent to any other ailment. A Vietnamese Buddhist abbot described AIDS as an illness:

> "It [AIDS] is a sickness like other sickness. . . . We don't look down [on it]. Need money to treat it, if no treatment, die. . . . Karma, [the person having AIDS] didn't do good last life. Buddha said, care for sick, homeless, it is good deed."

Traditional norms also include the close-knit ties of family and kinship networks. At times, even with the intense stigma associated with AIDS, the strong social support networks within families in the Latino/a and Vietnamese communities in Orange County provide care for persons who have AIDS. A priest commented on the supportive nature of one Latino/a family even given the socially unacceptable behavior of its members:

> "I think that people are very compassionate to their relatives. For example, the family that I met, even though this, ah, young man who was 29 years old, even though he had been married in the past, and had been using drugs, and stealing from them, and doing so many things, they still took him back. They were taking care of him."

The existence of kinship ties and caring also means, however, that those individuals who cannot access these resources are deemed "outsiders" and are often invisible to the community. The close-knit ties of family networks and the overriding norm of productivity and work constituted the primary reasons for the predominant belief among all the residents interviewed that homelessness was not an issue for the Latino/a and Vietnamese communities in Orange County. Indeed, when I asked them about the seriousness of the homelessness issue for their communities, the leaders often asked me about homelessness "in" their community or outside. Inside their communities, there was generally the claim that homelessness was not a problem, that social support networks housed those individuals who needed shelter. As one Latino stated:

> "[In the city of Santa Ana, the] Civic Center is a great place to find any kind of homelessness you want. Just go out there—you don't see Latinos out there."

Further, many of the leaders indicated that homeless people did not have families and were primarily from outside their communities. As one Vietnamese Catholic priest mentioned:

> "Now, we have a group who takes care of the homeless in Santa Ana. They come here from here to Santa Ana to give food and to serve meals on every Friday. These people are Vietnamese, but the homeless people they feed are not Vietnamese."

In addition, the leaders often argued that an immigrant work ethic in addition to the shelter provided by family and friends ensured that Latino/a and Vietnamese residents were not among the growing ranks of the homeless in Orange County. As one Latino physician argued:

> "You're not going to [find Latinos on skid row]. You're not going to because it's not an acceptable thing. The work ethic is there among the first generation, new arrivals. . . . So you are not going to find a lot of people out in the street, because they are going to be trying to get a job. The other thing is that if the people come into this country usually they are coming into a support situation whether it be family or someone from the same region or whatever, and I think it is expected within our culture that you are going to be contributing and contributing through employment and through work and you are not really going to be a drain to anyone. . . . That's just unwritten rules."

One primary source of the intense stigmatization of homeless people and individuals living with HIV or AIDS is the danger associated with the conditions. With respect to HIV and AIDS, there is a widespread perception within both the Latino/a and Vietnamese communities in Orange County that AIDS is an invasion—not only of the polluted to the pure, but also of an undesired influx of Anglo, Westernized societal values into Vietnamese and Latino/a culture. The danger associated with invasion by AIDS was expressed in much more intense ways among the Vietnamese individuals interviewed than among the Latinos and Latinas. Many of the Vietnamese religious leaders interviewed indicated that they felt dual pressures concerning AIDS: one set of pressures posed by the life-threatening dangers and stigma of the condition, and a second set of pressures emanating from the unfamiliar traditions of "Western" society associated with the behaviors that serve to spread HIV. As an expression of these dual pressures, many of the Vietnamese religious leaders believed that harboring traditional norms and community values would eliminate the risk of contracting HIV and AIDS. The strength of cultural norms was often seen as a shield protecting community members from AIDS. This belief was particularly evident among the Vietnamese church leaders, and it spanned multiple religious affiliations throughout the Vietnamese community. A Vietnamese Catholic priest argued:

> "AIDS is a problem for other people, but [not] for the Vietnamese Catholic. . . . Traditions are still strong enough to keep the children away from those deadly disease[s]."

In addition, a Vietnamese Lutheran minister stated:

> "They [Vietnamese people] are aware of the danger [of AIDS]. I think it is because it reflects a clear distinction between the Asian values, moral values, and the Western moral values. It involves the free sex, the careless sex that is not commonly heard [of] in Vietnam."

A Vietnamese Buddhist abbot believed that AIDS would follow the influence of non-Vietnamese traditions and values, particularly among younger generations:

> "[Community members] are concerned. Maybe [the] young generation [is more] influenced by American culture, style, system. Some have American boyfriend and girlfriend. But [this is] not problem with adults."

Indeed, acculturation and immersion in Western culture and values has played a complex role in the development of community-specific attitudes toward AIDS and homelessness in Orange County. There is the perception among the Latino/a and Vietnamese residents that AIDS and homelessness are linked to younger, more acculturated individuals who believe less fervently in traditional values, are more likely to behave in ways that would place them at risk of AIDS transmission, and are more likely to be representative of being "American." As one Latino physician commented:

> "[T]he majority of people that I would see homeless that are Latino are people that are most likely second generation, third generation. And I think that's because they fall more into our, more the middle American model, where maybe they were employed and they lost their job or they become discouraged, they got on drugs, they came back from the war and they become IV drug abusers, or they just had mental dysfunctions that did not

allow them to really support themselves or however through poor interactions with family they wind up on the street."

Although the metaphor of invasion permeates understanding of homelessness and HIV/AIDS in both communities, the Catholic church in the Latino/a community has apparently taken a more pro-active approach in dealing with AIDS in particular by providing education and awareness programs concerning HIV, AIDS, and sexuality. Such efforts indicate that priests within the Catholic church, rather than trying to use religion as a shield, have been working toward the demystification of AIDS. As a Latino priest put it:

> "[I]n the churches we have been, maybe aggressive is not the right word, but we have done a lot of education. . . ."

> "They [young people] are becoming more aware of the sexual community out there, homosexuality. A lot of questions about homosexuality are being asked in young adult meetings and . . . they are about 'What's the church's position about that?,' 'What about those people?,' and those types of things. I mean it is bubbling to the surface."

Perhaps the most important element framing Latino/a and Vietnamese attitudes toward HIV/AIDS and homelessness is personal culpability. In terms of HIV/AIDS, as the previous quote indicates, its linkage with homosexuality plays a primary role in its understanding. Although studies have indicated that Latino/a and Vietnamese individuals are at high risk of contracting AIDS, most notably gay men but increasingly heterosexual women (Carrier, Nguyen, & Su, 1992), there is still the predominant belief that AIDS is linked solely to homosexuality. For example, one Latina stated:

> "[T]hey [community members] blame it [AIDS], and seem to continue to attach it, to lifestyle, to the fact that it's a gay disease."

With the association of AIDS with homosexuality or other socially unacceptable behavior comes the perception that persons who acquire HIV and AIDS are somehow to blame for their conditions. This personal responsibility for acquiring HIV and AIDS contributes to the exclusion of persons living with HIV/AIDS and their invisibility within the Latino/a and Vietnamese communities. For example, one Vietnamese community service director described the distinction often made by Vietnamese residents between AIDS and mental disability:

> "Whereas HIV and AIDS that's, . . . you know, voluntary behavior."

The close association between AIDS and homosexuality in both communities has contributed to the intense stigmatization of AIDS. The physical dangers associated with AIDS coupled with the cultural and community threats associated with homosexuality make HIV and AIDS that much more dangerous to members of the Vietnamese and Latino/a communities. With the widespread belief that AIDS is confined to the homosexual population, nonhomosexual individuals perceive themselves as not being at risk and may then behave according to this belief. This perception of the confinement of AIDS tends to interact with moral standards for behavior (especially heterosexual males' behavior) held by respected social institutions, at times resulting in unwanted and increasingly dangerous outcomes. One Latino physician described one possible interaction between the cultural beliefs concerning acceptable male behavior and the influence of churches:

> "The culture states that men may actually be, you know, out playing around, but the Church doesn't necessarily condone that they protect themselves. You know, so you've got this conflict of maybe somebody going out, but not necessarily taking precautions and picking up a disease."

The perception of personal culpability also played a significant role in the lack of acceptability for homeless persons in these two communities. Given the prevailing assumption that the social networks defined by Latino/a and Vietnamese cultural norms will always provide shelter, individuals who cannot access shelter often carry the stigma of personal culpability. As a Vietnamese Catholic priest commented:

> "There may be some homeless cases because they came here alone, or they are divorced or they are teenagers who come alone or they came here with family and don't deal with rules that the family set up for them, so they ran away. In these cases, they might become homeless."

The housing available to many low-income Latino/a and Vietnamese households is often overcrowded, but it still provides a means of staying off the streets. As one Latina commented on overcrowding and homelessness:

"I lived like that when I came to this country and it just like, well that's what you've got to do until you make the money, you know, you don't ever think that they want to live like that forever. . . . I find that people come into an area where there are people from the same village or their same super-extended families and friends and so they feel an obligation to take care of each other. You do hear, at least in the newspaper, in the newspaper I heard of a person with a Latino name being called a transient and that's interesting to me because I don't know Latino transients. I see transients, what I consider transients near the market where I shop, near the stores when I go buy clothes, around where I work and none of them are Latinos, so I don't know, I guess because you don't have your own place you then the larger community calls, the mainstream community calls you transient, a vagrant, a homeless person. But within the Latino/a community you don't hear that term."

HUMAN SERVICE DELIVERY AND JUSTICE FOR ALL

This chapter has explored the dynamics of distinction that influence community response toward human services and service-dependent populations, particularly in populations self-identified by race or ethnicity. The Orange County residents interviewed expressed many of the perceptions of nonproductivity, dangerousness, and personal culpability associated with people who are homeless or living with HIV/AIDS that underlie broader community responses to human services. These attributions of "difference" to homeless people or those living with HIV/AIDS are used in the Latino/a and Vietnamese communities in exclusionary, rejecting ways, but may also activate caring and supportive reactions by family and friends.

Exploring such responses is vital for creating a human service delivery system that provides equity for communities and service-dependent populations. Justice in terms of facility siting is not as simple as equal distribution across communities, municipalities, or states (Flax, 1993; Young, 1990). There are neighborhood considerations and client circumstances that must help to determine what justice means in terms of human service facility siting. For example, is justice in facility siting defined by an equal distribution of human services across space (e.g., fair-share policies) (Dear & Wolch, 1987), spatial concentrations of facilities and services (e.g., service hubs) (Wolch & Dear, 1993), some combination of these two, or perhaps, the reduction of human services together with a focus on the underlying causes of homelessness, AIDS, and mental disability (the NIABY, or "not in anybody's backyard," alternative) (Heiman, 1990)? The contextual definition of justice has become an increasingly impor- tant issue, with the perception of injustice concerning the siting of human services and environmental hazards serving to activate locational conflict across the United States. With calls for environ- mental justice, in particular, communities identifying themselves ra- cially or ethnically are becoming active participants in this emerging politics of facility siting.

To explore the complexities underlying such responses, it is nec- essary to move beyond the conceptualization of community opposi- tion as selfish and reactionary and to build on past work in geogra- phy that has tried to untangle the dynamics underlying community rejection. In this chapter, a focus on difference provided a useful way of accessing some of the complexities underlying attitudes among two racially self-identified communities in Orange County. What it showed specifically was that the stigmatization of homelessness and HIV/AIDS in these two communities reflected both rejecting and accepting facets, that the "otherness" defined by homelessness and AIDS had multiple aspects associated not only with the conditions themselves but also with community marginalization and cultural self- identity, and that while both homelessness and HIV/AIDS are causes for concern in these two communities, they are generally seen as prob- lems for other communities and indeed as emanating from "outside" the community. Thus, landscapes of stigma in these two communities might be strongly defined by facilities serving homeless persons and individuals living with HIV/AIDS. Homelessness and HIV/AIDS do constitute significant and growing issues for both communities, but to acknowledge their importance and legitimacy also means a neces- sary change in the communities' self-identity. No longer could homelessness be seen as a problem merely for those outside the kin- ship network; the acknowledgment of HIV and AIDS as relevant is- sues might signify that Anglo values have permeated these two com- munities.

In general, what this analysis has indicated is that changing the perception and community response to human service facilities for homeless persons and individuals living with HIV and AIDS might also require fundamental shifts in community self-identity and in the definition of the constitution of "difference" and "otherness." In the future, using such an analytical approach may indicate possible av- enues not only for understanding why communities react in the ways that they do but also for developing human service delivery systems that are accepted as equitable and fair by all involved.

ACKNOWLEDGMENTS

This research was supported in part by a grant from the National Science Foundation, Program in Geography and Regional Science (No. SBR-9308857), and by a University of California–Irvine Faculty Fellowship. I thank David G. White and the editors for their helpful comments on a previous draft. Any omissions or errors remain my responsibility.

NOTES

1. "Managed care" is a system of health care services reflecting the twin goals of cost control and maintenance of quality of care. In a "fee for service" model, individuals incur costs for medical services provided by doctors selected by that individual. The doctors are then reimbursed for these services in part by the individual and in part by his/her insurer. In a managed care situation, which may include health maintenance organizations (HMOs), preferred provider organizations (PPOs), or independent practice associations (IPAs), the managed health care company would pay doctors or medical groups a set monthly fee for each member or subscriber using their practice. Each member/subscriber in subscribing to the managed care company agrees to use that company's providers for all covered health services.

2. This argument, however, has been disputed by Blau (1992).

3. The literature on housing policy during the 1980s and early 1990s is far more extensive than can be included in this chapter. See Blau (1992) for a concise review of this literature as it pertains to homelessness.

4. While daily mobility is oftentimes limited, residential mobility may be very high due to the instability of shelter and housing within such populations (Wolch et al., 1993).

5. There is a growing literature that assesses knowledge and attitudes among populations self-identifying racially or ethnically. See, for example, DiClemente, Boyer, and Morales (1988), Flaskerud and Nyamathi (1989, 1990), and Mays and Jackson (1991).

6. This extends the arguments made by Lake (1993) with respect to community opposition concerning development and environmental hazards.

7. Personal culpability is very much linked to the differentiations made between deserving and undeserving groups. There is an extensive literature on this issue and the "culture of poverty." See, for example, Katz (1989) for a discussion of the origins of the characterization of "undeserving poor."

8. Each interview included questions about the seriousness of homelessness and AIDS among Latino/a and Vietnamese residents; about how culture, tradition, and religion play a role in structuring community

response to homelessness and AIDS; and about how likely Latino/a and Vietnamese residents would be to accept a facility for homeless persons or people with AIDS in their neighborhoods. The length of the interviews ranged from 30 minutes to 1½ hours. Each interview was conducted at the religious or civic leader's office or facility. For a more detailed discussion of the methodology, see Takahashi (1997c).

REFERENCES

Abrahamson, A. (1991, November). Been down so long jail looked like up to him. *Los Angeles Times*, p. A1.

Ainlay, S. C., & Crosby, F. (1986). Stigma, justice and the dilemma of difference. In S. C. Ainlay, G. Becker, & L. M. Coleman (Eds.), *The dilemma of difference: A multidisciplinary view of stigma* (pp. 17–38). New York: Plenum Press.

Alreck, P. L., & Settle, R. B. (1985). *The survey research handbook.* Homewood, IL: Irwin.

Baer, W. C. (1986). Housing in an internationalizing region: Housing stock dynamics in Southern California and the dilemmas of fair share. *Environment and Planning D: Society and Space, 4*, 337–360.

Baumohl, J. (1989). Alcohol, homelessness and public policy. *Contemporary Drug Problems, 16*, 281–300.

Blasi, G. (1994). And we are not seen: Ideological and political barriers to understanding homelessness. *American Behavioral Scientist, 37*(4), 563–586.

Blau, J. (1992). *The visible poor: Homelessness in the United States.* New York: Oxford University Press.

Blendon, R. J., & Donelan, K. (1989). AIDS, the public and the NIMBY syndrome. In D. E. Rogers & E. Ginszberg (Eds.), *Public and professional attitudes towards AIDS patients* (pp. 19–30). Boulder, CO: Westview Press.

Bullard, R. D. (Ed.). (1994). *Unequal protection: Environmental justice and communities of color.* San Francisco: Sierra Club Books.

Burt, M. R. (1992). *Over the edge: The growth of homelessness in the 1980s.* New York: Russell Sage Foundation and Urban Institute Press.

Burt, M. R., & Cohen, B. E. (1989). *America's homeless: Numbers, characteristics, and programs that serve them.* Washington, DC: Urban Institute Press.

Carrier, J., Nguyen, B., & Su, S. (1992). Vietnamese American sexual behaviors and HIV infection. *Journal of Sex Research, 29*(4), 547–560.

Cox, K. R. (1989). The politics of turf and the question of class. In J. Wolch & M. Dear (Eds.), *The power of geography* (pp. 61–90). Boston: Unwin Hyman.

Dear, M. J. (1992). Understanding and overcoming the NIMBY syndrome. *Journal of the American Planning Association, 58*(3), 288–300.

Dear, M., & Gleeson, B. (1991). Community attitudes toward the homeless. *Urban Geography, 12*(2), 155–176.

Dear, M., & Laws, G. (1986). Anatomy of a decision: Recent land use zoning appeals and their effect on group homes locations in Ontario. *Canadian Journal of Community Mental Health, 5*(1), 5–17.

Dear, M., & Taylor, S. M. (1982). *Not on our street: Community attitudes toward mental health care.* London: Pion.

Dear, M., & Wolch, J. (1987). *Landscapes of despair: From deinstitutionalization to homelessness.* Princeton, NJ: Princeton University Press.

DiClemente, R. J., Boyer, C. B., & Morales, E. S. (1988). Minorities and AIDS: Knowledge, attitudes, and misconceptions among black and Latino adolescents. *American Journal of Public Health, 78*(1), 55–57.

DiRado, A. (1994, February 4). Appeals court voids Santa Ana ban on camping by homeless. *Los Angeles Times,* p. A27.

Dolan, M. (1995, April). State justices uphold tough homeless law. *Los Angeles Times,* p. A1.

Fink, P. J., & Tasman, A. (Eds.). (1992). *Stigma and mental illness.* Washington, DC: American Psychiatric Press.

Fischer, P. J. (1988). Criminal activity among the homeless: A study of arrests in Baltimore. *Hospital and Community Psychiatry, 39*(1), 46–51.

Flaskerud, J. H., & Nyamathi, A. M. (1989). Black and Latina women's AIDS related knowledge, attitudes, and practices. *Research in Nursing and Health, 12,* 339–346.

Flaskerud, J. H., & Nyamathi, A. M. (1990). Effects of an AIDS education program on the knowledge, attitudes and practices of low income black and Latina women. *Journal of Community Health, 15*(6), 343–355.

Flax, J. (1993). *Disputed subjects: Essays on psychoanalysis, politics and philosophy.* New York: Routledge.

Gallagher, M. L. (1994). Homeless—not hopeless. *Planning, 60*(10), 18–21.

Gallup Organization. (1995). *Homeless but not hopeless: A Los Angeles Mission report on what Americans believe about homeless people, their problems, and possible solutions.* Lincoln, NE: Author.

Gilderbloom, J., & Applebaum, R. (1988). *Rethinking rental housing.* Philadelphia: Temple University Press.

Gilman, S. L. (1988). *Disease and representation: Images of illness from Madness to AIDS.* Ithaca, NY: Cornell University Press.

Goffman, E. (1963). *Stigma: Notes on the management of spoiled identity.* Englewood Cliffs, NJ: Prentice-Hall.

Goldberg, S. B. (1994). Homeless victory: Santa Ana law criminalizes status. *ABA Journal, 80*(April), 102–103.

Graham, L., & Logan, R. (1990). Social class and tactics: Neighborhood opposition to group homes. *Sociological Quarterly, 31*(4), 513–529.

Green, D. E., McCormick, I. A., & Walkey, F. H. (1987). Community attitudes to mental illness in New Zealand twenty-two years on. *Social Science and Medicine, 24*(5), 417–422.

Hanson, S., & Pratt, G. (1995). *Gender, work, and space.* London: Routledge.

Harrison, B., & Bluestone, B. (1988). *The great U-turn: Corporate restructuring and the polarizing of America.* New York: Basic Books.

Heiman, M. (1990). From "not in my backyard!" to "not in anybody's backyard!": Grassroots challenge to hazardous waste facility siting. *Journal of the American Planning Association, 56*(3), 359–362.

Herek, G. M., & Glunt, E. K. (1988). An epidemic of stigma: Public reaction to AIDS. *American Psychologist, 43*(11), 886–891.

Hoch, C. (1991). The spatial organization of the urban homeless: A case study of Chicago. *Urban Geography, 12*(2), 137–154.

Hopper, K., & Baumohl, J. (1994). Held in Abeyance: Rethinking homelessness and advocacy. *American Behavioral Scientist, 37*(4), 522–552.

Jones, E. E., Farina, A., Hastorf, A. H., Markus, H., Miller, D. T., Scott, R. A., & French, R. de S. (1984). *Social stigma: The psychology of marked relationships.* New York: Freeman.

Jones, J. P., III, & Kodras, J. E. (1990). Restructured regions and families: The feminization of poverty in the U.S. *Annals of the Association of American Geographers, 80*(2), 163–183.

Katz, M. B. (1989). *The undeserving poor: From the war on poverty to the war on welfare.* New York: Pantheon Books.

Keigher, S. M. (Ed.). (1991). *Housing risks and homelessness among the urban elderly.* New York: Haworth Press.

King, M. B. (1993). *AIDS, HIV and Mental Health.* Cambridge, UK: Cambridge University Press.

Kunkel, L. E., & Temple, L. L. (1992). Attitudes towards AIDS and homosexuals: Gender, marital status, and religion. *Journal of Applied Social Psychology, 22*(13), 1030–1040.

Lake, R. W. (1993). Rethinking NIMBY. *Journal of the American Planning Association, 59*(1), 87–93.

Laws, G. (1992). Emergency shelter networks in an urban area: Serving the homeless in metropolitan Toronto. *Urban Geography, 13*(2), 99–126.

Lee, B. A., Lewis, D. W., & Jones, S. H. (1992). Are the homeless to blame? A test of two theories. *Sociological Quarterly, 33*(4), 535–552.

MacKinnon, K. (1992). *The politics of popular representation: Reagan, Thatcher, AIDS, and the movies.* Cranbury, NJ: Associated University Presses.

Mair, A. (1986). The homeless and the post-industrial city. *Political Geography Quarterly, 5,* 351–368.

Massey, D. (1984). *Spatial divisions of labor: Social structures and the geography of production.* New York: Methuen.

Mays, V. M., & Jackson, J. S. (1991). AIDS survey methodology with Black Americans. *Social Science and Medicine, 33*(1), 47–54.

McDevitt, T. M., Sheehan, E. P., Lennon, R., & Ambrosio, A. (1990). Correlates of attitudes toward AIDS. *Journal of Social Psychology, 130*(5), 699–701.

Myers, D., Baer, W. C., & Choi, S.-Y. (1996). The changing problem of overcrowded housing. *Journal of the American Planning Association, 63*(1), 66–84.

Palmer, J. L., & Sawhill, I. V. (Eds.). (1982). *Perspectives on the Reagan experiment.* Washington, DC: Urban Institute Press.

Phillips, K. (1990). *The politics of rich and poor: Wealth and the American electorate in the Reagan aftermath.* New York: HarperCollins.

Pomerance, L. M., & Shields, J. J. (1989). Factors associated with hospital workers' reactions to the treatment of persons with AIDS. *AIDS Education and Prevention, 1*(3), 184–193.

Pulido, L. (1996). *Environmentalism and economic justice.* Tucson: University of Arizona Press.

Ringheim, K. (1990). *At risk of homelessness: The roles of income and rent.* New York: Praeger.

Rogers, T. F., Singer, E., & Imperio, J. (1993). Poll trends: AIDS—an update. *Public Opinion Quarterly, 57,* 92–114.

Rowe, S., & Wolch, J. (1990). Social networks in time and space: Homeless women in skid row, Los Angeles. *Annals of the Association of American Geographers, 80,* 184–204.

Segal, S. P., Baumohl, J., & Moyles, E. W. (1980). Neighborhood types and community reaction to the mentally ill: A paradox of intensity. *Journal of Health and Social Behavior, 21*(4), 345–359.

Smith, C. J., & Giggs, J. A. (Eds.). (1988). *Location and stigma: Contemporary perspectives on mental health and mental health care.* Boston: Unwin Hyman.

Smith, C. J., & Hanham, R. Q. (1981). Any place but here! Mental health facilities as noxious neighbors. *Professional Geographer, 33,* 326–334.

Solomon, P. (1983). Analyzing opposition to community residential facilities for troubled adolescents. *Child Welfare, 62*(4), 361–366.

Sontag, S. (1988). *AIDS and its metaphors.* New York: Farrar, Straus & Giroux.

Takahashi, L. M. (1997a). Representation, attitudes, and behavior: Analyzing the spatial dimensions of community response to mental disability. *Environment and Planning A, 29,* 501–524.

Takahashi, L. M. (1997b). When does race matter? Exploring socio-demographic variation in attitudes toward controversial facilities. *Urban Geography, 18*(5), 451–459.

Takahashi, L. M. (1997c). Stigmatization, HIV/AIDS, and communities of color: Exploring response to human service facilities. *Health and Place, 3*(3), 187–199.

Takahashi, L. M., & Dear, M. J. (1997). The changing dynamics of community attitudes to human services. *Journal of the American Planning Association, 63*(1), 79–93.

Toro, P. A., & McDonell, D. M. (1992). Beliefs, attitudes, and knowledge about homelessness: A survey of the general public. *American Journal of Community Psychology, 20*(1), 53–80.

Tringo, J. L. (1970). The hierarchy of preference toward disability groups. *Journal of Special Education, 4,* 295–306.

Veness, A. R. (1993). Neither homed nor homeless: Contested definitions and the personal worlds of the poor. *Political Geography, 12*(4), 319–340.

Wolch, J., & Dear, M. (1993). *Malign neglect: Homelessness in an American city.* San Francisco: Jossey-Bass.

Wolch, J. R., Rahimian, A., & Koegel, P. (1993). Daily and periodic mobility patterns of the urban homeless. *Professional Geographer, 45*(2), 159–169.
Young, I. M. (1990). *Justice and the politics of difference.* Princeton, NJ: Princeton University Press.

CHAPTER 7

Sexuality and Urban Space

GAY MALE IDENTITY POLITICS IN THE UNITED STATES, THE UNITED KINGDOM, AND AUSTRALIA

Lawrence Knopp

A growing body of academic work is considering the ways in which sex and sexuality are related to urbanization (Bech, 1993; Binnie, 1992a, 1993; Chauncey, 1994; Knopp, 1992, 1995; Wilson, 1991). This is in part an outgrowth of various queer, feminist, postmodern, and poststructuralist critiques of conventional social science (Geltmaker, 1992; Kobayashi & Peake, 1994; Lees, 1994; Soja, 1989; Rose, 1993). The latter, it is argued, has focused on naive mappings of sexual spaces (primarily ones defined as "gay"—see Castells, 1983; Ketteringham, 1979; Lauria & Knopp, 1985; Levine, 1979; Weightman, 1980; Winters, 1979) while remaining conspicuously silent about the ways in which these spaces (and urbanization processes in general) are sexed, gendered, racialized, and sexualized in the first place. Critiques have therefore focused on exposing the unacknowledged power relations lurking behind these various silences, on destabilizing pregiven social categories (e.g., "man," "woman," "black," "white," "heterosexual," "homosexual") and on establishing the ways in which such categories, while fluid, are nonetheless both constitutive of and constituted by sociospatial processes such as urbanization (see, e.g., the edited collection by Bell & Valentine, 1995).

While the most critical dimensions of this work have their roots in humanistic fields such as history (e.g., Chauncey, 1994), comparative literature (e.g., Munt, 1995), and cultural studies (e.g., Grosz, 1990), the specific concern with urbanization as often as not has its roots in one form or another of critical social science. The Marxist-inspired work of geographer David Harvey (1973, 1985, 1989, 1992) and that of several feminist and lesbian/gay urbanists (e.g., Adler & Brenner, 1992; Bondi, 1992; Brown, 1994, 1995; Geltmaker, 1992; Moos, 1989; Peake, 1993) have been particularly influential. Thus many of those writing about sex/sexuality and urbanization (especially in geography) are engaged in a fundamentally interdisciplinary project, one which draws heavily on critical traditions in both the humanities and the social sciences.

This chapter was conceived very much in that spirit. Through a discussion of gay male identity politics in several English-speaking cities around the world, I wish to demonstrate the utility of an approach to urbanization that synthesizes humanistic and social scientific perspectives. Material power relations, operating at the local, national, and international scales, figure prominently in my analyses. But so too do questions of meaning and culture, especially as they are articulated in and through local contingencies (i.e., "places"). Indeed, the two are simply different sides of the same coin. This is because, in the contemporary world at least, place-based questions of meaning and culture have themselves become material stakes in the processes and practices we have come to call urbanization.

THE SOCIAL AND SPATIAL DYNAMICS OF URBANIZATION

"Urbanization" is a contentious and problematic term. Empirically, it refers to a diverse set of events, experiences, meanings, and artifacts and the various social processes that shape (and are in turn shaped by) them. Primary among these are the growth of cities and the emergence of certain related lived experiences and cultural forms. Avoiding for the moment the issue of how meaningful or useful the concept "urban" might ultimately be theoretically,[1] it cannot be disputed that in the minds and imaginations of many people "the urban" (if not urbanization) is something quite real. For purposes of the present discussion, then, I am treating urbanization as a useful object of analysis that can fruitfully be conceived of as the unfolding and inscription of social relations and meanings in space, at densities and scales that are at once sufficiently large and complex as to feel overwhelming and almost incomprehensible, yet which remain navigable and meaningful in many particular respects from the vantage points of people's daily lives. This includes, but is in no way limited to, the creation and destruction of built environments (Paris, 1983). Thought of somewhat more broadly, it involves the creation and destruction of "places" or sites (both material or abstract[2]) that provide people with a contradictory experience of ontological security (due to their perceived stability and "reality") and *in*security (due to their complexity and ephemerality).

From his Marxist perspective, Harvey sees this process as arising fundamentally out of a tension between the spatially fixed nature of many capital investments (including investments in particular social structures) and the need for capital generally to remain mobile (and hence competitive). He argues that in the contemporary "postmodern" phase of capitalist development places have become increasingly ephemeral and unstable, due to new technologies of transportation, communication, and organization that have rendered capital more mobile than ever before. These conditions have massively accelerated processes of restructuring and diminished, therefore, the ability of places to remain stable and to offer ontological security. One of the ironies of this process, however, is that while roving capital undermines the stability of particular places (and hence place-based identities) it also becomes much more sensitive to the particularities and nuances of place. Indeed, the proliferation of such place-based differences is, according to Harvey, as much a necessary feature of contemporary capitalist social relations as their obliteration.

Various of Harvey's critics—including especially many feminists— have argued that this analysis disembodies the social relations it describes, thus reducing them to a single abstraction called "class." In so doing, other axes of power such as race, gender, and sexuality are implicitly discounted as in some sense or other subsidiary to, or derivative of, these class relations. This then perpetuates those aspects of the power relations involved which work to the advantage of dominant groups other than capitalists. What needs to happen, these critics argue, is for the mutual constitutions of social relations such as class, gender, race, and sexuality to be recognized right from the start. Thus "class" must be seen as always sexed, gendered, racialized, and sexualized, and in turn for sexuality, say, to be seen as always "classed," sexed, gendered. In this way the complex configurations of interests that are served (and victimized) by a social totality which is not only capitalist but also racist, patriarchal, and heterosexist can be more fully understood and combated.

Transformations in research concerning "gay" geographies demonstrate the effects these critiques have had. Much of the work done in the late 1970s and 1980s (including some of my own—see, e.g., Knopp, 1990a, 1990b; Lauria & Knopp, 1985) treated a "gay" identity as relatively unproblematic, focused on locating gay communities in urban space, and explained the emergence of such areas in terms primarily of various economic and political processes. More recent work, meanwhile, has been aimed at developing a framework which takes the mutual (and variable) constitutions of class, race, gender and sexuality much more seriously (see, e.g., Knopp, 1992, 1994, 1995). Drawing on the work of many feminists, postmodernists and poststructuralists (e.g., Bech, 1993; Blasius, 1994; Kobayashi & Peake, 1994; Lees, 1994; Rose, 1993; Soja, 1989; Wilson, 1991), I have argued recently that the construction and essentialization, through social practices, of variable human differences and experiences (e.g., the creation of categories such as "capitalist," "worker," "man," "woman," "black," "white," "gay," and "straight") is a fundamental mechanism of social control. Control over various aspects of the production, reproduction and distribution of values (all broadly defined to include cultural as well as material products) is most easily exercised when people can be categorized and forced to conform as members of supposedly homogeneous groups. Thus, for example, the gendering, racializing and sexualizing of various spatial divisions of productive and reproductive labor have always been crucial to the practices which constitute class. But it can also be said that class practices have been crucial to the constitution of various gendered, racialized and sexualized identities, and that this has served the interests not only of capitalists but of men, "white" Europeans, and "heterosexuals" (among others).

It follows that the contradictions in the urbanization process which Marxists like Harvey (and other "modernist" and/or structuralist social scientists) identify must also be seen as sexed, gendered, racialized, sexualized, etc. For example, the cross-class "structured coherences" that Harvey stresses (1985, pp. 139–144), which supposedly arise to protect long-term, spatially-fixed investments in places, must be seen as communities of interest defined by variable configurations of racial, sexual and gender interests, not just class interests. They serve not only the interests of local capital but of particular "fractions" and coalitions of male, female, black, white, gay and straight interests as well—coalitions which, incidentally, may or may not be consistent with the interests of "men," "whites" and "heterosexuals" in society overall. Similarly, gender-based spatial divisions of labor which are designed to facilitate the exploitation of working-class men and women may not only precipitate class warfare, but resistance to gender and sexual oppression as well.

In the contemporary era, with all its instability and fluidity, many potentially disruptive forms of difference emerge from these contradictions. Most are very rapidly appropriated and co-opted by more flexible dominant interests in their continual search for new and more effective means of social control and self-service. Classic examples include the transformation of certain aspects of urban ethnic and minority youth cultures into market niches. At the same time, other forms of difference, including some which may have been designed primarily to advance the interests of dominant groups (e.g., some religious "cult" movements), are appropriated by groups and movements with much more radical, counterhegemonic agendas.

Furthermore, the proliferation of all this difference, as a crucial defining feature of contemporary places and place-based identities, has rendered struggles over symbols and representation virtually indistinguishable from more "material" stakes in urbanization. Struggles over the *meanings* of places have everything to do with how places grow and develop, how they function within systems of power relations, and how they shape and reshape social relations generally. For example, the ways in which certain gay and black neighborhoods are sexualized and racialized (as, e.g., either "light" liberated consumption zones or "dark" sexually dangerous jungles) can have a profound impact on investment, disinvestment, migration, and other location decisions. Similarly, local struggles over social policies governing sexual behavior, discrimination in housing and employment, adoption and same-sex domestic partnership benefits, while contested largely on cultural grounds, have very clear material consequences, both for the particular places involved and for other places (and the people whose social relations constitute them). The point is that the distinction between the material and the representational or symbolic is increasingly untenable in a world characterized by so much fluidity in meanings and identities.

GAY MALE IDENTITY POLITICS IN U.S., BRITISH, AND AUSTRALIAN CITIES

In illustrating the utility of this perspective, I am drawing on research conducted over several years in one Australian, two U.S., and two British cities. These are Sydney, New South Wales, Australia; Minneapolis, Minnesota; New Orleans, Louisiana; Edinburgh, Scotland; and London, England. Each features a distinct setting and scale for an analysis of the relationships between sexual identity politics and certain aspects of urbanization. The six cases reflect at least four different forms that these relationships take. Each of these is embedded within fairly traditional discourses and social practices (especially those relating to race, class, gender, and nation formation), and each is present to some degree or other in every one of the cities studied. At the same time, certain of these forms tend to be associated somewhat more with the U.S. cities, certain others with the British cities, and another with the Australian city, due in no small measure to the unique nation-building projects that constitute part of the six cities' wider social contexts. I offer here a glimpse into ways in which these relationships work in different contexts and why.

Territorialization, Empowerment, and the Control of Space

In the three U.S. cities (and to a somewhat lesser extent in Sydney and London), dominant[3] forms of gay male identity politics are strongly linked (ideologically, if not in practice) to the infiltration by gay men of mainstream economic and political institutions and the related construction and economic development of territorial spaces. These spaces function only secondarily as sites of gay sexual or other cultural expressions. This is perhaps best illustrated by the fact that the predominantly white, mostly middle-class men who have created these spaces represent them to the "outside" (read "heterosexual") world almost exclusively in disembodied and desexualized terms, while appealing politically to similarly disembodied popular abstractions that are deeply embedded in many mainstream political and cultural discourses: economic and individual freedom, personal rights, personal responsibilities, equality of opportunity, freedom from discrimination, equal access to services, etc. At the same time, they deploy strongly sexualized representations (images of seminude male bodies, for example), and at times even emphasize the politics of sexual practice and sexual freedom, in their portrayals of these spaces as functional and meaningful *places*, to other gay men. The result is a form of urbanization in which struggles over sexual resources, opportunities, and meanings are strategically embodied, disembodied, and otherwise manipulated spatially by both gay-identified and non-gay-identified actors to advantage particular class, gender, sexual, and other interests.

This general model plays itself out particularly clearly in Minneapolis and New Orleans (though in sometimes strikingly different ways), and in somewhat more muted ways in London and Sydney. In Minneapolis (a relatively low-density, predominantly white, middle-class, and affirmatively "liberal" city in terms of its post-World War II political culture), certain conflicts over municipal policies relating to race, gender, and sexuality were won by social issue liberals, including gay men, in the late 1970s and early 1980s. This was one of the factors leading to a consolidation of middle-class gay political power, and the emergence of gay-identified residential and commercial spaces in the city, in the 1980s and 1990s. One of the most visible conflicts occurred between 1979 and 1985 and involved police department policy toward the enforcement of vice laws affecting gay men (see Knopp, 1986, 1987).[4] While gay activists were split over how to respond to perceived double standards and abusive practices of the police department, they were ultimately successful in forcing a favorable change in official police policy on the issue. This was due to a combination of tactics by at least two gay political factions. One favored a confrontational approach that forced the police and city government generally to talk about the issue of sexual freedom and to confront contradictions in dominant social constructions of gender and sexuality, as well as of taken-for-granted notions like "public" and "private." The other favored a pluralist, interest-group-based strategy of bringing pressure through powerful institutions such as the city council, the office of the mayor, and the local Democratic party, and of deemphasizing issues like sexual freedom, gender, sexuality, and the definitions of "public" and "private." Interestingly, this tactical divide did not mirror a larger liberal versus radical philosophical divide between the factions. Indeed, many of the tactical "radicals" were also wedded philosophically to a vision of gay community development that was strongly predicated upon place creation in the form of neighborhoods with a distinctly gay identity, private accumulation, and the economic development of urban space more generally; liberal gay "insiders," meanwhile, were often drawn from the ranks of tenants-rights and other non-gay-specific community-based groups, and espoused a more social democratic, integrationist (and hence less place-based) ethos.

The gay victory on the police policy issue was quickly followed by a consolidation of political power by the more integrationist and liberal faction. Ironically, however, this power *was* strongly territorially based and resulted in a more-or-less permanent place in city (and state) politics for liberal, largely middle-class urban gays. This is evidenced by (among other things) the elections of an openly gay city councilor and two openly gay members of the Minnesota state legislature from Minneapolis constituencies containing higher-than-average concentrations of gays and lesbians. These successes came at a cost, however. Over the course of the 1980s and early 1990s Minne-apolis became increasingly identified (and isolated) as a bastion of institutionalized liberalism at a time when much of the rest of the state was showing strong signs of rejecting such a consensus.[5] The city's (and especially certain of its neighborhoods') increasingly dis-tinct identity as a place laden with very particular sexual and other cultural meanings became more and more central to official economic development strategies, while other local policies, in spite of being administered by supposedly "liberal" city governments, took on an increasingly lean and mean character. Economic development initia-tives focused on entertainment and tourism (particularly through the vehicle of "public–private partnerships" and other promotions of "place"), while resources for housing, neighborhood revitalization, and basic service delivery (arguably indicators of a very different no-tion of place) have been consistently retrenched. Perhaps more ger-mane to the issues being explored here, though, is the fact that main-stream gay politics in Minneapolis has generally supported, and at times profited from, these initiatives (despite the political roots of many gay insiders). At the same time, issues of sex and sexual free-dom, even in particular place-based contexts such as parks, are still virtually never on mainstream gay activists' agendas (in spite of the fact that they are frequently featured in representations of urban gay life that circulate among gay men). Instead, a premium is placed on issues of equal rights in the abstract, which as often as not reduces to the freedom for white middle-class gay men in the city to consume and/or accumulate, especially within those zones of the city (increas-ingly, all of it) which have become established as "gay-friendly" turf, at least for those with the means to consume sexual freedom as a commodity. Meanwhile, sites where sexual freedom can be practiced by a wider cross section of the gay population, such as bathhouses, have been forced to close. Others, such as certain public restrooms and public parks that have traditionally functioned as sites for anony-mous sexual encounters, have become much more tightly policed. Similarly, resources for HIV treatment and prevention have been re-duced, and a city-sponsored plan to grant insurance and other ben-efits to domestic partners of city employees has been ruled invalid by the State Supreme Court.

In New Orleans, a much poorer, majority-black, and much less "liberal" city than Minneapolis, a somewhat different permutation of this relationship between gay male identity politics and urbanization has evolved. In the 1970s and 1980s, a bid for economic and political power by predominantly white gay men took place there as in Minne-apolis. But this bid for power involved an attempt specifically to accumulate wealth through real estate development while promoting gay community development (primarily among white men) in a particular neighborhood (Knopp, 1990a, 1990b). In this sense the strategy was much more place based than that of Minneapolis from the start. Building on a foundation laid by sexual refugees and advocates of historic preservation in the 1960s and early 1970s (many of whom were also middle-class white gay men), shrewd gay developers and speculators began investing in the neighborhood's gentrification (Figure 7.1). Because access to capital was controlled by very culturally conservative local interests at the time, this entailed illegal schemes to defraud financial institutions by manipulating property appraisals. It also involved legal and illegal subsidies to young gay service-sector workers (and others) to become homebuyers and renters in the neighborhood, as well as the development and subsidy of neighborhood-based gay community institutions and resources.

Until the illegal property appraisal schemes were discovered, which was at roughly the same time that the economic potential of the neighborhood became fully realized, the project was enormously successful. The Marigny neighborhood (as it is called) developed a strong gay identity through the concentration in it of gay bars, restaurants, guest houses, a bookstore, and other commercial enterprises

FIGURE 7.1. Gay gentrification in New Orleans.

catering to a predominantly gay clientele. A plethora of other formal and informal organizations and institutions, some specifically organized around gay interests and others not, also developed in the neighborhood. Interestingly, a gay-owned real estate firm, which put together many of the fraudulent deals in the area, itself became a neighborhood landmark and informal gay community social center.

Once the distribution of power and profits in the neighborhood was restored, by legal intervention, to its pregentrification pattern, however, the area's symbolic importance in terms of local gay identities began to wane. The once-powerful gay real estate firm was dismantled, its owner was fined and put on probation, and the gay community of the neighborhood began to fracture along class lines. Many of the neighborhood's poorer gay residents were forced out by rising housing costs, and increasing numbers of heterosexuals and other non-gay-identified people began moving into the area.

In other senses, though, the neighborhood and the events that led to its identification as a gay-friendly place have had lasting effects. Public and private officials recognize the potential of gay money and gay votes in the area. A more affordable neighborhood immediately adjacent to the Marigny neighborhood has become a new locus of some middle-class gay home-buying fervor. Several bars and other gay-oriented businesses remain in the neighborhood as well. Moreover, outside the very tourist-oriented French Quarter, New Orleans' Marigny neighborhood is probably the only place in the city that is popularly recognized as being the base for any kind of gay economic or political clout at all.

So in New Orleans the relationship between gay identity politics and urbanization is articulated almost entirely through the workings of the place-based entertainment and real estate economies of certain neighborhoods in which predominantly white, male, and middle-class gay culture constitutes the core of a marketing strategy. As in Minneapolis, the *politics* of sex are quite marginalized in all of this—even within the gay "community" itself, and even though sexual freedom is very much a part of the image that these neighborhoods (and New Orleans as a whole) market to "outsiders" every day. Unlike Minneapolis, in New Orleans there have been relatively few efforts to parlay local economic clout into interest group-based political power. Indeed, gay identities are arguably less politicized overall in New Orleans than in Minneapolis. Rather, they tend to be organized almost entirely around accumulation and consumption, in a political culture where these are revered above all else as the ultimate sources of personal freedom and identity.

These politics of social and economic empowerment through

territorialization, place creation, and the control of space are evident to a lesser degree in most of the other cities as well. London, for example, features several relatively small-scale gay commercial zones (such as around Old Compton Street in the West End), and Sydney features a fairly large commercial and residential zone centering on Oxford Street and the surrounding inner-city neighborhoods of Darlinghurst, Surry Hills, and Paddington. These all function, in part, as bases for the achievement of a certain amount of economic and political power within their respective urban environments and beyond. However, in both London and Sydney this particular form of gay male engagement with space is much less prevalent than other forms. In Edinburgh, meanwhile, a gay community empowerment effort informed by this strategy is also present but is much less implicated in patterns of urbanization than are more straightforward responses to oppression.

Geographies of Oppression, Discrimination, and Harassment

The forging of identities through the economic and political colonization of territorial spaces (and the related creation of gay-identified *places*) is much facilitated by class, racial, and gender privilege. Thus, gay male identity-formation projects that embrace this strategy are particularly successful in contexts where there is a critical mass of middle-class white men (such as the cities and societies under consideration here).[6] But even where these conditions exist certain others may render the strategy ineffectual. In Edinburgh, for example, a socially conservative local culture has produced strong resistances to gay male visibility and power. Instead, the contesting of everyday urban spaces for various social, political, and even sexual purposes (including, frequently, transgressive ones) is much more central to gay male identity formation than empowerment through the economic and political colonization of particular spaces. Such conflicts over the sexual meanings and practices associated with urban space, as well as efforts by various interests, especially economic and nationalist, to turn such conflicts to their advantage, are well reflected in patterns of urbanization. A conflict in the late 1980s and early 1990s in Edinburgh illustrates this quite neatly (Knopp, 1997).

Edinburgh is a more middle-class, conservative, and Anglicized city than most others in Scotland. At the same time, it is the historic seat of government in Scotland and a symbol of many "things Scottish" including the Scottish legal system, one of the defining institutions of Scottish identity (McCrone, 1992). Historic preservation in the city's core and surrounding middle-class neighborhoods, as well as the segregation of working-class populations and council housing into peripheral areas, has been a prominent feature of urban development since at least the 1960s. In the 1980s, Thatcherite economic policies including the deregulation of financial institutions precipitated a wave of reorganization in which large quantities of capital were invested in highly speculative, short-term real estate projects in the city. Other policy changes, such as reforms in administration of housing allowance programs for indigent youths, resulted in homeless young men becoming vulnerable to unscrupulous landlords.

These circumstances came together in the late 1980s and early 1990s in the context of a sex scandal focused on the Scottish judiciary. The local tabloid and mainstream presses, in cooperation with certain local police officers, circulated reports alleging that the legal profession in Scotland (including the Scottish judiciary) had been infiltrated at its highest levels by a "magic circle" of gay lawyers and judges who were conspiring to "pervert justice." The chief offenses alleged to have been perpetrated and protected by these lawyers and judges were mortgage fraud, housing allowance fraud, and various sex crimes. While after several years of investigation these allegations were found to be baseless, the discourse surrounding the scandal and investigations drew on and cultivated popular notions of a link between a geography of sexual subversion in Edinburgh and various threats to the established order in Scotland including Scottish identity itself, through a threat to the sanctity of the Scottish legal system.

Mainstream and tabloid press reports constantly invoked metaphors of movement and penetration, and made reference to a huge number of specific sites in Edinburgh to legitimate the existence of a conspiracy. Sites referenced included fraudulently acquired residential properties where sex "crimes" were alleged to have taken place; gay bars and clubs; hostels and B&Bs ("bed-and-breakfast" lodgings) where the sexual exploitation of youths was alleged to have taken place; and various sexual "cruising grounds" including, notably, the road in front of the Scottish Office, where judges were allegedly procuring male prostitutes. This had the effect of literally grounding the allegations in urban space, and of course it did suggest a geography of gay male life in Edinburgh. So in this case the discursive construction of gay spaces and places was much more straightforwardly a strategy of oppression than of resistance.

Indeed, gay responses to this onslaught were divided and not at all particularly spatial. Some activists challenged dominant constructions of criminality that were implicit in this discourse by arguing that many of the offenses alleged deserved neither a response nor justification. They focused most of their rhetoric instead on questions of sexual freedom, ethics, and the hypocrisy of those supposedly defending Scottish "justice" from "perversion" (including more "mainstream" gay activists). Others attempted to distance gay men as a group from the criminal activities being alleged, denying where possible the significance of the sites offered up as evidence of a gay conspiracy by the police and press. But these individuals, like mainstream gay activists in the United States, focused primarily on abstract, disembodied, and delocalized issues of rights, responsibilities, and freedom from discrimination.

One important effect of these events was to deflect attention from certain other aspects of the social, political, and spatial contexts in which they took place. Neither the police, the press, politicians, nor gay activists of either tactical persuasion ever seriously addressed the issues of deregulation and administrative reform that made many of the alleged abuses possible. As a result, many dominant groups in the local land and housing markets never saw their interests and privileges seriously questioned (much less threatened). Political strategies focusing on the sexual meanings of and practices in particular urban spaces and places, meanwhile, were critical to the success of this diversion. Indeed, they were at least as crucial to the outcomes described here as the place-based liberal and entrepreneurial forms of gay politics were to the outcomes described in the U.S. cities. Furthermore, they were deployed (successfully) almost exclusively by the agents of oppression, not resistance.

The Cultural Politics of Resistance

Another form which the relationship between gay male identity politics and urban space takes is an active resistance to the dominant sexual codings of urban spaces through the appropriation of such spaces by gay men for specifically gay, and often explicitly sexual, purposes. In some cases this happens even in repressive environments such as Edinburgh, where certain "cruising grounds" (and other sites for gay male sexual encounters) have become well established. In such cases, however, the contest is often relatively low-profile and circumscribed; if and when the alternative sexual uses of a space become widely publicized, representatives of the dominant culture are usually able to reappropriate the space in their own image. Thus processes of oppression still dominate in the creation of "gay geographies" in these cities. In certain others, however, such as London and Sydney, such conflicts can be an ongoing and tremendously important element in the process of gay male identity formation.

London features a great deal of this sort of conflict. The city is huge, and there exists a correspondingly enormous and diverse set of gay male (and related) sexual subcultures, organized particularly (though hardly exclusively) around both commodified and noncommodified forms of sexual consumption (Binnie, 1992b). Compared to U.S. cities of comparable scale (e.g., New York and Los Angeles), London's many sites of sexual consumption are quite dispersed geographically. While relatively small-scale gay commercial zones have developed in a few areas, such as around Old Compton Street in the West End, much more common are small and discreetly situated collections of establishments in very diverse settings (ranging from the upscale and trendy borough of Islington, to the somewhat transient and "sleazy" Earl's Court area in the west, to the quite diverse Brixton area in south London, where predominantly white gays and a substantial number of non-gay-identified blacks share neighborhoods). Service-oriented organizations and institutions, especially AIDS service organizations, are also important but tend to be geographically dispersed, small-scale, and poorly supported. Similarly, the entire Greater London area has very few full-service gay and lesbian bookshops. The largest is located in a very upmarket area (Bloomsbury) with no other identifiable gay institutions nearby—save for one pub and a park, Russell Square, where a modest amount of gay male cruising takes place at night (Bell, Binnie, Cream, & Valentine, 1994).

What is much more common in London, as a source of gay male identity and a feature of gay male identity politics, is the phenomenon of gay men challenging and appropriating, through both their actions and their self-representations, everyday spaces and places for specifically and openly transgressive purposes. Frequently these include attempts to convert (or defend) certain public spaces as sites for various forms of nontraditional sexual behavior. Other attempts are made simply to expose and subvert the dominant sexualizations of public and semipublic places such as streets, parks, and clubs, as well as the more abstract spaces of popular culture. Thus struggles such as a recent one to protect the use of bushes and toilets in Hampstead Heath (a large park in the very upmarket Hampstead area) for specifically sexual purposes, and the continued highlighting of the *Spanner* case (which involves an appeal to the European High Court of the conviction and imprisonment of several British men for engaging in consensual sadomasochistic sex) through demonstrations such as 1993's "S&M Pride March," are probably much more powerful shapers of gay men's consciousnesses and identities in London and the United Kingdom generally than are more liberal political strategies (Figure 7.2). They are symbols of a clear, unequivocal, and tangible form of oppression from which the primary form of escape often seems to be defiance.

Similarly, the London-based British gay press is more characterized by discussions of how to develop and define an appropriate and distinctly gay sexual ethic and style, as well as other internal, often cultural debates, than with discussions of how to achieve particular political ends within British society. Even in those arenas where gay culture is clearly engaged with and informed by traditional economic and political institutions, for example, in mainstream popular culture, especially popular music and the "clubbing" scene, it is clear that the transgressive homoeroticization of these sites, not their symbolism as icons of economic or political "success," is the source of much of their popularity.

These features of gay male culture and identity in London, which can also be found, at smaller scales, in the other cities studied, constitute what I call a "cultural politics of resistance." This is a form of social practice that involves the contesting of dominant values outside formal political and economic institutions. At the same time, there is a deep and consciously strategic aspect to this form of cultural resis-

FIGURE 7.2. "No sexual freedom, please. We're British"—placard in Central London.

tance and identity formation. The British group Outrage, for example, while modeled in some ways on American "direct action" groups like Queer Nation and Act-Up, and founded by an Australian-born activist, Peter Tatchell, probably exploits and exposes contradictions in non-gay-identified cultural spaces such as Parliament and the Anglican church more shrewdly and effectively than do its U.S. counterparts. Recently, for example, Outrage was successful in forcing a high-ranking Anglican church official to declare his sexual "ambiguity."

In terms of urbanization, these sorts of identity politics result, as in Edinburgh, in a relative lack of engagement with many of the formal institutions of power with which other, especially American, gay male communities do typically engage. But this does not mean they are irrelevant to the processes we call urbanization. On the contrary, these various conflicts over sexual meanings in space have produced urban and other cultural forms that are arguably much more openly sexualized and sexually expressive, and in that sense liberated, than their counterparts elsewhere. To be sure, few of the articulations of gay male identity politics and urbanization discussed here have produced anything in the way of effective resistance to certain other power relations (e.g., class, gender, and racial ones), but this does not alter the fact that they shape urban physical and cultural landscapes in important ways.

Urban Spectacle, Social Democracy, and the Management of Success

A fourth and final form that the relationship between gay male identity politics and urbanization can take involves the management and celebration of political successes, including the production of gay-oriented spectacles in city centers, such as each of these cities' annual gay and lesbian pride celebrations. It is perhaps best represented, however, by Sydney's annual Gay and Lesbian Mardi Gras.

In Sydney, the largest and arguably the most economically and culturally diverse center of population in Australia (Horvath, Harrison, & Dowling, 1989), the links between this form of identity politics and urbanization may at first glance appear similar to the place-based, territorial empowerment model discussed above. For example, Sydney has at least one well-defined, visible gay male commercial and residential district in and around Oxford Street and the neighboring suburbs of Darlinghurst, Paddington, and Surry Hills, as well as two or three somewhat less visible and more "mixed" ones in the modestly gentrified suburbs of Glebe, Annandale, and Newtown (Leese, 1993; Wotherspoon, 1991). In a process similar to that which was described in Minneapolis, the Oxford Street concentration has served as a staging ground for very successful campaigns to achieve economic and political empowerment at both the local and national scales. The area's Member (MP) of the New South Wales Parliament, for example, is a non-party-affiliated woman who, while straight-identified, has been a relentless and uncompromising voice for gay political rights *and* sexual freedom. When it appeared in early 1995 as if she might hold the balance of power in forming a new state government in New South Wales, she threatened to hold the process hostage until she secured assurances from potential coalition partners that a reform package including full recognition of same-sex partnerships would be passed.

But Sydney's experience can be distinguished from the territorial empowerment model by (among other things) the way in which gay male identity politics there have *not* been disembodied and desexualized, in spite of an enormous range of U.S.-style liberal successes. A liberal gay political agenda has been very rapidly accommodated into a recent social democratic project in Australia. This project has commanded a more or less bipartisan consensus at the federal level and is largely institutionalized in local Sydney area (but not necessarily New South Wales State) politics as well. The consensus involves substantial government commitments—at least as compared with Britain and the United States—to multicultural programming and policies which extend to gay and lesbian groups. HIV and AIDS education and prevention campaigns that target gay men, for example, are comparatively well funded and among the most effective in the "developed" world (Figure 7.3). Furthermore, their sometimes graphic sexualization is generally accepted not just as necessary from a public health standpoint but as the "right" thing to do from the standpoint of respecting a minority culture. Similarly, Australian immigration policies allow for the same-sex partners of Australian nationals and permanent residents to immigrate on the basis of "affectional ties"; the federal and most state governments now recognize gay relationships as families and/or de facto "marriages" (indeed, the next Australian census will officially count them as such); and gay institutions of all kinds, even sex clubs, are generally allowed full participation in and access to most public facilities and institutions (especially, again, in Sydney). When a group of Christian conservatives backed by a number of federal MPs from both major parties, for instance, objected to the broadcast of the annual Sydney Gay and Lesbian Mardi Gras on national television in 1994, the state-run Australian Broadcasting Company simply refused to budge, citing its mission to reflect the full diversity of Australian society in its broadcasting. This was quite remarkable given the fact that the Mardi Gras parade and party are in

FIGURE 7.3. "Choose Safe Sex"—poster in Central Sydney.

many ways spectacular displays of sexual and gender transgression (McNeil, 1994; Seebohm, 1994). Floats in 1994, for example, included a giant erect penis straddled by hat-waving cowboys, a mock dungeon with shackled, nearly bare-bottomed men in leather, and numerous floats advertising sex clubs. The Mardi Gras is also widely touted both as a minority-culture, event and as a strongly sexualized, tourist attraction. At Sydney's famous Opera House and Circular Quay, for example, banners advertising the Mardi Gras in January prominently feature the names of corporate sponsors, which include sex establishments.

All of this translates into a politics of what I call "managing success" on the part of gay men in Sydney. It manifests itself in, among other things, the production of celebratory spectacles, now as often for non-gay-identified as gay-identified consumption, and in efforts to maintain the gay identities of gay-sponsored or initiated spaces, places, and events. Fear of the loss of identity through assimilation and integration, rather than through repression, is a common preoccupation in gay establishments along Oxford Street, for example (Figure 7.4). Similarly, the all-night Gay and Lesbian Mardi Gras party, which follows the annual parade, has become so popular with non-gay-identified people that in 1994 the organizers began restricting access to members of the predominantly gay Mardi Gras organization, their guests, and (significantly) tourists.

In terms of urbanization, then, Sydney features an articulation with this particular form of identity politics that is surprisingly social democratic. Only in a few other places might one find such a highly sexualized *and* politically successful gay male culture in an urban environment—perhaps in Amsterdam, Copenhagen, or San Francisco. This is, of course, not without its own problems and contradictions. But the fact remains that celebrations of an embodied and sexualized gay culture and a set of political successes in Sydney, strongly linked but nevertheless extending well beyond the boundaries of certain gay-identified territories, have shaped that city's identity and patterns of development.

FIGURE 7.4. A gay "Safe Place" sticker in the window of a restaurant on Oxford Street, Sydney, an area whose gay identity is increasingly under threat.

DISCUSSION: URBANIZATION AND SEXUALITY IN "PLACE"

These variations in the ways in which urbanization and processes of gay male identity formation are linked suggest strong connections to the evolution of class, gender, sexual, and other relations of power at a variety of spatial scales and in the context of specific locales (or "places"). It is, of course, impossible to do justice to the full range of scalar and other articulations producing these various "gay male geographies" in the space available here. Instead, my discussion focuses attention on a set of processes operating primarily at the scale of nation-states. This should not be construed as implying that nation-building and other "national-scale" processes and power relations are intrinsically more important than those operating at other scales. On the contrary, the national scale is highlighted precisely because of its utility in posing the links *between* processes operating at a *variety* of scales (Taylor, 1994, pp. 43–48).

It is perhaps no coincidence that the "success management" form of articulation is particularly evident in Sydney. Marilyn Lake (1994) has pointed out that Australian national identity in general has been linked historically to specific discourses and practices related to race, gender, and sexuality. As she describes these, they also appear to be deeply spatialized. She argues that as both a colonized and a colonizing people in a multicolored and multicultural region of the world, white Australians were involved during much of the 19th and 20th centuries in a nation-building project through which they distinguished themselves from both the "Old World barbarians" of Britain and the "Stone Age primitives" of the South Pacific. Foremost among the differences emphasized were white Australians' opposition to an allegedly widespread British practice of trafficking in white female sex slaves. (Opposition to the British class system would seem to be an obvious feature as well, though Lake does not discuss this.) Defending the white race, and in particular white women, against both the barbarous "Old World" practice of "white slavery" and its "primitive" local counterparts thus became part of a larger project of advancing white supremacy in the South Pacific. This combination of egalitarianism, racism, and sexism was then reflected and reproduced in a variety of formal and informal institutions in Australian society, including the "white Australia" policy on immigration, a particularly complex electoral system including proportional representation, strong labor unions, and a highly eroticized cult of heterosexual masculinity.

The "turn" toward multiculturalism and social democracy in Australia, which has so relatively easily accommodated the predominantly liberal demands of gay people, actually has roots in these traditions and can be read, ironically, as an extension of them. Since the onset of global recession, Australians have become increasingly aware of their precarious position in the world economy. The abandonment of the "white Australia" policy in the 1970s and the embracing of a particularly Asian-focused, but highly flexible, form of multiculturalism are probably more concessions to the reality of Australians' present situation than a signal of any fundamental change in racial, sexual, or gender attitudes. The new ethic is one which is willing to tolerate certain transgressions against the "old" order provided that this results in a perpetuation of the "good life" overall to which most Australians have become accustomed. Nowhere in Australia is this perspective more institutionalized than in Sydney, where economic development strategies, property markets, and the production of highly sexualized cultural symbols, representations, and performances intersect on an almost daily basis to construct that city and its neighborhoods as unique places.

Of course, the "success management" form of articulation is not limited to Sydney. It is present, to varying degrees and in different ways, in most, if not all, of the cities studied. This reflects, at the very least, the variable impact of post-World War II liberalism and recent global restructurings, across all of the societies in which these cities are located. Gay male identities in New Orleans, for example, are also shaped by highly sexualized spectacles such as that city's own Mardi Gras and its strong historical and geographical links to French and Spanish colonialism in the Caribbean, as well as to Catholicism. And while this reflects a complex set of linkages that may in superficial ways be similar to those operating in Sydney, other processes that are more specifically "American" are also at work and would appear to have an even stronger impact on the construction of gay male identities there.

These specifically "American" processes, meanwhile, are linked to a set of foundational discourses that, on the surface, would also appear to have much in common with those of Australian society (and Sydney's local culture in particular). They involve, for example, a myth of classlessness born of a liberal opposition to the British class system and a set of social practices, including slavery and citizenship rights based on race, gender, and property ownership, which are fundamentally classist, racist, and sexist. But the nature of these traditions' engagements with space and their expressions institutionally have been quite different than in Sydney. American liberal institutions, including a particular form of federalism with so-called checks and balances between branches of government, have fundamentally revered the

individual as an economic agent and have viewed property ownership as the ultimate form of free individual expression and democratic participation in society. While rhetorically this venerated individual is represented as abstract and disembodied, he (sic) is almost
universally represented in practice, in both formal institutions, such
as the law, and informal ones, such as myth and folklore, as white,
male, and heterosexual. Those icons of American individualism, the
cowboy and the land developer, for example, are both almost always
represented as straight white men. And each is viewed as a heroic
figure in part because of the way in which he achieves "freedom" and
self-expression through the domination of nature and control/de-
velopment of space. To the extent that women, nonwhites, and sexual
dissidents have traditionally been viewed as part of nature, and thus
something less than fully human in American and other Western societies, this spatial strategy for achieving freedom has also been about
enforcing a particular racial, gender, and sexual order. To be sure,
this is articulated through the prism of local contingencies, but the
result is often consistent in the sense of reproducing a familiar array
of oppressions in a way that is similar in form, at least, if not in all of
its particulars.

One of the great tensions in American society, then, seems to
arise from the contradiction between democratic ideals (narrowly and
abstractly conceived) and more undemocratic "real world" outcomes.
Formal political power is checked at every turn, but civil and other
institutions offer virtually no protection, to either groups or individuals, from the consequences of economic or cultural power becoming
concentrated. Nowhere is this tension more evident than in struggles
against cultural oppression. Struggles over civil and citizenship rights
of the 20th century notwithstanding, most of the gains of women,
nonwhites, nonheterosexuals, and even workers in U.S. society have
come when they have been cast in terms of individual rights and freedoms, and when demands have been backed by some kind of territorially based economic and political power. The movement for women's
suffrage, for example, made its earliest gains in parts of the isolated
and sparsely populated West, and contemporary feminist and lesbian
cultures frequently have strong territorial bases as well—especially, as
several studies (Adler & Brenner, 1992; Beyer, 1992; Grebinoski, 1993;
Novatney, 1997; Rothenberg & Almgren, 1992; Rothenberg, 1995)
have shown, in otherwise marginalized urban and rural areas. This
makes these areas' inhabitants, like many of their gay male counterparts, "pioneers" of a sort. The struggles against both slavery and Jim
Crow also had strong territorial political bases, and contemporary
middle-class African American cultures and communities often have

close associations with the colonization of inner-ring suburbs or formerly all-white middle-class neighborhoods in cities. The dominant forms of gay male culture in the United States, with their strongly politicized territorial bases and links to political-economic practices such as gentrification, are very much in keeping with this tradition (even while they vary considerably with local histories, geographies, and other contingencies).

These particularly "American" articulations of urbanization and gay male identity formation also find expression in Britain and Australia, as the "pink economies" of Sydney's Oxford Street and London's gay male commercial enclaves suggest. But the peculiarly depoliticized, yet still comparatively radical, forms of both place-based domination and place-based cultural resistance present in London and Edinburgh appear to reflect a set of forces that are, in many respects, distinctly British. The generally repressive institutional environment of British society, which often quite straightforwardly serves to enforce rigid racial, gender, and sexual orders as well as the class system, seems on the face of things to do so primarily in the service of class. But this kind of analysis is of course overly simplistic and functionalist, as the links between Scottish identity, the Scottish legal system, and the "magic circle" affair shows. Such institutions and practices are also tied to a much broader and ongoing project of nation building in the United Kingdom, one in which "Britishness" is defined in racial terms as well as in terms of the class system (Gilroy, 1991). Jon Binnie (1992b, 1994) and David Bell (1995) have each argued that "Britishness" is also defined in terms of a particular set of heterosexual identities and practices; and Nuala Johnson (1994, 1995) has discussed the gendering of this project as it pertains to Anglo–Irish relations. Add to this the class system's association with a landed aristocracy, and the fact that space is itself a scarce commodity on that small island, and it is perhaps no surprise that forms of cultural resistance have focused on the contesting of everyday spaces and places at a microscale, rather than struggles aimed at accessing formal power through the permanent control and transformation of space at larger scales.

But this begs the questions of why these forms of both domination and resistance are so strongly sexualized and why the self-consciously radical politicization of sexualized cultural resistance is, as I think I have correctly observed, disproportionately the province of middle-class, urban (and specifically center-city) white gay men. This may be due, in part, to the relative lack of social mobility in Britain. Because of this, the opportunity costs associated with sexual defiance in these social and spatial contexts are, in a certain sense, low. There is simply less of a *reason* to desexualize gay culture in an environment where institutional vehicles for social mobility, based on desexualized abstractions, are relatively absent. Related to this, there are fewer alternatives to sex as a basis on which to define gay culture in Britain than in either the United States or Australia. Gentrification and other territorially based economic and political practices are less feasible, and so is participation in an officially sanctioned project of "multiculturalism." Finally, dominant interests in British society may actually be more comfortable and familiar with middle- and upper-class urban radicals—especially white male sex-radicals—than with working-class, nonwhite, nonurban, and female ones. It can accommodate them personally while undermining their critiques of the class system, urbanization, and possibly even patriarchy, by labeling them as hypocrites (for indulging their privilege) or "eccentrics" and tolerating them. Hence it may not be as dangerous to be a middle-class urban sex-radical in Britain—especially if one is white, male, and in London—as it is to be a working-class, nonwhite, nonurban, or female one.

CONCLUSION

I am interpreting the relationships between urbanization and dominant forms of gay male identity politics in these six cities as embedded within very traditional discourses and social practices at a variety of scales, from nation-building projects to local economic development strategies and processes of place creation. These are, in turn, deeply gendered, sexualized, racialized, and class structured. These identities do have inherently radical potential and content, but in all of the contexts discussed I am interpreting this as fairly effectively neutralized by institutions that offer opportunities for survival to middle-class, urban, white gay men. Does this mean that middle-class, urban, white gay men in these places are simply agents of a set of conservative interests? In some ways, yes. But this kind of contradictory position always exists when a population that is marginalized in one way but not others struggles to survive and thrive. And the situation is not without its costs even to those who are supposedly co-opted. The urban white working classes of the United States, for example, are implicated in a form of racism that has provided them with certain privileges as whites while dividing them from others with whom they share certain class interests. The consequences of this division have clearly been visited upon American workers as a whole in the past two decades or so. Similarly, middle-class, urban, white gay men's participation in classist, sexist, and racist discourses and practices in these various places has certainly driven a wedge between us and other non-heterosexually-identified people. In the long-run this has cleared the way for the relatively unimpeded rise of a powerful antigay Right determined to roll back the few very minimal gains that, in recent years, we have begun to make.

A more useful conclusion is that in all the cities reviewed dominant gay male cultural identities are profoundly structured by interlinked discourses and deeply entrenched, strongly interconnected (yet contingently articulated) practices of class, race, gender, and sexual relations. These have evolved in unique ways over time and space but seem to serve the common purpose of protecting the interests of capital and white heterosexual masculinity. If we are to challenge this effectively we must understand both the depth of these interconnections and the historically and geographically specific forms that they take.

NOTES

1. See Knopp (1995) for a defense of "the urban" as a theoretical object of analysis.

2. I recognize that this distinction is problematic. Again, see Knopp (1995).

3. By "dominant" I mean those which are most visible and powerful vis-à-vis non-gay-identified institutions and politics and which either claim or are treated by other powerful interests in society as representative of gay men as a whole.

4. These had to do primarily with sexual activity that was taking place in adult bookstores, gay bathhouses, and certain public parks.

5. Most recently, in 1994, a very conservative, Christian Coalition-backed former broadcaster was elected to the U.S. Senate from the state of Minnesota over a conventional liberal, who carried less than 10 of the state's 87 counties.

6. Actually, certain other economic and demographic conditions—especially the job structures of local economies—are also important (see Lauria & Knopp, 1985).

REFERENCES

Adler, S., & Brenner, J. (1992). Gender and space: Lesbians and gay men in the city. *International Journal of Urban and Regional Research, 16,* 24–34.

Bech, H. (1993, June). *Citysex: Representing lust in public.* Paper presented at the Geographies of Desire Conference, Netherlands' Universities Institute for Coordination of Research in Social Sciences, Amsterdam.

Bell, D. (1995). Pleasure and danger: The paradoxical spaces of sexual citizenship. *Political Geography, 14,* 139–153.

Bell, D., Binnie, J., Cream, J., & Valentine, G. (1994). All hyped up and no place to go. *Gender, Place and Culture, 1,* 31–47.

Bell, D., & Valentine, G. (Eds.) (1995). *Mapping desire.* London: Routledge.

Beyer, J. (1992, August). *Sexual minorities and geography.* Paper presented at the 27th International Geographical Congress, Washington, DC.

Binnie, J. (1992a, September). *Fucking among the ruins: Postmodern sex in postindustrial places.* Paper presented at the Sexuality and Space Network Conference on Lesbian and Gay Geographies?, University College, London.

Binnie, J. (1992b, September). *An international cock-tail party: The spatiality of fetishism.* Paper presented at the Sexuality and Space Network Conference on Lesbian and Gay Geographies?, University College, London.

Binnie, J. (1993, July). *Invisible cities/hidden geographies: Sexuality and the city.* Paper presented at the Social Policy and the City Conference, University of Liverpool.

Binnie, J. (1994, August). *Invisible Europeans: Sexual citizenship in the new Europe.* Paper presented to a special session on Gender and the Politics of International Migration, Regional Conference of the International Geographical Union, Prague.

Blasius, M. (1994). G*ay and lesbian politics: Sexuality and the emergence of a new ethic.* Philadelphia: Temple University Press.

Bondi, L. (1992). Gender symbols in urban landscapes. *Progress in Human Geography, 16,* 157–170.

Brown, M. (1994). The work of city politics: Citizenship through employment in the local response to AIDS. *Environment and Planning D: Society and Space, 26,* 873–894.

Brown, M. (1995). Sex, scale and the "new urban politics": HIV-prevention strategies from Yaletown, Vancouver. In D. Bell & G. Valentine (Eds.), *Mapping desire* (pp. 245–263). London: Routledge.

Castells, M. (1983). *The city and the grassroots.* Berkeley: University of California Press.

Chauncey, G. (1994). *Gay New York: Gender, urban culture, and the making of the gay male world, 1890–1940.* New York: Basic Books.

Geltmaker, T. (1992). The queer nation acts up: Health care, politics, and sexual diversity in the County of Angels. *Environment and Planning D: Society and Space, 10,* 609–650.

Gilroy, P. (1991). *There ain't no black in the Union Jack: The cultural politics of race and nation.* Chicago: University of Chicago Press.

Grebinoski, J. (1993, April). *Out north: Gays and lesbians in the Duluth, Minnesota–Superior, Wisconsin area.* Paper presented at the Annual Conference of the Association of American Geographers, Atlanta, GA.

Grosz, E. (1992). Bodies—cities. In B. Colomina (Ed.), *Sexuality and space* (pp. 241–253). New York: Princeton Architectural Press.

Harvey, D. (1973). *Social justice and the city.* Baltimore: Johns Hopkins University Press.

Harvey, D. (1985). *The urbanization of capital.* Baltimore: Johns Hopkins University Press.

Harvey, D. (1989). *The condition of postmodernity.* Cambridge, MA: Blackwell.

Harvey, D. (1992). Social justice, postmodernism, and the city. *International Journal of Urban and Regional Research, 16,* 588–601.

Horvath, R., Harrison, G., & Dowling, R. (1989). *Sydney: A social atlas.* Sydney: Sydney University Press.

Johnson, N. (1994). Sculpting heroic histories: Celebrating the centenary of the 1798 rebellion in Ireland. *Transactions of the Institute of British Geographers, 19,* 78–93.

Johnson, N. (1995). Cast in stone: Monuments, geography and nationalism. *Environment and Planning D: Society and Space, 13,* 51–65.

Ketteringham, W. (1979, April). *Gay public space and the urban landscape: A preliminary assessment.* Paper presented at the Annual Meeting of the Association of American Geographers, Philadelphia, PA.

Knopp, L. (1986, May). *Gentrification and gay community development: A case study of Minneapolis.* Paper presented at the Annual Meeting of the Association of American Geographers, Minneapolis, MN.

Knopp, L. (1987). Social theory, social movements and public policy: Recent accomplishments of the gay and lesbian movements in Minneapolis, Minnesota. *International Journal of Urban and Regional Research, 11,* 243–261.

Knopp, L. (1990a). Some theoretical implications of gay involvement in an urban land market. *Political Geography Quarterly, 9,* 337–352.

Knopp, L. (1990b). Exploiting the rent-gap: The theoretical significance of using illegal appraisal schemes to encourage gentrification in New Orleans. *Urban Geography, 11,* 48–64.

Knopp, L. (1992). Sexuality and the spatial dynamics of capitalism. *Environment and Planning D: Society and Space, 10,* 651–669.

Knopp, L. (1994). Social justice, *sexuality* and the city. *Urban Geography, 15,* 644–660.

Knopp, L. (1995). Sexuality and urban space: A framework for analysis. In D. Bell & G. Valentine (Eds.), *Mapping desire* (pp. 149–161). London: Routledge.

Knopp, L. (1997). Rings, circles and perverted justice: Gay judges and moral panic in contemporary Scotland. In M. Keith & S. Pile (Eds.), *Geographies of resistance* (pp. 168–183). London: Routledge.

Kobayashi, A., & Peake, L. (1994). Unnatural discourse: "Race" and gender in geography. *Gender, Place and Culture, 1,* 225–243.

Lake, M. (1994). Between Old World "barbarism" and Stone Age "primitivism: the double difference of the white Australian feminist. In N. Grieve & A. Burns (Eds.), *Australian women: Contemporary feminist thought* (pp. 80–91). Oxford: Oxford University Press.

Lauria, M., & Knopp, L. (1985). Toward an analysis of gay involvement in the urban renaissance. *Urban Geography, 6,* 152–269.

Lees, L. (1994). Rethinking gentrification: Beyond the positions of economics or culture. *Progress in Human Geography, 18,* 137–150.

Leese, A. (1993). *The spatial distribution of subcultures: Gay men in Sydney.*

Undergraduate thesis, Bachelor of Town Planning Program, University of New South Wales, Kensington, NSW, Australia.

Levine, M. (1979). Gay ghetto. *Journal of Homosexuality, 4,* 363–377.

McCrone, D. (1992). *Understanding Scotland: The sociology of a stateless nation.* London: Routledge.

McNeil, P. (1994). The Sydney Gay and Lesbian Mardi Gras party: Masquerade and muscle culture. In R. Aldrich (Ed.), *Gay perspectives II: More essays in Australian gay culture* (pp. 223–244). Sydney: University Printing Service.

Moos, A. (1989). The grassroots in action: Gays and seniors capture the local state in West Hollywood, California. In M. Dear & J. Wolch (Eds.), *The power of geography* (pp. 351–369). Boston: Unwin Hyman.

Munt, S. (1995). The lesbian *flaneur.* In D. Bell & G. Valentine (Eds.), *Mapping desire* (pp. 114–125). London: Routledge.

Novatney, D. (1997). *Settlement patterns of gays and lesbians in Duluth and Superior.* Undergraduate senior project, Department of Geography, University of Minnesota–Duluth.

Paris, C. (1983). The myth of urban politics. *Environment and Planning D: Society and Space, 1,* 89–108.

Peake, L. (1993). Race and sexuality: Challenging the patriarchal structuring of urban social space. *Environment and Planning D: Society and Space, 11,* 415–432.

Rose, G. (1993). *Feminism and geography: The limits to geographical knowledge.* Cambridge, UK: Polity Press.

Rothenberg, T. (1995). "And she told two friends": Lesbians creating urban social space. In D. Bell & G. Valentine (Eds.), *Mapping desire* (pp. 165–181). London: Routledge.

Rothenberg, T., & Almgren, H. (1992, August). *Social politics of space and place in New York City's lesbian and gay communities.* Paper presented to the 27th International Geographical Congress, Washington, DC.

Seebohm, K. (1994). The nature and meaning of the Sydney Mardi Gras in a landscape of inscribed social relations. In R. Aldrich (Ed.), *Gay perspectives II: More essays in Australian gay culture* (pp. 193–222). Sydney: University Printing Service.

Soja, E. (1989). *Postmodern geographies: The reassertion of space in critical social theory.* London: Verso.

Taylor, P. (1994). *Political geography: World-economy, nation-state and locality.* Harlow, Essex, UK: Longman.

Weightman, B. (1980). Gay bars as private places. *Landscape, 23,* 9–16.

Wilson, E. (1991). *The sphinx in the city.* London: Virago.

Winters, C. (1979). The social identity of evolving neighborhoods. *Landscape, 23,* 8–14.

Wotherspoon, G. (1991). *City of the plain: History of a gay sub-culture.* Sydney, Australia: Hale & Iremonger.

CHAPTER 8

Sexing the City

Liz Bondi

There now exists a considerable body of feminist scholarship concerned with urban environments (see McDowell, 1993a, 1993b, for a review). Within this work, urban landscapes are generally viewed as the product of patriarchal gender relations. Interpretations vary in detail: sometimes, the influence of men—as planners, as architects—in the creation of urban forms is highlighted, implying that women live in an environment that is literally man-made (e.g., Roberts, 1991); sometimes the emphasis is on the persistence of stereotypical views of gender roles within the assumptions guiding urban design, which have particularly detrimental effects on women (e.g., Tivers, 1985); sometimes the urban environment is seen more as a product of conflict over gender divisions, expressing rapidly outmoded moments in the continuous renegotiation of gender roles (e.g., Mackenzie, 1989).

Since its inception, this tradition has been attentive to empirical differences among women, most especially to differences of class, race, and ethnicity. However, it has become increasingly apparent that many of these acknowledgments of difference are not in fact adequate because the conceptual frameworks being used tend to set up class, racial, and ethnic norms that position certain groups (typically middle-class, white, Western women) as the standard from which others differ. This is deeply ethnocentric. Consequently, within contemporary feminist studies, a good deal of effort is being devoted to dealing with difference conceptually as well as empirically (see, e.g., Ramazanoglu, 1989; Bacchi, 1990; Spelman, 1990; Mohanty, Russo, & Torres, 1991; hooks, 1992; Ware, 1992; West & Fenstermaker, 1995). To date, the main way in which this has been tackled is through a notion of the mutual constitution of different dimensions of power and domination and of different aspects of identity. As Linda McDowell (1991, p. 126) puts it:

> Just as in the past we have pointed out the inadequacies of add-
> ing in gender as another variable in conventional analyses of
> geographical problems, neither can the experiences of Black
> women simply be incorporated into feminist analyses by adding
> in the differences between, say, West Indian and Asian women.
> Herein lies the contradiction at the heart of feminist politics
> and theorizing: how to deal with the *contradictory* bases of divi-
> sions between women. Black and White women may have inter-
> ests in common with each other but they also have interests that
> cut across these common ones. The same point is valid for divi-
> sions based on class position. (emphasis in original)

Thus, McDowell argues that gender is constituted differently for women and men of different classes, races and so on, and she conceptualizes gender as fragmented by the existence of other dimensions of social differentiation and inequality so that there are multiple identities within the categories "women" and "men."

In this chapter I approach related issues from a different angle. I focus on the relationships between sex, gender, and sexuality, and in so doing seek to add to the fracturing of gender categories. Rather than thinking in terms of the social construction of difference through multiple dimensions of power, I draw on feminist readings of psychoanalysis to evoke decentered, fragmented, and self-contradictory conceptions of the human subject. In particular, I argue that gender is far more complex than implied by the categories "women" and "men," and that aspects of gender relate in complex ways to sex and sexuality. The strategy I adopt inevitably invokes dichotomies, for example, between sociological and psychoanalytic perspectives, between externally constituted identities and internally experienced selves, or most simply between "outside" and "inside." But it is my intention to unsettle these dichotomous formulations even as I deploy them and so to foster less rigid understandings of gender (see also Bondi, 1997).

To develop my case, in the next section I argue that existing feminist interpretations of urban landscapes have, in the main, adopted a concept of gender that has tended to close off questions about sex. I then discuss some contemporary contributions to feminist theory in order to reopen some of the boundaries between sex, gender, and sexuality. Finally, I offer a partial and schematic analysis of two urban landscapes affected by gentrification in order to illustrate something of the potential implications of all this for feminist urban studies.

GENDERED AS DE-SEXED

Feminist geographers have been strongly influenced by a distinction between sex and gender in which the former refers to biological differences and the latter refers to socially created distinctions (see also Longhurst, 1995). One of the attractions of this distinction is that it has allowed us to focus on gender as something entirely separable from biological sex. For example, in a pathbreaking textbook, the Women and Geography Study Group of the IBG (Institute of British Geography) stated:

> We use the term "gender" to refer to *socially created* distinctions between femininity and masculinity, while the term "sex" is used to refer to biological differences between men and women. . . . [W]e are concerned to introduce . . . a geography which explicitly takes into account the socially created gender structure of society. (1984, p. 21, emphasis in original)

This notion of gender as separable from sex continues to dominate work in urban studies concerned with gender issues. Some analyses focus on women and men as categories of people, divided also by class, race, ethnicity, and so on. One such example is Alan Warde's (1991) discussion of gentrification as consumption in which he argued that the emergence of gentrifiers is best understood in terms of changes in gender divisions within particular fractions of the middle class. He emphasized the distribution of paid work and domestic labor between women and men, and conceptualized women's and men's behavior in terms of rational responses to external economic and cultural pressures. In so doing he fostered the impression that gender is constituted principally through divisions of labor in paid employment and unpaid domestic work. In the context of repeated and familiar understandings of gender that associate it with these forms of work and not with other facets of life, this perpetuates the idea that gender is dissociated from anything sexual—that it is "sex-free."

Other studies have emphasized how gender divisions vary geographically and historically and have examined how different versions of femininity and masculinity are constructed and negotiated. An example is my own discussion of gentrification in which I argued for a shift away from gender as a category toward consideration of gender as a social process (Bondi, 1991). While arguing against the treatment of gender as a fixed attribute of individuals and advocating instead a relational concept of gender, like Alan Warde I drew particular attention to changes in the position of women in the family and the labor market. Only when discussing cultural production did I refer to sexuality, at which point I cited heterosexual imagery associated with gentrification (p. 195). However, the aim of this brief discussion was to *extract* representations of gender rather than to engage with issues of sexuality:

> [F]rontier mythology . . . casts the urban pioneer as a hero whose heterosexual masculinity can scarcely be in doubt . . . [and] that which is encountered, whether viewed as an urban wilderness or as an eroticized "other" is feminine. . . . The highly polarized representations of masculinity and femininity embedded within these accounts sit uneasily with claims that gentrification entails a "loosening of . . . sexual apartheid." (Bondi, 1991, p.195)

In the context of a predominantly "sex-free" concept of gender, this passage reads as a short reconnoiter into the territory of sexuality in order to demonstrate the persistence of conventional representations of masculinity and femininity. Having made the point, I rapidly retreated to the familiar (safer?) terrain of gender. Thus, the move served to reinforce my commitment to a concept of gender devoid of anything sexual.

While the expressed intention of the sex–gender distinction widely adopted in feminist urban studies has been to exclude questions of biological sex and to emphasize that gender divisions are socially constructed, one of the effects has been to exclude questions of sex in the sense of sexuality and sexual practice. Put another way, we have tended to be insensitive to the double meaning of "sex": while intending to set aside sex in the sense of biological difference, we have also set aside sex as cultural practice. Thus, despite the feminist claim that "the personal is political" and despite the related feminist critique of a public–private dichotomy, by relying on a concept of gender *as opposed to* sex we have largely avoided matters often regarded as personal or private. Maybe one of the reasons for this is that we remain somewhat bashful, perhaps embarrassed, or even squeamish, about sex, preferring instead to deal with a disembodied, de-sexed and de-eroticized concept of gender (see also Bell, 1991). In making this claim I want to emphasize that I am not arguing that it is because feminist geographers are committed to social analysis that we have largely avoided questions of sex and sexuality. Rather, I am suggesting that the term gender has invoked a particular approach to the social that downplays if not excludes such issues.

In recent years this has been counteracted in certain ways. Most importantly, the development of a body of gay and lesbian studies of the city has begun to transform urban studies itself (a small selection of contributions to this work include Lauria & Knopp, 1985; Adler & Brenner, 1992; Knopp, 1992; Bell, Binnie, Cream, & Valentine, 1994; Bell & Valentine, 1995; Forest, 1995; Quilley, 1995). Prominent within this work are studies concerned primarily with previously neglected groups, typically defined in terms of sexual orientation. This approach continues a tradition of examining categories of people rather than issues of sexual practice and desire. One consequence of this is that these studies do little to challenge the notion that markers of identity, including sexual orientation as well as gender, are separable from sexual practice. However there are important exceptions to this, that seek to show how sexuality permeates all aspects of life including urban space. For example, Gill Valentine (1993) has shown how dominant forms of heterosexuality are inscribed on urban space to the particular detriment of lesbians. And Rachel Pain's analysis of sexual violence and fear of crime reinforces a view of urban space as sexualized in a manner deeply oppressive to women (Pain, 1991). Other studies view the sexual qualities of space more positively. While many relate to men's experiences, and especially to gay men's experiences of urban life, a few also stress the opportunities afforded to women (see, e.g., Bell et al., 1994; Wilson, 1991). While this work does not directly address the concept of gender, it certainly undermines the "sex-free" tendency that has developed in feminist urban studies. My intention in this chapter is to contribute to this increasingly wide-ranging work that in one way or another sexualizes the city by exploring further the interconnections between sex, gender, and sexuality.

SEX, GENDER, AND SEXUALITY

The concept of gender that I have argued dominates feminist urban studies has been subject to criticism within contemporary feminist theory. I discuss in turn some points relating to the sex–gender distinction, to the complexity of gender, and to the relationship between gender and sexuality. In so doing I make the case for understanding sex, gender, and sexuality as complex and complexly related terms.

The Sex–Gender Distinction

The sex–gender distinction has been subjected to a powerful and wide-ranging critique. The distinction is generally attributed to psychological research on transsexualism, which argued for the primacy of gender over sex in the formation of identity as feminine or masculine (Stoller, 1968). It was widely taken up in feminist scholarship from the late 1960s onward for two related reasons. First, it offered a straight-forward framework within which to refute claims that sought to natu-ralize (to attribute to biology) differences between women and men, and within which to argue for the overriding significance of gender. Secondly, and following from this, it offered a basis on which to advo-cate forms of social change that would emancipate women.

While the sex–gender distinction undoubtedly played an impor-tant role at a particular moment in feminist theory and feminist prac-tice, in recent years an increasing number of commentators have be-gun asking whether it has outlived its usefulness (for one of the earli-est such comments, see Edwards, 1989, p. 1). I do not attempt to present a comprehensive critique in this chapter but merely point out three lines of argument.

First, the last three decades have not provided convincing evi-dence of the liberatory potential of gender: just because it is socially constituted doesn't mean that gender can be changed any more eas-ily than sex (Evans, 1994). This is one factor in the increasing interest feminists have shown in psychoanalytic theory, which has been used both as an adjunct to social analyses of women's subordination and as a means for exploring the limits of sociopolitical interventions (for an example of the former see Mitchell, 1974, and for an example of the latter see Gallop, 1982; for more general discussions of the con-tribution of psychoanalysis to feminism, see Brennan, 1991, and Gatens, 1991).

Secondly, the construction of a sex–gender distinction, in terms of the biological versus the social, links it closely to oppositions be-tween nature and culture and between the body and the mind. Within this kind of framework there seem to be two possible interpretations of the relationship between sex and gender. Either gender corresponds directly to sex, implying that culture serves to elaborate or embellish nature. Or gender invokes an idea of the transcendence of mind over body, in which case the gendered mind floats free of the sexed body. In both cases it is not clear why we need a sex–gender distinction at all. If, as in the first case, gender necessarily follows from sex, how can we distinguish the one from the other? We may wish to challenge existing sexual stereotypes, but this is likely to be hampered rather than advanced by debates about where sex ends and gender begins. Conversely, if, as in the second case, gender is wholly disconnected from sex we can deal with a mind that is untrammeled by bodily con-cerns. But such a mind would surely not be divided by gender. In practice, feminists have shown how the universal human being to which the latter position appeals is implicitly male. The point is that the sex–gender distinction reinforces a system of conceptual dichotomies that covertly position maleness or masculinity as the human norm (see, e.g., Jay, 1981; Lloyd, 1989; Butler, 1990; Grosz, 1994; Moore, 1994).

Thirdly, the sex–gender distinction implies that biology and therefore sex are somehow presocial or free of the social. But feminist critiques of science have convincingly demonstrated that biological thinking is steeped in social thinking: theories and assumptions about the nature of society pervade attempts to explore the nature of nature (see, e.g., Harding, 1986; FitzSimmons, 1989; Haraway, 1990; Soper, 1995).

These criticisms of the sex–gender distinction require that we reexamine the interplay between mind and body and between the social and the biological. In other words, we need to take embodiment seriously, a point now being made by several feminist geographers (e.g., Rose, 1993; Longhurst, 1995; McDowell & Court, 1994; Cream, 1995; Johnston, 1996). In so doing, the idea of gender becomes rather more complex than is generally admitted within feminist urban studies. Here, I draw on Judith Butler's (1990) analysis *Gender Trouble*, into which I enter via psychoanalytic theory (see also Butler, 1993).

The Complexity of Gender

For Sigmund Freud, femininity and masculinity—our identities as women and men—are difficult psychical achievements that depend upon the repression of sexual desires and that are always problematically connected to anatomy. Precisely how the creation of gendered subjects is theorized varies between versions of psychoanalysis, but all suggest that subjectivity is necessarily fractured. In other words, we are not coherent, unified beings, but operate with internal splits, sometimes within the level of consciousness (in which case we experience ourselves as divided, as argued by object relations theorists), and sometimes because of the influence of unconscious wishes (which are likely to disrupt or contradict our conscious sense of self, as argued by Lacanian theorists). In this context, "gender . . . identities are precarious, provisional and constantly undermined by the play of desires" (Weeks, 1985, p. 148). Rather than expressing some intrinsic existential reality, gender identities are more like masks or fictions we create in order to sustain myths about our subjective integrity, which we need to operate within our rule-governed social milieus (on womanliness as masquerade, see Rivière, 1986, a paper first published in 1929, and the commentary on it by Heath, 1986).

The notion of internal fracturing is sometimes viewed as problematic for a feminism sensitive to differences among women because it appears to undermine the coherence of experientially grounded statements of identity in terms of class, race, and so on, as well as gender. Certainly, if we accept subjective fragmentation as a condition of human existence, we must acknowledge that there are no coherent, authentic identities integral to our beings. But this does not mean that we can do without myths of identity, and I would argue that class, gender, sexual, and racial identities are politically as well as existentially necessary fictions (see Fuss, 1989) . From this perspective, a feminist politics of difference can be strengthened by understanding something of how these strategic rather than ontological forms of identification work.

The mask-like quality of gender is highlighted where conventional codes are transgressed, for example, in transsexualism, or in drag, or in butch/femme lesbian identities. These deploy a "distinction between inner and outer psychic space . . . [to] . . . mock . . . both the expressive model of gender and . . . the notion of a true gender identity" (Butler, 1990, p. 137). In the case of drag, the cross-dresser is in effect adopting a feminine appearance as the surface for an underlying masculine embodiment, but in so doing suggests precisely the opposite: that the surface appearance is masculine but the inner essence is feminine. The contradiction between these two statements destabilizes the distinction between inner and outer, between essence and appearance, between original and imitation. In so doing, drag and other transgressive forms also unsettle the presumption of heterosexuality associated with normative versions of gender identity (see also Epstein & Straub, 1991; Bell et al., 1994).

While it takes transgression to generate this confusion, the effect is to point up the complexity of gender in general. In Judith Butler's words:

> The performance of drag plays upon the distinction between the anatomy of the performer and the gender that is being performed. But we are actually in the presence of three contingent dimensions of significant corporeality: anatomical sex, gender identity, and gender performance. If the anatomy of the performer is already distinct from the gender of the performer, and both of these are distinct from the gender of the performance, then the performance suggests a dissonance not only between sex and performance, but sex and gender, and gender and performance. As much as drag creates a unified picture of "woman" (what its critics often oppose), it also reveals the distinctness of those aspects of gendered experience which are falsely natural-

ized as unity through the regulatory fiction of heterosexual coherence. In imitating gender, drag implicitly reveals the imita-
tive structure of gender itself—as well as its contingency. Indeed,
part of the pleasure, the giddiness of the performance is in the
recognition of a radical contingency in the relation between sex
and gender in the face of cultural configurations of causal uni-
ties that are regularly assumed to be natural and necessary. In
place of the law of heterosexual coherence, we see sex and gender as denaturalized by means of a performance which avows
their distinctness and dramatizes the cultural mechanism of their
fabricated unity. (1990, pp. 137–138; see also Gatens, 1991)

This account suggests that far from abandoning any distinction between sex and gender in favor of a singular sex–gender concept, we
need to differentiate further within, and admit more complexity to,
the sex–gender framework. In its conventional form, the sex–gender
distinction assumes both a straightforward separation between the
biological and the social and a one-to-one correspondence between
them. What I am arguing for instead is a conceptualization that highlights complex tensions and interconnections among what Butler
terms anatomical sex, gender identity, and gender performance. Put
another way, there is an awful lot of difference within the gender of
every individual occupying a particular position defined by gender,
class, race, ethnicity, and so on. (Of course class, race, and ethnicity
are not straightforward categories either, so that there are many other
sources of difference too; see Moore, 1994.)

Gender and Sexuality

Dominant myths about gender eclipse this difference and fuse together gender and sexuality. Thus, heterosexuality is integral to normative versions of gender identity: within a Freudian framework, the
achievement of femininity or of masculinity includes an adoption of
heterosexual object choice and heterosexual intercourse as sexual
aim. This fiction of heterosexual coherence, as Butler expresses it,
whereby heterosexuality appears to be integral to gender identity, is I
think implicit in the unduly coherent and sex-free concept of gender
that dominates feminist urban studies. Symptomatically, heterosexual
orientation is assumed unless otherwise stated. Moreover, where issues of sexuality become explicit, the tendency is to move to a diametrically opposite position in which sexual orientation is treated as
an entirely independent system of differentiation that cuts across gender. The more complex concept of gender for which I have argued

demands a more nuanced approach to questions of sexuality and of the relationship between gender and sexuality. Here I draw out three points from Eve Kosofsky Sedgewick's *Epistemology of the Closet* (1991).

First, while it is undoubtedly important to maintain a distinction between gender and sexuality, which can then be deployed in ways similar to the use of class and gender or class and race as mutually constitutive dimensions of identity and structures of power, gender and sexuality are in certain respects intimately, indeed definitionally, connected. As Sedgewick (1991, p. 31) puts it, "without a concept of gender there could be, quite simply, no concept of homo- or hetero-sexuality."

This observation implies that the relationship between gender and sexuality is qualitatively different from that between, say, gender and class. But the second point I wish to make questions this by resisting the widespread conflation between sexuality and what is generally called "sexual orientation," that is, a binary distinction between homosexual and heterosexual object choice. The term "sexuality" is surely much broader and richer than this implies. Sedgewick offers a lengthy list of potentially significant aspects of sexuality—facets of sexual desire and sexual practices— that need not be directly related to gender or sexual orientation and that might turn out to be more closely related to, say, class or race. Again, we are faced with a lot more difference than is often acknowledged. In summary, Sedgewick (p. 27) argues that "[t]he study of sexuality is not coextensive with the study of gender; correspondingly, antihomophobic inquiry is not coextensive with feminist inquiry. But we can't know in advance how they will be different."

Thirdly, Sedgewick observes that sexuality necessarily invokes associations with biological sex in its reference to "physical sites, acts and rhythms associated . . . with procreation . . . and species survival" (p. 29). But, at the same time, as Freud argued, "the sexual nature of human sexuality has to do precisely with its excess over or potential difference from the bare choreographies of procreation" (p. 29). Thus, sexuality occupies "the full spectrum of positions between the most intimate and the most social, the most predetermined and the most aleatory, the most physically rooted and the most symbolically infused, the most innate and the most learned, the most autonomous and the most relational" (p. 29). This reinforces the importance of tensions and interconnections within the complex nexus of sex, gender, and sexuality.

SEXING THE CITY

These observations about sex, gender, and sexuality challenge the rather narrow interpretation of gender that I have argued dominates feminist urban studies. Quite what the full implications of this challenge might be I do not hazard to guess; neither do I offer anything approximating to an agenda for research. Instead, I seek to sketch out some of the possibilities of a broader and more nuanced interpretation of sex, gender, and sexuality through an empirical study of representations of gentrification, focusing especially on representations of two areas subject to gentrification.

In the course of research on gender and gentrification in the Scottish city of Edinburgh, I have been examining the gender symbolism of some specific urban environments, including two inner-city areas, one of which is very much in transition (the waterfront area of Leith) and one of which is almost wholly gentrified (the area of Stockbridge). In this section, I argue that the notions of conquest and domestication capture some of the cultural meanings associated with their gentrification. I consider the relevance of these terms to the appearance and marketing of owner-occupied residential properties and explore their relevance to representations of prostitution in the two areas, which are significant to the gentrification process in both cases, albeit in rather different ways.

The metaphors of conquest and domestication have strongly sexual connotations. Archetypally, conquest is associated with men and a masculine sexual role, in contrast to domestication, which is associated with women and a feminine sexual role. Thus, conquest alludes to the active pole of an active/passive polarity. It implies detachment from, objectification of, a predatory attitude toward, and the exploitation of that which is conquered. Domestication, by contrast, is associated with taming the wild (in this case the sexual urges of men), and with using subtle skills (feminine wiles) to pacify a brutish aggressor. In its successful accomplishment, domestication is suggestive of intimate connections and interdependence between the domesticator and that which is domesticated, in contrast to the distance between subject and object implied by conquest (see also Kolodny, 1975, 1984). The domestication metaphor alludes to monogamous heterosexual marriage, in which the sexual is intricately connected to emotionally significant relationships, whereas conquest alludes to sexual encounters sharply separated from other relationships. This is very close to one of Sedgewick's dimensions of sexuality: "For some people, it is important that sex be embedded in contexts resonant with meaning, narrative and connectedness with other aspects of life; for other people it is important that they not be; to others it doesn't occur that they might be" (Sedgewick, 1991, p. 25). These sexual connotations have a good deal of resonance in representations of Leith and Stockbridge, respectively. By examining their operation I explore some of the complex connections between the concepts of sex, gender and sexuality.

Urban Conquest in Leith

Leith was once a flourishing port, and its many fine Georgian and Victorian buildings testify to the affluence of its merchants and industrialists during the 18th and 19th centuries. But for most of the working-class population, residential conditions were very poor. Much of the working-class housing built in the 19th and early 20th centuries suffered chronically from neglect by private landlords. The expansion of public sector housing from the 1920s onward led to a good deal of slum clearance. However, the housing that replaced the crumbling tenements was not, in all cases, a great improvement. In particular, as elsewhere in Britain, many of the apartment blocks built in the post–World War II period proved extremely problematic because of inappropriate and poor quality design and management (Dunleavy, 1981; Roberts, 1991). Meanwhile, through the 20th century the area experienced a progressive and deep decline in its economic fortunes culminating in the closure of the last dockyard in the late 1970s. As well as great economic hardship, this prompted population out-migration, fostered by local authority housing policies, that encouraged movement to other parts of Edinburgh.

The gentrification of Leith began in the early 1980s, prompted principally by the availability of public-sector finance designed to support the diversification of a severely depressed local economy (cf. A. Smith, 1989). Developers seized upon the opportunities this provided to initiate potentially lucrative residential projects. These included conversions of disused industrial buildings, such as warehouses and factories, and newly built complexes, on or close to the waterfront (see Figure 8.1a, b). This process caused little if any displacement of local people but led to an influx of middle-class owner-occupiers. By the mid-1980s, the new upmarket residential complexes stood cheek by jowl with patches of vacant land, derelict buildings, the residuum of former industrial activities, and the concrete monstrosities that house what remains of the local working classes (Figure 8.1b). Since then many of the gap sites and derelict buildings have disappeared. But local working-class people remain, as do the high-rise apartments and deck-access blocks in which many of them live.

(a)

(b)

FIGURE 8.1. Gentrification in Leith (1987). (a) Urban dereliction and early signs of gentrification. (b) Residential projects on the waterfront, with high-rise public-sector housing behind.

The marketing of the new housing units in the waterfront area has frequently emphasized the area's industrial heritage and in particular its nautical associations. This is evident in the names of developments, such as "Admiral House" and "The Cooperage," and is elaborated in many of the sales brochures. For example, one residential development is described thus: "Timber Bush—so called because of the area being the site of wood importation from France in the days going back to the Auld Alliance—the word 'Bush' deriving from the French for market—*debouché*. . . . In more recent times the busy Port was the base for Whalers who voyaged round the world on their epic journeys." Brochures also refer positively to nonresidential land uses in the area, which are increasingly directed toward the incoming owner-occupiers: restaurants, architects' offices, and so on are now rather more in evidence than other commercial activities.

Through this kind of marketing pitch, the area is represented in a manner resonant with ideas of the urban frontier and of urban pioneering (see N. Smith, 1986, 1990). This is emphasized by the use of photographic images similar to those presented in Figure 8.1b. Thus, incoming house purchasers are positioned as participants in the conquest of an industrial urban landscape where only the "intrepid" would choose to settle. Prospective home buyers are invited to identify themselves with 18th- and 19th-century adventurers and entrepreneurs, invariably men. This construction of incomers underlines their social distance and profound difference from "local" people. Implicitly, the urban environment including its existing residents is positioned as the passive, feminine Other, to be conquered by the active, masculine, gentrifying subject (see Rose, 1993).

The potential for class conflict between these groups is considerable but remains effectively contained (Bondi, in press). However, the area is locally renowned for conflict over another issue, namely, prostitution. Prostitution is so strongly associated with the life of a seaport that it is implicitly invoked by the heritage eagerly claimed in promotional brochures about the waterfront developments in Leith. Moreover, representations of prostitution in the local press bear some striking resemblances to representations of gentrification promoted by developers and selling agents.

To local residents and the local press, prostitution in Leith means transactions secured on the streets: it means women plying their trade in public places; it also means, in colloquial parlance, "kerb-crawling" (or, in U.S. English, "curb-crawling" or "cruising") by prospective clients. The new residential developments are reputed to have resulted in some microscale shifts in the places where this occurs, presumably as a result of police activity, but this has if anything height-

FIGURE 8.2. A street corner where "kerb-crawling" has been reported (1991).

ened the conflict with local working-class residents (see Figure 8.2). Newspaper representations emphasize almost exclusively the nuisance caused by prostitution, and especially by kerb-crawlers propositioning women residents:

> Terrified women in Leith are being mistaken for prostitutes by an army of menacing kerb-crawlers. . . . Women returning from a night out at the bingo, or leaving their homes to go to work in the evenings, are finding themselves targets for men who wind down their car windows and ask "Are you open for business?" . . . Some of the streets most heavily infested with kerb-crawlers . . . are residential areas with tenement blocks housing dozens of families. (*Edinburgh Evening News*, Saturday, October 26, 1991)

Such representations position men as predators hunting for sex, and masculine sexuality as a form of conquest. The object of their desires is sexually passive and readily symbolized by the body of a woman. As press coverage indicates, any female body can perform this function. The numerous individual stories recounted in local newspapers focus on women positioned as victims of unwanted sexual propositions. These women are presented as mothers, as wives, as workers, as bingo players, and so on, but never as overtly sexual beings. References to the bingo, to bus journeys, and to "young mums pushing baby buggies and carrying bags of shopping" (*Edinburgh Evening News*, Saturday, October 26, 1991) suggest strongly that it is working-class women who are the victims of "kerb-crawlers" rather than the inhabitants of gentrified properties, who are far more likely to travel to and from their homes by car. The prostitutes themselves are largely ignored by the newspapers but within this regime take up a position of transgressing social norms by visibly embracing a role generated by men's sexual desires.

The "kerb-crawlers" whose behavior prompts such concern are, like the incoming owner-occupiers, represented as adventurers or urban pioneers, in this instance searching for overtly sexual pleasures. While the opprobrium of the local press is reserved for the former, their discursive positions remain much the same. Both are portrayed as active, desiring sexual subjects, who occupy a masculine subject position (Henriques, Hollway, Urwin, Venn, & Walkerdine, 1984). This applies to women who take up the position of gentrifiers, as well as to men. Butler's distinction between different dimensions of gender is very useful in the interpretation of such contradictions. Thus, within her framework, the female gentrifier embodies the distinction between "the anatomy of the performer [female] and the gender that is being performed [masculine]" (see the quotation above from Butler, 1990, p. 137). How women choose to negotiate this in practice is beyond the scope of this analysis. This interpretation emphasizes the presence of multiple and potentially conflicting dimensions of gender, which, in this case, operate within the context of an insistently heterosexual regime dominated by a predatory, objectifying version of masculine sexual desire.

Urban Domesticity in Stockbridge

A different form of urban pioneering took place in Stockbridge in the late 1960s and early 1970s. At that time, middle-class professionals began to purchase artisan cottages dating from the late 19th century, most of which still lacked standard amenities and many of which were in a very poor state of repair. The new owner-occupiers upgraded and refurbished them with the assistance of local authority improvement grants (Kersley, 1974). Prices began to rise, with spin-off effects in other parts of Stockbridge, including areas of tenement apartments built in the late 19th century for Edinburgh's expanding middle-classes, and the mews, which had originally been stables and coaching accommodation for large Victorian townhouses (Figures 8.3a, b). The latter, with unusual frontages along narrow cobbled streets, provided an environment particularly attractive to gentrifiers. Upgrading was undertaken by individual owner-occupiers, and through the 1970s

(a) (b)

FIGURE 8.3. Gentrification in Stockbridge (1991). (a) Nineteenth-century tenements originally built for middle-class occupation. (b) Stockbridge mews.

and early 1980s countless apartments were described by selling agents as "full of potential," "in need of renovation" and so on.

Changes in the social composition of Stockbridge resulted partly from a transfer of property from private renting to owner occupation. By the early 1980s the area was predominantly middle class, and by the mid-1980s the area was almost fully gentrified. Selling agents frequently describe the area as "fashionable," emphasizing both its "excellent location"—very close to the city center—and its "convenience"—home to a wide range of retail outlets from newsdealers and corner shops, through supermarkets, to a substantial number of specialist retailers selling handknits, brass fixtures, and so on (which convey the impression that particular styles of homemaking activity are accorded high value both socially and economically). These descriptors combine to suggest a distinctive style of residential neighborhood in which domesticity is an integral element of an assertively *urban* lifestyle (c.f. Mills, 1993). This representation is underpinned by the architectural form, which supports both high residential densities and miniature gardens in the form of flower boxes (see Figure 8.3b). Thus, prospective house purchasers are positioned as consumers of both urban culture and domestic pleasures.

Comparing Stockbridge with Leith suggests that domestication may be an outcome of processes through which poverty and poor people have been erased. However, what is of more direct concern here is that the representation of Stockbridge outlined invokes a very different version of heterosexuality from that associated with Leith. In particular, through the domestication metaphor, it accords priority to a feminine sexual role characterized by intimacy, monogamy, and connectedness.

As in Leith, prostitution plays a role in the reputation of the area. However, its significance is historical rather than contemporary. For more than 40 years a local woman, Mrs. Dora Noyce, ran a brothel in the area. It was not closed down until after her death in 1977, by which time the neighboring properties in the row of substantial Georgian houses had all been upgraded and commanded considerable prices (Figure 8.4). In the few weeks before its final closure, the brothel and its history attracted considerable press coverage. Although it came to be viewed as a nuisance after Dora Noyce's death, it was also represented as having been a largely well-run business. Typical of local sentiments are these comments contained in a letter to a local newspaper from a next-door neighbor: "I confess to having felt something of affection for Dora Noyce. . . . At least she was prepared to accept re-

FIGURE 8.4. The street on which Dora Noyce's brothel was once situated (1991).

sponsibility for what occurred within and outside of her premises. . . .
It may well be that Mrs Noyce was right when she always claimed that
she offered a necessary social service" (letter to *The Scotsman,* August
26, 1977).

This notion of prostitution as a "social service" draws on representations of sexuality different from those evident in the street-trad-
ing case affecting Leith. Here, prostitution is about making male sexuality safe. It is about reining in, rather than letting loose, the predatory, sex-hungry male. Although still defined in terms of men's sexual
needs, women become more active agents since they are endowed
with the skills to tame and to satisfy the men they service (cf. Hart,
1995). While the model of masculine sexuality underpinning these
ideas is still one couched in the same terms as the conquest metaphor, prostitution is now represented as a process of domestication.

In the years that have elapsed since the brothel closed, it has
become part of the constructed heritage of the area. The story appears to add a touch of spice to the reputation of this now well-estab-
lished middle-class area. It helps to make the area exciting rather
than staid. It suggests that not so long ago this area was an urban
frontier. At the same time, the process of selective recuperation, in
which prostitution is represented more in terms of domestication than
predation, both endorses and is endorsed by the high value attached
to homemaking. This typifies the gentrification process itself, which
in different ways in different places deploys a wide array of artifacts
and images to invoke deeply romanticized versions of history, within
which issues of social identity and social status are often central (see,
e.g., Jager, 1986; Ley, 1987; N. Smith, 1990; Jacobs, 1992; Mills, 1993).
In so doing, gentrification transforms history into heritage, and un-
tamed urban wilderness into domesticated urban landscapes.

These representations place gentrifiers in the same discursive
position as prostitutes working discreetly and skillfully inside well-run
brothels. Both are portrayed as engaged in relationships in which
"feminine" skills of patience, attention to detail, and so on are employed to satisfy potentially unpredictable clients. This places men
who buy into owner-occupation in this area in a contradictory position so far as gender is concerned. Consequently, Judith Butler's distinction between the gender of the performance, the gender identity
of the performer, and the performer's anatomical sex is very useful
once more, opening up fascinating questions about the experiences
and perspectives of the gentrifiers (men and women) themselves.

CONCLUSION

As I have illustrated, the representations of prostitution just discussed relate to the different ways in which prostitutes obtain clients and clients find prostitutes. Potentially they relate to different clientele, although Mrs. Noyce's Stockbridge brothel is reputed to have serviced many of the sailors who might equally well have been serviced by prostitutes working the streets in Leith, where today's "kerb-crawlers" are described as smartly dressed and as driving smart cars. However, I am not so much concerned with these aspects of prostitution as with the images of gender and sexuality these representations impart to the urban landscapes with which they are associated.

In conclusion I pick up briefly on two of the points I drew out from current feminist debates about sex, gender, and sexuality. First, the conventional emphasis on gender and radical exclusion of sex is of little help in elaborating the interpretations presented here. It seems to me more useful to consider tensions within and between different aspects of gender. To use Judith Butler's terms, the metaphors of conquest and domestication assume a direct mapping between gender performance (the sexual roles), gender identity (their association with women and men), and anatomical sex, within a model of heterosexual complementarity and coherence. To understand the operation of these metaphors it is essential to distinguish between these aspects of sex–gender because the seamlessness of the model is mythical, not least because, as I have indicated, both women and men are actively involved as gentrifiers in contexts represented in terms of both "conquest" and "domestication."

Thus, my second point is that the connotations of conquest and domestication illustrate the presence of multiplicity even within the most archetypal representations of gender and sexuality. To elaborate, the conquest and domestication metaphors stand for a complex series of oppositions: masculine/feminine, active/passive, subject/object, detached/connected, single/married, autonomous/interdependent. There are potential tensions here. For example, "married" does not correspond to "feminine" but presumes a union between man and woman. The potential tension between these metaphorical associations is suppressed through an asymmetry in the treatment of masculine and feminine sexuality. Whereas the former is represented as autonomous and self-defined, the latter is represented as existing only in relation to, and as defined by, men's sexual needs. Thus, the dichotomy between supposedly equal and opposite sexual roles coexists with a dichotomy between separation and union because, whether its opposite or in union with it, femininity is always subordinated to masculinity rather than vice versa.

Recognition of this asymmetry is central to feminist analysis; challenging it is essential to feminist politics. The conquest/domestication metaphors code one of the urban landscapes I am interested in as masculine, the other as feminine. But if feminine sexuality exists only in relation to masculine sexuality, then the apparent femininity of the domesticated landscape must be qualified. However, the analysis I have offered allows all this to be reversed: in both conquest and domestication representations of prostitution, masculine sexuality is definitionally dependent on women and feminine sexuality. This unsettling of conventional representations of gender identity and sexuality is a necessary precursor to articulating counterhegemonic versions. I do not embark on this task here, but I hope that this limited example at least suggests some of the possibilities that ensue from opening up the concept "gender."

ACKNOWLEDGMENTS

The research on which this chapter is based was made possible by a grant awarded by the Economic and Social Research Council (No. R/000/23/2196), whose financial support is gratefully acknowledged. Much of the research was undertaken by Nuala Gormley, who deserves all the credit and none of the blame for the use I have made of primary sources. Thanks are due also to Marion Markwick, who first introduced me to the metaphors of conquest and domestication as descriptions of landscapes of gentrification. And, finally, thanks to Jane M. Jacobs for her stimulating and encouraging comments on an early draft and her assistance in the final revisions.

REFERENCES

Adler, S., & Brenner, J. (1992). Gender and space: Lesbians and gay men in the city. *International Journal of Urban and Regional Research, 16*, 24–34.

Bacchi, C. L. (1990). *Same difference.* Sydney: Allen & Unwin.

Bell, D. (1991). Insignificant others: Lesbian and gay geographies. *Area, 23*, 323–329.

Bell, D., Binnie, J., Cream, J., & Valentine, G. (1994). All hyped up and no place to go. *Gender, Place and Culture, 1*, 31–48.

Bell, D., & Valentine, G. (Eds.). (1995). *Mapping desire.* London: Routledge.

Bondi, L. (1991). Gender divisions and gentrification. *Transactions of the Institute of British Geography, 16*, 190–198.

Bondi, L. (1997). In whose words? On gender identities, knowledge and writing practices. *Transactions of the Institute of British Geography, 22,* 245–258.

Bondi, L. (in press). Gender, class and urban space: Public and private space in contemporary urban landscapes. *Urban Geography.*

Brennan, T. (1991). An impasse in psychoanalysis and feminism. In S. Gunew (Ed.), *A reader in feminist knowledge* (pp. 114–138). London and New York: Routledge.

Butler, J. (1990). *Gender trouble.* London: Routledge.

Butler, J. (1993). *Bodies that matter: On the discursive limits of "sex."* New York: Routledge.

Cream, J. (1995). Re-solving riddles: the sexed body. In D. Bell & G. Valentine (Eds.), *Mapping desire* (pp. 31–40). London: Routledge.

Dunleavy, P. (1981). *The politics of mass housing in Britain 1945–1975.* London: Clarendon Press.

Edwards, A. (1989). The sex–gender distinction: Has it outlived its usefulness? *Australian Feminist Studies, 10,* 1–12.

Epstein, J., & Straub, K. (Eds.). (1991). *Body guards.* London and New York: Routledge.

Evans, J. (1994). *Feminist theory today.* London: Sage.

FitzSimmons, M. (1989). The matter of nature. *Antipode, 21,* 106–120.

Forest, B. (1995). West Hollywood as symbol: The significance of place in the construction of a gay identity. *Environment and Planning D: Society and Space, 13,* 133–157.

Fuss, D. (1989). *Essentially speaking.* London: Routledge.

Gallop, J. (1982). *The daughter's seduction.* Ithaca, NY: Cornell University Press.

Gatens, M. (1991). A critique of the sex–gender distinction. In S. Gunew (Ed.), *A reader in feminist knowledge* (pp. 139–157). London and New York: Routledge.

Grosz, E. (1994). *Volatile bodies.* Bloomington and Indianapolis: Indiana University Press.

Haraway, D. (1990). *Primate visions: Gender, race and nature in the world of modern science.* New York: Routledge.

Harding, S. (1986). *The science question in feminism.* Ithaca, NY: Cornell University Press.

Hart, A. (1995). (Re)constructing a Spanish red-light district: Prostitution, space and power. In D. Bell & G. Valentine (Eds.), *Mapping desire* (pp. 214–228). London: Routledge.

Heath, S. (1986). Joan Rivière and the masquerade. In V. Burgin, J. Donald, & C. Kaplan (Eds.), *Formations of fantasy* (pp. 45–61). London: Methuen.

Henriques, J., Hollway, W., Urwin, C., Venn, C., & Walkerdine, V. (1984). *Changing the subject.* London and New York: Methuen.

hooks, b. (1992). *Black looks: Race and representation.* London: Turnaround.

Jacobs, J. (1992). Cultures of the past and urban transformation: The Spitalfields Market redevelopment in East London. In K. Anderson & F. Gale (Eds.), *Inventing places: Studies in cultural geography* (pp. 194–214). Melbourne: Longman Cheshire.

Jager, M. (1986). Class definition and the esthetics of gentrification: Victoriana in Melbourne. In N. Smith & P. Williams (Eds.), *Gentrification of the city* (pp. 78–91). Boston: Allen & Unwin.

Jay, N. (1981). Gender and dichotomy. *Feminist Studies, 7,* 38–56.

Johnston, L. (1996). Flexing femininity: Female body builders refiguring the body. *Gender, Place and Culture, 3,* 327–340.

Kersley, S. R. (1974). *Improvement grants: Their contribution to the process of gentrification.* BSc Thesis, Department of Town and Country Planning, Heriot–Watt University, Edinburgh.

Kolodny, A. (1975). *The lay of the land.* Chapel Hill: University of North Carolina Press.

Kolodny, A. (1984). *The land before her.* Chapel Hill: University of North Carolina Press.

Knopp, L. (1992). Sexuality and the spatial dynamics of capitalism. *Environment and Planning D: Society and Space, 10,* 651–670.

Lauria, M., & Knopp, L. (1985). Toward an analysis of the role of gay communities in the urban renaissance. *Urban Geography, 6,* 152–169.

Ley, D. (1987). Styles of the times: Liberal and neo-conservative landscapes in inner Vancouver, 1968–1986. *Journal of Historical Geography, 13,* 40–56.

Lloyd, G. (1989). Woman as other: Sex, gender and subjectivity. *Australian Feminist Studies, 10,* 13–22.

Longhurst, R. (1995). The body and geography. *Gender, Place and Culture, 2,* 97–105.

Mackenzie, S. (1989). *Visible histories.* Montreal: McGill–Queen's University Press.

McDowell, L. (1991). The baby and the bath water: Diversity, deconstruction and feminist theory in geography. *Geoforum, 22,* 123–133.

McDowell, L. (1993a). Space, place and gender relations: Part I. Feminist empiricism and the geography of social relations. *Progress in Human Geography, 17,* 157–179.

McDowell, L. (1993b). Space, place and gender relations: Part II. Identity, difference, feminist geometries and geographies. *Progress in Human Geography, 17,* 305–318.

McDowell, L., & Court, G. (1994). Performing work: Bodily representations in merchant banks. *Environment and Planning D: Society and Space, 12,* 727–750.

Mills, C. (1993). Myths and meanings of gentrification. In J. Duncan & D. Ley (Eds.), *Place/culture/representation* (pp. 149–170). London and New York: Routledge.

Mitchell, J. (1974). *Psychoanalysis and feminism.* Harmondsworth, UK: Penguin.

Mohanty, C. T., Russo, A., & Torres, L. (Eds.). (1991). *Third World women and the politics of feminism.* Bloomington: Indiana University Press.

Moore, H. (1994). "Divided we stand": Sex, gender and sexual difference. *Feminist Review, 47,* 78–95.

Pain, R. (1991). Space, sexual violence and social control: Integrating geographical and feminist analyses of women's fear of crime. *Progress in Human Geography, 15,* 415–431.

Quilley, S. (1995). Manchester's "village in the city": The gay vernacular in a postindustrial landscape of power. *Transgressions, 1,* 36–50.

Ramazanoglu, C. (1989). *Feminism and the contradictions of oppression.* London and New York: Routledge.

Rivière, J. (1986). Womanliness as masquerade. In V. Burgin, J. Donald, & C. Kaplan (Eds.), *Formations of fantasy* (pp. 35–44). London: Methuen. (Original work published 1929)

Roberts, M. (1991). *Living in a man-made world.* London: Routledge.

Rose, G. (1993). *Feminism and geography.* Cambridge, UK: Polity Press.

Sedgewick, E. K. (1991). *The epistemology of the closet.* Hemel Hempstead, Hertfordshire, UK: Harvester Wheatsheaf.

Smith, A. (1989). Gentrification and the spatial constitution of the state: The restructuring of London's docklands. *Antipode, 21,* 232–260.

Smith, N. (1986). Gentrification, the frontier, and the restructuring of urban space. In N. Smith & P. Williams (Eds.), *Gentrification of the city* (pp. 15–34). Boston: Allen & Unwin.

Smith, N. (1990). New city as new frontier: The Lower East Side as Wild West. In M. Sorkin (Ed.), *Variations on a theme (park)* (pp. 61–93). New York: Hill & Wang.

Soper, K. (1995). *What is nature? Culture, politics and the non-human.* Oxford: Blackwell.

Spelman, E. V. (1990). *Inessential woman.* London: Women's Press.

Stoller, R. J. (1968). *Sex and gender.* London: Hogarth.

Tivers, J. (1985). *Women attached.* London and Sydney: Croom Helm.

Valentine, G. (1993). (Hetero)sexing space: Lesbian perceptions and experiences of everyday spaces. *Environment and Planning D: Society and Space, 11,* 395–413.

Warde, A. (1991). Gentrification as consumption: Issues of class and gender. *Environment and Planning D: Society and Space, 9,* 223–32.

Ware, V. (1992). *Beyond the pale: White women, racism and history.* London: Verso.

Weeks, J. (1985). *Sexuality and its discontents.* London: Routledge.

West, C., & Fenstermaker, S. (1995). Doing difference. *Gender and Society, 9,* 8–37.

Wilson, E. (1991). *The sphinx in the city.* London: Virago.

Women and Geography Study Group of the IBG [Institute of British Geography]. (1984). *Geography and gender.* London: Hutchinson.

CHAPTER 9

Sites of Difference

BEYOND A CULTURAL POLITICS
OF RACE POLARITY

Kay Anderson

The linkages between culture and material life in Western societies are increasingly the focus of a research agenda that bears the title of "critical human geography" (Painter, 1995). Such a field does not seek to freeze a subdisciplinary division of human geography but rather aims to explore lines of conceptual and methodological convergence among cultural, political economy and feminist perspectives. In particular, this geography is developing a critical interest in identity and power, subjectivity and position, entitlement and privilege, as shaped by the mutually constitutive relationships between "the cultural" and "the material." Systems of signification (such as those surrounding race) and economic and political structures of inequality are taken as being thoroughly interdependent, and there is a refusal to oppose the positions of culture and economy.

Evidence for disciplinary convergence into such a critical human geography hails from both cultural and economic geography. On the one hand, a number of cultural geographers are seeking to heed criticisms about "evacuating the social" (Gregson, 1993) and averting the study of "lived relations" (Chouinard, 1994)—what another writer has called the "descent into discourse" (Palmer, 1990)—by grounding identities and other representational forms in the political struggles surrounding their material production (e.g., Jacobs, 1992; Mitchell, 1994). It is acknowledged that such struggles bear witness not only to a cultural politics of difference but often also to nondiscursive factors of class formation and capital that play a role in shaping the stakes and outcomes of such struggles.

At the same time, concepts of distributive justice, urban policy, and politics are increasingly being reformulated from a materialist direction to address questions of difference, identity, and culture (Revill, 1995). In this move, class is still regarded as a conceptual necessity for understanding the dynamics of society, but the restructuring of the economy and the decline of old class identities is seen to coincide with a dispersal of subjectivities that are not easily coded into the old positions of Left, Right, and Center (Mercer, 1990). Current challenges for analysis thus seem to surround the coupling of theoretical critique with the plural sources of oppression and antagonism in contemporary capitalist societies, that is, with their mutual economic and ideological determinations.

In this chapter I attempt to meet those challenges by working strands of culture and economy into the analysis of racialized spaces. As I have previously demonstrated (Anderson, 1991, 1993), racialized identities are often configured in spaces where the boundaries between cultural differences are inscribed. Just as the body holds in nondiscursive grounding the social inscriptions of "sex," so do sites of difference inject a material presence into the discourses (e.g., of race and gender) that condition cultural hierarchies. This should not be taken as implying that the cultural boundaries between categories of difference are forever stabilized in space. Cultural boundaries do not exist a priori; they are a product of articulation between different elements of experience and subjective position (Bhabha, 1994). It follows that in specific moments particular identities are foregrounded, transgressed, and sometimes subverted through negotiations that have come to bear the name of "identity politics" (Rutherford, 1990). And in such negotiations, the spatial relations of difference can also be reconfigured.

This chapter begins with a brief review of conceptualizations of race and racism in urban studies, spanning ecological through recent constructivist perspectives. I then propose a move that goes beyond the essentialist modeling of Self and Other that tends to characterize current constructivist geographies of race and racism. Implicit in such a move is the location of race positionings within other fields of oppression, including those of class and gender. In this case, I seek to open out the study of racialized sites and identities by contextualizing the relations of class and capital in which they are inserted. Elsewhere I have undertaken a similar enlargement of race narratives with reference to the gender positionings that trouble overdetermined stories of race polarization (Anderson, 1996).

In what follows I extend the autocritique of my earlier work *Vancouver's Chinatown* (Anderson, 1991) by foregrounding the economic stakes in racialized place meanings in contemporary China-towns in a range of Western cities. Consistent with poststructuralist critiques of the centered subject, I seek to destabilize the fixed positionings of a racialized dichotomy by highlighting moments in the recent history of two Chinatowns, in New York City and Melbourne, when class-based interests and alliances crosscut the racial divide. A story constructed out of such moments not only weaves together threads of culture and economy, I will argue, but also unsettles the narrative ghettoization of racialized spaces as eternally Othered.

The second section of the chapter further explores the theme of racialized difference in an Australian inner-city district that in appearance resembles the classic "ghetto" of the American city. Again, I seek to displace the binary logic of center–margin models that position such sites of racialized poverty within an ethnic explanatory frame of "domination" and "resistance." Such an ethnic frame can be inadequately nuanced to the cultural and economic determinations of such sites of difference. More specifically, I will argue that struggles over living conditions in Redfern (a district in the Sydney metropolitan area) have created a local culture of housing/service provision in the cracks of urban redevelopment regimes. Neither inside nor outside the dominant regime of colonial capitalism, neither traditional nor assimilated, Redfern "striates" (Minh-ha, 1990) the transparent gaze and development trajectory of metropolitan capitalism and consciousness.

RACE AND THE CITY: BLACK IS BLACK AND WHITE IS WHITE

Race and racism have been closely examined features of Western cities for decades. The subjects have long attracted media attention, while in the academy their study has reflected the evolution of analytical perspectives in the social sciences at large. From the time Robert Park (1924) argued that profound social distance gradients operated between blacks and whites in American cities, urban geographers mapped the spatial patterns generated by race and racism. In the ecological tradition of research—ascendant through the positivist era of the 1950s and 1960s—residential segregation by race was measured using a range of indices that sought to quantify its extent and form (e.g., Burnley, 1975; Jackson & Smith, 1981; Peach, 1975; Peach, Robinson, & Smith, 1981). Some research effort turned on determining the relative significance of class and race in explaining patterns of segregation (implicitly assuming that the two factors were analytically independent) (e.g., Farley, 1986). Others studied the dynamics of urban housing markets: how they became "split" along racial lines, and the roles of financial institutions and real estate agents in shaping the "dual" housing market (e.g., Berry, 1979; Palm, 1985). There was also widespread interest, particularly in the United States, in the neighborhood transition that was said to occur when blacks "invaded" white neighborhoods (e.g., Clark, 1980; Rose, 1972).

By now the critique of positivism in human geography is so well developed that there is little merit in rehearsing it here. Moreover, in the rush to challenge the presumption of objectivity in positivist geography, one should not foreclose the possibility that its quantitative methodologies can be integrated with more recent, interpretive forms of research on race and the city. The spatialities of race consciousness should continue to interest urban geographers, perhaps especially in the United States, where the city–suburb distinction is so profoundly encoded with race meanings and practices (Davis, 1992).

More troubling, however, is that research questions such as Waddell's (1992)—"the influence of race on urban spatial structure"—continue to be so uncritically framed in the pages of reputable geography journals. While some geographers who once advocated ecological forms of race analysis have diversified their analytical course (e.g., Peach, 1984), others (such as Waddell) still tacitly endorse nonscientific classifications of identity by implying that "races" can be actually distinguished by biologically or culturally relevant criteria (see the critique by Berg, 1993). Here such geographers reinforce the doubly spurious notion that "races" exist as immutable things and that racial inequality has its ultimate origins in differences given at birth. They also overlook a fresh body of work that has refused to invest race with its own explanatory status, arguing that "race" is something which must itself be explained. Here I refer to the recent body of work concerned with the social construction of race and racism— work which has sought to conceptualize racial segregation as a culturally and politically negotiated process (e.g., Anderson, 1991; Smith, 1989). It is also work which I will argue has been less successful in assimilating non-discursive factors of class formation and capital into its explanatory frame.

EAST IS WEST AND THE SOCIAL CONSTRUCTION OF RACE

The insight that race identities are constructed out of specific historical and political contexts prompted a radical revision of theorizing about racial segregation in cities. It required geographers to adopt a more rigorous approach that critically examined the discursive leap made in Western cultures from visible differences to something more fundamental which has been called "race." It was a move that went beyond describing the spatial forms produced by commonsense notions of difference to deconstructing the processes of exclusion and inclusion out of which segregated cities were produced, both symbolically and materially.

Such work has gone a long way to restoring cultural process to the center stage of explanation in urban "race relations" (see Harrison, 1995). It has also opened up important new substantive concerns, for example, the conventionally neglected configurations of whiteness (e.g., Frankenberg, 1993). Perhaps most persuasively, constructivist studies of race have highlighted (in conjunction with those of gender relations) the *multiple* faces of social power. If power was once seen in the narrow terms either of a workplace relation born in the contract between labor and capital or of formal institutionalized politics, the force of Michel Foucault's and Antonio Gramsci's more broadly based conceptions of power has by now been widely authorized in human geography (e.g., McLaughlin & Agnew, 1986; Philo, 1992). The concept of "cultural hegemony," understood in all its cultural and instrumental dimensions (Said, 1978), has been especially useful in articulating a more inclusive concept of social power that I (for one) found useful in dislodging the grip of primordialist understandings of districts called "Chinatowns" in Western settings.

The recent tradition of constructivist race research has not been without its weaknesses, however. For one thing, it has been less successful in relating the cultural and material aspects of race and race-based inequality in such a way as to demonstrate their mutual structuring. A cultural politics of race polarity—implicit in dualistic us/them models of European hegemony—has tended to overwrite the interconnections of race positionings with other sources of identity, power, and oppression. Such positionings have tended to be uncritically assimilated into a hegemonic narrative whole. It follows that fresh, if unwitting, forms of reification creep into race research where us/them binaries are abstracted from their wider social relations. Social orders like European hegemony begin to appear to function like grand systems and tidy totalities, rather than complex and often contradictory disunities.

As a related point, the fictionalized collectivities of "black," "white," "European," or "Asian" that positivists and social constructivists work with (in quite different ways) tend to obscure the subjectivities of identities internal to those categories. So, whereas the critique of Western feminism by black, postcolonial, and lesbian writers has upset consensus notions of the category "woman" and patriarchy (e.g., hooks, 1981; Larbalestier, 1991; Butler, 1990), recent race research—including that by anticolonialists such as Said (1978) and Clifford (1988)—has reinforced modernist premises of an ordered (racialized) reality whose subject positionings are, for the most part, fixed and undifferentiated (cf. Anthias & Yuval-Davis, 1992; Donald & Rattansi, 1992). The multiple axes of identity that constitute subject positions and never neatly align in stable and coherent ways (Haraway, 1991, p. 170) are thus explained away.

In the following section I seek to problematize the polarity of race identities upon which rests the cohering argument of my earlier work *Vancouver's Chinatown* (Anderson, 1991). I aim to undertake such an autocritique by feeding into Chinatown stories, from a few settings, the social location of class and the context of capital's recent restructuring under advanced capitalism. By extension, the section critiques other work in race relations that disengages race identities from other historically situated oppressions such as those surrounding gender, class, and sexuality. Without discrediting work that specifies the contribution that race-based oppression makes to structures of inequality, the section seeks to foreground the *multiplicity* and *mobility* of subject positionings, including those of race and class.

DIFFERENCE AND CAPITAL:
CHINATOWN BEYOND ORIENTALISM

Just as it is possible to read the Chinatown story in terms of an epistemic regime of race, it is also fruitful to narrate it as a site of conflict over shifting identifications and economic stakes. Certainly the distinctions of class, gender, ethnicity, generation, language, and so on that have pluralized the Western world's Chinatowns suggest that notions of a stably positioned racialized identity—pitted in dichotomous relation against a coherent European oppressor—require some refinement.

In the early Chinatowns of North America, such as in Vancouver, British Columbia, Canada, there existed a socioeconomic pyramid at the apex of which stood a tiny minority of men of capital. They were some of Vancouver's wealthiest individuals from the time the city was incorporated in the 1880s (Wickberg, Con, Johnson, & Wilmott, 1982; Yee, 1988). The wider cultural and legal liability implied by the racial category "Chinese" may well have been the asset of merchants who in that Chinatown had a captive force of Chinese laborers at their disposal (Chan, 1983). This bloc of workers, unprotected by white unions and subject to onerous immigration (head) taxes, often labored under punitive contracts for their Chinese bosses. There were also many unpaid workers, including women, who worked long hours sewing buttonholes and doing much of the handwork for Chinese tailors (Adilman, 1984). The experience of those workers was shaped by their subordinate status in an array of oppressions. Notable among them were the wider social relations of class and race in which the Chinatown subeconomy was inserted, as well as the communal hierarchies of class and gender.

That such oppressions have persisted to the present is evident in many other North American Chinatowns. The women workers of Chinatown in early Vancouver prefigured today's sweatshop workers, whose notoriously exploited labor in Chinatowns such as New York City's tell of class and gender conflict that has only recently prompted agitation for reform on the part of Chinese women workers (Kwong, in press). Indeed the gender and, as we shall see, ethnic division of labor within New York City's Chinatown has reached levels of entrenchment that warrant further attention as follows.[1] Not only do we glimpse a more complexly differentiated minority than the oppressed victim of race narration, but in situating Chinatown within a wider social field, the district is displaced from its essential alterity within an ethnic explanatory frame.

Changes to U.S. immigration laws in the 1980s brought capital and labor to New York City that transformed the once tiny six-block district of Chinatown on the Lower East Side, situated virtually in the shadow of Manhattan's Wall Street skyscrapers. What in the 1960s was a district of small restaurants, gift shops, dry goods stores, and residence for some 15,000 people, had by the late 1980s become a base of garment and textile factories, restaurant chains, and real estate speculation among properties that housed some 250,000 people. The ethnic mix of the district had also widely diversified by the late 1980s to include people not only from mainland China but also from Hong Kong, Taiwan, Vietnam, and Malaysia (to name only the major sources).

The growing concentration of garment trades in Chinatown since the 1980s reflected wider processes of capital restructuring on the part of U.S.-based corporations. While some garment and textile manufacturers relocated factories to non-Western countries, some remained home, notably in immigrant communities where unregulated economies exist. In New York City's Chinatown, where labor is increasingly casualized, such a subeconomy is well developed. Currently the wage levels in the district stand at approximately $2 (U.S.) per hour (while the official minimum hourly wage as of September 1,

1997, is $5.15), a 12-hour day is common, and the withholding of wages has, according to the Chinese Staff and Workers Association of Chinatown, become a common "accounting practice" (Kwong, 1994a). It is a practice that a women's committee of the association began to confront in 1991 with campaigns for back wages and consciousness-raising sessions.

There are also ethnically differentiated relations within the category "Chinese" that are erased by characterizations of a stably bound (racialized) minority. Penetrating the least-skilled ends of Chinatown's trades in New York City are growing numbers of non-Cantonese-speaking, undocumented workers from the Fuzhou province of mainland China (Kwong, 1994b). Such workers, themselves racially othered as inferior "snake people," now congregate in the new "foreign" section of the district near the employment agencies on East Broadway. These are the residents who—echoes of the indentured labor system that brought thousands of railway workers to California in the late 19th century (Barth, 1964)—are indebted to the contractors who organize their illegal entry to the United States. In turn, Fuzhou immigrants work for almost any wage to pay off debts running as high as $35,000(U.S.). The preferred choice of many Chinatown employers, Fuzhou workers rarely report their adverse working conditions and wages due to their undocumented immigration status. Meanwhile, documented Chinese workers find it increasingly difficult to get any work at all.

Such ethnic- and gender-differentiated relations within the Chinatown enclave lead us to consider the possibility that other oppressions—quite apart from the relation that places whites in a deterministically antagonistic relationship to Chinese (Anderson, 1991)—might be as decisive in shaping everyday experiences inside the enclave. Not all the realities and aspirations of the lives of Chinatown's residents and workers are exhausted by the fact of racial subordination, not least because of Chinatown's nesting within regimes of production and accumulation.

What emerges from this discussion of social relations within the subeconomy is the utility of exploring the changing cultural logics of production relations in sites of difference such as Chinatown. Diverse idioms of difference, gender and ethnic, are the cultural resources of the accumulation process under conditions of capital's restructuring. Culturally shifting markers of difference become encoded through the production process as the building blocks of recurrent production and accumulation cycles (see also Jackson, 1992). This is not to invoke the crudely functionalist model of causation that polarizes base and superstructure and derives the latter (difference) from the needs of the former (capital). The mutable signifiers of difference require their own critique and explanation *within* the fluid cultural universe of Chinatown. Rather, it is to insist on collapsing the conventional split in critical consciousness as between the economic and the cultural—to work against their rigid and immobile juxtaposition, and to demonstrate the dynamic "in process, in time" (Abrams, 1982) of their thoroughly mutual structuring.

Certainly, in the quest to unsettle sharply dichotomous race interpretations of Chinatown, one should be careful not to make the reverse error of erasing altogether the cultural context of racial scripting in which Chinatown is inserted. For all that the concept of race is ontologically empty, it has an undeniable vitality as a social reality. In the case of New York City's Chinatown, the New York State Labor Department has turned a blind eye to the casualization of labor and Dickensian conditions within the Chinatown subeconomy (Kwong, 1994b). One official of that department stated in 1992 that "in the underground economies of the ethnic enclaves of the Vietnamese, Cuban, Dominican, Central American, and Chinese, it is a case of immigrants exploiting immigrants. We can't be expected to protect those who are too docile to come forward" (Kwong, 1994b). It is surely the case, therefore, that the scripting of immigrants in racial terms and the encoding of Chinatown as an "ethnic" space in the speech and practices of such officials feed into the complex matrix of oppressions currently shaping this district's fortunes. Just as "culture seems to be the prison of 20th century Aborigines" (Muecke, 1992, p. 18), where anything that happens for Australia's Aborigines is read in terms of an Aboriginal identity (see later), so too the race typification of "Chinese" works to obscure other vectors of power that have the enclave as their protection. It follows that to write a more inclusive Chinatown story requires one to draw on the reciprocal determinations of (at least) class *and* race, economy *and* culture.

Chinatowns offer other windows on the interconnections between difference, class, and capital. Turning to Australian cities, one finds the same doctored Oriental streetscapes that bear the name of "Chinatown" in North America (Anderson, 1990). Chinatown has indeed been a most mobile representational form. From Brisbane to Sydney, Melbourne, and Adelaide, Chinese entrepreneurs and non-Chinese urban planners have instigated neighborhood redevelopment schemes that have in turn been underwritten by state and local governments. Paradoxically, capital and the state have grown attracted to difference. What once prompted stigma on the part of governments and consumers, now sells, under conditions of postmodernity (Rutherford, 1990, p. 11). This is no more apparent than in the ethnic enclaves that have been made to stand as emblems of the East in the West. At sites called Chinatowns, Chinese language, culture, cuisine, and artifacts have been torn free of their original referents and turned into spectacles in a power relation that constitutes a cultural and commercial appropriation of meanings (Anderson, 1993).

The Melbourne case bears more careful scrutiny in the context of this chapter's objectives, however. There, the Chinatown upgrading scheme of the mid-1970s saw Councillor David Wang, a Hong Kong-born entrepreneur and Australian citizen, join force with Mayor R. Walker and a Chinese architect to transform Little Bourke Street into central Melbourne's "Window on the East." Stage 1 of Chinatown's redevelopment proceeded, complete with Chinese-style decorative lanterns and pavings dotted with Oriental motifs. The alliance that brought about Chinatown's revalorization, then, was founded in a correspondence of economic and political interests that cut across the racial divide. Such an alliance—all the more common in Australian Chinatowns at a juncture when Hong Kong capitalists are seeking safe havens for their investment—suggests a few theoretical points. First, it complicates neat stories of unilateral hegemony and appropriation on the part of a putatively undifferentiated European oppressor. Second, it turns our critical eye to the overlapping fields of economic and ideological determination in which Chinatown is inserted. And, finally, by opening out the Chinatown storyfield to take in the district's location within wider processes of class formation and capital's restructuring, the district's narrative positioning as eternally (racially) othered is displaced.

Not only were there class-based alignments between Chinese and non-Chinese parties to support Chinatown's upgrading on the one side, but a joint interest was also struck between Chinese and non-Chinese groups in the struggle that ensued to *halt* Chinatown's redevelopment on the other. In 1976, an organization of small Chinatown shopkeepers formed to fight the plan to erect pagodas that, in the words of the Chinese-origin architect, would be "replicas of traditional Chinese entrances." The use of an ahistorical concept of Chinese culture as an ideological device for reconfiguring race was not lost on them. In the view of the retailers, some of whom lived in the district, "the project is entirely dubious. We want to be treated as Australians and with dignity. . . . We don't want to bring back the image of an opium-smoking mahjong-playing people which the whole concept of Chinatown encourages" (*The Australian*, August 22, 1976). Significantly, given the interests of this chapter, the retailers' grievances were heard. The Melbourne branch of an influential left-wing builders' laborers' organization, intent on disrupting development it found politically undesirable refused to build the pagodas out of an anticapital solidarity with the shopkeepers. The joint challenge eventually prevailed over government and capitalist agendas, and Stage 2 of Chinatown's redevelopment was halted.

Once again, then, complicities arose across racialized boundaries that, for all their continuing force in Australian society, resist being pinned down in statically authorial (us/them) locations. And this is not just a matter of theoretical argument. Out of the provisional positionings that I have mapped in this section—inconsistent positionings that are contradictory to those neatly mapped in bipolar race formulas—lie the possibility not only of fresh Chinatown stories but of alternative political alliances and futures.

DIFFERENCE AND POVERTY: ABORIGINAL REDFERN BEYOND "RESISTANCE"

Just as Chinatowns are complex sites of difference, so the settlement of Aboriginal people in the inner-city blocks of Redfern in Sydney, Australia, defies texting in the dichotomous terms implied by an overdetermined structure of "domination" and "resistance." Unlike Chinatown, however, Redfern is no commodified place. It is a site of racialized poverty whose "difference" is of interest to this chapter for what it says about the twin (cultural and economic) bases of struggle in class- and race-stratified societies.

Redfern is home to some 400–500 residents of diverse Aboriginal origins who pay rent to the Aboriginal Housing Company (AHC) which since 1973 has had legal title to the (approximately 70) terrace houses and land bounded by the inner-city streets of Eveleigh, Vine, Louis, and Caroline (Figure 9.1). In that year, the Commonwealth government of Australia, seeking to legitimate itself in the language of welfare, equity, pluralism, and self-determination for indigenous people, granted Redfern Aborigines funds to purchase a block of inner-city housing. The grant followed a sustained struggle on the part of local Aborigines and some non-Aborigines intent on securing shelter for the growing number of destitute Aborigines in central Sydney. The settlement thus grew out of a partnership between a federal government in Canberra with particular ideological requirements and a group of local (white and black) activists armed with social justice and land rights agendas. Agitation over Aboriginal welfare in Sydney had steadily grown following the migration from rural areas in the 1950s and 1960s, and had already seen the establishment in the area of an Aboriginal Legal Service and Aboriginal Medical Service. There

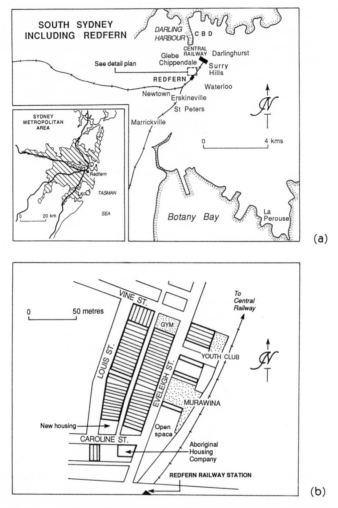

FIGURE 9.1a and 9.1b. Location of Redfern and properties owned by the Aboriginal Housing Company.

also existed a number of arts, music, and sporting organizations in the area, most notably the Redfern All Blacks football club.

Today, the district clings to the edge of the rapidly expanding commercial frontier of Australia's premier city, with dramatic views north to the impressive skyline of Sydney's central business district and within meters of the wave of gentrification sweeping Victorian terrace houses. The apparently eccentric location of the block of Aboriginal housing is certainly one of the striking things that arouses geographical curiosity in the district. It is a settlement embedded within the economic and social restructurings of the postmodern city, yet present—seemingly defiantly so—as a noncommodified space. During 1991/92, the eccentric juxtapositions of people and place prompted me to investigate the formative processes that brought the block of housing into existence (see Anderson, 1993). Then, in 1994, in two weeks of interviews, I spoke with 20 tenants who live in the block of Aboriginal housing, including the only member of the board of directors of the AHC who lives on the block. I was accompanied by an Aboriginal assistant known to the majority of tenants but who was not himself a resident. The interviews took the form of 1- to 2-hour conversations based on questions formulated by myself and a few members of the board of directors of the AHC. In what follows I seek to interweave some of the threads that emerged from the interviews and earlier archival research,[2] with the theoretical concerns of this chapter.

Since 1973, Redfern has acquired a field of meaning that resonates far beyond the tiny pocket of Aboriginal settlement and into the imaginations of Australians across the country. Although Aborigines constituted less than 5% of the total population of the local government area Redfern at the 1991 census, it is widely held by white and some black Australians that blight, crime, poverty, substance abuse, truancy, vandalism, youth disaffection, and despair have found their natural habitat on that district's streets. Deeply implicated in the construction of such a selective image of the district have been the various agencies of law enforcement and the media that have consistently represented it through the filter of negative racist imaginings (Cunneen, 1990). Mediated as such, the district has been made to stand as the icon of a degenerate Aboriginality whose original referent has been erased in the movement to city life (Langton, 1981). A by-product of "detribalization," so the representation goes, Aboriginal Redfern has become "our" Harlem, "our" archetypal slum.

Redfern is indeed a racialized place. Through narration it has become positioned within white Australia's dominant regimes of representation and its often lurid languages of urban violence and decay. The ideological materials for the construction of Redfern's Aboriginality have been shaped by such powerful colonial discourses, that a content analysis of media representations of the district would be unremarkable in the consistency of its (derogatory) themes. But implicit within such a one-dimensional race conceptualization of Redfern (and by extension other racialized ghettoes) is a model of power relations that is insensitive to the complexity of social relations out of which Aboriginal Redfern has been structured. A model of

pure and stable dominant and oppositional subject positionings—
one that gives ethnic personality to both—seems to risk casting "domination" and "resistance" in essentialist (culturalist) terms (e.g.,
Cowlishaw, 1988; for a critique see Rowse, 1993). Yet, two centuries of
colonial capitalism in Australia have seen black and white struggles
over living conditions whose cultural and economic bases are impossible to separate and futile to prioritize. In this context, and however
much we might like to recuperate the Aboriginal subject as a pur-
poseful agent, not everything about Aboriginality should be read as
"counterhegemonic," whether manifest as acts of cultural persistence
or overt challenge to white power. Such a reading risks leaving us
with an understanding of Aboriginal experience in relativist terms, as
operating inescapably within the parameters of an ethnic structure of
race polarity. And yet the everyday, place-specific realities of Australia's
heterogeneous Aboriginalities are more complex and contradictory. In
some moments and settings, for example, and perhaps especially in cities where housing and property markets generate intense competition
for space and shelter, subjugation can generate both emancipatory *and*
disempowering responses, liberating *and* negating forms of struggle, social organization *and* disorganization. Such are the complexities where
race and class costructure society and space.

The case of Redfern, Australia's first housing cooperative, has
certainly been read by scholars as testimony to the "resistance" of the
oppressed (Bishop, 1992; see also Hollinsworth, 1992; Keefe, 1988;
Morris, 1988). Its presence at the heart of white, urban, capitalist
Australia has been championed as the mobilization of a resurgent
Aboriginality for territory against the invasive oppressor (despite the
fact that the housing project evolved out of joint black–white efforts
in a context of new federal government policies). It is possible, however, to criticize the resistance paradigm constructively by conceptualizing the district in alternative ways—as, for example, the localized
struggle of a racialized underclass to control and define more fully
the terms of its own living conditions. The culture of service/housing
provision that has evolved at Redfern, with both Aboriginal and non-
Aboriginal input, is a local, ethnic, and class-based enterprise. It allo-
cates most of its housing to Aborigines on a needs basis, that is to
destitute people who have been most disenfranchised by the relations of colonial capitalism.

Aboriginality is therefore not the only ideology integral to the
workings of this district, though it is often invoked by black adminis-
trators of the AHC as a language of public address and appeal. Redfern
is known by many black Australians as the "black capital" of the country. Yet while for some tenants this status is a source of identity and

pride, others see it more cynically as the resource of a pan-Aboriginal movement that does not connect with their everyday life and in which they express little political interest. For some of those tenants, Redfern is more appropriately conceived as a "city mission," a place where the economic dependency bred in the rural missions of the 1930s and 1940s has been transferred to Sydney. Once again, then, the identity construct "Aboriginal" needs to be located within the wide and heterogeneous social field crafted out of class, race, and other structures of difference. It follows that we can avoid retextualizing Redfern within a narrow racialized frame of reference (without discounting either the salience of race definition in the life experiences of its residents, or the expressive processes of cultural identification of the range of ethnicities in Aboriginal Redfern).

Resistance readings of "the ghetto" have other theoretical and practical costs. Not least, they risk implicitly valorizing much of the dysfunctional behavior that can occur in such districts of racialized poverty as Redfern. Truancy, substance abuse, gasoline (petrol) sniffing, vandalism, and other everyday acts of restless struggle tend to be elevated as heroic reversals of colonial power (when surely there are other actions more conducive to Aborigines' physical and psychological survival). Here, resistance readings, for all their emphasis on agency and more dynamic understandings of culture and identity, have more in common than might be acknowledged with an older "culture of poverty" school of thought (Lewis, 1966). That school of cultural determinism, in conceptualizing pathology as a behavioral adaptation to poverty—a coping mechanism passed on through generations—underlined the ultimately functional quality of pathologies for those in their grip.

More recently, the concept of "transculturation" (Pratt, 1992) has been coined to denote the process by which the "dominated" select codes and materials from dominant cultures. The process is distinct from "assimilation" and is invoked to highlight the capacity for resistance of colonized peoples. In the case of Redfern's Aborigines, such a perspective, while alive to aspects of the oppositional culture that have evolved there, overstates the scope for negotiation and organization of people whose poverty has not been manufactured by the terms through which Aboriginal people have been defined. Such poverty is not, for example, the cultural invention of the white census. Rather, it is the result of two centuries of crushing marginalization within the relations of colonial capitalism. The point suggests the more general merit of collapsing perspectives on sites of difference that, on the one hand, offer a portrait of the world from the vantage point of their subjects and, on the other, attend to the structures of inequality in which those subjects are multiply positioned and variably constrained.

The complexities inherent in struggles over living conditions that occur at sites of racialized poverty defy neat modeling within the standard antinomies of social theory, whether of culture and structure, race and class, or resistance versus domination. They also challenge assumptions of order that undergird much of social science. Certainly the vocabulary of the underclass in social science has lacked political imagination, moving little further than models of the exotic poor on the part of cultural determinists, and the victimized poor on the part of structuralists (Marks, 1991). The latter emphasize the lack of income-producing employment in the shift from manufacturing to service societies in an increasingly globalized economy (e.g., Massey & Eggers, 1990).

A part way forward has been offered by Wilson's (1987) notion of cultural adaptations with structural origins. I however prefer to turn a conceptual spotlight to *sites* of racialized poverty, discursively and spatially located in what de Lauretis (1987, p. 25) calls those "in-between-spaces." Adapting that concept, these are the minoritized spaces carved in the interstices of discursive regimes (of in Redfern's case, capital, race, gentrification, and redevelopment). At such sites reside the structural tensions of communities incorporated within structures of race, class, politics, and administration but not fully determined by them; communities shaped by but not wholly assimilated to colonialism's cultures. Such a community is Aboriginal Redfern, located at the margins in the very heart of the metropolis. There, the homogenizing trajectory of capitalist redevelopment practice is intercepted. The scopic regime of metropolitan consciousness is striated. Dominant space is unmapped. But as I have been suggesting, I wish to see this rupture less in terms of "Aboriginality," about "them" as a resistant ethnic force, or of the needs of the "center" to have itself reflected in the "margin" (Bhabha, 1990). Such readings, in their abstraction, serve only to reinvent dichotomous models of identity and race polarization.

Rather, I wish to think about such sites as places where difference is materially inscribed in struggles over living conditions. Difference—the marked subject of oppression past and present—is encoded in the built environment, not as *itself* but as a *process of struggle* embedded in the between-spaces of metropolitan capitalism. In the enactment of such struggles, space is transformed into place. But I resist calling such contestations "cultures of struggle" (as if they have some shared outlook born of a unitary identity, perhaps "resistance"), out of recognition of three things: the heterogeneous variety of subjectivities in minoritized spaces; the interdependent economic, cultural, and political determinations of struggle; and their often contradictory outcomes and effects.

Each of the tenants I interviewed is grappling in different ways to reconcile the injuries of alienation from a racially and class-stratified society with the exigencies of everyday life in Redfern. Approximately two-thirds of the total number of rent payers on the block are women who head households of on average four to five permanent persons, mostly children and young adults. One of the dominant language groups on the block is Banjalang, but a wide range of other place-based dialect groups is present, including Eora people (Sydney region), Wiradjuri (Nowra), Kamlaroi (Dubbo and Moree), and many other groups from throughout New South Wales and Queensland. Redfern is a meeting place for ethnically diverse Aborigines, many of whom base themselves with relatives on the block during visits to Sydney. Aboriginal traditions of duties to share are observed by most tenants, though while some generously throw open their doors to visitors, others choose not to shop during the visits of relatives in order to protect household income. Fifty percent of the total number of tenants on the block are unemployed and eligible for pensions of various kinds, including single-parent and sickness benefits; a tiny minority of long-standing residents has independent jobs; while the remainder earn (minimal) wages in exchange for work in local Aboriginal enterprises funded by the federal government's Community Development Employment Program (CDEP). The tenants live in mainly three-room terrace houses in various states of disrepair, ranging from properties in need of minor repairs to plumbing and wiring, through to homes with holes in walls, broken windows, rickety roofs, and unstable floors and ceilings. The large majority of terraces have "defaced" exteriors, though only some of the tenants were concerned about the appearance of their homes. Their abiding concern was the structural condition of their homes and those on the block as a whole.

Since 1974, the block of terraces has undergone a succession of renovation, rebuilding, and improvement ventures. The AHC progressively bought up decrepit houses on the block and then undertook renovation programs using Aboriginal labor (where possible) and Commonwealth grants. The management, training, and administrative challenges in such ventures were considerable, and the AHC's records contain periodic complaints of incompetence from grant-giving organizations and of nepotism in employment and tenancy access from tenants. The challenge of balancing income from (the minimal) rents against maintenance has been especially delicate for the

AHC, which is seen resentfully as a "black landlord" by many tenants. The problems were compounded from the mid-1980s when violence with police and local white residents (the Redfern Home-owners Association) greatly disrupted the AHC's activities and the lives of tenants. As the confrontations deepened and media coverage grew more sensational, serious consideration was given by federal government bodies in the late 1980s to encouraging the AHC to sell its stock and disperse the block. The embattled AHC—landlord, welfare worker and community resource—weathered this period of scrutiny, however, and continues its rent-deficit operation today.

Most of the tenants with whom I spoke are among the more permanent residents on the block. The majority had spent at least 5 years there, and a minority had lived there since the housing project began in 1973. A sense of familiarity with the block was, however, one of the few sentiments the tenants held in common. The quest to generalize and abstract is an artifact of the research agenda wholly inappropriate to Redfern (and probably many areas). When asked about safety on the block, for example, some tenants declared they confidently leave their children alone at home in the knowledge others will look out for them; other tenants claimed rape of young girls on the block was so prevalent that they constantly feared for their safety. In response to questions about "police targeting" of the block, some claimed that Redfern is where police go to exercise their muscle, whereas others regretted that police turn a blind eye to the block and are slow to respond to incidents. When asked about the responsiveness of black organizations in the area, including the AHC, some tenants claimed the AHC had their interests at heart; others slammed the organization for charging rent, for being remote and incommunicative, and for failing to maintain properties. For every positive observation the tenants made about life on the block, there was an equivalent range of negative ones. One contradictory image lodged in my mind is of a woman placing flour, sugar, and cigarettes in the refrigerator "so the rats wouldn't get them" and simultaneously telling me she wouldn't live anywhere else in Australia even if she had the choice. Drugs, poverty, housing conditions "fit for dogs," and "car dumping" were singled out as the worst problems on the block; on the other hand, the Redfern Aboriginal Cooperative (funded through the CDEP program), the Eveleigh Street vegetable garden, and the sense of excitement and unpredictability of life on the block were things that attached residents positively to the block. Did the block constitute a "community"? For some, assuredly "yes"—especially during "Knock-out Week," when Aboriginal people from throughout New South Wales came to Redfern for annual football play-offs. For others, "no"—"Just look at the place." Also there was the rift, often noted, between the "transients" on Eveleigh Street and the "uptown niggers" (with permanent jobs) on Louis Street. Some saw the block as "home"; others perceived their place of birth as home; still others considered that they had multiple homes, including Redfern.

Some degree of consensus arose in relation to views about the future of the block. While very few expressed an interest in Aboriginal politics (only a tiny minority vote in ATSIC[3] elections, for example), all were concerned about the possibility of the block passing out of Aboriginal hands and into those of developers. In that sense, issues of identity and material circumstance fused, though not, I would argue, in a politically abstract sense of "resistance." Although most tenants are aware of the commercial value of the site and the visual rupture the block currently presents to upmarket, inner Sydney—one claiming "it's good for whites to have to see us this way"—the focus of their various, fitful struggles for expression is less "Aboriginality" as a generalized emancipatory rhetoric than the specific, local referent of the block itself. Redfern is a *place* where Aborigines are collectively engaged in everyday efforts to recast the terms and conditions of their material existence. This process of redefinition, born in struggles surrounding identity and poverty, is not necessarily or always enacted cooperatively. The conflicts of opinion and interest among tenants, and between tenants and the AHC, attest to that. Nor does struggle necessarily take the consistent form of empowering, emancipatory strategies. In only some senses, including the considerable land rights victory it represents, is Aboriginal Redfern a "self-determination success story." At Redfern some of the most dispossessed members of Australian society have indeed been afforded the means for postcolonial survival. But the formidable constraints exerted by a history of class and race oppression make for a more contradictory record than that offered up by resistance and other narratives framed in strict ethnic terms. The current conflict surrounding the future of the AHC operation[4]—in which tenants are considering invoking land rights legislation to halt plans to demolish their homes by their Aboriginal landlords (*The Australian,* January 17, 1996, p. 9)—attests precisely to the complex entanglements of race and class in the structuring of Aboriginal Redfern (Figure 9.2).

CONCLUSION

In this chapter I have sought to bring together strands of culture and economy to the analysis of racialized sites of difference. The chal-

FIGURE 9.2. The most recent struggle to retain Aboriginal housing in central Sydney has been registered in Canberra, Australia's capital. (Photograph by Nick Gill)

lenge issued by this volume—to acknowledge, on the one hand, the spaces and voices of difference opened up by a decentered human geography and, on the other, the complex faces of power and inequality that condition fragmented cities—invites fresh ways of conceptualizing such sites. In particular, it encourages a style of thinking that breaks with the dichotomous culture/identity models that have enjoyed a long (though manifestly variable) history in theorizing about race and the city. Of course, by situating racialized sites in wider contexts of, for example, class and capital restructuring, the elegance of the ethnic explanatory frame implicit in fashionable (if fatally abstract) concepts of "hegemony" and "resistance" is sacrificed. But through enlarging the narrative grid, as I have tried to do in this chapter, not only is a window offered on a more complexly differentiated and positioned subject, there is also the possibility of offering fresh stories that displace stale scenarios of otherness and marginality. "Knowing about the terrain," claims Haraway (1989, p. 295) "on which raced self/other have been constructed within western culture at particular historical moments is a prerequisite for remapping the possible ground for new stories." That is, breaking the logic of binarism is not just to unsettle stories and languages of polarity but also, we can hope, the material structures of inequality they reinscribe.

ACKNOWLEDGMENTS

I wish to acknowledge with thanks the secretary and directors of the Aboriginal Housing Company (AHC), who granted me access to view company records and interview its tenants. To the people on the block who kindly afforded me time for the interviews and to Rex Marshall, research assistant, I am also grateful. Thanks are due to Julie Kesby for assistance with proofreading, formatting, and referencing, and to Peter Jackson for comments on a draft. The financial support of the Australia Research Council is gratefully acknowledged.

NOTES

1. I wish to acknowledge here not only the research of Peter Kwong (Asian American Studies, Hunter College, City University of New York) but also the time we spent in, and insight he gave me on, New York City's Chinatown.

2. The records to which I refer include primary data from government sources relating to Redfern at local, state, and national levels. I was also given special access to view documentary community sources such as the AHC's own records.

3. The Aboriginal and Torres Strait Islander Commission (ATSIC) is the federal organization, administered by both Aborigines and non-Aborigines, that oversees grants to Aboriginal organizations and activities.

4. Since this chapter as gone to press, there have been concerted efforts on the part of the New South Wales government and the Aboriginal Housing Company to disperse tenants and redevelop the district as (what is called) "Black Chinatown." See Anderson (forthcoming).

REFERENCES

Abrams, P. (1982). *Historical sociology*. Bath, Somerset, UK: Pitman Press.

Adilman, T. (1984). A preliminary sketch of Chinese women and work in British Columbia 1858–1950. In B. Latham, R. Latham, & R. Pazdro (Eds.), *Not just pin money* (pp. 53–78). Victoria, British Columbia, Canada: Camosun College.

Anderson, K. (1990). Chinatown re-oriented: A critical analysis of recent redevelopment schemes in a Melbourne and Sydney enclave. *Austra-lian Geographical Studies, 28*(2), 137–513.

Anderson, K. (1991). *Vancouver's Chinatown: Racial discourse in Canada, 1875–1980.* Montreal: McGill–Queen's University Press.

Anderson, K. (1993). Place narratives and the origins of inner Sydney's Aboriginal settlement, 1972–73. *Journal of Historical Geography, 19*(3), 314–335.

Anderson, K. (1996). Engendering race research: Unsettling the self/other dichotomy. In N. Duncan (Ed.), *Bodyspace: Destabilizing geographies of gender and sexuality* (Chap. 12). London: Routledge.

Anderson, K. (forthcoming). Reflections on Redfern. In E. Stratford (Ed.), *Australian cultural geographies.* Melbourne: Oxford University Press.

Anthias, F., & Yuval-Davis, N. (1992). *Race, nation, gender, colour and class and the anti-racist struggle.* London: Routledge.

Barth, G. (1964). *Bitter strength: A history of the Chinese in the United States, 1850–1870.* Cambridge, MA: Harvard University Press.

Berg, L. (1993). Racialization in academic discourse. *Urban Geography, 14*(2), 194–200.

Berry, B. (1979). *The open housing question: Race and housing in Chicago, 1966–1976.* Cambridge, MA: Ballinger.

Bhabha, H. (1990). The other question: Difference, discrimination and the discourse of colonialism. In R. Ferguson, M. Gever, T. Minh-ha, & C. West (Eds.), *Out there: Marginalization and contemporary cultures* (pp. 71–88). New York: New Museum of Contemporary Art; Cambridge, MA: Massachusetts Institute of Technology.

Bhabha, H. (1994). *The location of culture.* London: Routledge.

Bishop, J. (1992). *History of the Aboriginal Housing Company Ltd.* MSc social work project, University of New South Wales, Kensington, NSW, Australia.

Burnley, I. (1975). Ethnic factors in social segregation and residential strati-fication in Australia's large cities. *Australian and New Zealand Journal of Sociology, 11*(1), 12–23.

Butler, J. (1990). *Gender trouble: Feminism and the subversion of identity.* New York: Routledge.

Chan, A. (1983). *Gold mountain: The Chinese in the New World.* Vancouver: New Star Books.

Chouinard, V. (1994). Reinventing radical geography. *Environment and Plan-ning D: Society and Space, 12*(1), 2–6.

Clark, W. (1980). Residential mobility and neighborhood change: Some implications for racial residential segregation. *Urban Geography, 1*(2), 95–117.

Clifford, J. (1988). *The predicament of culture: Twentieth-century ethnography, literature, and art.* Cambridge, MA: Harvard University Press.

Cowlishaw, G. (1988). *Black, white or brindle: Race in rural Australia.* Melbourne: Cambridge University Press.

Cunneen, C. (1990). *Aboriginal–police relations in Redfern; With special reference to the "police raid" of 8 February 1990: Report commissioned by the National*

Inquiry into Racist Violence. Sydney: Human Rights and Equal Opportunity Commission.

Davis, M. (1992). *City of quartz: Excavating the future in Los Angeles.* New York: Vintage Books.

de Lauretis, T. (1987). *Technologies of gender: Essays, films and fiction.* London: Macmillan.

Donald, J., & Rattansi, A. (Eds.). (1992). *"Race," culture and difference.* London: Sage, in association with the Open University.

Farley, J. (1986). Segregated city, segregated suburbs: To what extent are they products of black–white socioeconomic differentials? *Urban Geography, 7*(2), 164–171.

Frankenberg, R. (1993). *White women, race matters: The social construction of whiteness.* Minneapolis: University of Minnesota Press.

Gregson, N. (1993). "The initiative": Delimiting or deconstructing social geography? *Progress in Human Geography, 17*(4), 525–530.

Haraway, D. (1989). Monkeys, aliens and women: Love, science and politics at the intersection of feminist theory and colonial discourse. *Womens Studies International Forum, 12*(3), 295–312.

Haraway, D. (1991). *Simians, cyborgs, and women: The reinvention of nature.* London: Free Association Books.

Harrison, F. (1995). The persistent power of "race" in the cultural and political economy of racism. *Annual Review of Anthropology, 24,* 47–74.

Hollinsworth, D. (1992). Discourses on Aboriginality and the politics of identity in urban Australia. *Oceania, 63*(2), 137–155.

hooks, b. (1981). *Ain't I a woman: Black women and politics.* London: South End Press.

Jackson, P. (1992). The racialisation of labour in post-war Bradford. *Journal of Historical Geography, 18,* 190–209.

Jackson, P., & Smith, S. (Eds.). (1981). *Social interaction and ethnic segregation.* London: Academic Press.

Jacobs, J. M. (1992). Cultures of the past and urban transformation: The Spitalfields Market redevelopment in East London. In K. Anderson & F. Gale (Eds.), *Inventing places: Studies in cultural geography* (pp. 194–211). Melbourne: Longman Cheshire.

Keefe, K. (1988). Aboriginality: Resistance and persistence. *Australian Aboriginal Studies, 1,* 67–81.

Kwong, P. (1994a). *The unwelcome immigrants.* Unpublished manuscript. (Copy courtesy of author)

Kwong, P. (1994b, October 17). China's human traffickers. *The Nation,* 422–425.

Kwong, P. (1994c). A model for organizing in the changing economy: Chinese staff and workers' association. *Social Policy, 25*(2), 30–39.

Kwong, P. (in press). Back to basics: Politics of organizing Chinese women garment workers. *Social Policy.*

Langton, M. (1981). Urbanising Aborigines: The social scientists' great deception. *Social Alternatives, 2*(2), 16–22.

Larbalestier, J. (1991). Through their own eyes: An interpretation of Aboriginal women's writing. In G. Bottomley, M. de Lepervanche, & J. Martin (Eds.), *Intersexions: Gender, class, culture, ethnicity* (pp. 75–91). Sydney: Allen & Unwin.

Lee, S. (1990). *Disappearing moon cafe.* Vancouver: Douglas & McIntyre.

Lewis, O. (1966). The culture of poverty. *Scientific American, 215,* 19–25.

Marks, C. (1991). The urban underclass. *Annual Review of Sociology, 17,* 445–466.

Massey, D., & Eggers, M. (1990). The ecology of inequality: Minorities and the concentration of poverty. *American Journal of Sociology, 95*(5), 153–188.

McLaughlin, J., & Agnew, J. (1986). Hegemony and the regional question: The political geography of regional industrial policy in Northern Ireland, 1945–1972. *Annals, Association of American Geographers, 76*(2), 247–261.

Mercer, K. (1990). Welcome to the jungle: Identity and diversity in postmodern politics. In J. Rutherford (Ed.), *Identity, community, culture, difference* (pp. 43–71). London: Lawrence & Wishart.

Minh-ha, T. (1990). Cotton and iron. In R. Ferguson, M. Gever, T. Minh-ha, & C. West (Eds.), *Out there: Marginalization and contemporary cultures* (pp. 71–88). New York: New Museum of Contemporary Art; Cambridge, MA: Massachusetts Institute of Technology.

Mitchell, D. (1994). Landscape and surplus value: The making of the ordinary in Brentwood, CA. *Environment and Planning D: Society and Space, 12*(1), 7–30.

Morris, B. (1988). Dhan-gadi resistance to assimilation. In I. Keen (Ed.), *Domesticating resistance: The Dhan-gadi Aborigines and the Australian state.* London: Berg.

Muecke, S. (1992). *Textual spaces: Aboriginality and cultural studies.* Kensington, NSW, Australia: New South Wales University Press.

Painter, J. (1995, April). "Going critical"—alternative organisations for radical geographers: Some personal thoughts. *Social and Cultural Geography Study Group Newsletter, Institute of British Geographers,* pp. 10–11.

Palm, R. (1985). Ethnic segmentation of real estate agent practice in the urban housing market. *Annals, Association of American Geographers, 75*(1), 58–68.

Palmer, B. (1990). *Descent into discourse: The reification of language and the writing of social history.* Philadelphia: Temple University Press.

Park, R. (1924). The concept of social distance. *Journal of Applied Sociology, 8,* 339–344.

Peach, C. (Ed.). (1975). *Urban social segregation.* London: Longman.

Peach, C. (1984). The force of West Indian island identity in Britain. In C. Clarke, D. Ley, & C. Peach (Eds.), *Geography and ethnic pluralism* (pp. 214–230). London: Allen & Unwin.

Peach, C., Robinson, V., & Smith, S. (Eds.). (1981). *Ethnic segregation in cities.* London: Croom Helm.

Philo, C. (1992). Foucault's geography. *Environment and Planning D: Society and Space, 10*(2), 137–161.

Pratt, M. (1992). *Imperial eyes: Studies in travel writing and transculturation.* London and New York: Routledge.

Revill, G. (1995, April). Social justice and the city: Conference report. *Social and Cultural Geography Study Group Newsletter, Institute of British Geographers,* pp. 12–13.

Rose, H. (1972). The spatial development of black residential sub-systems. *Economic Geography, 48,* 43–65.

Rowse, T. (1993). Rethinking Aboriginal "resistance": The community development employment program (CDEP). *Oceania, 63*(3), 268–287.

Rutherford, J. (1990). A place called home: Identity and the cultural politics of difference. In J. Rutherford (Ed.), *Identity, community, culture, difference* (pp. 9–27). London: Lawrence & Wishart.

Said, E. (1978). *Orientalism.* New York: Random House.

Smith, S. (1989). *The politics of "race" and residence: Citizenship, segregation, and white supremacy in Britain.* Cambridge, UK: Polity Press.

Waddell, P. (1992). A multinomial logit model of race and urban structure. *Urban Geography, 13*(2), 127–141.

Wickberg, E., Con, H., Johnson, G., & Wilmott, W. (1982). *From China to Canada: A history of the Chinese communities in Canada.* Toronto: McClelland & Stewart.

Wilson, W. (1987). *The truly disadvantaged: The inner city, the underclass and public policy.* Chicago: University of Chicago Press.

Yee, P. (1988). S*altwater city: An illustrated history of the Chinese in Vancouver.* Vancouver: Douglas & McIntyre.

CHAPTER 10

Contesting Social Relations in Communal Places

IDENTITY POLITICS AMONG ASIAN[1] COMMUNITIES IN DAR ES SALAAM

Richa Nagar
Helga Leitner

Social divides and diverse ways of life are an age-old characteristic of cities. Religious, caste, class, racial, and ethnic divisions, distinctive to different societal systems, have always been inscribed in urban space. Examples include the religious ghettos and guild quarters of medieval European cities, the imperial quarters of colonial cities, the squatter settlements of the urban poor in contemporary Third World cities, and the racial ghettos of 20th-century American cities.

Traditionally, many urban scholars have been content with documenting the ways in which social divides are inscribed in the patterning of urban space. And, indeed, residential segregation along class, racial, and ethnic lines is empirically well documented. In contrast, the significance of the social differentiation of urban space, in and of itself, for the construction and reconstruction of social identities and for relations of domination and subordination among different social groups has been relatively neglected (exceptions include Harris, 1984; S. Smith, 1993). Research that has taken such questions on board has shown, for example, that racially segregated neighborhoods are an important source of racial identity and security, and thus potential empowerment. At the same time, however, racial segregation may be oppressive and disempowering because it involves relationships among groups of individuals with varying access to political influence and economic resources (Ford, 1994, p. 1844). We show in this chapter that the neighborhoods and communal places of a particular social group not only reinforce social identities and power relations but they themselves become important sites of struggle and negotiation over identities and over relations of domination and subordination, inclusion and exclusion, privilege and deprivation, both among and within different social groups.

Most writing on identity and difference in the Western context has tended to emphasize race, class, gender, and sexuality as the main nodes around which identities are formed. Our focus on the South Asian (henceforth referred to as Asian) communities in postcolonial Dar es Salaam, Tanzania, however, underscores the need to look at other axes of difference. Race, class, gender, and sexuality, by themselves, can be inadequate to understand social action of people whose identities and experiences are defined just as saliently by their caste, religious, or sectarian affiliations. Our examples also highlight how religion, sect, and caste are not merely people's individual self-perceptions; rather, they form both principal nodes around which communities are organized and controlled, and defining points for the power struggles that take place.

In this chapter we explore not only one but multiple axes of difference. Numerous intersecting social identities (those of race, class, caste, religion, and sect) and power relations between Asians and Africans and within the Asian communities have been played out, contested, or imposed in communal places of Dar es Salaam. The focus will be on the social experiences of Asian communities, and strategies used by them to resist and accommodate to pressures of African authorities on communal boundaries and places. Emphasis will also be placed on cross-caste alliances and fissures among Asian communities in the struggle for control over living space. The case studies presented in this chapter will demonstrate the complex relationships between multiple, fluid, and intersecting social identities, interests, and places, as well as the sociopolitical practices of individual and collective actors.

The fieldwork for this study was conducted between 1991 and 1993 in Dar es Salaam. Personal narratives and life stories of more than 200 Asian men and women of diverse religious, caste, class, linguistic, and sectarian backgrounds, in addition to participant observation and gathering of archival records, provided insights into the manner in which people perceived and experienced their multiple social relationships and constructed their identities and communities in different contexts. In-depth interviews were conducted in Gujarati, Hindi/Urdu, and English and participant observations were carried out in people's homes, temples, community halls, and clubs during the course of everyday life and during communal gatherings, weddings, and religious and secular festivals (see Nagar, 1995).

IDENTITIES, POWER RELATIONS, AND PLACE

Generations of urban scholars have been concerned with the importance of such social categories as race, ethnicity, and class as the ordering principles of social life and in patterning urban space. Traditionally, studies focusing on the diversity of social worlds and urban neighborhoods, for example, along race, ethnic, and class lines, have tended to essentialize these social categories by ascribing observed behavior and spatial distributions to membership in a particular social group. Thus race, ethnicity, and class have been treated as fixed and unproblematic.

Recent feminist, postcolonial, and poststructuralist thought has challenged the notion of fixed social categories, emphasizing both their socially constructed nature and the contingency of social action and experience more generally (Anzaldúa, 1987; Rosaldo, 1989; Scott, 1986). Central to this reconceptualiztion is the notion of identity and its relationship to power, discourse, and sociopolitical action.

Identities are people's understandings about themselves that mold the meanings they attribute to their social worlds and which in turn shape sociopolitical action and practices (Nagar, 1995, p. 296). Identities are constructed out of the multiple and shifting social relationships in which people are embedded (Somers, 1992, p. 607). Ethnic, gender, class, or racial identities are therefore not fixed profiles of traits but a fluctuating composition of difference with multiple intersections that are constantly transformed in the continuous play of history, culture, and power (Hall, 1987; Jha, 1991; Lowe, 1991; Watts, 1992).

Such an understanding enables us to view identities and communities as unstable and changing in their signifying practices and in their relationships with each other. It also challenges such simple binary oppositions as between male and female, white and nonwhite, Hindu and Muslim. It allows us to see communities as specific yet simultaneously uneven and unclosed, and individuals as embodying a variety of differences without essentializing any one of their identities (Lowe, 1991, p. 32). It is only by conceptualizing community in this way, that we can understand how the processes and structures that hold a community together coexist with the politics of power and difference that are continuously played out within it.

The term "community," whether based on race, religion, class, caste, or gender, often evokes the erroneous idea of a homogeneous and harmonious group that shares a set of values and has common interests. In this chapter we challenge the dominant notion of Tanzanian Asians as a homogeneous community of exploitative male traders and demonstrate that a community, no matter how it is defined, is also characterized by dissension, disharmony, and power hierarchies that celebrate some people and groups and marginalize others.

Power relations thus are integral to a relational conception of identity and community. They are inscribed in dominant discourses, institutional structures, and practices that rigidify certain identities and communities and deemphasize others, thus defining rules of exclusion and inclusion. For example references to different Asian communities such as "Goan," "Ithna Asheri," and "Hindu" constitute problematic and unstable categories, because members of those groups are simultaneously embedded in multiple and changing social relationships. At the same time, however, communal organizations and sociopolitical and discursive processes have operated over time to impart a structure and continuity to these categories, and to strengthen and reinforce people's identities as members of these communities (Nagar, 1995, p. 297).

Dominant rules of exclusion and inclusion are subject to change as a result of altered contextual realities and social agency. For example, as will be elaborated on in the next section, the Africanization and nationalization policies of the postcolonial Tanzanian government challenged the dominant rules of exclusion and inclusion by attempting to redefine the social boundaries and power relations between Africans and Asians. At the same time, individuals and communities have to be seen as active social agents in constructing their identities through the life experiences and discourses into which they are inserted and the sociopolitical practices they engage in. It is these processes that we understand to be identity politics.

While we stress the importance of an identity approach in understanding sociopolitical action, we disagree with Somers' argument that in order to understand social action we need to substitute the concept of identity for that of interest (Somers, 1992, p. 607). We contend that neither identities nor interests are pregiven, but rather they are both articulated in the course of the struggles of everyday life and are circumscribed by contextual realities. In the two case studies that follow, we explore how racial, class, caste, and religious identities and material interests combine and disrupt one another to guide in complex ways the evolution of social relations and sociopolitical practices.

Establishing relations between identity politics and place and space has become an increasingly venerable inquiry. Recent post-modernist, postcolonial, and poststructuralist writing has employed geographical metaphors heavily in an attempt to unravel the inter-play between history, culture, and power in identity formation and politics. Thus, for example, much feminist writing begins with calling for a need to "locate" the female subject (Clark, 1993, p. 139). Simi-larly, recent discussions on the politics of difference have focused on "deconstructing both margin and center" to reconstitute "new spaces of opportunity" (hooks, 1990, pp. 149–152; Soja & Hooper, 1993, p. 191). While we appreciate the widespread application of spatial meta-phors for comprehending the contours and meaning of social iden-tity formation and politics, and while we do not claim that the meta-phorical and the material belong in separate realms, this chapter emphasizes the importance of material spaces in identity politics.

It has generally been acknowledged that social identities are rooted in places (Hall, 1987, 1989; Lowe, 1991), and several geogra-phers have highlighted the manner in which places help define the identities and boundaries of various social groups (Bell, Binnie, Cream, & Valentine, 1994; Keith & Pile, 1993; Pratt & Hanson, 1994). The relationship between people's identities and place is, however, a complicated one. Places are important in the construction of social identities and are integral to identity politics in multiple ways. With respect to identity formation, places such as neighborhoods and com-munal places are symbols of identification and power relations. As such they reinforce community identities and power relations. The example of communal places of the Asian communities in Dar es Sa-laam may serve as an example. Neighborhoods, temples, community halls, clubs, and bars define the social worlds of the different sections of Asian communities in Dar es Salaam. These places play a major role in building and sustaining a deep sense of belonging to their caste, religion, or sect among the people. Regularly held social and religious gatherings in these places enhance the centrality of the com-munity in people's lives. Close and distant relatives, best friends, mari-tal partners, and (quite frequently) customers and clients come from the same religious community, and people's social, religious, and eco-nomic lives revolve around their communal places. In this way com-munal places form the nuclei in which people interact with each other, first to build their multiple communities and networks and define their religious, caste, class, racial, and gender identities and, second, to secure their material reproduction. Communal places are also important in reinforcing existing power hierarchies, for example, between the Asian community members and the African servants who clean their temples, mosques, and community halls, and between the upper-class or upper-caste community leaders and the commoners (Nagar, 1997).

What is less obvious and also has been given less attention in the literature is the significance of communal places as sites of struggles and negotiations over social identities/boundaries and power relations within and between communities. The examples presented in this chapter demonstrate that place-based struggles are simultaneously struggles for and negotiations over identity, social boundaries, and material reproduction and that the appropriation and control of space is central in this process. This suggests that space and place are not just passive arenas in which things (social relations) happen (Keith & Pile, 1993, p. 2), but rather play an active role in the complex constitution and articulation of social relations. In this sense, identity politics become identity politics of place.

THE CHANGING POSITION OF THE ASIAN POPULATION IN POSTCOLONIAL TANZANIA

The formation and reformation of social identities and sociopolitical practices constitutes not only an intriguing form of social agency (M. P. Smith & Tarallo, 1993) but is circumscribed by changing contextual realities.

For this reason, it is important to locate the migration and settlement of South Asian communities in Tanzania within the larger process of colonization. Colonial societies of East Africa have been described as systems that hinged on racial separatism between Africans, Asians, and Europeans (Tandon, 1965). The colonial system of racial separatism and hierarchy encouraged Asian merchants, traders, and civil servants to occupy a middle rung in the social hierarchy, with Europeans at the top and Africans at the bottom. In the economic sphere, Asians dominated commercial activity while Africans were discouraged from participating in commerce by the Credit to Natives Ordinance of 1931 (Coulson, 1982, p. 61). Asian traders and shopkeepers were involved in buying agricultural produce from African peasants and selling them imported manufactured goods. The top and middle rungs of the civil service were disproportionately staffed by European and Asian civil servants (Nyerere, 1973, p. 269; Shivji, 1976, p. 69). With respect to education, generally the best educational facilities were for Europeans and the second best for Asians, Africans being the worst off educationally (Coulson, 1982; Trebon, 1980).

After Tanganyika's independence (1961) and the Zanzibar revolution (1964), this racial hierarchy was the first thing to be attacked.[2] The adoption of an Africanization policy and of socialist nationalization policies (1967–1976) aimed at rectifying racial disparities between Africans and non-Africans in order to bring greater equality between different social groups. Five Asian ex-civil servants said in their interviews (conducted by Richa Nagar in October and November, 1992) that due to the Africanization of the civil services, a large proportion of Asian civil servants either lost their jobs or lost the scope for further advancement, and some started emigrating to Britain (Shivji, 1976). In the sphere of education, the Africanization policy eliminated the divided system of education based on race and integrated the education system for Africans, Asians, and Europeans. In March 1967, a move was taken to replace non-African headmasters with African headmasters in 31 of Tanzania's 84 secondary schools in order to facilitate the policy of self-reliance in education (*Tanganyika Standard* [Dar es Salaam daily newspaper], March 15 and 16, 1967). The 1969 Education Act brought all schools under government control and eliminated all entry restrictions based on the grounds of race or religion, the only exception being schools established purely for religious instruction (United Republic of Tanzania, 1969; *Tanganyika Standard*, October 10 and December 17, 1969; *The Standard* [Dar es Salaam daily newspaper], March 14 and 23, April 20 and 25, June 25, 1970). Nationalization of economic activities, as part of the adoption of socialist policies in Tanzania between 1967 and 1976, resulted in the nationalization of many Asian enterprises. In 1967, all commercial banks, insurance companies, and major industries, including food-producing and milling industries, were nationalized. Licenses held by large-scale Asian export–import traders were revoked, and all export, import, and wholesale trade was brought under the State Trading Corporation. In 1968, Asian private traders were phased out of agricultural marketing. Private shopkeepers were seen as "capitalists and racketeers" who hoarded commodities and "exploited the toiling masses," and peasants and workers were urged to "fight capitalism" by eradicating the Asian middlemen (*Daily News* [Dar es Salaam daily newspaper], April 27, 1972). Finally, the nationalization of buildings in 1971 meant that many rich and middle-class Asians lost their properties. The majority of the buildings acquired by the government (2,908 by November 1972) belonged to members of the Asian commercial bourgeoisie (Fimbo, 1974). These changes, combined with an increasingly racialized discourse in the early 1970s, generated an exodus of over 50,000 Asians from Tanzania to the United Kingdom, Canada, and India in the decade of the 1970s.[3]

After the onset of the economic liberalization period in Tanzania in 1984, however, the erstwhile Asian "exploiters" came to be regarded by African politicians and businessmen as suitable investors and partners in joint ventures, leading to a return of some upper- and middle-class Asians to Tanzania beginning in the late 1980s. At the same time, however, the rise of multiparty politics in Tanzania resulted in calls for "indigenization," or the transfer of economic power to "indigenous" people, and popular antagonism against Asian people surfaced loudly in the media and daily life (Nagar, 1993).

Africanization and nationalization policies enacted by the postcolonial Tanzanian government effectively challenged the power relations and social boundaries between Africans and Asians and the privileged status of Asians in Tanzania. An important part of this process has been periodic attacks on Asians for their racist, exclusionary institutions and behavior toward Africans. Before we present the story of responses by Asian communities to these changed contextual realities, a brief characterization of the Asian communities in Dar es Salaam and the place-specific context is in order.

THE ASIAN COMMUNITIES IN DAR ES SALAAM: A STORY OF DIVERSITY

In the late 1950s, the Asian population of Tanganyika was about 76,500. Of these, approximately 30,000 lived in Dar es Salaam (Khoja Shia Ithna Asheri Jamaat, Dar es Salaam, 1969). According to the latest 1988 census (United Republic of Tanzania, 1990), the population of the city was 1.4 million; at the time of this research in 1993, Asians there numbered about 35,000.[4] Thus, the city's Asian population increased slightly between the 1950s and the late 1980s, despite the large-scale emigration of Asians from Tanzania during the 1960s and 1970s. There are several reasons for this. In the wake of the Zanzibar Revolution of 1964, which challenged the Asian and Arab dominance, about 10,000 Zanzibari Asians moved to the mainland. The majority of them came to Dar es Salaam due to both its physical proximity to Zanzibar and the relatively strong presence there of Asian communal and familial networks. In the 1970s and 1980s, many Asian families moved from the interior to Dar es Salaam to take advantage of the relatively better economic opportunities and educational and health care facilities. Most recently, the city's Asian population has slightly increased as a result of some return migration from overseas.

Contrary to the tendency by African and European people to bracket the Asian population in Tanzania into a homogeneous entity, the Asian population of Dar es Salaam consists of a diversity of communities defined by differences in religion, caste, class, sect, language, place of origin, and race. In 1993, Hindus, Ithna Asheris, and Bohoras (both Ithna Asheris and Bohoras are Shiite Muslim groups), numbering approximately 10,000, 7,500, and 7,500, respectively, were the most populous Asian communities. Goan and Sikh communities with about 700 and 250 members, respectively, constituted the smallest Asian communities.

The majority of the Hindus and Muslims in Dar es Salaam trace their origin from the western Indian states of Gujarat, many from the district of Kutch and the Kathiawar peninsula in that state. Hindus form about 30 subcommunities, defined primarily on caste lines. Muslim communities include different sects and subsects, the most numerous being the Ithna Asheris, Bohoras, Ismailis, Sunnis, and Memons. Goans, from the ex-Portuguese colony of Goa (now a state of India), follow the Roman Catholic faith. Followers of the Sikh faith from Punjab form another distinct community. The examples in this paper are drawn primarily from the Ithna Asheri, Hindu, and Goan communities.

Upper-class Ithna Asheris and Hindus in Dar es Salaam have been mainly involved in business and trading since colonial times. Lower-class Hindu and Ithna Asheri men work as shop assistants and clerks for big businessmen of their communities. Many also work as foremen and skilled laborers, whereas others own small repair shops. It is common for lower- and middle-class women from all Asian communities to work as schoolteachers, seamstresses, and caterers. Some women also work as vendors, domestic servants, cooks, and midwives.

With the infiltration of migrants from Zanzibar and the interior, both the Ithna Asheri and Hindu communities in Dar es Salaam increased in size during the last decade, and their communal institutions and organizations also expanded. The caste divisions in the Hindu community became stronger with greater in-migration. Several lower-caste groups, for example, Rana, Bhoi, Divecha, Vanand, and Suthar, enlarged in size, which in turn led to greater organization and identification along caste lines. Caste divisions overlapped to a considerable degree with class differences, with the recently migrated lower castes such as Rana, Bhoi, and Divecha being among the poorest castes, and upper castes such as Lohana, Bhatia, and Patel being among the wealthiest. At the same time, the umbrella organization of the Hindus, Hindu Mandal, which controlled health facilities and was in charge of religious instruction and marital disputes for the Hindu community, became a powerful influence on the entire Hindu community. Hindu Mandal is led by relatively rich and upper-caste Hindu men, and many lower-class and lower-caste Hindus ex-press discontent with it.

Although the institutions of the Ithna Asheri community are also dominated by upper-class men, it has been more successful than the Hindu community in providing welfare services to its lower- and middle-class members in the form of subsidized housing, loans, and educational and health services. Also, unlike the Hindus, the absence of caste-based rifts among the Ithna Asheris has led to a strong iden-tification by its members as Ithna Asheris across class and gender lines.

Goans mostly worked as clerks, managers, and accountants dur-ing both colonial and postcolonial times, although some have recently ventured into business. The Goan community shrank considerably in Dar es Salaam due to continued emigration, however. Consequently, Goan communal organizations are relatively weaker than those of Hindus and Ithna Asheris and do not affect the economic, political, and social aspects of the lives of their members to the same extent as in the Hindu and Ithna Asheri communities.

To this day, Dar es Salaam remains a racially segregated city with clearly marked Asian and African residential areas (see Figure 10.1). In 1993, approximately 80% of the Asians lived in and around the commercial heart of Dar es Salaam, in the city center and the adjoin-ing areas of Kisutu, Upanga, and Kariakoo.[5] Although the national-ization of private buildings in 1971 did make room for Africans to settle in the city center and in Upanga, the majority of Africans still live away from the city center in areas such as Magomeni, Manzese, Temke, Ilala, Buguruni, Ubungo, Mwenge, and Kinondoni. Very few Asians live in African neighborhoods, with the exception of Kariakoo and Oyster Bay. Kariakoo is the most racially mixed residential area of middle- and working-class people in Dar es Salaam. Oyster Bay, occupied by Europeans during colonial times, is now a racially mixed upper-class neighborhood dominated mainly by homes of ministers, managers of government banks and agencies, officers of multinational companies, and rich businessmen (Iliffe, 1979).

As one might expect based on this pattern of residential segrega-tion, the communal institutions and places of the Asian communities in Dar es Salaam are concentrated in the city center. Figure 10.2 shows the location of communal places such as temples, community halls, clubs, bars, and beaches, which define the social, religious, and eco-nomic worlds of the different sections of Asian communities in Dar es Salaam.

The centrality of communal places in the everyday lives of Asians imparts them enormous meaning as sites of struggle where power relations between various social groups are negotiated and where the

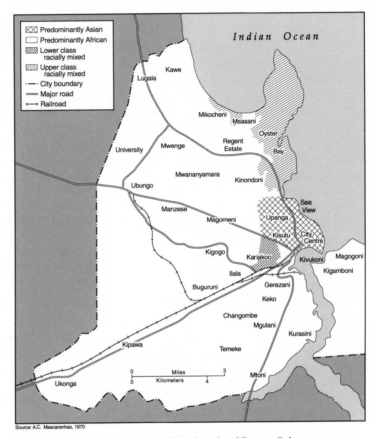

FIGURE 10.1. Neighborhoods of Dar es Salaam.

politics of identity are played out. In the following sections we focus on two such struggles: the first took place soon after independence and was centered around the redefinition of the boundaries of Asian communal places, whereas the second occurred more recently around control over a lower-caste Hindu settlement in Dar es Salaam.

DEFENDING AND RENEGOTIATING COMMUNAL BOUNDARIES AND PLACES

As outlined above, in the power hierarchy and the system of racial separatism of colonialism, Asians occupied the position of a privileged minority with its distinct and separate institutions. Asian religious groups operated as separate bodies, and the government com-

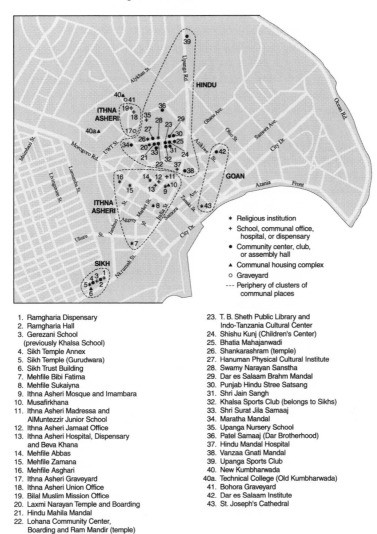

FIGURE 10.2. Asian communal places in Dar es Salaam.

1. Ramgharia Dispensary
2. Ramgharia Hall
3. Gerezani School
   (previously Khalsa School)
4. Sikh Temple Annex
5. Sikh Temple (Gurudwara)
6. Sikh Trust Building
7. Mehfile Bibi Fatima
8. Mehfile Sukaiyna
9. Ithna Asheri Mosque and Imambara
10. Musafirkhana
11. Ithna Asheri Madressa and
    AlMuntezzir Junior School
12. Ithna Asheri Jamaat Office
13. Ithna Asheri Hospital, Dispensary
    and Beva Khana
14. Mehfile Abbas
15. Mehfile Zamana
16. Mehfile Asghari
17. Ithna Asheri Graveyard
18. Ithna Asheri Union Office
19. Bilal Muslim Mission Office
20. Laxmi Narayan Temple and Boarding
21. Hindu Mahila Mandal
22. Lohana Community Center,
    Boarding and Ram Mandir (temple)
23. T. B. Sheth Public Library and
    Indo-Tanzania Cultural Center
24. Shishu Kunj (Children's Center)
25. Bhatia Mahajanwadi
26. Shankarashram (temple)
27. Hanuman Physical Cultural Institute
28. Swamy Narayan Sanstha
29. Dar es Salaam Brahm Mandal
30. Punjab Hindu Stree Satsang
31. Shri Jain Sangh
32. Khalsa Sports Club (belongs to Sikhs)
33. Shri Surat Jila Samaaj
34. Maratha Mandal
35. Upanga Nursery School
36. Patel Samaaj (Dar Brotherhood)
37. Hindu Mandal Hospital
38. Vanzaa Gnati Mandal
39. Upanga Sports Club
40. New Kumbharwada
40a. Technical College (Old Kumbharwada)
41. Bohora Graveyard
42. Dar es Salaam Institute
43. St. Joseph's Cathedral

municated with Asians through the leaders of their religious communities. With the departure of the British, however, their status changed from a privileged to an unwanted minority. Soon after independence, African leaders castigated the Asians for living exclusive social lives and for not mixing socially with Africans, and Asian communal clubs and societies became the main targets of criticism. The Ministry of Home Affairs ordered the Asian clubs and societies and other racial institutions to amend their constitutions and remove any racial links from their names, or disband (*Tanganyika Standard*, November 21, 1964). The government also expressed concern about "the actual nature of the activities" carried out by Asian religious associations and about the fact that they did not even open their membership to fellow Asians, let alone Africans (*The Standard*, December 15, 1964).

> If they did not allow fellow Asians to join, it was difficult to see how they could tolerate people of another race. . . . The Regional Commissioner, Mr. S. Kitundu, said that Asians should consider themselves one with the indigenous people. If they did not watch out, they would be like people sitting on dynamite.

The male leaders of the various Asian organizations, who usually made decisions on matters affecting their communities as a whole, responded to these criticisms and pressures in a number of ways.[6] The first was a simple "decommunalization" of the names of their organizations and clubs. Thus, the Goan Institute became the Dar es Salaam Institute, the Goan Community became the St. Xavier's Society, Patel Brotherhood became Dar es Salaam Brotherhood, Hindu Sports Club became Upanga Sports Club, and the Hindu Volunteer Corps became Indo Tanzania Cultural Center.[7]

Second, the Asian clubs partially opened their doors to outsiders. Members of any racial and religious group were allowed to become members, visit the bar, participate in games and parties, and eat in the canteens. For example, the Goan Institute, which had resolved in 1955 not to permit any non-Goan guests to attend its events unless especially invited by the management (Goa Portuguese Community, Dar es Salaam, 1955), no longer disallowed outsiders on the grounds that they were not Goan. It is worth noting, however, that the decision-making powers over admission remained in the hands of the respective communities for whom the clubs had been established, which helped to keep the number of outsiders minimal. A male leader of the Goan community (interviewed on February 14, 1993) remarked:

> "We try to keep this ratio [of 75% Goans and 25% non-Goans] in check so that we may not lose our identity. . . . When we have a new application, the committee can say, 'Yes, we accept you' or 'No, we cannot accept you.' We don't have to give any reasons [for acceptance or rejection]. We can just say no [on the grounds] that the background [of the applicant] is not good. . . . So we can find the reasons to keep you out."

As a result, with the exception of the Dar es Salaam Institute (DI, formerly Goan Institute), which had only 1% African members according to its 1992 membership record, all other clubs continued to remain almost exclusively Asian, even though in theory they had opened their doors to Africans. A senior male member of the Goan community (interviewed on October 20, 1992) remarked:

> "In the beginning, we were afraid that Africans would pour into our club. At that time, most Goans regarded Africans as just houseboys and Ayahs—they had never mixed with or seen intellectual Africans. But as it turned out, most of the non-Goan members were Asians and there were hardly any Africans. [Africans] themselves feel that they cannot fit into our society. They have their own culture, their own people. Very few of them like it in the DI. They prefer their own [clubs]. Most of our non-Goan members are Asian [men] from communities where it is not allowed to drink publicly. Otherwise the DI is still Goan in character and, so far, all the posts in the committees have been held by Goans."

Third, in response to government pressures to open their organizations, various leaders of Hindu castes forged an ingenious strategy that allowed them to maintain their caste identities and boundaries. In the case of caste-based organizations, opening their doors to outsiders, even in theory, would have been synonymous with destroying the very purpose of their existence. A resourceful Hindu businessman who was involved in devising the strategy (interviewed on July 27, 1993) explained its origin in the following manner:

> "We [Hindus] had community halls owned by different castes and the government officials could have used them whenever they wanted to. But we didn't want to lose control over our places. I and some other people in the Hindu community had [personal] connections with ministers. So I asked them [ministers] what to do and they advised me. Although Tanzanian government did want to do away with communal and racial places, at the same time the government's policy was to not interfere with the affairs of any religious body. So we used that loophole and erected a small temple in our [caste-based] communal complex. We advised other castes to do the same thing. The idea became popular and almost all the castes adopted it."

Thus in postcolonial Tanzania, where the government had explicitly committed itself to respect the religious diversity of its peoples, the easiest way for caste-based organizations to retain their exclusivity was to redefine their communal spaces as religious spaces. They accomplished this by constructing little temples in the community halls.

This story of the redefinition of communal spaces offers a pointed example of the Hindu communities' response to a changing political context. In response to the threats from outside, members of different Hindu caste groups joined together to devise a strategy that would help them to maintain control over their communal places and as such maintain their caste-based Hindu identity.[8]

African attacks on Asians as exclusive and racist also affected relationships among different sections of the Asian community. For example, the Goan community in Dar es Salaam, while homogeneous in terms of religion (almost 100% of them being Roman Catholic), was deeply fragmented on class lines. This fragmentation was manifested in separate, exclusive organizations. The "Goan Community" organization (now St. Xavier's Society) was mainly run by men who worked in the civil service. The Goan tailors had their own organization, the "St. Francis Xavier's Tailors Society," which also had carpenters and cooks as members. Until the 1950s, Goan tailors were barred from membership in the Goan Institute (Goa Portuguese Community, Dar es Salaam, 1964). A Goan man whose father was a tailor (interviewed on August 12, 1993), recalled:

> "We Goans didn't just despise Seychelloise, we despised our own Goans. Tailors were not considered to be fit for the civil servants' society. [It was said about tailors that] they may know how to dress people, but they didn't know how to dress themselves. They just knew how to drink, sing and get drunk. The constitution of the Goan club [Goan Institute] clearly stated right through the 1950s that tailors and their children could not be members of the club. It was the civil servants who ran the entire show."

This class division within the Goan community, manifested in exclusionary communal institutions and places, however, began to be questioned in the postcolonial period. The Africanization of the civil service and thus the elimination of the Goan civil servant class, combined with soaring criticism of the Asian communities' exclusiveness by the postcolonial Tanzanian government, generated feelings of insecurity among the Goan community leaders sufficient to stimulate moves toward reducing divisions within their community (Goa Portuguese Community, Dar es Salaam, 1962; accounts of five Goan informants interviewed in Dar es Salaam in 1992–1993). For example, the Goan Institute (now Dar es Salaam Institute), which was perceived by non-Goans as the main communal place of the Goans, opened its doors to lower-class Goans. In this way, the Goan community leaders initiated the process of deemphasizing its class boundaries in response to outside pressures to secure the survival of the community as a whole.

The above examples have shown that class boundaries within Asian communities became more permeable as a result of changed political conditions and that, by and large, leaders of the Asian communities were successful in devising strategies that enabled them to maintain the exclusivity of their communal boundaries and places vis-à-vis Africans. This illustrates how internal divisions become less trenchant when the community is under external threat.

STRUGGLES OVER THE CONTROL OF LIVING SPACE: THE CASE OF THE KUMBHARWADA SETTLEMENT

In Gujarati, Kumbharwada literally means "the place where potters reside." The first Kumbharwada settlement emerged in the 1940s and 1950s in central Dar es Salaam (see Figure 10.2), with houses made of tin sheet roofs and bamboo poles to house Hindu potters along with some other poor, lower-caste Hindus. Some 50 families resided within the temporary fenced boundary of Kumbharwada, the majority of them working as manual laborers, artisans, housewives, domestic servants, and shop assistants. In the mid-1960s low-caste Hindus from Zanzibar and other homeless low-caste Hindus from Dar es Salaam, as well as some African and Zanzibari Arab families, started living in tin-roofed homes just outside the Kumbharwada fenced boundary.[9]

During the early 1970s this settlement was demolished to make way for a technical college. In 1973, the Tanzanian government provided the Kumbharwada residents with a plot of land on Olympio Street in Upanga for a temporary settlement (see Figure 10.3). Since then, this area, measuring less than two blocks, has accommodated 52 low-caste Hindu families in 35 houses and has served as a workplace for several of its residents who repair cars and make car seat covers for a living. Within this settlement, the Kumbharwada residents have established a one-room temple in the house of a Divecha family (the majority of the residents are from the Divecha caste), and an open area for gatherings during festivals and weddings. The gatherings are attended by not just the residents but also by several poor Hindus from Kariakoo, especially from the Divecha caste.

Cognizant of their temporary status, and in an attempt to pro-

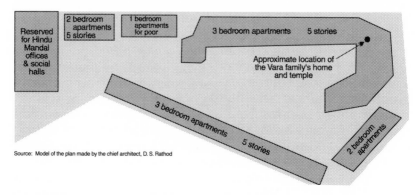

Source: Model of the plan made by the chief architect, D. S. Rathod

Source: Model of the plan made by the chief architect, D. S. Rathod

FIGURE 10.3. A sketch of the planned Kumbharwada housing estate as of August 1993.

tect their living and work space, representatives of Kumbharwada residents made repeated pleas to the government to allot the land permanently to them, but to no avail. In 1988, the Tanzania Assemblies of God attempted to convince the government that the Kumbharwada was a squatter settlement which should be demolished so that they could build a church, a dispensary, and a multipurpose complex. At first, the Tanzania Assemblies of God received the government's permission to take over the area and the Kumbharwada dwellers were once again ordered to move, this time to the African neighborhood of Tabata (Shree Hindu Mandal, Dar es Salaam, 1991).

Faced with the uprooting of their settlement and community, and fully aware of their powerless position, the Kumbharwada residents sought support from among the larger Hindu community. They approached the Hindu Mandal, the umbrella organization for Hindus led by high-caste and upper-class Hindus, to come to their support. One man (interviewed on August 1, 1993) recalled the thinking among Kumbharwada residents that precipitated this action:

> "We found ourselves in a weak position . . . because . . . the Assembly of God was a registered organization. When we realized our weak bargaining position, we had to involve the Hindu Mandal in our matters because Hindu Mandal was also a registered body. So, even though we felt distant from the Hindu Mandal because it is led by the rich and influential Hindus, we had to ask Hindu Mandal for help. . . . It was the choice between Assembly of God taking over the entire area versus collaborat-

ing with Hindu Mandal. We went for the second option because that was the only way to save our homes."

The Hindu Mandal came to their rescue and made a case to the government that Kumbharwada was not a squatter settlement and that its residents were entitled to live on that land. Between 1988 and 1990, the Hindu Mandal in collaboration with the Kumbharwada Residential Society entered into a struggle with the Tanzania Assemblies of God over control of the Kumbharwada settlement, with both parties making various appeals and reappeals to the Ministry of Lands. Finally, in 1990, the Hindu Mandal sent a petition containing the story of the old and new Kumbharwada to Tanzanian President Ali Hassan Mwinyi and an appeal to the world headquarters of the Assemblies of God. Following receipt of this petition, President Mwinyi visited Kumbharwada in May 1990 and subsequently the Kumbharwada plot was allocated to the Hindu Mandal (Shree Hindu Mandal, Dar es Salaam, 1991).

The battle of the Kumbharwada residents to protect their living space was not over, however. Although the space was protected against usurpation by the Assembly of God, the government had conferred control over the land to the Hindu Mandal rather than the Kumbharwada residents. This, in turn, engendered another conflict, this time along class and caste lines, between the Hindu Mandal and the Kumbharwada residents.

Once the Hindu Mandal had gained control of the land, it appointed a committee of eight Hindu men, including an architect, an engineer, and a contractor, to design a Kumbharwada Housing Project with the objective of safeguarding the area against future usurpation. This committee proposed to replace the one-story dwellings with multistoried apartment buildings and to secure all the corners of the plot in order to leave no further scope for allocation of the land to any other party (see Figure 10.3).[10] The apartment buildings being constructed during the time of this research in 1993 contained one-, two-, and three-bedroom units. After the completion of these buildings, a new office and community center for the Hindu Mandal was to be built. A member of Hindu Mandal's management committee (interviewed on October 29, 1992) explained the rationale behind the plan:

"The shanty dwellers do not have any money to pay for the construction. So first, apartments will be constructed for rich Hindus. Once the rich pay up, more construction will take place to house the shanty dwellers, either in low-priced flats or free one-bedroom complexes. . . . The Kumbharwada dwellers will lose their land to rich Hindus, but since they are poor they are not strong enough to stop organizations like the Assembly of God from trying to wipe them out. And they don't have the money to replace their huts with permanent structures which would not be so vulnerable to demolition. So acquisition of their plot by Hindu Mandal is their best option in the given circumstances."

However, a Kumbharwada resident (interviewed on August 1, 1993) read the situation differently:

"I am not happy with the way things are going now. The rich Hindus will end up gaining far more from this than us. . . . [Hindu Mandal people] are saying that those of us who can't afford to buy a flat, will get one room for free to live in. That makes sense to them, but it doesn't appeal to people like me. I may be poor, but why should I suffocate in a free room that will be given to me as a big favor when I have my own bigger place now? . . . We are still negotiating with Hindu Mandal. Half of the Kumbharwada Housing Committee is made up of our people. . . . And we are determined to not give up any more than what we have already given up."

One Kumbharwada family has become directly involved in the confrontation with the Hindu Mandal. The Varas, in whose home the Kumbharwada temple is located, have refused to move their temple and home from their present location, thereby thwarting Hindu Mandal's planned construction at that site. The chief architect of the Kumbharwada Housing Project (interviewed on August 16, 1993) lamented that, because of the Vara family's conflict with the Hindu Mandal, the project was going to take much longer than the Hindu Mandal officials had estimated.

The end of the struggle over control of Kumbharwada between the residents and Tanzania Assemblies of God thus paved the way for another class- and caste-based struggle between the residents of Kumbharwada and the Hindu Mandal. The Kumbharwada residents attempted to defend their own homes and communal space, while the Hindu Mandal pressed for full implementation of its proposed plan, which in the eyes of the Hindu leaders constituted a more efficient development of an underused area and one that they saw as benefiting the entire Hindu community.

The story of Kumbharwada exemplifies pointedly how people's actions are influenced by multiple, fluid, and intersecting social identities and material interests. Which of them assumes salience at a particular point in time and in a particular place is socially constituted as individuals and collectivities respond to cultural codes, material conditions, and relations of domination and subordination. In order to defend the Kumbharwada settlement against non-Asian intruders, the Kumbharwada residents felt compelled to form a strategic alliance across class and caste lines with the Hindu Mandal. The willingness of the Hindu Mandal to get involved in the struggle can be interpreted as an act to come to the rescue of Hindu sisters and brothers. And indeed, officially, the Hindu Mandal presented its action on behalf of the Kumbharwada residents as an act of Hindu solidarity. At the same time, Hindu Mandal's involvement can be interpreted as a calculated move to gain control over inner-city property and thus to further its material interests. As we have seen, the alliance between Hindu Mandal and the Kumbharwada residents broke down as soon as the Kumbharwada area was secured against non-Asian intruders. It was then that class and caste divisions and the unequal power relations associated with these divisions became salient again as the dominance of the Hindu Mandal was challenged by the Kumbharwada residents.

CONCLUSION

These narratives of social experiences and sociopolitical practices of Asian communities in Dar es Salaam have demonstrated that in addition to race and class, religious and caste identities form central nuclei around which communities are built, social lives of groups are organized and controlled, and power relations are contested. This does not mean, however, that we just have to add these categories to an investigation of difference in city life, since the examples have also shown the significance and complexity of multiple, fluid, and intersecting identities based on race, class, religion, and caste. The narratives also illustrate that we need to understand the actions and struggles of individuals and collectivities as simultaneously rooted in both social identities and material interests. Which of these assume salience at a particular point in time and a particular place is socially constituted as individuals and collectivities respond to cultural codes, material conditions and relations of domination and subordination.

Different places and spaces, however, cannot be thought of as simple stages on which these processes are played out, because the appropriation of place and control over material space are in fact central pivots in struggles for and negotiations over identities, social boundaries, and material reproduction. Communal institutions and places, such as community halls, temples, clubs, and neighborhoods of various Asian communities, were the sites of conflicts and struggles along race, caste, class, and religious lines: between the Tanzanian state and Asian community organizations, between the Tanzanian Assembly of God and Hindus, and between different castes and classes of the Hindu communities. The struggles discussed above with men as the chief players were centered around the issue of formal control over secular and religious communal institutions and places—for example, whether or not the Hindu temples and caste halls could remain exclusive, or whether the Kumbharwada belonged to the residents, the Tanzania Assemblies of God, or the Hindu Mandal.[11]

The outcome of these struggles led to a reconfiguration of the places in question and to the formation of new alliances. For example, in the case of Kumbharwada there was a temporary alliance among Hindus of different castes and classes to construct community "cohesiveness" in the face of external threats. Overall, however, there has been little change in prevailing norms and ideologies of the Asian communities and in the social and spatial relations between African and Asians. Asians' social activities and everyday life experiences continue to revolve primarily around their religious, caste, and sectarian institutions and places. For most of the Asian middle class, the only Africans with whom day-to-day interactions occur are African domestic servants, vendors, and employees working in Asian shops and businesses. Africans present in communal institutions such as temples, mosques, and clubs are there primarily in their capacity as servants, symbolic of their exclusion from mainstream social life of the Asian communities.

The racially mixed public primary and secondary schools do little to loosen the rigidity of this racial divide. As schools were desegregated and nationalized soon after independence, Asians began to open new private secondary schools. With the recent economic hardships and the deteriorating state of public schools, several private primary and nursery schools have also been started by the Ismaili, Ithna Asheri, and Hindu communities. Although these private schools are open to all in theory, they are dominated by Asian students whose parents can afford to pay the fees relatively more easily than can most Africans. Thus the social circuits of Asian children remain primarily confined to their own racial group.

No matter what angle we view them from, Asian communities in Dar es Salaam continue to operate in a social world that is generally far removed from that of the African communities with whom they share the physical space of the city. Furthermore, the discursive and nondiscursive practices of the majority of the members of Asian communities construct their own race, religion, sect, and language as superior, pure, and separate from the Africans, who are constructed as the impure and inferior "other." In times of economic and political crises, African resentment against Asian racism, economic privilege, and social and spatial exclusivity is easily stirred and manifested in negative stereotyping of all Asians as "exploitative," "disloyal," "self-interested," and "opportunistic" (Nagar, 1995).

The foregoing analysis suggests how difference on the lines of race, religion, caste, and class is interpreted differently by individuals and collectivities alike. These interpretations of difference and the ways in which they are acted upon can only be understood within the context of existing structures and relations of domination and oppression. The case studies discussed above show how multiple and intersecting social identities and power relations between Asians and Africans and within the Asian communities have been enacted, contested, and imposed in communal places and neighborhoods of Dar es Salaam. The strategies used by Asian communities to resist and accommodate to pressures of African authorities on communal places, as well as the cross-caste alliances and fissures among Asian communities in the struggle for control over Kumbharwada, illustrate how complex sociospatial processes intimately connect places to the sociopolitical practices of individual and collective actors and to their multiple, fluid, and overlapping social identities and interests.

ACKNOWLEDGMENTS

This research was supported by a grant from the National Science Foundation (No. SES-9205409) and a Davis Fellowship from the Department of Geography, University of Minnesota. We are grateful to Mui Le for his help with cartographic production.

NOTES

1. Throughout this chapter, the term "Asian" refers to people who are originally from what are now India and Pakistan.

2. Toward the end of the colonial period in Zanzibar, the Zanzibari society was polarized along the lines of Arab "haves" and African "have nots." Arabs owned most of the fertile, arable land with clove and coconut plantations, while most of the Africans living on such land were squatters whose security depended largely on their Arab landlords. Trade and commerce

was largely in the hands of Asian merchants who played a negligible direct role in politics. The British formed a small minority, mostly engaged in administration.

The end of the colonial era in Zanzibar saw the rise of Arab and African nationalisms and intense party politics. On December 10, 1963, Zanzibar formally became independent, but the majority of Africans saw it as independence for Arabs only. Finally, the Afro Shirazi party in collaboration with the Umma party carried out a bloody revolution that overthrew the sultanate on January 12, 1964.

The Revolution aimed to bring about social and economic equality for Zanzibari Africans and to eradicate feelings of racial superiority and class privilege among Asians and Arabs. After the Revolution, the majority of the movable and immovable property of Asians and Arabs was confiscated (Fair, 1993), all land was nationalized, all clubs based on religion, race or wealth were taken over by the government, schools were nationalized, the Clove Growers' Association was nationalized, and state shops were opened (Martin, 1978).

3. This number has been estimated on the basis of more than 30 interviews with Asian women and men from different communities and on the basis of information provided by an ex-employee of British Airways.

4. Estimates for 1993 are based on *Hindu Link,* Vol. 3 (published by Shree Hindu Mandal, Dar es Salaam, April 1991); *Biennial Report, 1988–89* of Khoja Shia Ithna Asheri Jamaat, Dar es Salaam (1991); interviews with the president of the Ithna Asheri Jamaat, Dar es Salaam (November 28, 1992), the treasurer of Saint Xavier's Society, Dar es Salaam (August 16, 1993), and the manager of the Sikh Temple, Dar es Salaam (July 11, 1993).

5. The Arusha Declaration (1967) which introduced state socialist ideals into the governance of Tanzania, aimed at the elimination of economic and social inequalities. All racial categories were removed from national statistical tables, abstracts, and censuses. For this reason, no census figures are available to show the present racial composition of different neighborhoods in Dar es Salaam. However, on the basis of 1988 census figures given for *Population in the regions by district and ward* (United Republic of Tanzania, 1990, p. 80), we have roughly estimated that some 30,000 Asians live in the wards of Kisutu, Upanga East, Upanga West, Kariakoo, Jangwani, Gerezani, Mchikichini, and Kivukoni.

6. With the exception of Goans, whose communal activities are not formally segregated on gender lines, almost all other Asian communities are characterized by gender segregation in their communal places. Asian communal organizations are male dominated. The office bearers of these organizations are primarily men, although women representatives head their own clubs or bodies that are responsible for organizing social and religious gatherings for women. For matters that affect the entire community, decisions are taken by the male leadership of the communal organizations, which also usually controls the finances.

7. This information has been obtained and verified through commu-

nal records, dates inscribed on communal buildings, and through interviews with community leaders.

8. Although the Muslim communities did have a few secular spaces, they were not as many or as prominent as the halls of the various Hindu castes. Due to the absence of numerous caste-based spaces among the Muslims, this kind of issue did not arise in their communities.

9. Conversation with a group of nine Kumbharwada residents, July 23, 1993.

10. This information is based on interviews conducted between October 1992 and August 1993 with the chairman of the Kumbharwada Housing Committee and a member of the management committee of Shree Hindu Mandal, Dar es Salaam.

11. Several women, who are often seen as "peripheral" in their communities, have used communal spaces to challenge the boundaries of these communities and the classed and gendered norms that are inscribed within them. These women have generally fought their battles alone without any support from the communal networks or structures. For further discussion on the gendered nature of the struggles in communal places, see Nagar (1995).

REFERENCES

Anzaldúa, G. (1987). *Borderlands/la frontera: The new mestiza.* San Francisco: Aunt lute Books.

Bell, D., Binnie, J., Cream, J., & Valentine, G. (1994). All hyped up and no place to go. *Gender, Place and Culture, 1*(1), 31–47.

Clark, H. (1993). Sites of resistance: Place, "race" and gender as sources of empowerment. In P. Jackson & J. Penrose (Eds.), *Constructions of race, place and nation* (pp. 121–142). Minneapolis: University of Minnesota Press.

Coulson, A. (1982). *Tanzania: A political economy.* Oxford: Clarendon Press.

Dar es Salaam Surveys and Mapping Division, Tanzanian Ministry of Lands, Settlement and Water Development. (1968). *City of Dar es Salaam, guide map* (3rd ed.).

Fair, L. (1993). A *house of mud, stories of stone: Tarab as an expression of struggles over class, gender and sexuality.* Paper presented at the Annual Conference of the African Studies Association, Boston.

Fimbo, G. M. (1974). Land, socialism, and the law in Tanzania. In G. Ruhumbika (Ed.), *Towards Ujamaa* (pp. 230–274). Kampala, Uganda: East African Literature Bureau.

Ford, R. (1994). The boundaries of race: Political geography in legal analysis. *Harvard Law Review, 107*(8), 1843–1921.

Goa Portuguese Community, Dar es Salaam (1955). *Minutes of annual general meeting,* February 15.

Goa Portuguese Community, Dar es Salaam (1962). *Minutes of emergency general meeting*, May 21.

Goa Portuguese Community, Dar es Salaam (1964). *Minutes of emergency general meeting*, October 6.

Hall, S. (1987). Minimal selves. *ICA Document on Identity, 6*, 44–46.

Hall, S. (1989). Cultural identity and cinematic representation. *Framework, 36*, 68–81.

Harris, R. (1984). Residential segregation and class formation in the capitalist city: A review and directions for research. *Progress in Human Geography, 8*(1), 26–49.

hooks, b. (1990). *Yearning: Race, gender and cultural politics*. Boston: South End Press.

Iliffe, J. (1979). *A modern history of Tanganyika*. Cambridge and New York: Cambridge University Press.

Jha, P. (1991). *Writing the nation: Hindi and the politics of cultural identity in colonial India*. Unpublished manuscript.

Keith, M., & Pile, S. (1993). Introduction part 1: The politics of place. In M. Keith & S. Pile (Eds.), *Place and the politics of identity* (pp. 1–21). New York: Routledge.

Khoja Shia Ithna Asheri Jamaat, Dar es Salaam. (1969). *Khoja Shia Ithna Asheri directory: 1969*. Dar es Salaam: Author.

Khoja Shia Ithna Asheri Jamaat, Dar es Salaam. (1991). *Biennial report: 1988–89*. Dar es Salaam: Author.

Lowe, L. (1991). Heterogeneity, hybridity, multiplicity: Marking Asian American differences. *Diaspora, 1*(1), 24–44.

Martin, E. B. (1978). *Zanzibar: Tradition and revolution*. London: Hamish Hamilton.

Nagar, R. (1993). Indigenization debate and Tanzanian Asians. *Africa World Review, May–October,* 24–25.

Nagar, R. (1995). *Making and breaking boundaries: Identity politics among South Asians in postcolonial Dar es Salaam*. PhD thesis, University of Minnesota, Minneapolis.

Nagar, R. (1997). Communal places and the politics of multiple identities: The case of Tanzanian Asians. *Ecumene, 4,* 3–26.

Nyerere, J. (1973). *Freedom and development: A selection from writings and speeches, 1968–1973*. Dar es Salaam: Oxford University Press.

Pratt, G., & Hanson, S. (1994). Geography and the construction of difference. *Gender, Place and Culture, 1*(1), 5–29.

Rosaldo, R. (1989). *Culture and truth: The remaking of social analysis*. Boston: Beacon Press.

Scott, J. (1986). Gender: A useful category of historical analysis. *The American Historical Review, 91*(5), 1053–1075.

Shivji, I. (1976). *Class struggles in Tanzania*. New York: Monthly Review Press.

Shree Hindu Mandal, Dar es Salaam. (1991, April). *Hindu Link, 3,* 14.

Soja, E., & Hooper, B. (1993). The spaces that difference makes. In M. Keith & S. Pile (Eds.), *Place and the politics of identity* (pp. 183–205). New York: Routledge.

Somers, M. (1992). Narrativity, narrative identity and social action: Rethinking English working-class formation. *Social Science History, 16*(4), 591–630.

Smith, M. P., & Tarallo, B. (1993). The postmodern city and the social construction of ethnicity in California. In M. Cross & M. Keith (Eds.), *Racism, the city and the state* (pp. 61–76). New York: Routledge.

Smith, S. (1993). Residential segregation and the politics of racialization. In M. Cross & M. Keith (Eds.), *Racism, the city, and the state* (pp. 128–143). New York: Routledge.

Tandon, Y. (1965). A political survey. In D. P. Ghai (Ed.), *Portrait of a minority: Asians in East Africa* (pp. 68–97). Nairobi, Kenya: Oxford University Press.

Trebon, T. J. (1980). *Development of the pre-independence educational system in Tanganyika with special emphasis on the role of missionaries.* PhD thesis, University of Denver.

United Republic of Tanzania. (1969). *Education Act, Tanzania Statutes, 1969.* Set 1, No. 50.

United Republic of Tanzania. (1990). *Tanzania sensa 1988, population census: Preliminary report.* Dar es Salaam: Bureau of Statistics, Ministry of Finance, Economic Affairs and Planning.

Watts, M. (1992). Space for everything (a commentary). *Cultural Anthropology, 7*(1), 115–130.

CHAPTER 11

Staging Difference

AESTHETICIZATION AND
THE POLITICS OF DIFFERENCE
IN CONTEMPORARY CITIES

Jane M. Jacobs

One of the features of contemporary cities often commented upon by analysts is the increased prevalence of the spectacle and processes of aestheticization. Urban transformations of all kinds are now understood to occur through the self-conscious exploitation of what might be thought of as cultural capital (Kearns & Philo, 1993, p. ix). Many types of urban change are taken into this ostensibly new cultural logic of city development: events-led planning, gentrification, the process of selling a city image, the expansion of sites of consumption, and even the rise of urban design as the new planning common sense. This transformation in the way in which urban development and change is understood to operate is regularly linked to the always voracious, but now more cleverly stylish, penetration of capital into the everyday lives of city dwellers. Relatedly, these processes of aestheticization and spectacularization are linked to the more complete grounding of capital accumulation in the sphere of consumption. Indeed, for many commentators the city of the spectacle is emblematic of postmodernity itself.

This chapter explores this specific understanding of the contemporary city in the context of postcolonial race relations. Aestheticization and spectacularization are often depicted as only ever working negatively: to override more real urban cultures (the appropriation of difference); as generating a proliferation of inauthentic diversity (depthless fragmentation); or as contributing to the production of new intensities of difference (social polarization). I wish to render problematic these commonly held views of the aestheticization of urban life. I argue that these perspectives overlook the multitude of ways a local politics of difference might brush against processes of spectacularization and aestheticization in the city. My aim is not to deny that urban processes may have entered into a new regime of signification, nor to rebuff the observation that in many contemporary cities there has been an intensification of the distinction between those who have and those who do not; rather, I reconsider the assumption that the aestheticization of city life only ever marks the familiar, albeit now more instrumentally semiotic, appropriative force of postmodern capitalism.

I elaborate this argument by exploring the cultural politics of urban space. By this I mean the various processes by which urban dwellers articulate their identities and interests through and in the spaces of the city. In existing accounts of the spectacular city this alternate cultural logic of urban space is relegated to the explanatory fringes. It is undeniable that cities are caught up in accelerated processes of globalization and that part of the way this manifests in urban space is through a cultural logic of image making. Yet cities are also sites where difference is amplified and where a situated politics of difference is acted out in a multitude of ways. There are many vectors of power at work in cities that structure how identity is articulated and rights and privileges are distributed. These vectors are not outside or incidental to the workings of capitalism, but they are often as not shaped by relations of difference whose complexity cannot simply be reduced to a narrow script of capital accumulation.[1] This is especially evident in processes of racialization and racial difference that are not simply outcomes of the uneven workings of capitalism but deeply embedded in historically constituted structures of power.

Empirical flesh is given to this argument by examining the way in which a racialized politics comes into contact with processes of aestheticization in contemporary Australian cities. Australian cities, as with cities in other settler colonies like South Africa or Canada, provide distinctive and useful variants on the First World city. These cities display many of the hallmarks of what is understood as postmodernity: gentrification, events-led redevelopment, city boosterism, self-conscious place making, and the emergence of various sites of spectacle (shopping malls, waterside redevelopments, theme parks). Yet these same cities are also products of a colonial past, and they exist in nations that are struggling toward a postcolonial future. In the Australian context the various aestheticized formations associated with cities that might be thought of as postmodern also negotiate a more local inheritance of (post)colonialism.[2] In the Australian context, British colonization resulted in Aboriginal people being dispossessed of their lands and marginalized from the emergent settler society. Until the 1950s Aboriginal people were encouraged to live away from urban areas on designated reserves and missions. Only those Aborigines who were judged to be suitable for assimilation into mainstream Australian society were deemed appropriate urban citizens. During the 1960s and 1970s the indigenous rights movement ensured, among other things, that Aboriginal people could become legitimate participants in urban life in Australia. Now small but politically vocal indigenous minorities live in most Australian cities. And while the more significant efforts to recognize Aboriginal rights to land have involved nonurban areas, as this paper will show, Australian cities have not been untouched by such postcolonial restructurings. To set processes of postmodernity into a context of postcoloniality necessarily and productively complicates the way each is understood. It challenges many of the assumed outcomes of processes of aestheticization by pointing to the unpredictable ways these come into contact with a situated politics that structures specific social differences.

RETHINKING THE HEGEMONY OF VISION[3]

In his account of the condition of postmodernity David Harvey (1989) elaborates the links between postmodernity, the restructuring of capital accumulation around consumption, and processes of aestheticization. As he so succinctly put it, "Postmodernism . . . signals nothing more than a logical extension of the power of the market over the whole range of cultural production" (Harvey, 1989, p. 62). Of course, Harvey's depiction of the condition of postmodernity draws heavily on Fredric Jameson's (1984) thesis about the cultural logic of Late Capitalism. For Jameson the defining feature of Late Capitalism has been the way in which culture has been appropriated and set to work as the fuel for the now semiotic motor of capital accumulation.

This transformation to a semiotic society, regulated by new regimes of representation and image making, is almost routinely given flesh by referring to the space of the city. In the city of consumption the manipulation of desire is paramount. As Featherstone (1991, p. 99) notes:

> The postmodern city is therefore much more image and culturally self-conscious; it is both a centre of cultural consumption and general consumption, and the latter . . . cannot be detached

from cultural signs and imagery, so that urban lifestyles, everyday life and leisure activities themselves in varying degrees are
influenced by the postmodern simulational tendencies.[4]

There is a central irony in this understanding of postmodernity: at
the same time that culture is placed center stage (as the new logic of
transformation), it is also divested of a more wide-ranging and everyday role in the lives of city dwellers. For example, Jameson and other
like-minded commentators place a predominantly negative inflection
upon the aestheticization of city space. For Jameson a once "semi-
autonomous" and authentic culture, is transformed into a hyperreality
of depthless culture. Similarly, real histories become "a series of per-
petual presents" (Jameson, 1984; see also Featherstone, 1992, p. 267).
For Sharon Zukin, aestheticized urban transformation, such as
gentrification or themed redevelopment, results in the dismantling
of "older urban solidarities," which are then replaced with consumption spaces "shaded by new modes of cultural appropriation" (Zukin,
1992, p. 221). In this view, the new cultural logic of global capitalism
simply works to estrange "real culture" from its more authentic, because more localized, origins. This now homeless vernacular is transformed into what Boyer (1992, p. 204) refers to as "the spectacle of
history made false."

Culture is certainly not centered in a productive way in these
accounts of the aestheticized city. Rather, here is a version of a far
more familiar positioning of culture as "mask," false consciousness,
or a "veil" over more "real" processes (Harvey, 1989, p. 87) . For David
Harvey the "urban spectacle" has been deployed to attract capital, to
augment entrepreneurialism, to legitimate change—in short, to act
as the more opaque face of new processes of accumulation and social
and political regulation. The city has become a "city of illusion" (Boyer,
1993, p. 111), a giant theme park (Sorkin, 1992; Zukin, 1991). In this
transformation, culture (understood as aestheticization) comes to
serve a decidedly modernist grand narrative about the new logic of
capital accumulation.[5]

There is a problematic relationship between the idea of the spectacular city of consumption and the notion of a politics of difference.
On the one hand, difference and diversity are acknowledged as fundamentally important components in this new aestheticized urban
logic. For example, it is acknowledged that new architectural and
urban design forms celebrate difference, selectively harvesting the
local and the past and reassembling the desired elements in an or-
chestrated pastiche. Similarly, cities wanting to court marauding capital
often emphasize ethnic diversity or local character as a way of com-
petitively marking their distinctiveness. And consumption industries

more generally intensify the diversity of their product in order to tap increasingly differentiated and discerning markets. Yet, on the other hand, this new diversity is often cast simply as a *play* of difference that is ultimately subordinate to the "cultural dominant" of consumption (Cooke, 1988, p. 479). In this sense the proliferation of difference is thought of as something which masks what is really a globalized cultural logic (King, 1993). Extending this argument, Jameson (1984, p. 61) has suggested that the proliferation of desires associated with this global culture of commodification has resulted in a "waning of affect" and a demise in "feeling . . . emotion, all subjectivity."

The emphasis that these accounts give to the *play* of difference as opposed to a *politics* of difference has not gone unremarked. Most notably David Harvey's account of postmodernity came under critical fire from feminist scholars like Rosalyn Deutsche (1991), Doreen Massey (1991), and Meaghan Morris (1992). Each argued that Harvey had failed to allow his account of the logic of the contemporary moment to come into contact with feminist ideas and political agendas or even, for that matter, alternately positioned articulations of difference. In particular, Morris' (1992, p. 258) response to Harvey is framed around the violence his account does to a productive notion of aesthetics and its role in meaningful politics of difference. As Morris notes, Harvey's meta-narrative of the cultural logic of capital "rewrit[es] as 'the same' all the differences" he sees as distinguishing postmodernity.

Such criticism might also apply to the way accounts of postmodern cities deal with other vectors of difference, including racialized difference. For example, Harvey's attempts to address race in the postmodern city demonstrate the assumption that "politics" has been transformed into "play," or that "affect" has become mere "effect":

> The geography of differentiated tastes and cultures is turned into a pot-pouri of internationalism that is in many respects more startling, perhaps because more jumbled, than high internationalism ever was . . . [T]his produces a plethora of "Little" Italies, Havanas, Tokyos, Koreas, Kingstons, and Karachis as well as Chinatowns, Latino *barrios*, Arab quarters, Turkish zones, and the like. Yet the effect . . . is to draw a veil over the real geography. (Harvey, 1989, p. 87)

At the hand of the cultural logic of capitalism, racial and ethnic difference and the associated processes of racialization are reduced to festivals, costume dramas, and sanitized and exoticized ethnic enclaves. Harvey even goes so far as to suggest that aestheticization works to pacify more unruly articulations of racial difference. Drawing on the example of the city of Baltimore, Harvey (1989, pp. 88–89) charts the way in which city officials invented a festival of "ethnic diversity" as a means of reclaiming downtown spaces that had previously been the site of less playful "urban spectacles" of "race riots."

For commentators like Harvey and Jameson, postmodernity has produced a political crisis. In these accounts, difference has no disruptive potential. It is only something that capitalism makes use of to give urban transformation an "accommodating face" (Kearns & Philo, 1993, p. 23). Difference is merely that which postmodernity disempowers by "ghettoizing . . . within an opaque otherness" (Harvey, 1989, p. 117). Dressed in the play of motifs and images that gesture to local pasts and celebrate other cultures, these new forms of urban transformation can guard against the "antagonism that might otherwise have surfaced from indigenous local populations" (Kearns & Philo, 1993, p. 23). Similarly, even as Soja (1989, pp. 74, 219) acknowledges new possibilities in a "postmodern politics of resistance" he, at the same time, despairs at the "numbing depoliticization" that has occurred in his beloved Los Angeles (see also Gregory, 1994, p. 307).

In his later work *Thirdspace* (1996), Soja self-consciously encounters theorists of difference in an attempt to elaborate his postmodern urbanism. At least part of *Thirdspace* concerns itself with processes of spectacularization in the "exopolis" of Orange County, California (1996). Soja, like Harvey and Jameson before him, comes to his views on processes of spectacularization under the influence of Jean Baudrillard (see especially 1983). Baudrillard's writings on the collapsed division between the real and the unreal and the emergence of the hyperreal, what he calls simulacra, has been undeniably important. At its most productive it contributes to uncoupling the chain of signification and revealing the often arbitrary alignments of signs and things. Yet his is also an undeniably cynical view of the consequences of this unsettlement of signification. While such an uncoupling might well stand at the brink of a subversive politics of difference, it is often taken to stand merely as a surprisingly uncomplicated indicator of capitalist mystification. Certainly Soja's analysis of Orange County wavers between these possibilities. He strives to replace cynicism with creativity. On the one hand he sees spetacularization as part of "creatively erosive postmodern urban geographies." On the other hand he still positions it as the mask of "corruption, deceit, greed, emptiness" (Soja 1996, pp. 278, 279).

Many of the preceding accounts of the postmodern city display an uncritical acceptance of the depoliticizing force of aestheticization. There is little sense of the ways in which the concerns of racial and ethnic minorities, say, might *not* be placated by the introduction of ethnic festivals, nor is there is any hint of how such groups might transform these new arenas of *play* into more familiar arenas of *politics*. Once having charted the displacement of politics by play, it is not surprising that these commentators on postmodernity display a certain nostalgia for the way it once was. They yearn for that time when there was "real" politics. They yearn for that time when they imagine an authentic local culture was better protected from the maraudings of global capital. They yearn for that time when, to coin the terminology of Raymond Williams, "residual" forms of cultural production could provide the ground spring for a counterhegemonic politics (see Jameson, 1984, p. 57). It seems that most commentators on postmodern urbanism have been quite at a loss when thinking about politics in this new regime of signification. For Harvey, postmodernity created a political dilemma based around the cleavage between the presumably always "reactionary politics of an aestheticized spatiality" and the now disempowered politics of "others" whose causes are articulated locally, whose political formations are fragmented, and whose struggles always risk being commodified (Harvey, 1989, p. 305).

This loss of politics is not a pregiven consequence of the aestheticization of contemporary society. It is, rather, a consequence of the way in which various commentators on postmodernity have conceptualized aesthetics, images, and signification. As both Deutsche (1991, p. 22) and Morris (1992, p. 265) have noted, these accounts of postmodernity refuse to see the realm of images and image making as meaningful practice: something which is socially produced, has politics, is material, and is productive. Moreover, there are still organized oppositions to urban redevelopments, no matter how clever their disguises. The logic of capital is regularly subverted by the everyday uses that urban dwellers make of their city spaces. In short, urban-based political processes continue at a variety of scales and around a wide range of issues. Indeed, the creation of spectacles and processes of aestheticization may even serve these other agendas in ways not envisaged in these existing accounts of the postmodern city.

Of course, playful appropriation is not the only framework through which race and ethnic difference are understood in contemporary accounts of postmodern cities. The discussion of the increasing levels of social polarization in postmodern cities also incorporates some attention to such vectors of difference. Lash and Urry (1994, pp. 145–146), for example, argue that "large numbers of immigrants" flow into the new and more sharply differentiated lower classes of the contemporary city. Within social polarization arguments, race and ethnicity become variant forms of class differentiation, an outcome of new distributional frameworks of advantage and disadvantage. Social polarization debates do alert us to important racialized outcomes in the postmodern city. Yet they tend to set these outcomes apart from the complexly embedded structures of power which ensure that the new underclass is indeed racialized. Moreover, the accounts of social polarization rarely attend to the various ways in which racialized groups might negotiate and subvert their historically constituted marginalization. So while social polarization accounts remind us that race matters in a most material sense in the sociospatial patternings of contemporary cities, they too deactivate the cultural politics of racialization. Keith and Cross (1993, p. 8), somewhat disturbed by the way in which race and ethnicity were being theorized in the context of the postmodern city, called for commentators to take more seriously the seemingly "taboo . . . architecture of power" associated with racialized differences. For them this adjustment would bring many so-called postmodern cities into contact with their colonial and neocolonial underbellies. In a similar vein, Paul Gilroy (1987, p. 228) made a plea for urban analysts to take seriously the "cultural politics" of race and racialization "as contending definitions of what city life is about."

In the remainder of this chapter I will examine some examples of the way in which processes of aestheticization intersect with a (post)colonial urban politics. My purpose here is twofold. First, I want to demonstrate the variability of processes of aestheticization in the contemporary city. Sometimes the making of an urban spectacle is just that, spectacular: in scale, in capital outlay, in political will. But aestheticization also has more diminutive articulations in the contemporary city, being manifest in localized urban design projects, in community arts initiatives, and in government-led place making and place-enhancement projects. The political effects that might attend megadevelopments which quite instrumentally utilize image making may not necessarily be associated with these alternate processes of aestheticization and place making. These alternate transformations of urban space may entail complex partnerships between local groups, the state, and private capital investors. They may even be part of quite genuine initiatives intended to create more inclusive urban spaces. Indeed, these more modest spectacles may even provide space for the articulation of those oppositional political forces for which so many analysts yearn. My second purpose in what follows is to demonstrate the unpredictable outcomes of processes of aestheticization at all scales. Be they the legitimating skin of capital accumulation or the result of a well-intended inclusionary planning, the political outcomes of the processes of aestheticization are by no means pregiven.

DISPLACING RACE

The Formula One Grand Prix encapsulates many of the features scripted into the logic of consumption characterizing postmodern cities. Here is a sports and leisure event that ranges across the globe, annually landing in those cities which have managed to woo Grand Prix organizers and convince them that they are adequately equipped to deal with such a prestigious event. The right to host the Grand Prix is fiercely sought after on the grounds that it brings enormous economic gains to the host city, increasing tourism and benefiting the service sector. Telecast worldwide, it is also an event that Grand Prix boosters claim can put a city "on the map." That the Grand Prix is a desired event was clearly illustrated in the recent struggle over which city should host the Australian race meeting. The city of Melbourne successfully wrested control of the event from the city of Adelaide, and this was cast by the conservative government of the state of Victoria as a economic coup of unprecedented proportions. Unlike many other Grand Prix circuits, the Melbourne circuit is located in the center of the city and uses existing road networks that run through a large park. Albert Park is now annually given over to the roar of Formula One racing cars.[7]

The Grand Prix meeting is an event that overflows into the urban spaces which surround it. In the case of the Melbourne Grand Prix it was anticipated that race goers would, at the end of the day, spill into the restaurant and club precinct of the nearby seaside area of St. Kilda. Like many seaside areas in contemporary cities, St. Kilda recently has been subject to efforts to revive and to stylize its image. Down-at-heel pubs have been transformed into bijoux restaurants and galleries, greasy cafés have reinvented themselves as "continental" cafés whose tables and chairs now spill onto the public pavements. The main street has been townscaped in ways that celebrate the diversity and "artistic" character of the community. The nearby Grand Prix event was not simply going to put Melbourne on the map but would also consolidate St. Kilda's role as one of the foremost entertainment areas of the city.

In the week preceding the inaugural Melbourne Grand Prix in March 1996, traders and local government officials in St. Kilda were busy preparing for the influx of race goers. In that week, in the early hours of one morning, a toilet block located in a small park at the end of the main restaurant street in St. Kilda was demolished. This was no ordinary toilet block. The building was covered with artwork depicting the Aboriginal flag, the important Aboriginal site of Uluru (Ayers Rock), and figures from creation stories of indigenous Australians. The toilet block stood in a small open space that was used by a group of about 30–40 local Aborigines as a meeting place (Figure 11.1). It is here that this small group of Aboriginal people talked, drank, dried out, and slept. It was a mobile and fluid group consisting of Aboriginal people from Melbourne as well as visitors from other parts of the country. Many of the group were homeless or relied on temporary housing, many were welfare dependent, and many were alcohol and drug dependent. Local community service groups regularly dropped in—providing wood for the communal fire and checking to see if anyone needed food, medical attention, or assistance in dealing with welfare agencies.

The "parkies" of Cleve Gardens were an increasingly anachronistic sight in the rapidly gentrifying restaurant precinct of St. Kilda. For some years the local traders had been complaining to the municipal authority about the parkies, calling for the area to be "cleaned up." Local community service groups, including Aboriginal services, had also expressed concern about the parkies and had attempted to pressure the municipal authority into providing better facilities for them. There was also concern, expressed by both Aboriginal and non-Aboriginal community service groups, that the parkies presented a negative and undesirable image of urban Aborigines to the wider public.

FIGURE 11.1. View of Cleve Gardens, St. Kilda, meeting place for local Aborigines and later defined by planners as a traffic island.

It was in the context of this mounting concern over the parkies that the local government passed a number of local "environmental" by-laws. The Environment Local Law No. 3, City of Port Phillip (1995), explicitly sought to "control activities which may be dangerous or unsafe or detrimental to the quality of life" in the municipality. The Streets, Roads and Other Public Places Local Law No. 4, City of Port Phillip (1995), enacted controls directed at keeping "peace, order and well being" in the foreshore area (including Cleve Gardens). Included in this local law was a provision that allowed the local authority to "regulate the use of reserves and other public places," including the power to "designate areas and times during which alcoholic beverages may not be taken into such areas." Although broadly applicable, these local bylaws had specific implications for the parkies. The provisions for the control of "nuisances and noise, odour and smoke emissions" directly implicated their use of open fires to keep warm and cook. The controls of drinking in public places was clearly a mechanism that could be used to regulate the current use of this open space by the parkies. If the parkies themselves were not "illegal," then certainly these local "environmental" laws ensured that specific aspects of the way they occupied this space were legislated to be so.

From 1994 to 1996 the local government established first a working group and then a task force to consider the fate of the parkies and of Cleve Gardens itself. Early initiatives did not envisage removing the parkies but proposed instead that Cleve Gardens be redesigned so that it might better serve their needs as well as ensure that a more "positive" image of Aboriginality was presented to the public. This plan did not assume that the parkies would be moved. It sought to improve facilities for the parkies by building a new toilet block, fireplaces, and even rudimentary shelters for those sleeping out. The initial scheme for Cleve Gardens also included landscaping and design features that were explicitly influenced by Aboriginal themes and motifs, albeit ones which drew solely from traditionalized versions of Aboriginal culture.

This relatively sympathetic approach to accommodating the parkies use of Cleve Gardens into the increasingly gentrified surrounds was short lived. This initial plan never eventuated and was ultimately shelved on the grounds that it was inappropriate: not only too costly but not necessarily in the interests of the parkies or the wider community. Included in the emergence of a less accommodating stance toward the parkies was the subtle redefinition of the open space in official discourses. Cleve Gardens transformed from a "park" to a "traffic island," a redefinition that not only justified claims that the area should not be overdeveloped but also that any human occupation of the park was "unsafe" (Port Phillip Council, 1995, p. 3). A 1995 discussion paper commissioned by the local government noted that the park had "become associated with anti-social behaviour resulting mainly from excessive alcohol consumption. Some of these behaviours are drunkenness, begging, harassment, violence and public hygiene issues associated with homelessness" (Port Phillip Council, 1995, p. 3). The report was careful to specifically state that this antisocial behavior was not necessarily associated with the Aboriginal parkies but also with other non-Aborigines attracted to Cleve Gardens. Despite this careful delineation between behavior and a racially categorized group, there is little doubt that the "anti-social behaviour" of this site was publicly coded as "Aboriginal."[8]

The local authority finally decided upon a multipronged initiative to solve the "problem" of Cleve Gardens. It was agreed that the site was not appropriate for its current uses and that parkies should be encouraged to use other, more appropriate (and less visible) open spaces in St. Kilda. To this end, a new (and better equipped) toilet block was constructed in another nearby park. Hostel accommodation for the parkies was also provided in a street further away from the main restaurant precinct. Free of its troublesome dwellers, Cleve Gardens itself was then to be "beautified" (City of Port Phillip, correspondence, March 4, 1996, in minutes of the Cleve Gardens Task Group, June 26, 1995). Some $A40,000 was allocated for the landscaping of the Gardens, which is to include market stalls for the sale of Aboriginal arts and crafts, Aboriginal-inspired pathways and walls featuring the artwork of a local Aboriginal artist, the replanting of the Gardens using native grasses and shrubs, and the construction of a "memorial and cultural marker." The "cultural marker," also to be designed by a local Aboriginal artist, is to pay homage to the Aborigines of the area, including some who had recently died.

In the local press much was made of the fact that the demolition of the toilet blocks at Cleve Gardens occurred in the week prior to the International Grand Prix. Although the synchronicity of these two events is remarkable, the demolition of the toilet block was simply one moment in a much longer history of local efforts to contain and regulate the Aboriginal presence in St. Kilda. In a context of the expansion and gentrification of this restaurant precinct, the parkies of Cleve Gardens had become increasingly anachronistic (Cresswell, 1996; Sibley, 1995). The pressure from local traders to "clean up" the area coalesced with the reformist visions of Aboriginal and non-Aboriginal bureaucrats who felt the parkies gave Aborigines more generally a negative image. Together these forces resulted in the Cleve Gardens parkies being constructed as aberrant, unclean, and dysfunctional. The arrival of the Grand Prix in Melbourne, and the planned role St. Kilda was to play in servicing the entertainment overflow from the event, energized this incremental trend toward excluding Aborigines from the main restaurant precinct (Sibley, 1995). St. Kilda is a highly diverse urban area in a nation that envisions itself as both multicultural and postcolonial. In this context, the complete erasure of an Aboriginal presence would be inconsistent with such a politics of inclusiveness. The tension between a drive toward exclusion and the desire for inclusionary difference resolved itself in the making of a sanitized, planned, and most disembodied indigenous garden. Here unruly embodied Aborigines were replaced by native vegetation, Aboriginal designs, and—most tellingly—a "memorial cultural marker."

PRODUCING OTHERNESS

In the example of Cleve Gardens urban Aborigines were displaced by the requirements of consumption-based industries, both local and global. Here embodied difference did transform itself into a playful, sanitized expression of inclusiveness. Here consumption-based development and urban Aborigines were cast as incommensurate things that had no business being proximate to one another. In this section I would like to turn to another example of the making of a site of spectacular consumption and the way it came into contact with urban Aboriginal interests.[9] In this case a consumption-based redevelopment actually helped to produce a specific articulation of difference in the form of Aboriginal claims for the spiritual significance of the redevelopment site. Faced with this opposition developers sought to incorporate specific, but ultimately unacceptable, forms of Aboriginality into their scheme. This example shows clearly that processes of aestheticization do not operate in any simple way to deactivate politics and legitimate change. Rather, this example shows exactly how such developments can activate a cultural politics of difference in which signification and material rights are complexly entwined.

During the 1980s in the city of Perth, Western Australia, a development partnership between the state government and private investors proposed a scheme to redevelop an old brewery site. Like many inner-city redevelopments of this time, the scheme envisaged transforming now redundant brewery buildings into a shopping, restaurant, and gallery complex. It was precisely the sort of redevelopment that is associated with the postmodern city. The 19th-century buildings were to be restored and made into the architectural centerpiece of the development. Initial plans included office space, a 450-vehicle parking lot, a 500-seat theatre, a museum display, a boutique brewery, various "multicultural" food outlets, and a "genuine Aussie pub." The function of the building was to center entirely around consumption, thereby marking that familiar reinvention of now defunct sites of production into places to eat, to buy art, to shop, and to be entertained. The redevelopment was to improve the city's attractiveness as a tourist destination, thus confirming that the economic survival of Perth, just like that of many other cities around the world, is increasingly reliant on service industries.

This redevelopment was actively opposed by local Aborigines who claimed that it would violate the resting place of the Waugal serpent, a dreaming creature responsible for the creation of many of the natural features over which the city of Perth had been built. In colonial nations like Australia the early development of cities had consciously sought to confine Aborigines to certain areas in the space of the city or exclude them from it. Aborigines were antithetical to the colonial project of creating familiar copies of home, to ordering these unknown spaces into knowable gridded plans, to making the colonial city the material embodiment of the pure idea of the imperial self. That such processes were only ever partially successful is evident in the modern-day claim by local Perth Aborigines to the spiritual status of this prime piece of city real estate. Not only did the descendants of the original inhabitants of the lands that became Perth survive (although often in the most marginal and economically deprived areas of the city), but so too did their sense of the spiritual significance of the land. For the non-Aboriginal residents of Perth and the development consortia, this claim for the spiritual significance of the brewery site was an unexpected return of an Aboriginal interest in lands that were presumed to be fully given over to urbanization.

In recent years Perth has, like many other cities, begun self-consciously to celebrate the diversity of the city. Under a local planning initiative called CityVision various planning experts have proposed a new city master plan that is to take Perth into the 21st century. This is, as the title of the plan suggests, very much an exercise in manipulating the visual qualities of the city. Historic buildings of the city's colonial past are celebrated along side the more recent traces of the diverse multicultural population. Ethnic food precincts and festivals are planned, and the distinctiveness of the city and its various localities is to be enhanced through a sympathetic combination of building restoration and townscaping. It was into this more self-consciously multicultural, historically referential and decidedly visual city that the proposal to redevelop the brewery came.

It might be expected that the city's new emphasis on the celebration and enhancement of difference would readily accommodate Aboriginal claims and interests. But it is in the specific coincidence between the impulse to redevelop and the impulse to register difference that most unlikely articulations of a politics of difference were generated. The development boom in Perth had resulted in the initiation of a systematic program of identifying and registering sites of Aboriginal significance (Vinnicombe, 1989). Of course, all of these sites already existed, but many were known only to local Aborigines or to archaeological experts. That is, these sites were "known" within the confines of what were essentially local knowledge systems. The systematic program of site identification and registration transformed these locally known sites into *public* sites—giving them legal protection under the Aboriginal Heritage Act, placing them onto official registers and maps, and ensuring that they entered into the planning equation for development in Perth. In this sense, the redevelopment push of the 1980s actually helped to produce the *public* and *legally sanctioned* Aboriginal site of significance.

City planning authorities were faced with the dilemma of reconciling the increased number of officially registered and protected sites of Aboriginal significance with the intensified redevelopment pressures. It was decided that it would be impractical to save all Aboriginal sites and that only the "most important . . . most representative or most informative" sites should and could be preserved in the urban context (Stawbridge, 1987/8, p. 18). The precise mapping of sites of significance and the designation of "real physical boundaries" were crucially important strategies in ensuring that Aboriginal interests and redevelopment interests could happily coexist (Strawbridge, 1987/8, p. 21). This desire to map precisely Aboriginal sites responded to the spatial logic of planning for development. It ensured that Aboriginal sites of significance were neatly defined, discrete parcels of land that might then be kept apart from other incompatible land uses. The registration of Aboriginal sites was a strategy that, on the one hand, recognized difference but, on the other, sought also to manage that difference.

This neatly managed incorporation of difference was severely unsettled by the struggle over the redevelopment of the brewery, a struggle which turned explicitly on the fact that Aboriginal land interests and developer aspirations occupied the same space. Efforts were made to map the precise location of the Waugal site in the hope that it could be conveniently separated from the main development site. But all efforts to map the exact location of this Aboriginal site were inconclusive, and redevelopment and the Waugal remained as promiscuous cohabitants of the same space: the former threatening to violate the latter, the latter threatening to halt the former.

The Aboriginal opposition to the redevelopment was intense and sustained. It included an 18-month reoccupation of land near the development site as well as various legal challenges to the legitimacy of a development that would place a registered, and legally protected, Aboriginal site of significance at risk. The developers attempted to placate the opponents by incorporating Aboriginal themes into their redevelopment plans. A new pathway, which was to lead from the parking lot to the main complex, was designed in the form of the Waugal serpent. It was proposed that an Aboriginal art collection be put on permanent display in the gallery. Both of these strategies to placate the Aboriginal protest worked through regimes of aestheticization. They were attempts to displace a racialized politics of opposition with a facade of inclusiveness. As such, these efforts to Aboriginalize the brewery redevelopment scheme accord well with current depictions of how culture and racialized difference are set to work within postmodern processes of legitimation. Yet in the case of the brewery redevelopment none of these strategies functioned successfully to dissipate Aboriginal claims over the site. Local Aborigines rejected these overtures of inclusiveness: their occupation of the redevelopment site continued, their legal challenges to the legitimacy of the redevelopment proceeded undeterred, and their resolve to see the area turned into a public parkland hardened. It was not the force of a clever capitalism dressed in the legitimating skin of an Aboriginalized aesthetic that finally defeated the Aboriginal protesters. It was, as has long been the case in Australia, the force of the law which finally found in favor of redevelopment and emptied the site of protesters.

This example of postmodern urban development both conforms with and deviates from the accepted accounts of how aestheticization functions in the contemporary city. Certainly, this redevelopment occurred under the logic of culture in the service of capital accumulation. It was a development that attempted to breathe new life into a dead industrial site by transforming it into a spectacular site of consumption. The spectacle was built most surely around a self-conscious incorporation of difference: ethnic restaurants, "Aussie pubs," and gestures to indigenous interests. And, certainly, there is evidence to suggest that the inclusion of signifiers of Aboriginality into the scheme was an instrumental attempt to pacify Aboriginal opposition. Furthermore, the way in which Aboriginality was incorporated into the development plans was limited to those dimensions which would supplement the main objectives of the development and augment its appearance of inclusiveness.

Yet none of these gestures worked to placate Aboriginal opposition to the redevelopment. Indeed, it is possible to read this redevelopment controversy, and the more general trends toward inclusiveness that were occurring in the broader revisions to the planning strategies for Perth, in exactly the opposite way. It may well be that processes of aestheticization and inclusive planning that gesture to difference actually work to produce an intensification of a politics of difference. For example, the efforts to map and plan for Aboriginal sites of significance actually ensured that Aboriginal claims over the city had a certain legitimacy which, even if eventually defeated, could not be entirely ignored. Similarly, the proposal to redevelop the brewery actually transformed locally held knowledges about the Waugal dreaming site into a highly politicized and uncompromising Aboriginal claim for that space. The efforts to map Aboriginal sites of significance in Perth and the proposals to symbolically Aboriginalize the brewery site did not do away with politics. They activated a postcolonial politics which had long been imagined as no longer of any relevance to the city of Perth.

TRACKING DIFFERENCE

An often unstated component of the arguments about the aestheticization and spectacularization of urban space is the issue of scale. It is those specific developments where grand spectacle combines with large-scale capital investment (the shopping mall, the theme park, and the spectacular event) that tend to provide the most secure evidence for the negative outcomes of aestheticization and spectacularization. This emphasis on developments and events of this scale overlooks the way in which processes of aestheticization and spectacularization are present at a variety of scales in contemporary cities. Nowhere is this more evident than in the growing importance of design and community arts in the sphere of urban planning. In this final case study I examine the way in which the aestheticized logic of urban design/community arts projects comes into contact with a postcolonial politics of difference. This is not simply a case of arguing that the smaller the scale, the more benign the effects. It is, instead, an acknowledgment that these other mechanisms of aestheticization can play a part in an activated urban politics. The example I draw upon to illustrate this point is a community arts/ urban design project which was conceived and built in the central business district of Melbourne in the early 1990s. Like the other examples I have drawn upon thus far, this case study demonstrates the way in which postmodern processes of aestheticization are complexly entwined with postcolonial political struggles.

In 1994 the City of Melbourne commissioned one Aboriginal and one non-Aboriginal artist to work together to produce what was entitled the "Another View Walking Trail." The Trail winds through the streets of the central business district, passing some 17 sites that include newly installed artworks as well as existing monuments and buildings. Many of the installations are quite modest in scale, and each site is marked only by a small plaque set into the ground. A guidebook with a detailed commentary about the Trail is available to the interested city stroller from tourist information outlets dotted about the city.

The Another View Walking Trail was devised and executed as a local articulation of the national goal of Aboriginal and non-Aboriginal reconciliation. The Council for Aboriginal Reconciliation, established in 1991 in order to achieve this goal, seeks to improve non-Aboriginal understanding of Aboriginal culture and Aboriginal experiences under colonialism (Council for Aboriginal Reconciliation, 1993, p. 1). A major function of the Council is to establish frameworks for reeducating non-Aboriginal Australians so that the nation might be more at one with itself. The pedagogical aims of reconciliation focus specifically on rearranging what is known about the birth of the modern nation of Australia and those who live in it. It attempts to bring the nation into contact with the "truth" of its past in order that there might be a certain "healing" in the present. From the outset it was intended that the official national commitment to reconciliation articulate itself "in smaller, practical, localized terms" through community-based initiatives (Council for Aboriginal Reconciliation, 1994, p. 5). Local government authorities and community groups throughout Australia were encouraged to initiate projects that accorded with the goals of reconciliation.

The Another View Walking Trail was one of many attempts to articulate reconciliation on-the-ground. In accordance with national goals, it sought to reeducate the public of Melbourne about the "true" history of the city and the nation. The Trail also sought to (re)-Aboriginalize city space symbolically by introducing Aboriginal imagery into the streetscape of a city which, like many Australian cities, had managed to relegate Aborigines to its margins. It was to chart a new geography of urban Aboriginality by producing artworks and narratives that challenged the conventional understanding of the city.

The way in which this community arts/urban design intervention worked to establish "another view" of the city was varied. In some instances new artworks were installed that spoke of the more violent and less grand aspects of colonial settlement. One artwork, for example, memorialized the first Aboriginal hangings at the Old Melbourne Gaol (i.e., U.S. "Jail"; Figures 11.2 and 11.3). Another installation of a Perspex casket containing bones and bullets was placed at the foot of the statue of one of the nation's early explorers. Other installations celebrated those Aborigines who actively resisted colonial settlement. In other instances, existing structures associated with imperialism, such as statues of Queen Victoria (Figure 11.4) or of early explorers and buildings like the law courts, the jail, and the remand center, were given different histories in the accompanying guidebook. Under this "other" visualization and narration these grand monuments of imperial triumph were transformed into monuments of Aboriginal suffering and loss. Other artwork sought to insert into the city streets expressions of Aboriginal creation beliefs such as the Rainbow Serpent story, the Seven Sisters Dreaming, or the Aboriginal story of the creation of men and women (Figure 11.5). These traditionally inspired works sought to uncover the lost cultural substrata of the city. They were self-conscious and deliberate attempts to articulate traditions long displaced by the space of city. By means of this diverse set of aesthetic and narrative strategies, the Walking Trail afforded "views" that counteracted and subverted the "known" his-

FIGURE 11.2. Totem pole artwork memorializing the first Aboriginal hangings at the Old Melbourne Gaol.

FIGURE 11.3. Detail of Aboriginal hangings artwork, showing noose.

tory and geography of the City of Melbourne. At some spots it took symbols of the dominant culture and destabilized their authority by presenting oppositional narratives of the events they represented. At others it reclaimed city space by inserting into the built environment strategic performances of Aboriginal tradition.

The Another View Walking Trail is an example of a quite different kind of aestheticization of urban space. It sought to create a legitimate space in which difference could be articulated. This was not simply in terms of traditionalized constructs of Aboriginality, although this certainly was one form that the artwork took. It also provided space for artworks with more troubled (and more clearly political) messages of Aboriginal suffering under colonialism. This example unsettles many of the assumptions that are associated with the processes of urban aestheticization. This spectacle served a nationally endorsed political agenda rather than the honed needs of profit

FIGURE 11.4. Statue of Queen Victoria that was incorporated into the Another View Walking Trail.

makers. Here the spectacle did not work as a "veil" but as a mechanism in the unveiling of a nation's past. Of course, I am presenting a very untroubled reading of this alternate manifestation of the aestheticization of urban space. It is one thing to observe that this particular project did much more than simply use difference as a disguise for processes of capital accumulation. But it is another thing to idealize this project as an example of how aestheticization might work to be unproblematically inclusive.

The response to the Trail suggests that this process of Aboriginalizing urban space succeeded less in its goal of producing a pathway to reconciliation than in activating non-Aboriginal expressions of resentment. Those artworks which were based around expressions of traditional Aboriginal views entered without controversy into the space of the city. These works conformed precisely to the ways in which non-Aboriginal Australians prefer to encounter their indigenous cohabitants—linked to a primitivized past which is viewed

FIGURE 11.5. Mosaic of Rainbow Serpent inserted into Melbourne's streetscape.

as more spiritual than political. But those artworks which addressed the bitter history of Aboriginal and non-Aboriginal confrontations, or which sought to subvert the narratives memorialized in the grand monuments of the city, met with considerable hostility. Rather than opening a pathway to reconciliation, these artworks generated controversy precisely because they attempted to adjust the "truth" of the nation. One press report dubbed this the "guilt trail" (Stevens, 1996, p. A15), and even before it was completed five of the planned artworks were withdrawn on the grounds that they were "too controversial" and "extremely confrontational" (City of Melbourne public art officer quoted in McKay, 1996, p. 1). The remains of the censored artworks that came to be placed along the Another View Walking Trail do give an alternate view of Melbourne that both inserts Aboriginality into the space of the city and subjects city space to a postcolonial political agenda. But those artworks which never made it onto the streets of Melbourne speak of a far more familiar—less reconciliatory—view of the space of the city and the nation.

This final example is intended to radically unsettle the assumptions that attend those who cast aestheticization simply as an instrumental mechanism in legitimating capital accumulation and deactivating politics. These artworks were intended to operate as local manifestations of a national agenda of reconciliation; they were commissioned for this explicitly political purpose. Of course the intended political effect of the Trail was subject to arbitrary fortunes. Rather than producing a calm state of reconciliation, it activated anxieties and worries among influential Melburnians who were concerned that their view of the city, and the stories which gave them authority over the city, were being destabilized. This unsettlement was activated not by a spectacularly grand aestheticized event, nor even by a claim by Aborigines to have their sovereign rights to the space of the city recognized, but by what was a quite modest aestheticized intervention in the design of city space.

CONCLUSION

In this chapter I have endeavored to reevaluate the way in which processes of aestheticization and spectacularization are thought about in the context of contemporary cities. In the first instance, I have argued that existing accounts of the postmodern city have tended to position these processes negatively, as part of the more cleverly semiotic face of capital accumulation. If these processes are linked to a politics of difference, such as ethnic or racial difference, then it is generally assumed that these differences are only displaced by or appropriated into new modes of consumption. In short, it is assumed that aestheticization is a mechanism whereby markers of difference are incorporated as the legitimizing skin of capital accumulation. Understood in this way, aestheticization operates to disguise unfriendly, exclusionary, and undemocratic redevelopments as just the opposite—friendly, inclusive, democratic. Moreover, it is often implied that this processes of staging difference works to displace or pacify a more real politics of difference.

One way I sought to challenge this existing view was by identifying a variety of forms that aestheticization and spectacle making take in contemporary cities. It is true that many of the large-scale sites of consumption that are typical of the contemporary city depend upon mechanisms of aestheticization. But it also true that aestheticization operates as the logic of many more modest urban transformations such as streetscaping, place making, and community arts projects. Some of these transformations assist in the selling of cities, but some may be addressing alternate agendas such as building identity or facilitating political formations among severely marginalized groups. In this more diversely motivated visual logic, it is not only the interests of big capital that are served. Aestheticization may also be the way in which national and local political agendas (be they agendas of inclusion or exclusion) are manifested.

The case studies drawn on in this chapter also unsettle the notion that aestheticization and spectacle making only result in exclusion and political pacification. As the case of the International Grand Prix event illustrates, this may well be an outcome of development that is more in tune with the aesthetic requirements of the international event than with obligations to local minorities. But equally, the case of the brewery redevelopment in Perth demonstrates that consumption-led spectacles which "play" with difference do not always succeed in deactivating a politics based around minority claims. It may well be the case, as in Perth, that such spectacular redevelopments activate political struggles that are fundamentally about how different interests should be registered (aesthetically and materially) in the space of the city.

Processes of aestheticization and spectacularization are not outside politics simply because of their scale, visual cleverness, or complicity with capital. Image making and processes of visualization are always also part of the way in which identities are formed, articulated, and contested. They are always open to reinterpretation and refusals. They may also operate in radically subversive ways, as part of political agendas that may effectively destabilize powerful interests. All processes of aestheticization are embedded in the material and political realities of city life that impart to them a productive instability. If these processes are prescripted as simply acting as the legitimating skin of capital accumulation, then these sometimes empowering complexities will be overlooked. But if the visual regimes of contemporary cities are thought about as activated spheres of practice in which various vectors of power and difference are meaningfully negotiated, then the story of the aestheticization of the city will unfold in ways that will defy the expected.

ACKNOWLEDGMENTS

I would like to thank Bev Kliger and Kate Kerkin of the School of Landscape, Environment and Planning at the Royal Melbourne Institute of Technology University for access to their data on Cleve Gardens. I would also like to thank Adrienne Barrett for her assistance with the background research for this chapter and Ruth Fincher for comments on an earlier draft.

NOTES

1. Kearns and Philo (1993, pp. 7–10) provide a useful historical explication of this point in *Selling Places: The City as Cultural Capital, Past and Present,* the volume they edited.

2. "Colonialism" and "postcolonialism" are complex terms whose meaning is still under considerable debate. I refer to colonialism as the processes of domination that were inaugurated during the imperial territorial expan-

sions of Europe in the 18th and 19th century but that may continue to shape structures of power and difference in the present. Postcolonialism in this chapter refers to far more than the formal state of sovereign independence from a colonial power. Nor do I use the term to indicate a sure state of being. Postcolonialism is best thought about as a set of diverse formations that work against colonial structures of power. They may be starkly oppositional (nationalisms, resistances of various kinds), but they may also refer to a range of formations (such as hybridity or mimesis) that work in subtle ways to subvert and unsettle colonial authority.

3. This heading takes the term "hegemony of vision" from a paper by Sharon Zukin entitled "Cultural Strategies of Economic Development and the Hegemony of Vision," presented at the Conference on Social Justice and the City: An Agenda for a New Millennium, School of Geography, Oxford University, March 14–15, 1994. (See also Zukin, 1991.)

4. While the current emphasis on consumption is regularly aligned with a distinctively different style of capital accumulation, it may be a process which is not that new. Featherstone (1992, p. 281) notes that a number of commentators on the 19th-century city had described the presence of "consumer-culture 'dream worlds'" in the emerging arcades and department stores. Featherstone concludes that "many of the features associated with the postmodern aestheticization of everyday life have their basis in modernity."

5. As Janet Wolff (1992, p. 555) so astutely notes, "looking at culture doesn't guarantee a postmodern perspective," and this is certainly not the outcome of Harvey's encounter.

6. The data for this section were kindly provided by Bev Kliger and Kate Kerkin of the School of Landscape, Environment and Planning at the Royal Melbourne Institute of Technology (RMIT University), Melbourne.

7. The arrival of the Grand Prix in this normally quiet area of the city was not unopposed. Middle-class residents whose houses adjoined Albert Park protested openly about the noise, the traffic problems, the privatization of their public amenity.

8. It was precisely such a conflation of antisocial behavior with Aboriginality that resulted, a few years earlier, in one local restaurateur banning an Aboriginal customer from entering his premises. The restaurateur later discovered he had banned a man who had recently been designated as Australian of the Year and who held an Order of Australia Medal!

9. A more detailed account of this case appears in my book *Edge of Empire: Postcolonialism and the City* (Jacobs, 1996).

REFERENCES

Baudrillard, J. (1983). *Simulations*. New York: Semiotext(e).

Boyer, M. C. (1992). Cities for sale: Merchandising history at South Street Seaport. In M. Sorkin (Ed.), *Variations on a theme park: The new American city and the end of public space* (pp. 181–204). New York: Noonday Press.

Boyer, M. C. (1993). The city of illusion: New York's public spaces. In P. L.

Knox (Ed.), *The restless urban landscape* (pp. 111–126). Englewood Cliffs, NJ: Prentice Hall.

Cooke, P. (1988). Modernity, postmodernity and the city. *Theory, Culture and Society, 5*(2–3), 475–492.

Council for Aboriginal Reconciliation. (1993). *Addressing the key issues for reconciliation: Overview of key issue papers No. 1–8.* Canberra: Australian Government Publishing Service.

Council for Aboriginal Reconciliation. (1994). *Footprints catalogue.* Canberra: Australian Government Publishing Service.

Cresswell, T. (1996). *In place/out of place: Geography, ideology and transgression.* Minneapolis: University of Minnesota Press.

Deutsche, R. (1991). Boys Town. *Environment and Planning D: Society and Space, 9,* 5–30.

Featherstone, M. (1991). *Consumer culture and postmodernism.* London: Sage.

Featherstone, M. (1992). Postmodernism and the aestheticization of everyday life. In S. Lash & J. Friedman (Eds.), *Modernity and identity* (pp. 265–290). Oxford: Blackwell.

Gilroy, P. (1987). *There ain't no black in the Union Jack.* London: Hutchinson.

Gregory, D. (1994). *Geographical imaginations.* Cambridge, MA: Blackwell.

Harvey, D. (1989). *The condition of postmodernity.* Oxford: Blackwell.

Jacobs, J. M. (1996). *Edge of empire: Postcolonialism and the city.* London and New York: Routledge.

Jameson, F. (1984). Postmodernism, or the cultural logic of Late Capitalism. *New Left Review, 146,* 53–92.

Kearns, G., & Philo, C. (Eds.). (1993). *Selling places: The city as cultural capital, past and present.* Oxford: Pergamon Press.

Keith, M., & Cross, M. (1993). Racism and the postmodern city. In M. Cross & M. Keith (Eds.), *Racism, the city and the state* (pp. 1–31). London and New York: Routledge.

King, A. D. (1993). Identity and difference: The internationalization of capital and the globalization of culture. In P. L. Knox (Ed.), *The restless urban landscape.* Englewood Cliffs, NJ: Prentice Hall.

Lash, S., & Urry, J. (1994). *Economies of signs and space.* London: Sage.

Massey, D. (1991). Flexible sexism. *Environment and Planning D: Society and Space, 9,* 31–57.

McKay, S. (1996, January 6). Massacre memorials "too confrontational." *The Age,* p. 1.

Morris, M. (1992). The man in the mirror: David Harvey's "condition" of postmodernity. *Theory, Culture and Society, 9,* 253–279.

Port Phillip Council. (1995, November). *Planning for future uses of Cleve Gardens: A discussion paper.* Melbourne: City of Port Phillip.

Sibley, D. (1995). *Geographies of exclusion.* London: Routledge.

Soja, E. W. (1989). *Postmodern geographies: The reassertion of space in critical social theory.* London: Verso.

Soja, E. W. (1996). *Thirdspace: Journeys to Los Angeles and other real-and-imagined places.* Cambridge, MA: Blackwell.

Sorkin, M. (1992). *Variations on a theme park: The new American city and the end of public space.* New York: Noonday Press.

Stevens, J. (1996, January 6). Another view of city's history. *The Age,* p. A15.

Strawbridge, L. (1987/8). *Aboriginal sites in the Perth metropolitan area: A management scheme* (Report for the Department of Aboriginal Sites, Western Australia Museum). Perth: University of Western Australia, Centre for Prehistory.

Vinnicombe, P. (1989). *Gooniniup: An historical perspective of land use and associations in the Old Swan Brewery area.* Perth: Department of Aboriginal Sites, Western Australia Museum.

Wolff, J. (1992). The real city, the discursive city, the disappearing city: Postmodernism and urban sociology. *Theory and Society, 21,* 553–560.

Zukin, S. (1991). *Landcapes of power: From Detroit to Disney World.* Berkeley, University of California Press.

Zukin, S. (1992). Postmodern urban landscapes: Mapping culture and power. In S. Lash & J. Friedman (Eds.), *Modernity and identity* (pp. 221–247). Oxford: Blackwell.

Zukin, S. (1994, March 14–15). *Cultural strategies of economic development and the hegemony of vision.* Paper presented at the Conference on Social Justice and the City: An Agenda for the New Millennium, School of Geography, Oxford University.

CHAPTER 12

Whose City?

GENDER, CLASS, AND IMMIGRANTS IN GLOBALIZING EUROPEAN CITIES[1]

Eleonore Kofman

A number of authors have highlighted the development and increased intensity of social polarization and exclusion, particularly marked in the major cities that are the strategic sites of the global economy (Castells, 1994; Friedmann, 1986; Fainstein, Gordon, & Harloe, 1992; Sassen, 1991, 1994a, 1995). For some (e.g., Castells, 1989) the dominance of the global city has resulted from the emergence of an informational mode of development and a space of flows; for others (e.g., Sassen, 1991, 1994a, 1994b) it is the restructuring and the production of financial services that makes these cities the key sites of authority and power in the global economy. Whatever theoretical framework is followed, the core idea is a restructuring of capitalism that expels the middle strata from the city and leads, on the one hand, to the expansion of higher-level professional and managerial classes and, on the other, to increasingly precarious and informal activities at the lower end, filled disproportionately by women and immigrants. These processes are instrumental in increasing segregation within such global cities. However, for Marcuse (1989, 1993) the notion of the dual city is highly problematic in that it obscures the relationships of power and profit in the city. Divisions in society exist along many lines such that dual cities would be best described as many cities coexisting in time and space, and interrelated with each other to produce a quartered city.

In this chapter I begin by outlining theorizations of the emergence of global cities and consequent social divisions and polarization. The literature is now so extensive that it is not possible to do it justice (for a review and evaluation of theoretical and empirical development in the past decade, see Knox & Taylor, 1995). I have chosen to focus on social divisions, difference, and inequality since this is one of the main axes along which the theory of global cities has been applied to European contexts. My initial concern is with the effect of global processes upon the internal structure of certain global cities, rather than how these cities constitute and concretize the global system (Beauregard, 1995, p. 232). I argue that, despite the growing attention to European modes of regulation and politics of planning and housing, the significance of gender divisions, the specificity of histories of immigration, and the contemporary insertion of immigrants and ethnic minorities within a broader economic and political context all continue to be underplayed in the analysis of European globalizing cities.

The impact of different welfare regimes in Europe, primarily derived from Esping-Andersen's typology (1990), has been noted (Dielman & Hamnett, 1994; Musterd, 1994), but the gendered nature of these regimes (Lewis, 1993; Kofman & Sales, 1996) has largely been ignored. Secondly, the role of women as agents in the transformation of the city is only slowly being acknowledged, whether it be in the context of gentrification (see Bondi, 1991, for a feminist reading) or in the debate around professionalization, polarization, and socioeconomic urban change (Breugel, Lyons, & Perrons, 1995; Hamnett, 1994a, 1994b). What is clear is that gender makes a difference to the nature of stratification and widening inequalities, a difference that cannot be measured in terms of the neutered and decontextualized individual. In relation to immigration and ethnic diversity, European cities do not contain anywhere near as high a proportion of immigrants and ethnic minorities as do comparable American cities, though immigrants are seen as forming part of the rising European underclass (Musterd, 1994). European societies in general do not see themselves as societies of immigration despite decades of substantial immigration.

An appreciation of the interaction of gender, immigration, and ethnicity is vital to understanding the new forms of social stratification in major European cities. I cannot, in the space available, present a comprehensive picture of these changes but shall restrict myself to some key elements that we researchers ought to bear in mind in establishing the nature of the new sociospatial geography of globalizing European cities. In the final section I consider the global city as a contested site and that the "right to the city" (Kofman & Lebas, 1996) might not be reserved just for the privileged, for there remains in these cities a capacity for social movements to fight against some effects of processes of exclusion and marginalization (Mayer, 1995).

This is not to say that for exponents of the dual or polarized city all possibilities of change or resistance have been closed off. For Sassen (1994a, 1996a), global cities are also contested sites in which, through reterritorialization and the new politics of identity, immigrant communities attempt to reclaim spaces. Castells (1994, p. 32), in an even more optimistic vein, concludes that "European cities, because they are cities and not just locales, could manage the articulation of the spaces of flows and the spaces of places, between function and experience, between power and culture, thus recreating the city of the future by building on the foundations of their past."

CAPITALIST RESTRUCTURING AND THE GLOBAL CITY

The conceptualization of global cities, initially designated as world cities, was strongly influenced by world systems theory and a critique of urbanization analyzed in national terms (Friedmann & Wolff, 1982). Friedmann (1986) set out an agenda for research starting from the view that such cities serve as the nodes of accumulation and concentration of international finance. The nature and extent of the city's integration into the spatial division of labor associated with the global economy would structure and differentiate their form. In addition, national pasts, policies, and cultural influences play a role in shaping such cities. The combination of spatial dispersal and global integration have given major cities a key strategic role as the centers of coordination and control in the current reconstitution of the world economy (Sassen, 1991), thus generating a new geography of centrality and marginality.

For Castells (1989) the current stage in the restructuring of capitalism is predicated on information technologies, in which the sources of economic, cultural, and political power in society are dependent upon the retrieval, storing, processing, and generating of information and knowledge. It is these changes which have produced the information mode of production that operates through spaces of flows, eliminating the meaning of historically determined places. Sassen (1991), on the other hand, contends that we should focus on the processes and workers who are required to produce the global city, rather than focusing on the disembodied outputs common to much research on the informational city. The circulation of capital in an economy that increasingly operates as a unit in real time has not ushered in the end of geography as some believe (O'Brien, 1992; see Martin, 1993, for a critique). On the contrary, the global city represents the concrete localization of contradictions and conflicts between opposing tendencies in the global economy (Sassen, 1994a) and constitutes an element of the dominant economic narrative about the city (Sassen, 1996a).

Global cities are particularly attractive sites for international migration both because of the expansion of professional and managerial classes and the availability of low-level, unskilled employment. The latter caters for the new consumption needs of the higher-income groups. The expansion of both ends of the employment spectrum has resulted in increased social and spatial polarization, most sharply manifested in cities such as Los Angeles and New York. Deregulation made finance so profitable that it took investment away from manufacturing, which also faced competition from Third World countries in certain sectors. What then tended to disappear as a result of the deindustrialization processes was the skilled manual middle-income jobs (primarily male), which from the early 1960s to the mid-1970s had largely accounted for job creation. At the same time, the expansion of the white-collar sector has been much slower, and more selective reindustrialization of high technology, lower-wage, and deunionized work have occurred (King, 1990, p. 27). Lower-wage jobs in maintenance, cleaning, tourism, clerical work, hotels, restaurants, and domestic service are the categories growing fastest. It is precisely the casualization and informalization of labor processes that have supplied the opportunities for flows of immigration, both legal and— to a notable extent—undocumented and illegal. The interaction and confrontation of ethnically, racially, and culturally different populations from economically poor societies and the rich core societies has thus taken place in global cities (King, 1990, p. 38).

Inflows of national and international workers generate massive needs for investment for social reproduction in housing, education, health, transportation, and welfare. Against this are the needs of transnational capital for economic infrastructure and its own social reproduction (Friedmann, 1986). Transnational elites increasingly seek to shape the city in their image and for their own needs. Again, possibly more in European than in American cities, these elites have both reinvested in the heritage of the city and developed new commercial and residential areas. These landscapes of power (Zukin, 1992) are not just the brash visualization of the material and symbolic aspirations of the affluent; they also affirm a (re)appropriation and consumption of the past.

EUROPEAN GLOBALIZING CITIES

Some major cities in Europe are emerging as the driving force of European societies at the same time as nation-states[2] are seen by some to be losing their power in this respect (e.g., Castells, 1994). Until recently, much of the research on global cities focused on the three major financial centers of the global system—New York, London, and Tokyo—and the model of global cities was largely derived from the American urban experience of large-scale immigration flows. It is only recently that continental European cities (Castells, 1994) in the Randstad (the central cities region of the Netherlands; see below—also Hamnett, 1994a), Paris (Sassen, 1994b), Frankfurt (Keil & Ronneberger, 1994) and now Berlin (Krätke, 1992) have begun to receive some attention as global cities.

Yet, in the case of major European cities, the appellation of "global" becomes even more problematic. It calls into question the nature of globalization, the term regionalization being preferred by some (e.g., Overbeek, 1994) in the context of the emergence of a tripolar world divided into three zones of economic power (North America, Europe, and the Asia–Pacific region), and the increasing pace of European integration. The multiplicity and multilayered scales at which different agents operate is also pronounced in the European context, where the local/global paradigm of the 1980s is deficient—not only theoretically (Beauregard, 1995; Smith, 1995) but practically. Cities are inserted into local, regional, national, supraregional (European Union), and global fields. Indeed, certain authors (e.g., Keil & Ronneberger, 1994), following Leborgne and Lipietz (1988), subscribe to a regional regime of accumulation and mode of regulation to explain the shift from the Fordist city to post-Fordist or after-Fordist[3] urbanization that involves new forms of spatiality and power. Applying the concept of globalization mechanistically tends to neglect the other aspect of global cities, that is, "their rootedness in a politically organized 'life space' with its own history, institutions, culture and politics" (Friedmann, 1995, p. 34), and marginalizes the specificity of national modes of regulation and welfare regimes (Burgers, 1996; Dielman & Hamnett, 1994) interacting with specific social structures.

European cities differ markedly in relation to the ways in which they embrace, acquiesce, adapt, and resist global forces (Beauregard, 1995, pp. 235–238; Keil & Ronneberger, 1994, on Frankfurt). As capital cities they retain a role in defining national identity, especially through the built environment, and are attractive as postimperial cities for Third World populations (King, 1990, 1995). For example,

Paris remains an unchallenged national intellectual capital (Rhein, 1996, pp. 46–51) over which different political forces strive to impose their physical and symbolic imprint. The city expresses the tension between the president as architect (Collard, 1992) and the economic and political forces behind the mayor (Carpenter, Chauviré, & White, 1994). The latter in particular have played a prominent part in converting the East of the city into an extended building site. The Randstad (Netherlands), including its financial center of Amsterdam, provides an unusually high proportion of social housing, though recent legislation signals a probable end to this situation (Priemus, 1995). The potential of Berlin to emerge as a global city has resulted from the reunification of Germany and the working out of a particular post-Fordist model of development and urban politics (Häussermann & Strom, 1994; Krätke, 1992; Lash, 1993). Nowhere, as Häussermann and Strom (1994) remark, are the tensions between the local and the national, the symbolic and the mundane, more striking than in Berlin. These differences modulate the reshaping of the city and struggles over the right to the city by particular strata and groups.

Centers of cities are seen as the battleground between the upper middle classes on the one hand, and the younger, educated countercultures that occupy the interstices of the urban fabric (Castells, 1994), on the other; they also house areas of immigrant concentrations. What has frequently happened is that the working class and earlier groups of immigrants, who had access to social housing, have been exiled to the peripheral areas in the process of redevelopment and gentrification (Carpenter et al., 1994; Keil & Ronneberger, 1994). These groups have lost the right to the city. As elaborated in a later section, struggles over housing, whether previously by squatters or now by the homeless, call most forcefully into question fundamental values pertaining to the appropriation of urban space. So too have these processes led to a discussion within a pluralist interpretation rather than in a neo-Marxist one about the emergence of an underclass (Haussermann & Sachmann, 1994; Musterd, 1994) in major European cities. The term "underclass" is defined by these writers as comprising that stratum of the population lacking an opportunity for social mobility and consequently subject to exclusion. As Wacquant (1993) points out, there is considerable danger in transposing an American concept to European contexts, and Woodward (1995) suggests that the notion of an underclass might well constitute a chaotic concept.

The emergence of the global city has also brought into being new familiar and unfamiliar social geographies (see Duncan, 1991, for London). Sassen (1991, p. 255) briefly suggests the study of the household, as a place of work with patterns that vary according to class and race, to be highly significant in understanding the transformation of global cities. High-income and the new two-career households tend to be locations of paid rather than unpaid housework. Low-income immigrant households on the other hand, are often places for paid industrial work and mostly unpaid housework. Castells (1994, p. 25), too, claims that "the transformation of households and the domestic division of [labor] are fundamentally changing the demands on collective consumption, [and] thus in urban policy . . . [childcare] is becoming as important an issue as housing in today's cities"—somewhat wishful thinking!

Certainly the entry of women into the labor force, and not just into the professional and managerial strata, has led to a greater demand for welfare services and paid domestic labor, but the means by which this is provided will vary from one (gendered) welfare regime to another. Law and Wolch[4] (1993) have examined the restructuring of welfare, community, and new household forms, and their implications for daily activity patterns and new forms of the built environment, in relation to class and gender privileges in American cities. This does not necessarily mean, however, that such changes have arisen from global processes. Drawing primarily from the New York situation, Marcuse (1989) deepens the analysis of sociospatial patterns in the interplay of gender and race through different household and familial configurations in his quartered city. (1) In the luxury city, women live as wives and members of minority groups only appear as service workers. (2) In the gentrified city, single-person households often predominate and women are accepted in the workplace. (3) The city of the traditional family is racially segregated; women, though regularly employed, are also traditionally mothers and "helpmates." (4) In the tenement city, women are often heads of households. Sassen (1996a, p. 27), too, speculates on the urban effect of female-led middle-class gentrification and a strong family base in immigrant communities in terms of an increased demand for family services.

Compared to national averages of household structures, single-person households are a significant and distinctive element of global cities. Female managers and professionals, far more than males, live in single-person or dual-career households (Sassen, 1991, p. 258). Men continue to live in more traditional familial structures. In 1990, 60.8% of persons living alone in Paris were female and 60.7% in the Île-de-France; 50.2% of single-female households in Paris were in paid work, 45.2% in the Île-de-France, and 32.2% in France as a whole. While the bourgeoisie never left Paris, the city has undergone rapid *embourgeoisement* (gentrification), especially in the eastern *quartiers.* Similarly, in Inner London fewer employed women, and especially professional (45.36%) and managerial (48.01%) women, tend to live with a male partner than do their counterparts in manual employment (between 53.6% and 65.7%) (Breugel et al., 1995). As elsewhere, women in London have been active agents in processes of gentrification (Bondi, 1991), although as Butler and Hamnett (1994) stress, it is the combination of class—especially certain sections of the middle class—and gender that underlies this process. In Paris and London, single women and dual-career couples, who are overrepresented compared to national averages, have either been attracted to or remained in the center, often by accepting lower-quality and smaller-size housing. Most studies of polarization and restructuring in global cities have tended to focus on income or occupational change of individuals, on the one hand, or on spatial change, on the other, without linking the two (Breugel et al., 1995; Musterd, 1994). Yet, as we have seen, households provide another unit of measurement.

So far, I have noted some of the preliminary attempts to incorporate a gender dimension into an understanding of the transformation of global cities, of which a crucial element has been the significance of international migration. Immigrant and ethnic minority populations, who constitute the majority in New York or Los Angeles, are not duplicated in European cities. So, for example, in the 1991 census, only 20% of Greater London and 25% of Inner London's population were from ethnic minorities, and 24% in Amsterdam (Hamnett, 1994, p. 408), whereas 13.7% were foreigners in 1990 in Greater Paris (Rhein, 1996, p. 47). French data refer to foreigners, or those without French citizenship. More than 38% of all immigrants in 1990 lived in the Île-de-France, an increase from 36.3% in 1982. The estimation of immigration is more problematic, especially with the opening up of internal European borders as well as the differences in definitions and paucity of data collection in many states (Salt, Singleton, & Hogarth, 1994; White, 1993). Furthermore, the focus on ethnic minorities or those groups who pose problems of integration in a national context, such as North African and other Francophone African-origin populations in France, tends to make these the groups singled out in studies and in the production of statistics about immigrants (Kofman, 1997). In Britain the emphasis on an ethnic minority and race relations paradigm tends to marginalize newer immigrant groups left out of statistics on ethnic minorities. More than ever, global cities have attracted a high percentage of the newer flows of immigration to fill domestic labor, construction, manufacturing, and commercial services jobs as well as welfare rolls. This pattern is characteristic both of the fourth wave of immigration in the United States and of European immigration after the suspension of mass labor migration in the mid-1970s. Large-scale immigration, however, continued in a number of major European cities through family formation and reunion (Kofman, 1996a; Rhein, 1996). In France, recent migrants from Southeast Asia, Francophone West Africa, and Turkey, more than the earlier flows of migrants from Algeria, Italy, Spain, and Portugual, have settled to a greater extent in the Île-de-France. Over two-thirds of permanent workers from the European Union and just under half from non–European Union countries settled in this region in 1993 (Lebon, 1994). The pattern in Germany, the powerhouse of the European economy and the principal state of immigration, is more decentralized and composed of a number of different flows with distinctive social rights (Blotevogel, Muller, Jung, & Wood, 1993; Jones, 1994). Thus in the three cities with the highest growth rates in information processing, the percentage of Turkish immigrants among the foreign population in the 1980s was lower by a third than the urban average (Kasarda, Friedrichs, & Ehlers, 1992). They, unlike southern European migrants, who enjoy European Union rights, confront far greater degrees of discrimination. In London, the segmentation of the labor market is strongly influenced by the immigration histories of specific ethnic groups (Hamnett & Randolph, 1992, p. 203).

One of Hamnett's objections to Sassen's thesis of social polarization in global cities is its dependence on the exceptionally high rates of immigration of American cities, in particular Los Angeles and New York. However, Sassen's (1991) conclusions do not depend exclusively on high levels of immigration. Informalization and casualization of the economy are not characteristics brought in by immigrants; she argues that immigrants are simply in a better position than others to take advantage of these changing structural conditions. Yet we should not forget that, even though immigrants and ethnic minorities may form a lower proportion of the population, they experience relatively high rates of unemployment and exclusion, which have contributed to a debate about the emergence of an ethnic minority underclass. For example, in Paris, 34.7% of the unemployed men and 23.9% of unemployed women in 1990 were non-French, although they only formed 15.8% of the population of the city. In Amsterdam, while average unemployment in 1992 for the indigenous Dutch amounted to 6.2%, it was much higher for Caribbean (18.6%) and Turkish (26.7%) populations (Burgers, 1996). Hamnett (1996) has subsequently shifted his critique of Sassen to her neglect of different welfare regimes that have commonly been divided, following Esping-Andersen (1990), into liberal (the United States and increasingly the United Kingdom), corporatist (Germany), and social democrat (Sweden). Yet, despite an acknowledgment of the distinctive profile of ethnic minority employment, there is no sustained analysis of the differential inclusion or exclusion of immigrant and ethnic minorities in specific welfare regimes. In a corporatist regime such as that of Germany, with marked social stratification and an ethnic concept of citizenship, immigrants and their children face high levels of discrimination in employment and welfare. Furthermore, a relatively high proportion of services are still produced by the family and in the household supported by a family-oriented welfare regime. Among immigrants, privatized familial welfare, such as elderly care, is even more marked (Lash & Urry, 1994, pp. 180–189). Welfare, of course, covers a number of interconnected aspects, ranging from transfer payments, subsidies, and services, whose management and provision generates public and voluntary sector employment. Unsurprisingly, the gender and immigrant/ethnic dimensions of these regimes have been largely ignored (Kofman & Sales, 1996).[5]

Too frequently immigrants and women are lumped together in discussions of the growth of the supply of unskilled labor. We need to be more discerning in our analysis, for both of these groups vary nationally in their characteristics and incorporation into the welfare state. For example, Breugel (1996) points out that older women and young people with reduced wage expectations have turned these groups into a renewed supply of cheap labor in Britain.

Despite the awareness that feminization of migration is one of the most striking characteristics of the past 20 years (Castles & Miller, 1993) and the existence of a large number of comparative and individual case studies (Buijs, 1993; Morokvasic, 1984, 1993; Phizacklea, 1983), women largely remain invisible in theories of international migration. The focus in main(male)stream European research has been directed to primary labor migration and, more recently, to refugees and asylum seekers, both of whom have been presented as predominantly male. Immigration regulations in many European countries have tended to treat women as dependents of men, often limiting their right as spouses to enter the labor market until they have lived in a country for several years, although this has changed in countries such as Germany (after July 1991) for those joining a worker with an unlimited residence permit (Boyd, 1996). While labor migration flows on the whole were initially heavily male, among certain groups there was a substantial female element. The variations in labor participation rates and unemployment among female immigrants has also to be taken into account. For example, Portuguese women in France migrated as part of labor migration and have a labor force participation rate that is higher even than French women. On the other hand, Turkish women have very low rates. Family reunification, which has been the means whereby immigrant populations have increased and ethnic communities have settled permanently after the official ending of labor migration, is seen at best as a supplementary contributor to labor supply, if not in the short term then certainly in the long term (Haut Conseil à l'Intégration, 1993). More recently the rotational forms of eastern European migration (Morokvasic, 1992, 1993), akin to seasonal migration, have been heavily female. In the newer eastern European migration, Polish women, for example, move regularly to Germany and combine work with family responsibilities. During a period of a supposed slowing down of migration from the mid-1970s, major European cities have developed a distinctive profile based on a disproportionate percentage of the new and more feminized immigration. Feminist literature on global processes has highlighted the degree to which women are part of the process of trading places in the world economy, whether it be in domestic labor, sex industries, or other services (Pettman, 1996; Sisson Runyan, 1996). There are 3000 marriage bureaus in Germany attracting Thai and Eastern European women. Some 20–30% of an estimated 2000 Thai women in Berlin are involved in prostitution, while Amsterdam and Frankfurt have become the centers of the modern slave trade where women from Latin America, Southeast Asia, Africa, and the Caribbean are rerouted to other European centers (Morokvasic, 1993, pp. 472–473). We see here the varied forms of commodification, exchange, and circulation that underpin the global economy (Kofman, 1996b; Pettman, 1996).

The inadequacy of an analysis of gender relations and divisions, whether in relation to immigrant or professional and managerial women, has considerable bearing on the current debate on polarization or professionalization in global cities, discussed previously. It is worth noting that much research on professionalization has concentrated on financial sectors, the driving force of global cities. In earlier work, the members of the transnational elite were seen as being predominantly males between the ages of 30 and 50 (Friedmann & Wolff, 1982), and the City of London was associated with masculinity and the male yuppie (Budd & Whimster, 1992; Fainstein et al., 1992). Even with the inclusion of women in studies of global economic processes, the emphasis on financial services continues through studies of producer services (McDowell & Court, 1994a, 1994b).

In the fastest-growing sectors such as finance, insurance, and real estate, low-paid jobs and differentials have substantially increased and are greater in London than for Great Britain as a whole (Breugel et al., 1995). In the case of London, women have not benefited to the same extent as men from the expansion of the upper echelons of these sectors, although they are employed full-time to a greater extent than elsewhere. There is evidence that major cities offer women more opportunities for social mobility, including movement from professional to managerial sectors of the service class (see Fielding & Halford, 1993, for southeastern England). In London and Paris women's share of professional and managerial employment has increased dramatically in 1980s, rising by 66.67% from 1982 to 1990 in the managerial and professional category in Paris and by 117% for professionals and 51% for managers from 1981 to 1991 in Inner London. The private sector even more than the public sector offers opportunities for high-level female professionals. The entry of an increasing number of women into higher-status jobs and at the lower end have opened up inequalities between women and households (McDowell, 1991). Breugel et al. (1995) also point out the casualization of professional groups, indicating a need to go beyond socioeconomic categories and investigate conditions of work, access to welfare, and the impact of cuts in welfare and increased unemployment in generating increasing polarization. Including women in the overall system of stratification might yield some insights into the supposedly "disappearing middle," likely to be heavily feminized due to the expansion of intermediate professions and the lower echelons of the higher professional and managerial categories.

It is not just financial sectors that have opened up these possibilities; global cities are also ideological controllers and cultural producers (King, 1993). Cultural production has become increasingly important in London's international role (King, 1990, 1995). Friedmann (1995, pp. 31–32) too stresses the importance of cultural producers for "ensuring the hegemony of transnational capitalism" and creating "a positive image of global capital accumulation." As with more general studies of social stratification in major cities, the middle strata in the cultural field, especially the nonglobally oriented, seem to disappear theoretically and empirically as the focus of studies.

King (1995), on the other hand, draws attention to the cultural influence of large numbers of immigrants from postcolonial societies attracted to global cities, and the subsequent reterritorialization of a diversity of cultures in these cities. Attention is beginning to be paid to cultural appropriation and resistance against dominant cultural practices and use of the built environment by transnational migrants and refugees (Sassen, 1996b; Smith, 1995). Furthermore, immigrant groups provide the variety (restaurants, entertainment, clothes shops, etc.) so frequently associated with world cities.

WHOSE RIGHT TO THE CITY?

Despite the power of groups linked to global activities in the restructuring of the city, urban conflicts continue. For Castells (1994, p. 25), city centers have become the battleground between upper middle class and territorially based countercultures. However, Sassen (1994a) feels that we still know little about how the new forms of inequality are constituted in the contested terrain of the city. Certainly, the expulsion of the working class from the center to the periphery of cities is not new; it was partly behind Henri Lefebvre's formulation of the right to the city in the late 1960s just before the events of 1968. Already by this time in Paris the popular classes were beginning to be driven out from the center to be allowed back merely as urban tourists. The young and unemployed come back to the rebuilt center (Les Halles/Forum) as tourists to the "Palm Beach of the poor," but they do not have the right of residence (Lefebvre, 1996, p. 210). The right to the city did not signify for him a temporary passage, although in his "utopia" he saw how the New Masters would appropriate space and, above all, time (Kofman & Lebas, 1996; for the United States see Law & Wolch, 1993). The right to the city was not merely a visiting card—it was about the right to appropriate space and participate in decision making (Kofman & Lebas, 1996, pp. 19–21), a situation in which exchange values had not usurped use values, and where the city could be added to other abstract rights of the citizen. Thus the right to and respect for difference and diversity in the city is an integral aspect of social citizenship (Christopherson, 1994).

In the 1970s, older immigrant groups too were expelled to the suburbs, as was also the case of Frankfurt, where the increase in foreigners was greatest in the periphery (Keil & Ronneberger, 1994). In Frankfurt the weakened Fordist middle classes have been squeezed between the upper-class elites and marginal groups who have taken back the street. At the same time, the discourse of equality has been replaced by the "renaturalization of racialized social and cultural difference" (Keil & Ronneberger, 1994, p. 153). The right to difference in relation to immigrants may not be about the right to residence in the city but about the incapacity by dominant groups to assimilate them. Originating as a left-wing slogan of social movements such as feminists and regionalists in the late 1960s and early 1970s in France, the "right to difference" was appropriated by the Far Right in the late 1970s and 1980s as the basis for arguments about incompatibility and coexistence within the same polity between indigenous and culturally different immigrant populations.

For the most marginal, even the interstices of urban spaces may be denied. Hassled and policed by the various agents of law and order, they find it difficult to even enjoy the right to their own estates let alone to have the cultural capital to negotiate the center, as depicted in Mathieu Kassovitz's film *La Haine* ("The Hatred"). Kassovitz originally thought of calling the film *Droit de cité* ("Right to the Estate/City"), playing on the dual key meanings of the term (Mongin, 1995). Certainly alliances have been formed between immigrant communities and the resident middle classes to oppose massive redevelopment, as in Belleville in eastern Paris, or in Frankfurt (Keil & Ronneberger, 1994, p. 164), where "socially marginalized agents, liberal middle-class groups and residual forces from old urban social movements" have mounted defensive action against the takeover of the central city. Yet, it has become far more difficult than in the 1960s and 1970s to sustain social movements (Mayer, 1994, 1995) against megaredevelopment projects and creeping, as well as rapid, processes of commercial and residential gentrification, particularly characteristic of larger cities. At a time when the image of place and the desire for clean and respectable, or at least controlled, "marginal" activities (drug dealing, prostitution) in cities is so important, increasingly draconian laws and measures against the homeless and travelers in public places have been enacted, as in Britain and France. European cities have not yet degenerated into fortresses where the street has been abandoned to the homeless, the poor, and the undesirable, ceasing to be a place of encounter, as in many American cities (Christopherson, 1994).

Notwithstanding, the homeless have defended their rights to the city in innovative ways. One of the most forceful campaigns launched in Paris was planned around the slogan the right to housing (*droit au logement*) as a fundamental right to residence in the city (Body-Gendrot, 1995). At a time when there are 5 million square meters of vacant office space in Paris and relatively little construction of social housing (2000 units per year), there are about 117,000 people homeless (Sarre & Maquart, 1995). An association called *Droit au logement* organized a spectacular mass squat in December 1994 in the middle of the 6th arrondissement, a fashionable area of Paris, a few months before the presidential elections. It was done with the intention of raising homelessness as an issue and forcing one of the candidates, Jacques Chirac, then the mayor of Paris and now the president of

France, to use a piece of existing legislation (originally passed in 1945 to deal with wartime shortages) that allowed justified expropriation of unused buildings for housing. This was not an isolated incident, for there have been a series of such actions in Paris and other major cities.

CONCLUSION

I have argued in this chapter that the transformations operating in European globalizing cities raise some fundamental issues for the conceptualization of "global cities" and that we need to connect class, gender, and immigration as they interact in household arrangements in understanding changes in urban spaces. An analysis of households not only adds a further dimension to our understanding of polarization and social stratification but brings out more clearly relations of power in employment, welfare, leisure, and other aspects of daily life.

Secondly, there has been a tendency in much research on global cities to simplify the processes of restructuring in such a way as to get rid of the middle strata, or the disappearing middle, and ignore the complexity of specific histories and immigrant experiences. This is not to deny the decreasing presence in these cities of groups associated with a Fordist regime, such as skilled manual workers. Differences in welfare provision, on the other hand, may enable those groups excluded from the labor market to maintain a presence in major cities despite the high cost of living and housing. Welfare, as I have argued, does not just cover transfer payments and subsidies but includes the provision of services, which generate the sources of female employment in intermediate professions. Furthermore, employment and welfare are usually analyzed as if immigrants do not experience discrimination and differential access. Just as immigrants supply labor for others, and among and for themselves in households and neighborhoods, so too are they implicated in welfare regimes. Far more research is required into the various effects of different welfare regimes in maintaining or reducing diversity in major cities.

Thirdly, the attention paid to occupation and employment fails to take adequate account of changes in housing, the built environment, and the right to the city that have become the major arenas of conflicts over whose city it is. Yet this conflict has not simply emerged with the transformations of the past two decades. At the time when Henri Lefebvre was writing in the 1960s, the housing question in Paris was still all important, and it has increasingly become so again today. The expansion of the financial sector and office building have demolished spaces that were, or might have been, devoted to housing. The right to the city is not just a matter of consumption in and of the city; the production of the built environment for the needs of financial services and residence may radically alter cities in a very short period of time, as can be seen so clearly in London or Paris.

NOTES

1. I hesitated in selection of the title of this chapter as to whether I should refer to major or global cities for several reasons. It is all too easy to get sucked into use of the word "global" and thereby impose, as King (1995) incisively comments, a conceptual category that confers status on particular cities in hegemonic states and establishes the standard against which other cities are to be measured. It furthermore reduces these cities to the operation of processes that correspond most closely to globalizing economic tendencies.

As we shall also see, it heightens the tendency to treat these cities as almost the exclusive sites of changes in welfare regimes, especially the development of neoliberal tendencies. It is too easy to link extremely arduous and poorly remunerated labor conditions with changes in global cities. Deregulation, worsening labor conditions, and reduction in welfare have as much to do with national conditions. So while the "scope for illegal working has widened with the contracting-out of cleaning in schools, offices, railway stations and airports . . . where cash-in-hand is the rule with no national insurance" (Milne & Nowicka, 1995, p. 10), this is not the exclusive prerogative of such cities.

2. There is a substantial literature on the ontological status of the state in social science disciplines, especially strong in international relations where the state reigned supreme for so long, and to its positioning in relation to global processes and international and regional institutions, such as the European Union and the North American Free Trade Agreement (NAFTA). The thesis of the retreat of the state is being increasingly refined to a reshaping of the state (Dunn, 1995; Müller & Wright, 1994).

3. "After-Fordism" is a term used by those who argue that a sustained mode of regulation has not yet replaced Fordism (Peck & Tickell, 1994).

4. Kofman and Sales (1996, p. 181) identify five trends with which new kinds of places and temporal rhythms of activity are associated: (a) polarization of earnings and household incomes; (b) marginalization of certain adults from both state support and the labor market; (c) incorporation of more women into wage labor; (d) reshaping of domestic labor; and (e) increased flexibility and variety in the hours and conditions of wage labor.

5. Taking gender into account forces us to reconsider the characterization of the regimes themselves. For example, treating France and Germany as corporatist regimes, as Esping-Andersen (1990) does, ignores the vital difference between women's participation in the labor market and access to

welfare. While Esping-Andersen (1993) has subsequently recognized the crucial role of gender in the development of postindustrial service structures, he focuses primarily on the creation of employment through the replacement of social reproduction in the household by services provided by the welfare state or the private sector. This has generated a large amount of unskilled service employment and enabled women to participate in paid labor outside the home.

REFERENCES

Beauregard, R. (1995). Theorizing the global–local connection. In P. Knox & P. J. Taylor (Eds.), *World cities in a world-system* (pp. 232–248). Cambridge, UK: Cambridge University Press.

Blotevogel, H., Muller, T., Jung, U., & Wood, G. (1993). From itinerant worker to immigrant? The geography of guestworkers in Germany. In R. King (Ed.), *Mass migration in Europe* (pp. 83–100). London: Belhaven.

Body-Gendrot, S. (1995). *Marginalization and political responses in the French context.* Paper presented at the European Research Conference on the Future of European Cities: Urban Restructuring in Europe—Citizenship and New Patterns of Social Integration in Wider Europe, Aquafredda di Maratea, Italy.

Bondi, L. (1991). Gender divisions and gentrification: A critique. *Transactions of the Institute of British Geographers, 16,* 190–198.

Boyd, M. (1996). Migration policy, family dependency and family membership: Canada and Germany. In P. Evans, T. McCormack, & G. Werkele (Eds.), *Remaking the welfare state.* Toronto: Toronto University Press.

Breugel, I. (1996). Gendering the polarisation debate: A comment on Hamnett's Social Polarisation, economic restructuring, and welfare state regimes. *Urban Studies, 33*(8), 1431–1439.

Breugel, I., Lyons, M., & Perrons, D. (1995). *Professionalisation, polarisation and feminisation in London.* Paper presented at the ESRC London Seminar, London School of Economics.

Budd, L., & Whimster, S. (1992). *Global finance and urban living.* London: Routledge.

Buijs, G. (Ed.). (1993). *Migrant women: Crossing boundaries and changing identities.* Oxford: Berg.

Burgers, J. (1996). No polarization in Dutch cities? Inequality in a corporatist country. *Urban Studies, 33*(1), 99–106.

Butler, T., & Hamnett, C. (1994). Gentrification, class and gender: Some comments on Warde's "Gentrification as consumption." *Environment and Planning D: Society and Space, 12,* 477–493.

Carpenter, J., Chauviré, Y., & White, P. (1994). Marginalization, polarization and planning in Paris. *Built Environment, 20*(3), 218–230.

Castells, M. (1989). *The informational city.* Oxford: Blackwell.

Castells, M. (1994). European cities, the informational society, and the global economy. *New Left Review, 204,* 18–32.

Castles, S. (1992). Migrants and minorities in post-Keynsian capitalism: The German case. In M. Cross (Ed.), *Ethnic minorities and industrial change in Europe and North America* (pp. 36–54). Cambridge, UK: Cambridge University Press.

Castles, S., & Miller, M. (1993). *The age of migration.* London: Macmillan.

Christopherson, S. (1994). The fortress city: Privatized spaces, consumer citizenship. In A. Amin (Ed.), *Post-Fordism: A reader* (pp. 409–427). Oxford: Blackwell.

Collard, S. (1992). Mission impossible: Les chantiers du président. *French Cultural Studies, 3*(2), 97–132.

Cross, M. (1992). Migration, the city and the urban dispossessed. In M. Cross (Ed.), *Ethnic minorities and industrial change in Europe and North America* (pp. 1–19). Cambridge, UK: Cambridge University Press.

Dielman, M., & Hamnett, C. (1994). Globalisation, regulation and the urban system: Editors' introduction to the special issue. *Urban Studies, 31*(3), 357–364.

Duncan, S. (1991). Gender divisions of labour. In D. Green & K. Hoggart (Eds.), *London: A new metropolitan geography* (pp. 95–122). London: Unwin Hyman.

Dunn, J. (Ed.). (1995). *Contemporary crises of the nation-state.* Oxford: Blackwell/PSA.

Esping-Andersen, G. (1990). *The three worlds of welfare capitalism.* Cambridge, UK: Polity Press.

Esping-Andersen, G. (Ed.). (1993). *Changing classes.* London: Sage.

Fainstein, S., Gordon, I., & Harloe, M. (Eds.). (1992). *Divided cities.* Oxford: Blackwell.

Fielding, A., & Halford, S. (1993). Geographies of opportunity: A regional analysis of gender-specific social and spatial mobilities in England and Wales, 1971–81. *Environment and Planning A, 25*(10), 1421–1440.

Friedmann, J. (1986). The world city hypothesis. *Development and Change, 17,* 69–84.

Friedmann, J. (1995). Where we stand: A decade of world city research. In P. Knox & P. J. Taylor (Eds.), *World cities in a world-system* (pp. 21–47). Cambridge, UK: Cambridge University Press.

Friedmann, J., & Wolff, G. (1982). World city formation: An agenda for research and action. *International Journal of Urban and Regional Research, 6*(3), 309–344.

Häussermann, H., & Sackmann, R. (1994). Changes in Berlin: The emergence of an underclass? *Built Environment, 20*(3), 231–241.

Häussermann, H., & Strom, E. (1994). Berlin: The once and future capital. *International Journal of Urban and Regional Research, 18*(2), 335–346.

Hamnett, C. (1994a). Social polarisation in global cities: Theory and evidence. *Urban Studies, 31,* 401–424.

Hamnett, C. (1994b). Socio-economic change in London: professionalization not polarisation. *Built Environment, 20*(3), 192–203.

Hamnett, C., & Randolph, B. (1992). Racial minorities in the London labour and housing markets: A longitudinal analysis, 1971–81. In M. Cross (Ed.), *Ethnic minorities and industrial change in Europe and North America* (pp. 173–204). Cambridge, UK: Cambridge University Press.

Haut Conseil à l'Intégration. (1993). *Rapport au premier ministre: Les étrangers et l'emploi.* Paris: La Documentation Française.

INSEE. (1994). *Les étrangers en France.* Paris: La Documentation Française.

Jones, P. N. (1994). Economic restructuring and the role of foreign workers in the 1980s: The case of Germany. *Environment and Planning A, 26*(9), 1435–1453.

Kasarda, J., Friedrichs, J., & Ehlers, K. (1992). Urban industrial restructuring and minority problems in the US and Germany. In M. Cross (Ed.), *Ethnic minorities and industrial change in Europe and North America* (pp. 250–275). Cambridge, UK: Cambridge University Press.

Keil, R., & Ronneberger, K. (1994). Going up the country: Internationalization and urbanization on Frankfurt's northern fringe. *Environment and Planning D: Society and Space, 12*(2), 137–166.

King, A. (1990). *Global cities: Post-imperialism and the internationalization of London.* London: Routledge.

King, A. (1993). Identity and difference: The internationalization of capital and the globalization of culture. In P. Knox (Ed.), *The restless urban landscape* (pp. 83–110). Englewood Cliffs, NJ: Prentice Hall.

King, A. (1995). Re-presenting world cities: Cultural theory/social practice. In P. Knox & P. J. Taylor (Eds.), *World cities in a world-system* (pp. 215–231). Cambridge, UK: Cambridge University Press.

Knox, P., & Taylor, P. J. (Eds.). (1995). *World cities in a world-system.* Cambridge, UK: Cambridge University Press.

Kofman, E. (1996a). *Female "birds of passage": A decade later—Gender, class and the politics of international migration in Europe.* Paper presented at a meeting of the International Studies Association, San Diego, CA.

Kofman, E. (1996b). Feminism, gender relations and geopolitics: Problematic closures and opening strategies. In E. Kofman & G. Youngs (Eds.), *Globalisation: Theory and practice* (pp. 209–224). London: Pinter.

Kofman, E. (1997). In search of the missing female subject: Comments on French immigration research in M. Cross & S. Perry (Eds.), *Population and Social Policy in France* (pp. 78–91). London: Pinter.

Kofman, E., & Lebas, E. (Eds.). (1996). Lost in transposition: Time, space and the city. In *Writings on cities: Henri Lefebvre* (pp. 3–60). Oxford: Blackwell.

Kofman, E., & Sales, E. (1996). Geography of gender and welfare in Europe. In D. Garcia Ramon & J. Monk (Eds.), *Women of the European Union: The politics of work and daily life* (pp. 31–60). London: Routledge.

Krätke, S. (1992). Berlin: The rise of a new metropolis in a post-Fordist landscape. In M. Dunford & G. Kafkalas (Eds.), *Cities and regions in the new Europe* (pp. 213–238). London: Belhaven.

Lash, S. (1993). Berlin's second modernity. In P. Knox (Ed.), *The restless urban landscape* (pp. 237–254). Englewood Cliffs, NJ: Prentice-Hall.

Lash, S., & Urry, J. (1994). *Economies of signs and space.* London: Sage.

Law, R., & Wolch, J. (1993). Social reproduction in the city: Restructuring time and space. In P. Knox (Ed.), *The restless urban landscape* (pp. 165–205). Englewood Cliffs, NJ: Prentice Hall.

Lebon, A. (1994). *Situation de l'immigration et présence étrangère en France 1993–1994.* Paris: La Documentation Française.

Leborgne, D., & Lipietz, A. (1988). New technologies, new modes of regulation: Some spatial implications. *Environment and Planning D: Society and Space 6*(3), 263–280.

Lefebvre, H. (1996). *Writings on cities: Henri Lefebvre.* (Introduced, selected, and translated by E. Kofman & E. Lebas). Oxford: Blackwell.

Lewis, J. (1993). *Women and social policies in Europe: Work, family and the state.* Aldershot, Hampshire, UK: Edward Elgar.

Martin, R. (1993). Stateless monies, global financial integration and national autonomy: the end of geography. In S. Corbridge, R. Martin, & N. Thrift (Eds.), *Money, power and space* (pp. 253–278). Oxford: Blackwell.

Marcuse, P. (1989). "Dual city": A muddy metaphor for a quartered city. *International Journal of Urban and Regional Research, 13,* 697–708.

Marcuse, P. (1993). Whats so new about divided cities? *International Journal of Urban and Regional Research, 17,* 355–366.

Mayer, M. (1994). Post-Fordist city politics. In A. Amin (Ed.), *Post-Fordism: A reader* (pp. 316–337). Oxford: Blackwell.

Mayer, M. (1995). *Urban restructuring, new forms of exclusion and the role of social movements.* Paper presented at the European Research Conference on the Future of European Cities: Urban Restructuring in Europe—Citizenship and New Patterns of Social Integration in Wider Europe, Aquafredda di Maratea, Italy.

McDowell, L. (1991). Life without father and Ford: The new gender order of post-Fordism. *Transactions, Institute of British Geography, 16*(4), 400–419.

McDowell, L., & Court, G. (1994a). Gender divisions of labour in the post-Fordist economy: The maintenance of occupational sex segregation in the financial services sector. *Environment and Planning A, 26*(9), 1397–1418.

McDowell, L., & Court, G. (1994b). Missing subjects: Gender, sexuality and power in merchant banking. *Economic Geography, 70*(2), 229–251.

Milne, S., & Nowicka, H. (1995, April 7). Illegal immigrants. *The Guardian,* p. 10.

Mongin, O. (1995, August–September). Regarde-les tomber: A propos de *La Haine* de Mathieu Kassovitz. *Esprit,* pp. 172–186.

Morokvasic, M. (1984). Birds of passage are also women. *International Migration Review, 18*(4), 886–907.

Morokvasic, M. (1992). Une migration pendulaire: Les Polonais en Allemagne. *Hommes et Migrations, 1155,* 31–36.

Morokvasic, M. (1993). In and out of the labour market: Immigrant and minority women in the labour market. *New Community, 19*(3), 459–484.

Müller, M., & Wright, V. (1994). Reshaping the state in western Europe. *West European Politics, 17*(4), 1–11.

Musterd, S. (1994). A rising European underclass? *Built Environment, 20*(3), 185–191.

O'Brien, R. (1992). *Global financial integration: The end of geography.* London: Pinter.

Overbeek, H. (1994). *Global restructuring and the emerging regional migration regime in Europe.* Washington, DC: International Studies Association.

Peck, J., & Tickell, A. (1994). Searching for a new institutional fix: The after-Fordist crisis and the global–local disorder. In A. Amin (Ed.), *Post-Fordism: A reader* (pp. 280–315). Oxford: Blackwell.

Pettman, J. (1996). An international economy of sex? In E. Kofman & G. Youngs (Eds.), *Globalisation: Theory and practice* (pp. 191–208). London: Pinter.

Phizacklea, A. (Ed.). (1983). *One way ticket: Migration and female labour.* London: Routledge & Kegan Paul.

Priemus, H. (1995). How to abolish social housing? The Dutch case. *International Journal of Urban and Regional Research, 19*(1), 145–155.

Rhein, C. (1996). Social segmentation and spatial polarization in Greater Paris. In J. O'Loughlin & J. Friedrichs (Eds.), *Social polarization in post-industrial metropolises* (pp. 45–70). Berlin: de Gruyter.

Salt, J., Singleton, A., & Hogarth, J. (1994). *Europe's international migrants. Data Sources, Patterns and Trends.* London: Her Majesty Stationery Office.

Sarre, G., & Maquart, D. (1995). *Ce que Paris nous dit.* Paris: Editions de l'Aube.

Sassen, S. (1991). *The global city: New York, London, Tokyo.* Princeton, NJ: Princeton University Press.

Sassen, S. (1994a). *Cities in a world economy.* Thousand Oaks, CA: Pine Forge Press.

Sassen, S. (1994b). La ville globale: Eléments pour une lecture de Paris. *Le Débat, 80,* 146–164.

Sassen, S. (1995). On concentration and centrality in the global city. In P. Knox & P. J. Taylor (Eds.), *World cities in a world-system* (pp. 63–75). Cambridge, UK: Cambridge University Press.

Sassen, S. (1996a). Rebuilding the global city: economy, ethnicity and space. In A. King (Ed.), *Re-presenting the City. Ethnicity, Capital and Culture in the 21st century Metropolis* (pp. 23–42). London: Macmillan.

Sassen, S. (1996b). Analytic borderlands: Race, gender and representation in the new city. In A. King (Ed.), *Re-presenting the city: Ethnicity, capital and culture in the 21st-century metropolis* (pp. 183–202). London: Macmillan.

Sisson Runyan, A. (1996). The places of women in trading places: Gendered global/regional regimes and internationalized feminist resistance. In E. Kofman & G. Youngs (Eds.), *Globalisation: Theory and practice* (pp. 238–252). London: Pinter.

Smith, M. (1995). The disappearance of world cities and the globalization of local politics. In P. Knox & P. J. Taylor (Eds.), *World cities in a world-system* (pp. 249–266). Cambridge, UK: Cambridge University Press.

Wacquant, L. (1993). Urban outcasts: Stigma and division in the black American ghetto and the French urban periphery. *International Journal of Urban and Regional Research, 17*(3), 366–383.

White, P. (1993). Immigrants and the social geography of European cities. In R. King (Ed.), *Mass migration in Europe. The legacy and the future* (pp. 65–82). London: Belhaven.

Woodward, R. (1995). Approaches towards the study of social polarization in the UK. *Progress in Human Geography, 19*(1), 75–89.

Zukin, S. (1992). The city as a landscape of power. In L. Budd & S. Whimster (Eds.), *Global finance and urban living: A study of metropolitan change.* London: Routledge.

CHAPTER 13

Social Polarization and the Politics of Difference

DISCOURSES IN COLLISION OR COLLUSION?

Katherine Gibson

Social polarization and representations of difference are two quite different discourses on contemporary social life that are currently influencing urban analysis and social policy. These two approaches embody quite different theoretical traditions and political imaginaries and have developed alongside each other without a great deal of contact (at least until now). It is my intention in this chapter to explore the points of convergence and divergence between analyses of social polarization and difference. My purpose in doing so is to provide some ways of thinking about the social policies loosely informed by these discourses that, I argue, are already in collision in the *Realpolitik* of urban practice.[1]

SOCIAL POLARIZATION

The interest in mapping and explaining social polarization particularly at the city scale appears to have had a radical renaissance in geography and urban political economy in the late 1980s and 1990s. It can be seen as part of a long-standing concern for urban inequality and ghettoization—a concern whose genealogy dates from at least the writings of Friedrich Engels and 19th-century social reformers, through to the Chicago School sociologists, and on to the welfare geographers' interest in social and spatial justice during the 1970s. Over the last 15 years the analysis of inequality has been heavily influenced by Marxian political-economic explanations put forward, for example, by David Harvey and others, who argue that inequality is a fundamental aspect of the structure of the capitalist mode of production and capitalist society.[2] More recently the understanding of social polarization as an accelerating process has been explained as a by-product of the global economic restructuring of capital and the formation of world cities.[3]

While in the 1970s makers of social policy, drawing upon liberal welfare theory, saw urban inequalities in terms of distributional malfunctions that could be eradicated by informed policy manipulation by the state, in the 1990s there is an acceptance by urban theorists and policymakers alike that the problems are systemic or global and largely out of any one government's control. Thus the "reemergence" of an interest in "social polarization" today signals a discursive shift in both explanation and potential for policy intervention—with polarization now woven into the hegemonic narrative of global capitalist restructuring and an acceptance that state intervention can only be ameliorative at best.

There is intense empirical interest in social polarization.[4] The growing literature is concerned with questions of comparison, relevance, and mapping: Is the social polarization that is taking place in New York and Los Angeles also occurring in European cities? Is there social polarization in Australian or Canadian cities? Is the middle really dropping out of the income distribution? Do we have an hourglass income distribution or an onion-shaped one? As much of this work focuses upon how to measure, who to include, expanding the number of cities studied, and so on, it affords endless opportunities for discussion, revision, and differentiation by technique. This chapter will not engage with the social polarization literature in its empiricist guise,[5] for what intrigues me is the curious level of conceptual interest that theorizing social polarization has aroused. I trace this concern to the disruption that contemporary social trends, described in terms of social polarization, pose to traditional class theory and the primary lineaments of (economic) difference it maps out. The literature on social polarization is largely a discourse about class and the reshaping of class relations. As Friedmann and Wolff (1982) put it, "the primary social fact about world city formation is the polarization of its social class divisions" (p. 322). As the term "polarization" implies, the analysis signals an increasing binary segregation, but not that of classical Marxian class theory between worker and capitalist (nor, indeed, their understudies, the lumpen proletariat and the petite bourgeoisie). The literature on social polarization documents the emergence of two groups who are difficult to describe in classical class terms. Bell (1973), one of the first to identify this change talked of a new class structure emerging from "post-industrial" society characterized by an expanding professional and managerial workforce. More recently, Sassen (1991) writes: "New conditions of growth have contributed to elements of a new class alignment in global cities— [composed] of a high-income stratum and a low-income stratum" (p. 13). Wright and Martin (1987) describe a slowing of the process of proletarianization and a quickening of the process of deproletarianization. Most recently, Lash and Urry (1994) have provided a good summary account of the class dimensions of social polarization:

> [T]he new lower class represents a sort of structural downward mobility for substantial sections of the organized-capitalist working class, as well as a set of structural social places into which large numbers of immigrants flow. . . . The new lower class takes its place at the bottom of a restructured stratificational ladder in which the hierarchy of capital and labour is replaced by a three-tiered ordering—a mass class of professional-managerials (alongside a very small capitalist class), a smaller and comparatively under-resourced working class, and this new lower class. Paradoxically this new quasi-Weberian pattern of social stratification is brought about by the eminently Marxian process of capital accumulation and effective positioning of new-lower-class agents by the dominant classes themselves. (pp. 145–146)

The polarization literature approaches difference in a way that sees it as primarily economic (no matter how much it may be associated with interesting cultural and ethnic dimensions), as distinguishing groups that are relatively internally homogeneous and structurally defined by contemporary processes of capital accumulation.

There is an interesting set of emotions associated with the polarization discourse—including loss and guilt, moral outrage and moral responsibility. Loss and moral outrage permeates discussion of the passing of the "traditional working class"; a sense of guilt enters into accounts of the rise of the "new professional managerial class" (to which, by the way, most commentators on social polarization belong); and a feeling of moral responsibility is expressed for the growing "underclass." Nowhere are these emotions more evident than in the huge literature on inner-city gentrification—the site of the most obvious examples of both social polarization and middle-class guilt:

> [A]dvanced services gentrifiers employ people in services, in restaurants, bars, taxis, cinemas, theatres, hotels, service-intensive boutiques. The new advanced-services middle classes then provide a market not only for one another, but also for the casualized labour of the new lower class. . . . [N]ew consumption-side practices of upper income groups *foster* new lower-class formation (Lash & Urry, 1994, pp. 164–165, emphasis added)

The implications of discourses of global restructuring and social polarization upon mainstream social and economic policies are schizoid to say the least. In much economic and urban policy, initiatives are designed to harness some of the new growth by, for example, promoting high-tech industry or repackaging a metropolis as a "world city," while in regional and social policy the focus is upon ameliorating the effects of polarization by, for example, instituting strategies for regional growth in disadvantaged areas or attempting to eradicate the underclass.[6]

DIFFERENCE

While urbanists and political economists concentrate upon the increasing social and economic polarization of society into two or three groups defined by their own internal, structurally designated sameness, other social and political theorists are writing in another vein about difference. Discourses of difference focus upon all those identities which are designated as Other to the social norm—that being the white heterosexual "middle-class" able-bodied young male who is granted universal subjecthood by Enlightenment political thought. Theories of difference highlight the social construction of gender, race, ethnicity, sexuality, ability, and age among other dimensions of the social field. While some theorists point to the inherent oppressivenes of these constructions, others highlight the inescapable role these constructions play in the constitution of identity and subjecthood (Young, 1990). Importantly, a politics of difference is not primarily aligned around the social cleavage of class but is enacted around the multiplicity of identity forming axes and processes of social life.[7] Difference politics need not be motivated by *ressentiment* and a fixation upon oppression but can foster the celebration of distinctive self-definition and cultures of difference. In urban analysis there has been an interest in mapping the spatial and cultural land-scapes created by this distinctive self-definition.[8] Iris Young's writings have been influential here, especially her notion of a heterogeneous public:

> The unoppressive city is thus defined as openness to unassim-ilated otherness. . . . A politics of difference lays down institu-tional and ideological means for recognizing and affirming dif-ferently identifying groups in two basic senses: giving political representation to groups' interests and celebrating the distinc-tive cultures and characteristics of different groups. (1990, p. 319)

In the shift in focus from assimilationism and antidiscrimination to bi- and multiculturalism and positive discrimination, the politics of difference can be seen to have infiltrated and affected social policy. There is now a validity to claims for different treatment and the need for positive means of identifying difference in many realms of social life. The recognition of key axes of difference have promoted and validated the interests of women, blacks, ethnic groups, gays and les-bians, the differently abled, and the aged in policy circles. And there has been a move in theory and practice to the recognition of the *difference within* each of these groups.[9]

While the literature on difference comes out of a somewhat dif-ferent tradition to that of Marxian political economy—one based in psychoanalytic theory, feminism, and poststructuralist political theory—there are points of contact that can be identified. The Marx-ist Louis Althusser's notions (1979) of "interpellation" and "overdetermination," for example, resonate with poststructuralist conceptions of identity and subjectivity as multiply constituted and always in process (1979). On the other hand, the political theorist Iris Young's designation of the five faces of oppression in which mate-rial exploitation still figures as a major form of oppression indicates an interest in reconciling her politics of difference with traditional class politics. Yet despite these points of contact there are significant divergences around political visions and social dynamics that I think it might be useful to highlight.

DIVERGENCES

When theorists of difference have an explicit political philosophy (not all have an emancipatory one as does Iris Young) it is often expressed as a vision of diversity and the tolerance of difference. Young poses city life, for example, as a normative ideal—by city life she means a sort of social relations defined as "the being together of strangers" (1990, p. 237). She writes, "In the city, persons and groups interact within spaces and institutions they all experience themselves as belonging to, but without those interactions dissolving into unity or commonness" (1990, p. 237). In contrast to this explicit and public political imaginary, theorists of social polarization are today more reluctant to voice their emancipatory visions. One could almost say that they no longer have them since the agent of emancipation in classical Marxian political analysis, the traditional working class, has been decimated and deproletarianized in the course of capitalist restructuring.

The vision of a classless society as a goal for social intervention (whether of a revolutionary or reformist nature) is seemingly unviable in the current context. Yet such a vision has not been wholly discarded. There is no recognition in the literature on social polarization (as there is in the discourse of difference) that polarization or class is an inescapable aspect of social life, as is gender, race, age, etc. Indeed the moral and emotional tenor of the polarization discussion implies a still-viable expectation that polarities and/or class can be eradicated. But beyond these faintly registered sensibilities and their very problematic relationship to political agency, I would characterize the political imaginary of urban political economy as devoid of any positive emancipatory vision but instead dominated by a very negative vision of the destructive threat of a politics of difference. In this imaginary that sees the source of power for the oppressed in solidarity and unity, difference denotes political fragmentation, disunity, and ultimately powerlessness.[10] In this sense the political imaginaries of a politics of difference and of social polarization are diametrically opposed.

Another divergence is around the theorization of social dynamics. Social polarization belongs to a discourse that is inherently historical. The emphasis is clearly upon development and change—upon theorizing the political impact of the increasing nature of this versus the decreasing nature of that. For example, is the working class growing or declining? Is capitalism strengthening its hold or loosening its hold over social and economic life?

Difference is a less temporally based discourse: there is no discussion of tendencies toward increasing or decreasing difference, but there is a sensitivity to the proliferation of multiple identities even within gender, ethnic, racial, and sexual identities. It would seem that poststructural theory has liberated the possibility of a greater proliferation of identities within categories such as that of woman, black, or the aged. For example, within feminism there is now a reluctance to talk of essential and shared characteristics of being a woman. Instead, there is much discussion of the many different ways in which sexuality is constructed, genders ascribed, and the female body inscribed.

Despite divergence between the profound historicism of one discourse and the seeming atemporality of the other, I discern an interesting incorporation of a logic or overarching dynamic affecting the proliferation of identities when theories of difference and social polarization are brought into relationship. That is, when these discourses actually collide, coming as they do from different theoretical traditions and political visions, there are traces of collusion that have interesting effects.

POLARIZATION AND DIFFERENCE: COLLISION OR COLLUSION?

Theories of difference can be seen in one light as an attempt to break from the stranglehold that economic and class theory has had over the constitution of social identity. Subaltern theorists of all sorts— feminists, African Americans, postcolonialists, gays, to name but some—have all argued for the separation of processes of gender, racial, and sexual constitution from processes of class definition and formation. While arguing for an interaction between these aspects of identity, there has been a sensitivity to the distinctive autonomy of these processes.

With the emergence of more complex theories of difference that highlight the differentiation within groups defined as Other, on the one hand, and the generation of a complex conception of social polarization and the reshaping of class divisions, on the other, we have seen an alarming abandonment of this traditional conceptual autonomy. What I find worrying is that the temporality of political economy (specifically the narrative of global restructuring) has incorporated and subsumed the atemporal discourse of difference. That is, these two distinctive discourses appear to collude in a story of economic dominance. Key to this collusion is the way in which commodification and consumption enter the social polarization story.

A central component of the social polarization thesis is the importance of consumption and lifestyle, particularly to the new professional managerial class. The importance of consumption is highlighted in the literature on gentrification in which there has been a complex debate about the explanations of inner-city revitalization. The debate goes like this: is gentrification fundamentally an economic phenomenon brought about by the rent gap and financial transactions liberated by the restructuring of production, or is it more likely a reflection of new styles of consumption, aesthetic values, and lifestyle, including changing gender relations and the heightened status of women in the paid workforce?[11] Or, has one provided the conditions of possibility for the Other, as Neil Smith (1987) argued when he wrote of the loosening of "sexual apartheid" being made possible by the economically determined emergence of gentrified inner-city areas? Liz Bondi (1991) weakly opposes such a conflation of gender "restructuring" to class restructuring, arguing that rather than assuming that gentrification "signals a shift in the power relations between men and women"—a formulation which subsumes a discourse on gender–sexual difference to the imperatives of a discourse centered upon economic change and historical progress (emancipation)—she would prefer to "consider how gentrification contributes to a reworking of gender divisions across . . . 'structures of patriarchy' "(p. 196), that is, to assume the inescapability of gender divisions and the complex and indeterminate relationship between economic processes and the transformations of masculinities and femininities.

A similar move to subsume discourses on difference to the discourse of economic restructuring is evident in the work on the political economy of flows of signs and symbols. For many contemporary theorists of postmodernity the distinctive aspect of late (postmodern) capitalism is the circulation not only of the traditional means of production—capital, labor, and commodities—but also the new means of economic exchange—information and images. Global or world cities are the hub sites where these flows of finance and information converge, reshaping the world political economy as we know it. With the ascendancy of information and communication structures it is the accumulation of information and images that, it is argued, fuels the economy. For example, Lash and Urry (1994), Massumi (1993), and Deleuze and Guattari (1987) argue that capital no longer only (or even predominantly) seeks investment sites based in material production processes but rather trades in images such that the commodity's value "is now defined more by the desire it arouses than by the amount of labour that goes into it. . . . The value of commodity-images . . . is attached more to their exchange and inclusive disjunction than to their material production" (Massumi, 1993, p. 200). Along with the surplus value embodied in a commodity and realized in the act of exchange is a noncapital form of "ghost surplus value": "more on the order of a prestige, an 'aura' style, 'cool,' the glow of self worth, 'personality' " (Massumi, 1993, p. 201). What Massumi (and Deleuze & Guattari, 1987) seem to be talking about is the trade of signifiers of subjectivity. As Massumi writes:

> Gender becomes increasingly negotiable, as new sexualities come onto the market. A body may be "transsexual," "bisexual," "asexual," "sex addicted," "sadomasochistic," or many other things. A whole service industry exists for each. Race sells (this season, wannabe rappers abound in white suburbia). It used to be that assuming or redefining an identity took a lifetime. Now it takes as long as it takes to shop for an image. (1993, p. 134)

In this formulation difference is something that is good for business.[12] The liberation and recognition of a multiplicity of identities via a celebratory politics of difference has, in the views of these theorists, been harnessed by the moneymaking imperatives of global capitalism. Indeed the capitalist axiomatic (to use Deleuze and Guattari's term) has invaded the entire social space, translating all nuances of subjectivity into image/commodities.[13] Both the new underclass and the new professional managerial class participate in the proliferation of imaged subjectivities, and this contributes to further political fragmentation and immobilization. It would seem that the discourse of social polarization has usurped the discourse of difference and that capitalism is the hands down winner.

Clearly the effects of this discursive invasion have significant implications for any political imaginary. It seems that within the hegemonic frame of global capitalism there can be no autonomous attempts to build a heterogeneous public based upon multiple and diverse identities that offer spaces for resistance to capitalism. Any such attempt is rendered benign by the newfound playfulness of capital's embrace.

My real concern here is to trace how we have produced such a politically debilitating and imperialistic scenario. As I see it, two of the factors contributing to this picture are the tendency to conflate all commodification with capitalism, and the inability of class theory to cope with the multiple class identities of individuals. In the remainder of this chapter I will take up the latter issue.[14]

CLASS AND MULTIPLICITY

While other aspects of subjectivity may be multiply constituted (e.g., I can enact my identity as a woman in a number of different ways within a single day, as well as over my lifetime), class is still constitued as a coherent and unified aspect of one's identity (one is working class or petit bourgeois, or now professional–managerial, or underclass). But, in fact, if we empty out the concept of class and reduce it to only the process of producing, appropriating, and distributing surplus labor, it is obvious that we all perform in many different sorts of class processes within one day, as well as over our lifetime.[15] The various mix of class processes we are involved in may include the capitalist class process of producing surplus value and having it appropriated, or distributing already appropriated surplus value. But it could just as easily include other modes of surplus labor production, appropriation, and distribution. Many of the other economic transactions we engage in may, in fact, not involve class transfers but may be overdetermined by other social relations involving power and oppression. To illustrate this point we could examine some hypothetical representatives of the emerging "classes" said to be at opposite ends of the social polarization process.

On the one hand, we have Lin and Van, a young Vietnamese couple who have recently migrated to a Pacific Rim world city and live in a public housing unit in an inner-city location. During the day Lin and Van both work as wage laborers cleaning houses for a contract cleaning company whose workers are nonunionized. Their baby is minded by an aunt who lives in the same housing complex. At night they take turns minding the child and performing household labor or working in the kitchen of a nearby restaurant owned by an uncle. This restaurant labor is provided as part of an understanding that when they are ready to set up their own business, as they are planning to do, they will be able to draw upon the financial assistance of this relation, at least being able to use his capital to enter the community *hui*—an informal financing scheme that operates in Chinese and Vietnamese cultural communities. Their affiliations with small business and Van's prior involvement in the South Vietnamese army influence this couple to support the most conservative political party at both provincial and national elections. Apart from the non-gender-specific sharing of housework and childcare, the gender roles assumed by Lin and Van are traditional and dominated by a discourse of heterosexuality—Van spends his leisure hours gambling and smoking with friends, and Lin sews and meets girlfriends who also have small children. Both utilize the cultural commodities specific to the Asian community, frequenting the Chinese-language video stores, local restaurants, and clubs.

These two members of the "new urban underclass" are involved in no less than four class processes. During the day their surplus labor is appropriated as surplus value in a capitalist class process. To be able to work, they appropriate the surplus labor of their aunt who looks after their child. This transaction is supported by a whole set of complex family social relations of obligation. During the evenings, household labor and childcare is performed as part of a communal class process in which the surplus labor of Van and Lin is equally shared between them. And other surplus labor is distributed to their uncle in return for a lump sum payment at a future date and his agreement to act as guarantor of their future business in which they will then become self-appropriators of their own surplus labor.

Just two blocks away from the public housing high-rise in which Lin and Van live, we find Karen and Kay, living together in an elegant Victorian house that they renovated from a boardinghouse into a beautiful gentrified mansion. Karen usually works as an investment consultant in a large financial institution in the city and earns a high salary complete with a package involving a car and a bonus (share in corporate profits). Presently she is on maternity leave with a 4-month-old baby. Kay works as a relief teacher in the public school system when she can get employment, and as a self-employed housepainter and artist the rest of the time. She has occasional exhibitions but makes very little money from her artwork. This lesbian couple have a very traditional division of labor in the home, with Karen doing all the cooking and household financial management and Kay doing the occasional household maintenance and outside work. The house is cleaned by contract cleaners. The couple are ardent supporters of the local left-oriented progressive political party and are active in the inner-city lesbian and feminist movements. Kay is a member of the teachers union. They regularly eat out and attend the movies.

These two members of the new "professional managerial class" are involved in multiple class processes. In her capacity as a financial manager, Karen participates in a distributional capitalist class process overseeing the movement of money into and out of both productive and unproductive investment opportunities. Her wage is supplemented by distributed class payments as part of a salary package that buys her allegiance to that particular firm. In her capacity as an activist in the local feminist community, Karen provides unpaid surplus labor voluntarily for fund-raising functions. At present she is producing surplus labor, which is appropriated in a traditional domestic class process providing childcare and housework for the maintenance of the household. Kay is involved in a number of class processes: as a wage laborer in a capitalist class process when she works as a teacher, as a self-employed worker in a self-appropriating class process when she takes on house-painting jobs; and as a craft worker in a self-appropriating class process when she does her artwork. At the same time she appropriates the surplus domestic labor of Karen, who looks after their child and cooks for the household.

According to the social polarization thesis, the economic differences between these two couples are related and the economic relation between these two couples is one of exploitation. As Young (1990, p. 218) writes, "exploitation [is broadly] defined as any relationship in which the results of the energies of one group systematically benefit another without reciprocation. The division between professionals and non-professionals enacts exploitation in this sense."

There are a number of important questions that arise when discourses of social polarization and difference collide, and this chapter concludes by raising, but not answering, some of them.

CONCLUSION

What might be the effect of conflating the process of social polarization with that of class exploitation? That is, what does it do to say that Karen and Kay create the "need" for Lin and Van and in doing so exploit them?

One effect is to eliminate the economic difference and diversity that the lives of these four individuals embody and to reduce their economic identity to that of only one of the economic processes around which it is multiply constructed. Another effect is to place these four people and the "groups" that they could be said to represent within the organizational grip/grid of global capitalism, thereby turning key aspects of their subjectivities—as, on the one hand, Vietnamese Pacific Rim migrants involved in an active ethnic and economic cultural community and as, on the other, lesbians involved in a redefinition of gender roles and sexualities within an alternative political community—into merely opportunities for greater profit making. A further effect is to close down the political imaginary liberated by the work of Young and others.

While I see much potential for an exciting give-and-take between the discourses of social polarization and the theories of difference, the current state of the collision between the two is worrying. Standing in the way of a fruitful engagement is the concept of class, something we all refer to with an unthinking ease but which has all but disappeared when we discuss almost any other aspect of social identity. Until the productive dis-ease that has been introduced into our discussions of gender or race by difference theorists is introduced into our language of class, the economic diversity that is as much an aspect of difference as anything else will remain suppressed both in knowledge and in policy practice. An essentialized economic sameness will commandeer diversity of all types and render it ineffectual. The time is ripe for development of an antieconomistic intervention into contemporary urban theory and policy and a restoration of some of the autonomy from the economic that discourses of difference have recently lost.

ACKNOWLEDGMENTS

I would like to note with much appreciation that the research that went into the writing of this chapter was funded by a grant from the Australian Housing and Urban Research Institute (AHURI). The original paper was published as part of AHURI Working Paper No. 6 (1996). I would also like to thank my co-researchers Jenny Cameron, Lauren Costello, Ruth Fincher, Margo Huxley, Jane Jacobs, Louise Johnson, and Mariastella Pulverenti for their helpful comments.

NOTES

1. I am not setting out to monitor, describe, or proclaim as true or false the processes of either social polarization or the constitution of difference as such. I am more concerned with the role these prevalent discourses are having on the ways in which we think about contemporary urban processes and intervene in them.

2. As argued, for example, by Harvey first in *Social Justice in the City* (1973) and still in *The Condition of Postmodernity* (1989).

3. As argued, for example, by Zukin (1991), Castells (1989), and Sassen (1991), to name just a few.

4. See, for example, work by Pinch (1993), Hamnett (1994), Baum and Hassan (1993), Fincher (1994), Murphy and Watson (1994), Marcuse (1989), and Pahl (1988), to name an unrepresentative sample of recent research.

5. The designation of this literature as empiricist is not to belittle the very important political role in influencing policy formulation that different maps of social inequality may have. It is, however, to dissociate from a belief in the possibility of an "accurate" map of polarization.

6. A new attempt at this latter task was evident in the recently deposed Australian federal Labor government's White Paper on Employment entitled *Working Nation*. This policy document explicitly forged a redefinition of citizenship in terms of one's actual or potential relationship to the labor market. One effect was that the so-called underclass could now be discursively eliminated by being redefined as no longer "discouraged" or "unemployable" but "unready" workers (Probert, 1994). Implicit in this redefinition is the assumption that the underclass can join the mainstream by being made "ready to work" via training.

7. Pratt and Hanson (1994, p. 10) point to the tendency for "work" and its contribution to identity to be elided in much current discussion of difference and subjectivity that is more characteristically focused upon nonwork aspects of life. Their analysis of a place- and work-based description of identity construction attempts to rethink these economic and geographical aspects of identity within a "difference" rather than a "class" frame.

8. In geography we have seen a renewed interest in studying ethnic space, gay space, ghetto culture, the space of homelessness, for example, in a manner reminiscent of but quite different in intent from the social ecologist's earlier interest in "deviant" social groups in space, such as street corner society, panhandlers, or urban villagers.

9. So now we see social policies that recognize difference being criticized in another round, for their inherent essentialism—that is, for the way in which they inadvertently treat all groups of difference as homogeneous, for example, all those of non-English speaking background as one, or all women as one, or all differently abled as one.

10. Such a negative sense of the politics of fragmentation is evident, for example, in the writings of Harvey (1989, p. 19).

11. See, for example, the work of Smith (1979), Warde (1991), Butler and Hamnett (1994), Ley (1994), Rose (1988), and Bondi (1991).

12. At the same time, to quote Massumi (1993, p. 201), this "schizophrenia" of postmodernity produces "the flowering of desire in play and experimentation, side by side with enormously widening social inequality and constant reminders of economic exploitation of the grimmest sort (homelessness, the 'permanent underclass' of the ghettoes, higher infant mortality in some city centers than in the 'Third World' and so on)."

13. Against this hegemonic or molar construction, Deleuze and Guattari (1987) do pose ways of escape via nomadology and the notion of "lines of flight." However, their attempts to capture a vision of subjectivity beyond or outside of the capitalist axiomatic are sketchy, to say the least (see Gibson-Graham, 1996, Chap. 4, for further discussion of this point).

14. For a discussion of commodification and its subsumption in political economic discourse to capitalism see Gibson-Graham (1996, Chap. 8).

15. This act of emptying out the concept of class is elaborated in the work of Resnick and Wolff (1987) and Gibson and Graham (1992).

REFERENCES

Althusser, L. (1979). *For Marx* (Ben Brewster, Trans.). London: Allen Lane.
Australia. (1994). *Working nation: Policies and programs.* Canberra: Australia Government Publishing Service.
Baum, S., & Hassan, R. (1993). Economic restructuring and spatial equity: A case study of Adelaide. *Australian and New Zealand Journal of Sociology, 29*(2), 151–172.
Bell, D. (1973). *The coming of post-industrial society.* New York: Basic Books.

Bondi, L. (1991). Gender divisions and gentrification: A critique. *Transactions of the Institute of British Geographers, New Series, 16*, 190–198.

Bondi, L. (1992). Gender symbols and urban landscapes. *Progress in Human Geography, 16*(2), 157–170.

Butler, T., & Hamnett, C. (1994). Gentrification, class and gender: Some comments on Warde's "Gentrification as consumption." *Environment and Planning D: Society and Space, 12*, 477–493.

Castells, M. (1989). *The informational city.* Oxford: Blackwell.

Deleuze, G., & Guattari, F. (1987). *A thousand plateaus: Capitalism and schizophrenia* (Brian Massumi, Trans.). Minneapolis: University of Minneapolis Press.

Fincher, R. (1994). *Australian urban systems: Trends and prospects in social disparities.* Report to the Australian Housing and Urban Research Institute, Melbourne.

Friedmann, J., & Wolff, G. (1982). World city formation: An agenda for research and action. *International Journal of Urban and Regional Research, 6*(3), 309–344.

Gibson, K., & Graham, J. (1992). Rethinking class in industrial geography. *Economic Geography, 68*, 109–127.

Gibson-Graham, J. K. (1996). *The end of capitalism (as we knew it): A feminist critique of political economy.* Oxford: Blackwell.

Hamnett, C. (1994). Social polarization in global cities: Theory and evidence. *Urban Studies, 31*(3), 401–425.

Harvey, D. (1973). *Social justice and the city.* Baltimore: Johns Hopkins University Press.

Harvey, D. (1989). *The condition of postmodernity.* Oxford: Blackwell.

Lash, S., & Urry, J. (1994). *Economies of signs and space.* London: Sage.

Ley, D. (1994). Gentrification and the politics of the new middle class. *Environment and Planning D: Society and Space, 12*, 53–74.

Massumi, B. (1993). *A user's guide to Capitalism and Schizophrenia: Deviations from Deleuze and Guattari.* Cambridge, MA: MIT Press.

Marcuse, P. (1989). "Dual city": A muddy metaphor for a quartered city. *International Journal of Urban and Regional Studies, 13*(4), 697–708.

Murphy, P., & Watson, S. (1993). Social polarization and Australian cities. *International Journal of Urban and Regional Studies, 18*(4), 573–590.

Pahl, R. (1988). Informal work, social polarisation and the social structure. *International Journal of Urban and Regional Research, 12*(2), 247–267.

Pinch, S. (1993). Social polarization: A comparison of evidence from Britain and the United States. *Environment and Planning A, 25*, 779–795.

Pratt, G., & Hanson, S. (1994). Geography and the construction of difference. *Gender, Place and Culture, 1*(1), 5–29.

Probert, B. (1994). Thinking about the White Paper: Problems for a working nation. *Australian Geographer, 25*(2), 102–109.

Resnick, S., & Wolff, R. (1987). *Knowledge and class.* Chicago: University of Chicago Press.

Rose, D. (1988). A feminist perspective on employment restructuring and gentrification: The case of Montreal. In J. Wolch & M. Dear (Eds.), *The power of geography: How territory shapes social life.* Boston: Unwin Hyman.

Sassen, S. (1991). *The global city.* Princeton, NJ: Princeton University Press.

Smith, N. (1979). Towards a theory of gentrification: A back to the city movement by capital not people. *American Planning Association Journal, 45,* 538–548.

Smith, N. (1987). Of yuppies and housing: Gentrification, social restructuring, and the urban dream. *Environment and Planning D: Society and Space, 5,* 151–172.

Warde, A. (1991). Gentrification as consumption: Issues of class and gender. *Environment and Planning D: Society and Space, 9,* 223–232.

Wright, E. O., & Martin, B. (1987). The transformation of the American class structure 1960–1980. *American Journal of Sociology, 93,* 1–29.

Young, I. M. (1990). *Justice and the politics of difference.* Princeton, NJ: Princeton University Press.

Zukin, S. (1991). *Landscapes of power: From Detroit to Disney World.* Berkeley: University of California Press.

Index